TRANSNATIONAL NETWORKING
AND ELITE SELF-EMPOWERMENT

A British Academy Monograph

British Academy Monographs showcase work arising from:

British Academy Postdoctoral Fellowships
British Academy Newton International Fellowships

Transnational Networking and Elite Self-Empowerment

The Making of the Judiciary in Contemporary Europe and Beyond

Cristina E. Parau

Published for THE BRITISH ACADEMY
by OXFORD UNIVERSITY PRESS

Oxford University Press, Great Clarendon Street, Oxford OX2 6DP

First edition published in 2018

British Library Cataloguing in Publication Data
Data available

Library of Congress Cataloging in Publication Data
Data available

Typeset by
Keystroke, Neville Lodge, Tettenhall, Wolverhampton

Printed in Great Britain by
TJ International Ltd, Padstow, Cornwall

ISBN 978-0-19-726640-3

Contents

List of illustrations

Figures

Tables

Preface

In *The Apology* Socrates says, 'The unexamined life is not worth living.' That means we ought to exert our capacity to transcend our ego-centrism and look back on our own behaviour as if through the eyes of another; and, becoming thus detached, be not bound by our wants and preferences, or our self-interest. A viewpoint objective to 'our own' is good for discerning where we may have strayed in our pursuit of The Good. So should it be with institutions, too. The unexamined institution is not worth perpetuating; the unexamined reform is not worth carrying out. And yet inquiry into the fate of Judiciaries in post-Communist Central and Eastern Europe has been rare and causal explanations rarer, although constitutional revisionists and institutional designers since the fall of Communism have striven to consolidate the third branch of government on a trajectory to join the global trend toward the expansion of the Judiciary power and the judicialization of politics.

This book is about the first step on that trajectory: the empowerment of the Judiciary through constitutional revisions to which Central and East Europeans paid absolutely no heed. It is an inquiry into why and how this could have come about, and what are the implications for democracy. Judiciary empowerment matters because it redirects this most venerable of all non-majoritarian institutions past adjudication of the guilt or innocence of ordinary subjects under legal certainty – the traditional role of courts – toward the making of public policy, with or without the consent of the governed, through 'finding' it in the constitution, the only legitimacy of which was the ratification of a supermajority. The question of who shall have the final word in case of conflict over basic law – viz. the Executive, the Legislature, the Judiciary, or the People – goes to the very heart of sovereignty and on whom it shall rest. Whoever has that final word is the sovereign for all practical purposes. Judiciary empowerment is now redistributing power to make public policy from the political branches of government – effectively 'us' insofar as we are represented – to the courts on all the most controversial decisions: topics as disputed as terrorism, asylum, prisoner rights, sex offenders, gay marriage, abortion, euthanasia, etc. This monograph, therefore, ought to be of interest to everyone, not just academics or policy practitioners.

The contribution of this monograph should not be underestimated because its theme in the first instance focuses on a particular geographical area. The interdisciplinarity of this work, and its not inconsiderable pioneering attempts should appeal to a wide audience. For scholars of law and politics and socio-legal studies, I have essayed to explain 'Why the recent spate of Judiciary revisionism?' My explanation should also appeal to those interested specifically in the evolution of judicialization across all of Europe, about which far less is known than about EU supranational judicialization, which has been written about in some depth. The complex causation that I discovered in the field centres on a community of elite legal professional networks and their lay 'constituents' who favour the judicialization of politics; it features their transnational networking, the sharing of common identities and discourse; a culture of consensus and a substantive agenda; self-empowerment through internally coordinated mutual dependency, and, above all, a paradigm of the power relations between the non-majoritarian courts and democracy. The judicializing phenomenon is global, and the causal nexus revealed may well apply to many other contexts. In Europe alone, countries with constitutional designs and political cultures very different from Eastern Europe (e.g. Britain, Norway) have been nudged toward the same paradigm.

For the academic audience within social science concerned with issues such as elite transnationalism and European integration beyond the EU, I hope to shed some light on how policy agendas are actually set, and how the public policy resulting from transnational networking can have a profound impact on entire regions. For practitioners of institutional design who are genuinely concerned to find solutions to real policy problems, I hope to convey the tremendous yet vastly underestimated merits of the classical design of inter-branch power relations which provided liberty and justice without making the Judiciary autonomous and supreme over everyone else, but which have been ignored out of irrational or ill-considered motives; and to help them reflect on the consequences of their intervention in countries whose history, culture, and mentality may be *sui generis* and who might be harmed in the long run by elite self-empowerment.

My hope is to raise awareness of issues that have been very little discussed in the law and politics literature, viz. the role of non-legal transnational networks like the metropolitan media and others; 'dormancy' or the lack of resistance from the political actors being disempowered (despite being the main 'veto players' in domestic politics); elite self-empowerment, and the unconscious egocentrism of human nature. So many of us scholars working in this field are scattered across disciplines and study one phenomenon from so many different angles. I wish to offer therefore a first adumbration of an integrating frame that may transcend the fragmentation of our knowledge, spread across specialisms and sub-disciplines and marred by a bedlam of theoretical variants on a few basic truths. I can attest to the high cost of interdisciplinarity, of trying to explain processes spanning multiple venues and levels of governance, of accessing primary and secondary data in a linguistically fragmented region. I chose early on to approach the matter synthetically not just analytically, endeavouring to illustrate the latent unity of the several law-and-whatnot disciplines and threads of inquiry. Just the attempt to speak to an audience larger than any specialism ought to be counted as in some measure an original contribution. Generalism is scarce and poorly rewarded, yet not without its uses, and even in cases where it may entail methodological imperfections, that is for its needfulness no bar to significant progress.

I owe thanks to many people, but above all, to my interviewees who contributed so much to my success. So much sincere effort and care, and sterling motives, I witnessed in so many of them! As to those closer to home, for his comments on the manuscript and insistence on my best I thank my long-standing friend and mentor, Jerry W. Bains; and thanks to my PhD supervisor Professor Gwendolyn Sasse (Oxford University) and Professor Conor Gearty (LSE) whose critical encouragement were pivotal. None of this research would have been possible without the support of the British Academy who generously funded the Postdoctoral Fellowship on which the primary fieldwork was done. Other funders that deserve mention are John Adams at the Foundation for Law, Justice and Society, the John Fell Fund at Oxford University, and the CoPolis project at Trento University. Many people besides have contributed moral and material support over the years, cumulatively advancing my intellectual and ethical enlightenment in ways not always obvious at the time, recounting all the way back to my transition from rural to urban Romania at the age of 14, from Romania to Britain at the age of 25, then through my progress in a culture which could not have differed more from my native Eastern Europe. I hope they will not disfavour being acknowledged: Popa Adela, Vasile Cionca, Ciprian Costăchioiu, Stanca Veştemean, the Lotrean Family, Ionuş Ioan, Anne-Marie Toader, Cristian Cărpinisan, Susan Buckingham-Hatfield, Alan Patterson, Simon Joss, Adam Fagan, Klaus Goetz,

Martin Lodge, James Hughes, Laszlo Bruszt, Denis Galligan, Richard Bellamy, and Ann Deighton. Finally my most heartfelt thanks are owing to my family – to Richard, Idris, and Freya – for bearing with me for so long with patience and understanding.

Abbreviations

ABA	American Bar Association
ABA-CEELI	American Bar Association – Central and Eastern Europe Law Initiative
CEE	Central and Eastern Europe
CC	Constitutional Court
CoE	Council of Europe
CCEJ	Consultative Council of European Judges (advisory committee to the Council of Europe made of apex court judges)
CDCJ	European Committee on Legal Co-operation (Steering Committee of the Committee of Ministers of the Council of Europe; an intergovernmental organ made of civil servants from the member states' Ministries of Justice)
CEPEJ	European Commission for the Efficiency of Justice (advisory committee to the Council of Europe made of civil servants from the member states' Ministries of Justice)
CIS	Commonwealth of Independent States
CJ-S-JUST	Group of Specialists on the Independence, Efficiency and Role of Judges (set up in 2007 to revise Council of Europe's 1994 Recommendation on Judicial Independence)
CJ-S-JUD	Group of Specialists on the Judiciary (set up in 2009 to revisit the 2007 revision of the 1994 Recommendation on Judicial Independence which had been liberally revised by CJ-S-JUST)
DG	Directorate-General of the European Commission
EC	European Commission
ECHR	European Convention on Human Rights
ECtHR	European Court of Human Rights
ECJ	European Court of Justice
EJA	European Judges Association
EP	European Parliament
EU	European Union

IAJ	International Association of Judges
ICC	International Criminal Court
IMF	International Monetary Fund
JC	Judicial Council
MEDEL	*Magistrats Européens pour la Démocratie et les Libertés*
MEP	Member of European Parliament
MoJ	Ministry of Justice
MP	Member of Parliament
MTA	Magistrates' Training Academy
NGO	non-governmental organization
OSCE	Organization for Security and Co-operation in Europe
SCt	Supreme Court
UN	United Nations
USAID	United States Agency for International Development

Introduction: Argument and methods

This monograph is about the singular, transnational and alien origins of the institutions of the Judiciary branch of government in the newly democratizing countries of Central and Eastern Europe (CEE). This is a region that comprises the Baltics (Lithuania, Latvia, and Estonia), the Visegrad Group (Poland, Hungary, the Czech Republic, and Slovakia), the states of former Yugoslavia (Croatia, Serbia, Slovenia, Bosnia, Montenegro, and Macedonia), as well as Romania, Bulgaria, and Moldova; not all of which have yet acceded to the European Union (EU). It is about the process of the introduction into the region and the remarkable empowerment of a 'turnkey' prefabricated Judiciary branch of government. All contemporary Judiciaries in CEE have been patterned on the same transnational template of institutional design which has laid a foundation for the judicialization of politics in CEE. The question arises, why was one Judiciary design preferred in CEE to the exclusion of all others? And why it was accepted so uniformly across the region despite its obvious detriment to the self-interest of those who ratified it? It is a puzzle that the empowerment of judges, so anomalous, was also so intense – here, where Civil law had historically prevailed, in which judges were Executive civil servants (Merryman and Perez-Perdomo 2007). This tradition had become depraved under Communism, which inured judges to subordination to the Party. The region's new Judiciary is an alien feature in a hostile landscape. CEE lacks the political culture which is favourable to Judiciary empowerment, viz. activist judges and rights advocates (Hirschl 2008).

The CEE countries are only following the West's headlong descent into a limitless expansion of Judiciary power, now a global trend outstanding for its ubiquity and significance (Tate and Vallinder 1995; Stone Sweet 2000). In a formal institutional sense, this empowerment has been exceptional. A tandem troika of Judiciary institutions (the Template) holds sway across the region: (1) a majority-jurist Constitutional Court (CC) with authority to 'strike down' legislative acts which it deems unconstitutional in its sole discretion;[1] (2) a Judicial Council (JC) composed, ideally, exclusively of 'magistrates' (judges and/or prosecutors), who autonomously govern Judiciary affairs from professional training to career appointments, and from promotions to discipline; (3) a Magistrates' Training Academy (MTA) monopolizing judicial education but exempt from Ministerial supervision. These institutions, adopted in CEE for the first time ever directly after 1989, were subsequently transformed by successive waves of constitutional revisions favouring judges over all other political actors.[2] The trend toward transferring ever more power to Judiciary institutions, even while imposing ever more restrictions on lay involvement in them, is unmistakable.

Judicial empowerment in the East is embedded in trends relating back to the Second World War at the latest, and earlier than that in the USA, the victor in that war. The fate of Judiciaries in Europe after the Second World War has profoundly influenced the fate of Judiciaries in post-Communist CEE. Judicialization in the West begat judicial empowerment in the East, which received a Template rooted notably in Western nations emerging from the experience of inter-war totalitarianism. A trend seemingly unique to the West is causally entangled with developments elsewhere – a state of affairs that has been invisible to those homed in on one or two aspects of CEE Judiciaries, but not to those whose approach is not even so much comparative as transnational and global.

The Template is anything but an academic exercise. Now settled public policy, it will have far-reaching consequences. Its institutions and universal norms are set to profoundly impact the real world. Above all, it systematically disempowers the majoritarian branches of government to make public policy in defiance of the Judiciary. Any public policy not forged outright by notably less accountable institutions under non-majoritarian influences will lie defenceless before the 'Judiciary veto'. Developments like these have inspired the claim that classical parliamentary supremacy (or alternatively of co-equal branches of government) is dead, supplanted by

[1] Whether they are penal laws or not; that is, what may be struck down are not only laws deemed to have violated the rights of the individual subject.

[2] It is true that Poland, Yugoslavia, and the Soviet Union instituted what they called 'constitutional courts' before the fall of Communism (Yugoslavia as far back as the 1960s); and these did function as such in some ways. But any pretensions to autonomy and supremacy, to say nothing of the judicialization of politics, were precluded by the Communist Party's 'leading role' in society.

'judicial supremacy', 'juristocracy', or 'governing with judges' (Stone Sweet 2000; Hirschl 2004; Whittington 2007). Judicial (self-)empowerment is of course necessary to this, but it may not be sufficient without a judicial activist mentality as will be shown below.

'Judicial empowerment' means those formal and informal Judiciary institutions which give judges latitude to make public policy as they deem fit, by subjecting democratic politics to their own control, a.k.a. 'judicialization of politics' (Tate and Vallinder 1995). The farther ambit of this term as to effects (not causes) lies outside the scope of this study. To study judicialization as such is to study the effects of empowerment through judicial rulings. The focus of this study shall be formal institutional design, for two reasons. Firstly, existing causal explanations of judicial empowerment by elected politicians are unconvincing in the light of new primary data. Secondly, in CEE, the reformers themselves spent most of their time, energy and material resources on institutional design, which they believed would bring about the protection of rights, the independence of the judiciary, and the rule of law (Open Society Institute 2001; American Bar Association 2002; Rekosh 2002).

The thesis: judicial empowerment is transnational elite self-empowerment

Judicialization as a mode of governance has come to play a significant role in the contemporary age. Much public policy in contemporary Europe is nowadays made by courts, in contrast to the state of affairs before the 1960s. If in the USA judicialization emerged from the bottom up (Hirschl 2008), in Europe it was no such organic evolution from indigenous tradition, but rather a modern, elite-driven project imposed from the top down through transnational networking for institutional redesign. From early on, the Federal government of the USA and its Judiciary has ruled over a vast empire; by contrast, non-Russian Europe is a continent roughly half the size of the USA and broken up into small states. For such a mode of governance to overspread Europe must have required transnational elite consensus and agency. The alternative would have seen judicial empowerment spring up spontaneously in each and every state, a confluence that is *prima facie* quite unlikely. Judicialization American-style could hardly have become a ubiquitous, quintessentially European trend without elite deliberation. In fact, European elites have been pursuing European integration through law for generations, using domestic and supranational Judiciaries as agents of change (e.g. Alter 2001). It is not surprising, then, that these elites would seek to specify the design of national Judiciaries, too, to the most minute punctilio.

It is a contribution of this study to take the foregoing conclusion and explanatory inference built on own and others' observations a few steps further. Judicialization is more than the empowerment of judges only; it empowers all those who are involved in it in the many ways that will be explored and explained hereinbelow. The Template is an important dimension of the overall self-empowerment of transnational elites, which is rooted in the programme of world peace through international law of certain nineteenth-century jurists. They were groping toward a power that stood above the nations in order to rein them in, and conceived the transnational harmonization of law and its internationally obligatory nature to act as such a power resource, a master 'capital instrument' for reaching their idealistic goals. But to get that far, they were obliged to socially construct a prior power to constitute the power of international and supranational law. It is argued that the transnational Template, seemingly an end *in se*, is actually only a means; its ulterior end is to empower the transnational elite network that created and is propagating it. Elite self-empowerment is therefore a crucial dimension of the causal nexus explaining the Template.

Elite self-empowerment exceeds the transnational Template or the judicialization of politics. Judicial empowerment can be fully understood only in a broader political context, as part of a general process of transferring public policy-making power from majoritarian to non-majoritarian institutions; for example, to central banks and regulatory bureaux not only to courts (Thatcher and Stone Sweet 2003); even to mass media, although this is much less theorized. This phenomenon passes under different labels in different fields: 'neo-democracy' (Gearty 2013), 'post-democracy' (Habermas 2012), the 'democratic deficit' (Marquand 1979; Mény 2003), 'the rise of the unelected' (Vibert 2007). Herein it is styled 'self-empowering elites' to home in on its political and social ontology.

'Elite self-empowerment' may seem a tautology: if elite, is it not empowered 'always already'? What matters about *this* self-empowerment is that it is self-interested in the manner neither of stylized rational actors nor of typecast villains. Some of the actors studied were observed to pursue purely corporate interests in the asocial manner of the dairy lobby; but equally true is that most of them were driven, often passionately, by deeply pro-social concerns, attested in both interview data and public discourses. To take action to entrench human rights, democracy, judicial independence, the rule of law in post-Communist CEE is a noble goal, one motivated by anything but self-empowering ambition (it is commonly supposed).

One stubborn fact remains, however; the means preferred by our networked elites to sustain these public goods betray a subtle undertow rarely studied or even noted by academe. Loftiness of intentions aside, it is ego-centric to presume to know best how to arrange matters which are not wholly 'professional' or technical, but known to have an irreducible political and moral dimension which ought therefore to be deliberated by all. Yet our elites scarcely question that to empower (themselves through) the Judiciary is the sovereign remedy to mankind's worst plagues. As national and international Judiciaries the world over are 'nudged', sometimes hectored, to accede to an elite transnational consensus on the relationship between the Judiciary and democracy, so those who originated that consensus are constructing therewith a sovereignty over the nation-states of Europe. Yet prior to this they had to construct a collective identity and self-image as champions of glorious ideals like human rights, the rule of law, good governance, democratization, etc. That their own self-empowerment is the panacea is their unexamined assumption.

The 'self-empowerment' of a network or an elite class is not always as strategic and instrumental in every respect as the label might suggest. The ego-centrism motivation must be at least partly unconscious. 'Unconscious' is meant in no uncertain terms: in the Constructivist sense that by socially mediated inurement one fails to notice the obvious or query the taken for granted especially as it concerns oneself, and in the plain and common sense of man's proneness to self-deception: 'the motivated desire to see the self and the world in ways that favor the self' (Chance and Norton 2015: 405). Nearly everyone overvalues his own knowledge and wisdom (Pinker 2015). If we take ourselves for granted as wiser and more knowledgeable than others, this will drive us to empower ourselves over those whom we deem incompetent and inferior. If deceptive, this deceives self first and then others. And yet the unconsciousness of the motivation is itself an objection. As Socrates reminds us, 'The unexamined life is not worth living'. All the more reason, then, for any elite minority, but especially a legal professional one, who pretend to decide amongst themselves what is best for all of society, to be cross-examined.

The will to power and its unconscious ego-centrism is perhaps 'first among many' of the commingled motives which all flesh inherits (Comfort

2003); and it manifests both individually and collectively. It is beyond the scope of this monograph to theorize the will to power in depth; it requires further research anyway. Even so, the author found that it wonderfully clarified the landscape to approach her subjects in a spirit of Constructivism: they were observed to be not wholly, straightforwardly instrumental in their choices. Political power is no innate or immutable social status or essential condition; it must be socially constructed and sustained. All the more Constructivist is that the self-empowerment is collective, and that the public spiritedness of it could not be gainsaid, even if the constructing society was an elite who resisted or evaded popular participation. This theorization is supported by the evidence presented in this monograph which shows that the strategic driver of the judicialization of domestic politics in Europe and its prerequisite judicial empowerment and institutional Template is a wittingly pan-European and transnational elite community of interest. This theorization is supported by the evidence presented in this monograph which shows that the strategic driver of the judicialization of domestic politics in Europe and its prerequisite judicial empowerment and institutional Template is a wittingly pan-European and transnational elite community of interest consisting of overlapping, interlocking professional associations, non-state actor coalitions, supranational functionaries which prominently feature jurists of every description. It is a veritable 'network community' of political and quasi-political actors, most having a legal background though not all. Their collaborations concentre inter alia on formal domestic constitutions especially the institution of the Judiciary, and are designed to empower judicial activists. The Network Community's activities promoting this objective span law, politics, and academia. The community has found it advantageous to organize itself through the medium of the organs of the Council of Europe (CoE), the 'cadre' or operational core around which it has evolved in the last thirty years. All these networked-in individual and collective actors are interdependent to such an extent, and with such potency, that even without formal jurisdiction, they can set national domestic agendas and get themselves regarded as *fontes et origines* of practical, politically consequential authority.

In principle, 'legal professional networks' advancing the interests *tout court* of the jurists who belong to them are distinguishable from a 'judicializing community', the overall elite movement (besides jurists) who promote the higher cause of judicial empowerment and judicialization. In practice, the collaboration between these two moieties is so seamless, they may be conceived as one transnational community sharing an *identity* and a *consensus* that entitles them, and an *agenda* that enables them to assume a *superintending* role in contemporary governance. 'Network Community' is the appropriate style for the phenomenon and will be preferred in this volume. Whenever occasionally it is relevant to distinguish its halves, the former terms – 'legal professional networks' for the world of jurists and 'judicializing community' for the 'infrastructure' of collaborators on whom judicial power ultimately depends – will be employed.

The Network Community shares general characteristics of all networks, which are manifolds of stable but informal and non-hierarchical relationships between individuals both inside and outside formal organizations. Networking enables each to avail himself of the resources of his own acquaintances (in the network) as well as of the acquaintances of acquaintances, to whatever depth may be feasible. The social fact of their having networked with each other for so long, cementing many interrelationships, itself constitutes the main asset and power resource of a network. A 'community' is a group of people within a larger society who are aware of holding common interests. Generally, networks exhibit more activity and specificity of interest and a tighter bonding than communities; they share a stronger 'we-ness' and members are more responsive to each other's influence. Activity, specificity, and bonding are more salient within any one network than between all those making up the community. The Network Community's transnationalism constitutes a voluntary process of transboundary interaction between members whereby cultural, social, intellectual, and other influences cross over from nation to nation without being vetted by higher control or authorized by hierarchical command or permission (Parau 2013c).

The Network Community interlocks with other European transnational communities, like the sister professional networks involved in other juridical issues, which gravitate around Brussels more than Strasbourg (Lahusen 2008; Vauchez 2008; Kauppi and Madsen 2013; Dallara and Piana 2016; Alter and Helfer 2017). Cognate networks exist in North America, Latin America, East Asia, and North Africa (e.g. Moustafa 2007), but none of them are likely as powerful, as they lack supranational organs capable of overmastering the national core Executives and providing a template of formal and informal behaviour. Thus, the Network Community may be understood to be part of a larger, global community featuring the cathexis of actors aware of each other's existence but located not just in different countries but on different continents – actors whose contacts and intercourse are persisting yet of variable frequency. Legal professionals in the USA, for instance, might as well be counted 'honorary members' of our Community, as they were involved directly in shaping Judiciary institutions in CEE directly after the fall of Communism – even if the intensity of their participation may have waned since then, compared to the Europeans – and perhaps never more 'honorary' than now, given their representation in the Venice Commission.

Transnational networking between judges was noted more than a decade ago by international relations scholars: 'Judges around the world are talking to one another: exchanging opinions, meeting face to face in seminars and judicial organizations, and even negotiating with one another over the outcome of specific cases' (Slaughter 2004: 66). Most instances of legal 'cross-fertilisation' are 'horizontal' (Slaughter 1994), as all nation-states are equally sovereign. Judges have been persuaded rather than obligated by external authority. But networking can be 'vertical', with supranational and international courts whose jurisdiction may be obligatory (Slaughter 2004). In its nature, networking conduces to convergence, as by 'comparing notes' judges are likelier to discover a meeting of minds. The resulting paradigm engages not only judges but a larger (but still class-bound) community of elites.

It is striking that the Network Community includes but a handful of politicians with legal background; they are the only elected politicians more than tangentially involved in judicial affairs (Parau 2013b). It is perhaps no surprise, as the Judiciary lends itself more to transnationalism than the Executive or Legislative, which are rooted more locally in their domestic constituencies. The prevalence of the Template, however, owes as much to the dormancy of all other veto players in parliaments and the permissive dearth of deliberation that followed (omission of agency) as to network co-optation or recruitment of essentially all of the active deliberants. This finding is in striking contrast to the widespread assumption that judicial empowerment is the outcome of delegation to courts as agents of majoritarian institutions whose members are fully engaged in Judiciary governance decisions (Stone Sweet 2002; Kelemen 2013).

What follows is a literature review that seeks to clarify the strengths and weaknesses thereof and the contribution of this study to the fund of knowledge. The causal explanatory literature on CEE Judiciaries remains unconvincing in its sketchiness and reductionist tendency. A key contribution is to show that only a nexus of interacting causes yields a rounded and empirically accurate explanation. The literature also typically overlooks the full spectrum of intentionality (whether defensive or offensive), ranging from malice aforethought to unconscious ego-centrism to utopianism. This is followed by a section that expounds the research design in detail. A book outline completes the introduction.

The state of the art and its discontents

To try to understand from the existing literature what has become of the Judiciary in Europe alone would require collating, comparing, and synthesizing theoretical claims and causal explanations that, each on their own, offer an incomplete story. Causal explanation is there to be found, but academe itself and its literature is fragmented by specialism. The elements of this Template are by the literature not understood to be elements of a whole, but treated in isolation, with nearly all of the focus on just one of them, the CC. Developments in the ordinary Judiciary are neglected as a matter of course.

All told, that literature on Judiciary empowerment in CEE over the last twenty-five years which seeks causal explanations has theorized a number of causal mechanisms, all of them (with the exception of EU accession conditionality) inspired by Western models: party bargaining and maximization of utility (qua judicial power); principal-agent delegation; judicial self-empowerment; hegemonic elites; accession conditionality and the incentives of EU membership; epistemic communities; and transnational judicial movements. These theories, and others which are also pertinent though they have not been derived in the context of CEE, are reviewed below.

Explanation is more scarce in the strictly legal literature, which for this reason is only briefly reviewed here. Some scholars who originate in the legal field, however, have fanned out into the broad plain that may be described as law and politics, and their work merits detailed review. Political science accounts are engaged next, and shown to be dominated by the Rational Choice paradigm borrowed from the literature on the West. Recently, however, political science inquiry has broadened its scope, suggesting more exotic causal mechanisms, including some belonging to constructivist strands of inquiry. The review ends with a critique of works that are more interdisciplinary in nature, the findings of which this monograph has corroborated, refined, and taken to the next level of theorization and normative critique.

Insights from legal scholarship

Legal scholarship seems the natural resort of those seeking insight into juridical affairs; however, legal scholars approach institutional developments as 'given', normal fixtures beyond their scope. Perhaps because lawyers are by trade servants of power, not its masters, the power politics behind institutional change is ignored. This body of literature is thus devoid of key concepts such as power relations, political motive, norm entrepreneurship, class identity, and the general tenor of social scientific explanation (e.g. Seibert-Fohr 2012; cf. Whittington 2000).[3]

Existing legal work on developments in the CEE region concerns CC jurisprudence almost exclusively (Schwartz 2000; Sadurski 2008, 2012). It is known that CEE has imitated the West, but crucial questions remain. Why were these institutional designs preferred to others? Who advocated them, and why? How should they have been entrenched in constitutions, if the politicians disempowering themselves could instead have reserved for themselves a role in constitutional interpretation?

For all its defects of social scientific method and purpose, however, this class of literature is sprinkled with scattered, unsystematic yet fascinating insights into these questions. US Law Professor Herman Schwartz's classic on CEE CCs is written from the perspective of a 'New Deal lawyer' (Schwartz 2000: 10). He omits scientific explanation, yet his own engagement as adviser in the design of CCs in the East is itself the next thing to primary data. And the classic works of Professor Wojciech Sadurski on CC jurisprudence touch on causality – 'constitutional borrowing', 'imitation of the West', 'vested interests and institutional self-aggrandisement' – and even run to normative critique of the 'self-congratulatory rhetoric' of constitutional law scholars and CC judges. Undoubtedly, these insights are of great value, but do not rise to the level of a systematic explanation (Sadurski 2008: xvi, 308–309). Sadurski does suggest that something profoundly important is taking place:

> The prevailing constitutional doctrine in CEE (as much as everywhere else in the world) portrays this [constitutional] interpretive task as a technical, arcane skill, where legal qualifications are key to the successful discharge of task. But as soon as we start to view constitutional interpretation as a constructive and creative task of infusing the abstract constitutional clauses

[3] Whittington notes that deeper questions about the power relations of the Constitution to the political system in the USA came from scholars outside the law schools.

> with political values in order to render them operative in specific cases the claim that lawyers enjoy a privileged insight into their 'real meaning' is undermined, and is revealed as a grab for power by the legal elites, particularly those represented in, or gravitating towards (as constitutional-law scholarship often does), constitutional courts.
>
> (Sadurski 2008: 295)

This is at least an opportune starting point. What follows will expand the analysis beyond the domestic scene, however, to capture the transnational nature of the 'power grab', and the equally important processes and roles of transnational elites, as well as the relation of CCs to other institutional trends that are part of the same phenomenon. Above all, the evidence and the inferential process through which insights such as the above have been arrived at will be laid out in profusion.

Rational Choice and utility maximization

Moving now to the political science literature, much that has been written on Judiciaries is deductive in method. The results are generally unsatisfactory for a reason: the generation of new and challenging theories too often is relegated to the periphery of the preoccupation with 'laws of [human] nature'. Rational Choice scholars are typical in deriving all explanatory conjectures a priori from the model, then looking, if not for confirmatory data, then for confirmatory interpretations thereof, not infrequently in the teeth of a disconfirming wider context. None the less, any political science perspective pays more attention to constructive agency than the doctrinaire law literature.

Electoral calculus

One class of political science theories relies on a rational model that features incumbent political parties' electoral calculus about their prospects of losing future elections, and the costs vs benefits of locking-in their policy preferences when out of power (Landes and Posner 1975; Ramseyer 1994). Notwithstanding their pre-eminence, these theories overlook too many contextual yet pivotal causal factors which attended, and derive their continuing effect from, the historical origins and consequent evolution of the Judiciary, at least in the Anglo-Saxon world. The institution originated in monarchical times; indeed, the common law of England and America rests on the system of writs instituted not by parliamentary consent but by the royal legislation of the twelfth century, well before anything like democracy existed (Maitland and Pollock 1899). This is a singular fact given the political revolutions that have intervened since then. Electoral calculus, whether a factor or not, touches neither origins nor why the legitimacy of a legacy Judiciary was never contested. Not only did democracy carry it forward without controversy (over the institution itself), there is also no trace of an 'institutional hiatus' – a period of historical time, however brief, when the Judiciary, too, was overthrown as a 'monarchical accretion', such that the democrats had to 'rediscover' its utility *to themselves* – which learning experience with electoral fortunes ought to imply. Otherwise, the continuation of the Judiciary's *historic* utility is a sufficient explanation, after which Ockham's Razor counsels against multiplying causal factors beyond the necessary. It has always been utile in mediating between the individual and the State. It is therefore a paradox how heavily democratic politicians have come to rely on the Judiciary by choice (unless the rational choice is *not* to govern), not in order to safeguard the individual from the State, but the opposite: to act in lieu of majoritarian institutions in designating classes of individuals culpable, so as to bring the power of the State to bear on them. In odd and stark contrast, the Judiciary of the monarchical past had no public policy-making role in today's activist sense; those courts would have dismissed much of contemporary litigation for lack of jurisdiction.

Applied by Ginsburg (2003) to democratizing regions like CEE, strategic electoral competition theory holds that politicians design CCs as an 'out-of-power insurance policy'. This was the stratagem used in the early USA by the administration of John Adams, who was packing the courts with party loyalists, most famously John Marshall himself, up until midnight on his last day in office, to lock in their Federalist policies in the wake of Thomas Jefferson's Democratic Republican electoral landslide in 1800 (Turner 1961).

The US experience notwithstanding, this explanation cannot be true of CEE (see also Kosař 2016). Even prior to research, good reason to doubt its accuracy exists, which may not be dismissed. All politicians have shorter time horizons than assumed, but those in CEE are shorter still. They rarely if ever think ahead about what will happen when they are out of power, but strive to pack the courts with their own loyalists in the expectation of favourable rulings whilst still in office. They demolish everything the previous regime built up, bending the Judiciary to their will right away whilst holding power affords the chance, as all previous experience teaches that nothing survives the successor opposition, who start over from scorched earth likewise, packing the courts with their loyalists (cf. Goetz 2005; Parau 2015c). No insurance policy can survive this political culture. The Rational Choice paradigm had to be strained to the limit to brook the sheer irrationality of especially CEE politicians, who by the by were observed, with stunning inconsistency, to have empowered the same Judiciary at their own expense with no self-benefit in exchange. Top-down, deductive studies like these assume too much and demonstrate too little about actual actors and their moves.

Rational Choice also claims power to explain the transformation of ordinary Judiciaries in CEE. Based on studies of electoral and presidential system design in CEE, Magalhães (1999) asserted that adoption of the Template's Judiciary Council is due to the incumbent party's maximizing its power. His explanation is lacking. Incumbents were observed revisiting the Template to try and eke out their power, but merely by tinkering with details. To rationalize it as maximization under the circumstances leaves unexplained why the circumstances were so limiting in the first place. It is part of a larger unaddressed question: why were East European politicians so keen to cede so much power to the Judiciary only months after the fall of Communism? One maximizes power by tightly reining judicial governance, not delegating it away without debate. The Template was rubber-stamped across the partisan spectrum right from the beginning of the constitution-making process, well before political parties were even properly founded, let alone fearing for their electoral fortunes.

Principal-agent delegation

In other Rational accounts, the JC has been attributed to domestic politicians delegating power to watchdog the Judiciary branch (Garoupa and Ginsburg 2009, 2011).[4] The idea that judges can be their own watchdogs is dubious at a theoretical level. It was found not to be the case in CEE; where constitutions cannot be taken at face value as mirrors of political reality; nor judges assumed to simply enjoy the receptiveness and patronage of

[4] Stone Sweet and others have made a similar argument in relation to CCs, endeavouring to replace the framework of principal-agent delegation with that of 'trusteeship' (Stone Sweet 2002; Sajó 2012). However, the analogy is tenuous, as trustees are accountable for breach of fiduciary duty in a way that CC judges are not. A higher law like the King's writ or statute of Parliament or written Constitution may be 'committed' to judges for interpretation, but the irreversibility of the commitment and the scope of judges' discretion in legal interpretation erodes the comparison with a trusteeship (Parau and Bellamy 2013).

the 'real' sovereign; nor even that elected representatives are anything more than shop-window mannequins. Judicial empowerment is therefore a conundrum indeed. The JC's very design evinces that it is no delegation of oversight for the abuse of which agents are held accountable by CEE politicians qua principals. It would be nearer the truth to call it the Judiciary's guard dog against democracy than democracy's watchdog over the Judiciary. That the JC ever was the agent of those who legislated it rests on the paradigmatic assumption that parliaments in CEE are actually in charge, not the playthings of other powers. The mass of ordinary politicians act in a manner contrary to how the paradigm predicts: they are 'dormant'– that is, asleep at the switch.[5] In regions where the Template has spread the most, parliaments are sidelined, leaving judges to elect their own government. MPs utterly neglect Judiciary institutional design and shrug off massive transfers of their own policy-making power, as if they had no use for it (Parau 2013a). The principal-agent model is a vacuous figment and empirically baseless. The author concedes that parliaments could in principle undo the deed and abolish JCs; in this hypothetical sense only might they be crammed into the category of delegation.

The Olympian stylization of Rational Choice has blinded scholars to *the* issue in politics: who gets to do what to whom, and whether the parties or politicians formally in power were the causes of anything; as well as blinding them to the agency of non-national and non-state actors. In theory, Rational Choice accommodates actors to settings, but its acolytes in this field are prisoners, in practice, of the principal-agent model of delegation. The key players in Judiciary institutional design proved to be not political parties nor parliaments nor elected politicians, but a transnational Network Community and its norm entrepreneurs (Parau 2015a).

Even if electoral calculus and delegation are not wholly inapplicable, they only explain the behaviour of a few domestic elites, who in CEE have all, or nearly all, been trained in law. Unpacking the causal agency that Rationalism takes for granted revealed that these few were the only electees involved in judiciary governance more than desultorily. This elite have been playing the judicialization game by themselves; which itself calls for explanation. Their counterparts are not their domestic opponents, but their

[5] Dormancy is systematic veto-player inaction or a permissive lack of deliberation by parliament/other domestic political actors. Within the scope of this volume, the author cannot do justice to this cause of judicialization in (especially Eastern) Europe, but will pursue it to the appropriate depth in the volume sequel hereto.

transnational and supranational allies. The games and actors that matter have already decamped from the domestic arena.

EU accession conditionality

Other Rational Choice explanations of Judiciary institutions in CEE attribute it to 'external incentives' of EU membership and 'accession conditionality'. Conditioning membership upon prior compliance with EU institutions, rules, and norms reshapes accession candidates' behaviour (Dimitrova 2004; Grabbe 2006). '[T]he credible promise of large material and symbolic benefits – particularly the golden carrot of full EU membership is generally effective in persuading national governments formally to adopt rules and institutions they would otherwise resist', like an empowered Judiciary (Magen and Morlino 2009: 229; see also Morlino and Sadurski 2010). But this theoretical mechanism is fraught with inconsistencies and unrealistic stylization; by themselves these motivators are insufficiently explanatory. The design of Judiciary institutions falls under 'democratic' not *acquis* conditionality (Schimmelfennig and Sedelmeier 2005), meaning the applicable norms do not exist but as nebulous principles like 'adherence to the rule of law' and 'sufficient judicial capacity to implement the *acquis*' (European Council 1993, 1995). The *acquis* itself is silent on the Judiciary. Lawfully, the European Commission may not exact upon accession candidates more rigorous specifications than those that bind existing member states. As shown below, accession conditionality does matter, chiefly because its lability has proved exploitable by Network Community entrepreneurs. For instance, the Romanian CC was inserted in the first democratic constitution of 1991 over the objections of MPs and local legal professionals with the rationale that it was an *informal* condition of accession to pan-European integrative organizations like the CoE. The Venice Commission had warned, 'You have to have a Constitutional Court if you want to join Europe' (Iorgovan 1998). Having just emerged, bewildered, from a half-century of Communist oppression, few nations in Eastern Europe could have resisted that.

Hegemonic elites

Rational Choice undergirds another theory of Judiciary empowerment in the literature which interprets 'agency' broadly to include the strategic interplay of several groups of elite actors, political, economic, and judicial. Developed in the context of Western democracies, this theory has had no following in the CEE context despite the clear relevance this monograph shows it has. The 'hegemonic preservation' theory is that judicial review is allowed because the dominant class (the bourgeoisie) fear losing their grip on power, and believe delegation to judges will shore up their legitimacy. The support of influential political elites remains the key factor in judicial empowerment through constitutionalization that results from 'a strategic pact led by hegemonic yet increasingly threatened political elites, who seek to insulate their policy preferences against the changing fortunes of democratic politics, in association with economic and judicial elites . . . [yielding a settlement that] reflect[s] a combination of the policy preferences and professional interests of these groups' (Hirschl 2004: 49). Judicial empowerment 'may elevate the symbolic status of a fairly cohesive professional stratum of judges, law professors, human rights organizations, litigation-oriented non-governmental organizations (NGOs), top lawyers, and law firms', whence legal professionals are its leading advocates (Hirschl 2004: 48–49). This theory, if true, allows this monograph to be seen sympathetically even from a Marxist perspective. It would falsify none of the author's conclusions (if anything, it would tend to verify them), which confirm hegemonic preservation theory to the extent of the elites under study; with the qualification that Hirschl presumes his *bourgeoisie* to be defensive reactionaries, whereas the author found hers very much on the offensive, confidently broadcasting the seed of judicialization. The reader should note this about the ideological background of such a framing: that in principle it favours neither left-leaning nor right-leaning elites, but criticizes both – which is the normative position of this monograph.

Hirschl errs also in what he omits. The elites are determined to rule not out of fear of the proletariat, but out of fear of the repercussions of their own internecine feuding as transpired most spectacularly in the World Wars. The 'bourgeois' elites have repaired to transnational networking and supranational governance in order to exert the leverage requisite to ruling with ease at the national level where dangerous military power still resides. Network solidarity is a solution to the internal problems of their own hegemony, which is not existentially threatened otherwise. National Judiciaries are at bottom just so many conveyor belts.

Self-empowering judges

Political-scientific explanations of judicialization in the West are sometimes based on the rationality of judges, the gist being that the utility to be maximized is the expansion and consolidation of a power to resolve other people's conflicts in ways that implement their preferred policy agenda; with judicial review and rights rulings enhancing their political influence and international prestige (Glendon 1993; Posner 1993; Shepsle and Bonchek 1997). In Europe, the hand that the supranational judges had in their own empowerment is well documented by scholars from both law and political science (Stein 1981; Weiler 1991, 1994; Burley and Mattli 1993). Judges indeed behave as power-maximizers given both means and motive, but the evidence from CEE and elsewhere is that judges are seldom in any position to maximize power unless *others* should institutionalize the Judiciary in ways that empower judges to empower themselves.

Beyond Rational Choice

Some recent political science literature acknowledges that classical Rational Choice motives are not a sufficient cause. Case studies have profiled causes ranging from the play of motives and factors rooted in prior, more intangible, constructivist processes, such as the need to shore up regime legitimacy; to ideology (e.g. legal positivism, French liberalism); and on to social psychological reactions to a recent trauma (Woods and Hilbink 2009; Erdos 2010). Multiple factors were found to interact to yield a more complex picture than the linear Rational theories just reviewed. These are advances in understanding, which this monograph builds on. Yet even this literature misses essentials, such as taking care not to confine oneself to domestic politics, for instance, nor to ignore transnational and non-state actors and supranational institutions. For the CEE region, this is a major omission, given its susceptibility to external influences. A critical reading of the data from similar regions such as Latin America suggests that causality there also transcends the nation-state (Woods and Hilbink 2009; Ingram 2016). Any advances in understanding the CEE region will therefore add significant value to this literature.

Transnational legal elites

A fraction of the literature stands out as being more sensitive to causation that overleaps the boundaries of the nation-state and prospects other agents than the stylized political actor to whom utility maximization is imputed. This 'alternative' literature has discovered a causation more transnational and sociological in nature. Karen Alter corroborates the author's thesis by highlighting evidence of pan-European communities of interest, especially the 'good European' jurists who projected and justified European Court of Justice (ECJ)-driven legal integration in the 1960s (Alter 2007). More recently, Alter and Helfer (2017) refined Alter's original understanding of 'jurist advocacy movements', which sounded at least akin to the Network Community of this monograph; viz. 'the group of lawyers, judges, academics, in-house counsels, and legally trained government and European officials who advocated for particular goals' (p. 229).[6] The role of these movements has never been better illustrated than by the comparison between the ECJ and the Andean Tribunal in Latin America. Modelled on the ECJ, the latter failed to attain anything like the same influence, as it lacked 'the sort of community building that Euro-law associations provided [to the ECJ]' (Alter 2008: 30; see also Alter and Helfer 2010). That the success of such tribunals depends on collective agency greater than even the whole corps of legal professionals; and that the collective actor is 'committed to a cause [that] extends beyond the pursuit of narrow self-interest' to the pursuit of 'specific policy and legal goals' (Alter and Helfer 2017: 229–230) are insights corroborated herein. What is missing from their account, however, is the Network Community's self-interest in the judicialization of all politics as a pathway to general governance and thus as collective self-empowerment beyond the more limited goal of regional integration through law. This is none the less self-empowerment, if in a form less visible than material coercion, because it is predicated on the premise that all would be well if only Ego ruled. A movement promoting 'originalism' that is as active, prestigious, and consequential as the Network Community has yet to emerge in Europe, though it may have crystallized in the USA (Teles 2009). This in itself is evidence that the universal agenda is elite self-empowerment, as originalism confines rather than 'liberates' Ego to make public policy from the bench; paralleling why the Template is preferred to viable alternatives (see Chapter 6).

[6] This author does not conceive of the Network Community as a mere advocacy coalition because the Network Community is more coherent and perdurable, whereas advocacy coalitions are heterogeneous collections of actors whose interests converge for the nonce on assorted issues; although the Network Community is quite capable of acting like an advocacy coalition if need be (e.g. the 'New Magna Carta' of 2014, a blueprint constitution for Britain, drafted by King's College London law faculty teamed up with sympathetic MPs). Incidentally, this illustrates a methodological predicament: academic terms like 'social movement', 'advocacy coalition', 'interest group' are to some extent arbitrary idealizations thought up by different scholars trying to make sense of a social reality that will never fit tidily into any linear model. In the social sciences, every model overlaps with every other, and the Network Community may be all of the foregoing at once.

Other of their inferential claims are of rather more dubious value. They start with the unnecessary assumption that nature and nurture stand in eternal opposition, and that international judges 'are not expansionist lawmakers by nature' (Alter and Helfer 2017: 228). It follows that to become as expansionist as they are now observed to be, they must have needed 'special nurturing' by the 'community' they identified. The Achilles heel of this line of inference is the assumption that nurture will generally teach judges political modesty and not otherwise, but for extraordinary (maybe supranational) intervention:

> The ECJ/ATJ's comparison reminds one of the 'nature' versus 'nurture' debate in child rearing. Is it the genes or the environment that shapes how an actor develops? Most international relations and international law scholars favor the nature side of this debate. They assume that judges are hardwired to increase their power. It is only limited opportunities or the fear of being sanctioned that inhibits judges' natural tendency to expand their authority. By contrast, nurture-based explanations assume that international courts typically apply the law in fairly straightforward and circumscribed ways. Expansionist lawmaking – which we define as judicial decisions that broaden the reach or scope of international law at the expense of national political discretion – requires, according to this view, special care and encouragement. (Alter and Helfer 2017: 202)

Nurture may not be 'hard-wired', but that only means it can be anything – more self-aggrandizing than nature. There is no default truth. The irony is that Alter and Helfer have in effect hard-wired nurture to always oppose nature and never complement or reinforce it, except through 'special' care and encouragement. Besides this unwarranted assumption, they have not inquired into the origins of the community they found, in order to discover the entire 'world' of who has been doing the nurturing, not only nowadays but also yesteryear; nor if the specialness of it has evolved over time and/or space. Above all, Alter and Helfer fail to address probably the most important issue of all: what is in it for the nurturers? These cracks in the foundation of reasoning vitiate some (not all) of the inferences built on them.

The nature-vs-nurture as debate drawn from the biological sciences has in fact played out rather differently there, where a consensus is now taken for granted that both play an equal role and indeed are critically interdependent and irreversibly entangled; that is, one cannot explain whole phenomena with nurture without reference to nature, and vice versa (Pinker 2002). It would be more empirically accurate and logically more robust to infer that *some* national cultures and traditions of governing – certainly in parts of the world such as Eastern Europe, South America, and even Britain – have long nurtured inhibitions overriding judges' expressing their natural will to power; while others enable judges' will to power. If reinforced by their co-nationals continually, the inhibitions that do exist will stay put, unless and until overridden by stronger influences. Indeed, it may well be that the un-inhibition of some cultures (like the American) is what, through prolonged influence, may override the inhibition of others (the traditional European). More than one mechanism may be able to override stably nurtured inhibitions: it is easy to imagine 'reverse nurturing'. Another possibility might be called 'interdiction' – that is, coming between national tradition and the incompletely 'nurtured' younger generation. This is exactly why the Magistrates' Training Academies in CEE are an essential part of the Template (see Chapter 6). If the previously conditioned inhibitions can be overridden, then one may find that the natural-born will to power will reinforce any nurturing of judicial activism and self-empowerment through expansion of jurisdiction. Alter and Helfer do explore the material and tangible relationship between the community and the international judges. But this is not all that matters; the whole syndrome of elite self-empowerment is in play and is definitive: their collective identity and solidarity, their culture of consensus, their ideology of perpetual peace through law, their common agenda to judicialize politics in the teeth of an undeniable democratic deficit, and above all, the unconscious egocentrism of assuming moral superiority over 'politics'. There transpired a whole causal nexus, not merely a few judges nurtured who knows why. Finally, it is also noteworthy that Alter and Helfer focus on international tribunals, omitting their 'parent' international governance organizations such as the CoE, let alone a *transnational* template of *domestic* judiciary design.

Alter's work transitions naturally to another important contribution, that of the socio-legal literature. Following Bourdieu, Antoine Vauchez and colleagues have looked at the role of Euro-lawyers in constructing the EU as we know it (Bourdieu 1987; Madsen and Vauchez 2005; Cohen 2007; Cohen and Vauchez 2007; Vauchez 2008; Kauppi and Madsen 2013). Examining legal professional networks in the EU, socio-legal scholars discovered valuable information about their nature and activity, and about the motives of certain actors in the legal sphere. Vauchez observed that they operate 'at the core of EU polity', which puts them in a 'favourable position [to] construct and legitimise a specific political order [and thus] redefine the relationship between law and political borders' (Vauchez 2008: 130, 132). He cautions against yielding to 'the self-proclaimed disinterestedness of Euro-law' as, in building Europe, Euro-lawyers have also 'built themselves'. Acting supranationally, they 'free themselves from their roles at the national level and [find] . . . new raisons d'être in a European polity in search of both professional models and political canons' (Vauchez 2008: 133). This literature engages with the contentious normative issues of 'elites' and 'power' that constitute the bulk of classical sociological work (Wright Mills 1956; Pareto [1901] 1991; Bourdieu 1996), about which legal academics are silent and contemporary political scientists dismiss as too normative. On the other hand, the systemic focus of sociological inquiry, while accounting well for certain sociological causes such as class and identity, can obscure specific causes that might supply answers to such quintessentially political-science questions as 'who does what to whom, how, and why?'

Transnational legal professional networks feature as explanations of judicial governance in CEE in the work of Daniela Piana and colleagues in the field of politics and socio-legal studies (Coman and De Waele 2007; Piana 2007a, 2010; Coman 2016; Dallara and Piana 2016). Piana (2009: 834) noticed 'epistemic communities' and 'policy networks' had assimilated judges, scholars, and 'legal experts' conferring 'legitimation', 'credibility abroad', and 'leadership at home' upon them. These actors exercised 'soft power' (left undefined, however) which caused changes to judicial institutions. This is an important factor, but Piana left unclear how precisely these networks exert causality. She rightly noted that judicial reforms in CEE continued along the trails blazed by the first constitutions made after the fall of Communism, but what was the role of networks in setting the Judiciary in CEE on those trails? How is it that CEE countries already conformed to a (proto-)Template right after 1989 and well before the Eastern enlargement of a decade later? One awaits joined-up explanation as to why institutions so remote from the tradition of CEE countries were adopted in the first place, so soon after their liberation from Communism.

In her earlier work, Piana conceptualized the transnational legal professional networks as an epistemic community (Piana 2007b, 2010). This is true only up to a point. The legal professional networks are only one element of the Network Community, which as a whole is more than merely an epistemic community, though it does arise from the real epistemic community of jurists in general. What is the difference then? In its original meaning, such a community prioritizes *episteme* over other interests and deploys set methods to fathom their class of questions (Holzner and Marx 1979). It is doubtful whether the Network Community seeks anything like objective truth in matters of judiciary institutional design (though this does not mean it never does so in other contexts) (see also Kauppi and Madsen 2013). An *epistemic* community would concern itself with 'knowledge' and its criteria and proof. The Network Community's goal – to forge elite consensus on a policy agenda facilitating pursuit of self-empowerment – is more ulterior and more political: it is collectively *chosen*, not discovered, although the power of collective action itself may have been discovered beforehand. Secondly, the Network Community is intentionally elitist in social achievement if not social origin, whilst epistemic communities ignore social and political class in principle. Thirdly, life outside the Network Community is not unthinkable; even some prominent elite jurists understand judicial governance differently from the Network. Indeed, the Network consensus, because it and any other consensus are political instead of truly epistemic, must be enforced by easing out heretics. In fine, the Network can only be an epistemic community in the revised sense of Haas (1992: 3): 'a network of professionals with recognized expertise and competence in a particular domain' who collaborate to solve policy problems *in their field of practice* (the possible sticking point even from Haas's viewpoint, as the ambit of the Network's common agenda transcends anything as banal as a field of practice). Thus, if our Network Community has an *episteme*, it is open to normative criticism for being an instrument of self-empowerment (cf. Lasch 1978). It may wish to enjoy the moral equivalent of an *episteme* to the extent that its Template is put beyond 'respectable' dispute (it might even be halfway there), but it has fallen short of 'closure' so far – partly due to its own epistemic vagueness about key terms in the pantheon, such as 'separation of powers'.

The most recent contribution to the socio-legal line of inquiry maps with some comprehensiveness the types of networks active in Europe in the field of judicial affairs, documenting their most tangible and visible activities. Dallara notes that legal networks outside the EU have been contributing to 'a gradual construction of a global legal system' through 'soft law documents', which they diffuse in the form of reports, opinions, best practices, and guidelines; which 'deal with crucial aspects of the judicial system organization and functioning such as judge status and role or guarantees of judicial independence', and are also 'involved in EU policy-making as well as mediation between supranational institutions and national judiciaries', which 'affect the circulation of models of judicial system organization' in Europe (Dallara 2012: 21–24). In their most recent work, Dallara and Piana go beyond the EU-centrism of their earlier work and include equally, if not more important, regional integrative organizations. Like the author, they point out that the agency of the legal professional elites orbiting the CoE has yet to be understood (Dallara and Piana 2016).

A compendious treatment of the manifold judicial network activities in Europe is an important step toward understanding; however, the authors remain within the discursive and interpretative boundaries set by the Network Community, portraying the networks as guardians of the rule of law who deploy their expert reputation and 'soft power of persuasion' to condemn and correct the sins against the Template of Fidesz in Hungary and Ponta in Romania. The interaction of those involved is investigated from the Network Community's viewpoint only. The acts of key players are documented in detail, but deeper empirical, theoretical, and ultimately normative questions are missed, as the Network's paradigm 'contains' the kinds of question that may be asked and the scope of the inquiry.

Crucial to social and political science is a critical approach to all actors, that raises awareness of the Network Community as also an issue in itself; for example, that the collective identity and assumptions about the judicial role in democracy that guide their policy programme may betray a will to power. In framing discourse exclusively in power-neutral, normatively uncritical terms like judicial *reform* or *securing the rule of law*, the literature skirts core political questions – whose reforms are these? whom do they (dis)empower? what motivates them? – and normative questions – what does it bode for democracy in the original sense of popular sovereignty? In the case of *Networking for the Rule of Law*, important normative issues are on the tip of the authors' tongue when they ask 'whether judicial networks are generators of epistemic communities'. The answer lacks sufficient empirical foundation and theoretical clarity, and vague inferences from the data are enmeshed in tacit normative preferences:

> Judicial actors have nowadays the opportunity to enter into expert-epistemic communities, whose influence targets in a homogenous manner all judicial actors serving in a country. Only those who represent judicial institutions by the transnational actors are directly affected by the ideas and the principles that circulate in an informal way in meeting, reporting, exchanging, and communicating activities. Surely in cases where the technical dimension is exchanged, it is crucial that this knowledge is legitimized by the fact of its having its origin from or through a judicial network as in the case of the Commission of Venice or in the case of the CEPEJ – giving to the knowledge a sort of qualification. This means the CEPEJ becomes – or may become – a leverage of change if used at home – in the national systems – by those actors who are willing to invest political and cognitive resources to promote a change which is in tune with transnational ideas.
>
> (Dallara and Piana 2016: para. 17.48)

Critical normative approaches remain scarce, generally, scholars being prone to strain to legitimate the Network Community's advance and consolidation; as by inventing untested forms of accountability for the shiny new Judiciary to justify the abolition of checks and balances; even going so far as to count as accountability any beholdenness of national judges to the transnational elite and Network Community, and *their* norm-setting power! '[T]he judicial network and the legal epistemic community draw the boundaries of new normative guidelines to which European judges will be held accountable in the future' (Piana 2010: 196). It is thought-provoking if the accountability of national judges has been trans- and supra-nationalized without the public's awareness, let alone consent. Here is where normative issues add depth to the analysis. What kind of accountability is this? What legitimates it? To whom, if anyone, are these accountants themselves accountable? Even if some of them are formal supranational institutions with an intergovernmental gesture in appointment of their vestigial organs by the member states (like the Parliamentary Assembly of the CoE), the chain of accountability is strung out to the point of superstition that runs from appointees of appointees back to those voters who bother to show up to infrequently periodic elections and still less frequent referendums.

Other authors have endeavoured to do justice to the empirical reality by engaging with both the Network Community's viewpoint and the domestic governments', yet oddly, even this has failed to yield a satisfactory explanation of why the *dramatis personae* acted as they did, not merely 'Who did what' (Coman 2014a). What supersedes this is an approach that will keep all actors equally at arm's length, yet wonder 'What in particular makes them tick?' – thereby reaching a conclusion that not only illumines but also edifies.

The research design

The purpose is to discover which causal mechanisms produced the Judiciary Template in CEE and how (the *explanandum*), and why this Template became so ubiquitous, contradicting a priori expectations of finding a diversity commensurate to the diversity of national cultures. The research is thus puzzle-driven, not method- or theory-driven (Shapiro 2005; Hancké 2009).

The author's preliminary observation of judiciary revisions in CEE warranted further inquiry into agency: backgrounds, beliefs, motives, etc. This was one of the author's few method-driven choices. Most of the causality consists of identifiable acts undertaken at this micro-level, without ignoring the fact that, of course, institutions – for example, opportunity structures; identities – will influence the willingness and capacity to act (Scharpf 1997; Hay 2002). The appeal of such an approach is greater, as nearly all research on judicial governance in CEE is methodologically structural, viz. political parties and accession conditionality, omitting actors from the picture; although gradually one is witnessing a slow turn in the literature to collective if not entrepreneurial agency.

The complexity of the causal nexus observed in the field, and the practical infeasibility of isolating so many tributary causes, steered the author away from any idea of probing one-dimensional correlations of variables. Correlation finding does not automatically open up the 'black box' of causal mechanisms and abductive inferences to the *best* explanation; it often cannot answer the question *how* it happened, only *that* it happened, and is just so likely to happen again (or not). This is not to gainsay the worth of conventional political science methods; correlations can certainly spotlight causal dependency, if they cannot always resolve it, for example, that party fragmentation in parliament correlates to empowerment of CCs. As with the Copernican revolution, interpretation is the key, not correlative data. Avoided also is standard small-N comparative methodology of country case studies, using methods of agreement or difference, because it is unsuitable for complex causality involving more than one factor (Lieberson 1991).

Open-ended exploration has the virtue of bringing to light causes never suspected, not just correlations of already suspected causes, a crucial yet neglected (sometimes even disrespected) side of social science (Gerring 2004), but it calls for a methodological repertory adapted to it. Hence the author's choice of three research strategies usual with qualitative research: process tracing, Grounded Theory, and normative comparison of norms. The result is a body of inference which is thoroughly inductive, or abductive as the case may be, that relies on informal logic (Toulmin 1958). For example, police and detective work is exemplary exploratory research. In law enforcement, the amount of data collected is enormous and the data set complete to exhaustion. The police are supposed to cast their net as wide as they can; that is, they interrogate everybody they can get hold of and listen to whatever they say. They follow up every little clue.

Process tracing

Process tracing excels at contributing to such research agendas as: (i) recognizing new phenomena; (ii) testing extant explanations and discovering new ones; (iii) exposing 'black box' causal mechanisms to probe how correlated variables might be interpolated or extrapolated; and (iv) detecting reciprocal causation and selection bias other than quantitatively (Collier 2011). However, process tracing has now been formalized to such a degree that the result is nearly as prescriptive as the top-down, variables-correlative approach (King et al. 1994). The author's research programme would have been poorly served by formalities meant to compete with statistical methods of testing known hypotheses. The exploratory nature of the research and the smoking-gun nature of the actual data rendered such methods supererogatory. Collier (2011) has noted that the method of elimination of inferences may discover in even the weakest tests enough decisional power to potentially 'solve' a case (which he illustrated with Sherlock Holmes's logic in Conan Doyle's *Silver Blaze*). It was unnecessary to be so elaborate for this study, as the interviewees themselves openly 'confessed to who done it'. Process of elimination is the most fertile in unexpected results: once the unsound has been eliminated, the truth is whatever is left standing (except if the researcher's nescience of unknown possibilities prevents subjecting them to elimination); *caveat inquisitor* who can never be certain every alternative has been eliminated. Here is the method of self-criticism: to eschew presuming the explanation left standing is absolute.

Process tracing is applicable to singular or recurrent events. The author applied it in its less formalized mode to seek the causes of Judiciary institutional design in a within-case analysis of Romania, a country literally familiar to the author, over the twenty-two years 1990–2012 in which it transitioned from Communist to second-wave EU accession candidate to member state. Process tracing focused the author on gathering 'causal-process observations': any bit of evidence, however small or rare, that might give insight into 'who did what to whom, when, why, and how?' Key facts about the identity of influential actors, their motives, strategies, power resources, and beliefs about themselves and what they were doing (cf. Scharpf 1997; Brady and Collier 2004) were duly revealed. The author let the inferences be suggested by the data; no prefabricated hypotheses were brought to the data for testing (cf. Yanow 2009). In this study, the basic causal observations of the singular event of the Judiciary and its design were made in Romania, and only later compared abroad and generalized in other European countries. The upshot was the discovery that Judiciary institutional revisions were driven by a causal nexus that differed markedly from other explanations in the literature. These findings in detail have been published separately to this book, though some of the evidence has been included here as well (see also Parau 2012, 2013a, 2015a). The nexus was exposed to falsification in other CEE countries, part of the same Enlargement, which vary in degree of integration into the EU and the West, viz. the Czech Republic, a first-wave candidate; Croatia, the newest EU member state; and Moldova, an EU aspirant. With the exception of the Czech Republic, which rejected the JC (though in practice the Judiciary is governed in quasi-JC manner; see Kosař 2017), the Template was achieved in every one, and inferentially so across the whole Enlargement region. Once this had become clear, the author widened the scope to Western Europe, where demonstrably kindred if more variable changes were found to be afoot; transforming the study into a cross-case analysis affording greater inferential leverage. Interviews of elites in Germany, Norway, Britain, Brussels, and Strasbourg evidenced that the same pattern or causal nexus was behind them all. The uniformity of the phenomenon itself rendered the 'improvident' case selection one where 'Romanian-style' institutional revisions were actually observed. Such a 'non-variance design', is legitimate if the purpose is 'gaining descriptive insight into a phenomenon about which researchers have little prior knowledge' (Munck 2004: 114). It proved serendipitous in that the author was expecting more variation, hence more methodological difficulty.

The countries beyond Romania were not researched to the same depth due to resource limitations, not least because of the language barrier. But the data, once begun to be collected, exhibited an unexpected homogeneity; whence *theory saturation* was reached so quickly that both Template and nexus were put beyond reasonable doubt wherever data were collected. Saturation allowed the author to avoid duplicating process tracing in all countries, which would have been logistically impossible. No refuting evidence, especially amongst the elites interviewed, was ever found. If future research should find to the contrary, it would be a welcome falsification of error. Further to this, if rank-and-file legal professionals should be found to hold beliefs divergent from the elites interviewed, then (fascinatingly) the latter will have proved singularly unrepresentative.

Saturation is a qualitative method for gauging the validity and reliability of data not randomly sampled (Glaser and Strauss 1967). There are many modes of saturation, but the ones which concern this study are data and theory saturation. Saturation can be a tricky concept in detail, as what constitutes 'data' or 'theory' can seem counterintuitive. Data are saturated when further collection yields no distinctly different observations.

Interview data from different persons in different places cannot be considered saturated: even if new informants said the same thing, it would still be coming from new places. To interview the same person until he repeats himself would be data saturation. Theory saturation is when new informants say things which *to the researcher* imply no new interpretations of events. Saturation was used by the author to gauge when her informants, explaining their and their peers' own acts and norms, wittingly or not were suggesting no better explanations than those the author had inferred herself from her informants, or had gleaned from the literature. The author *inferred* data saturation in each country from the repetitiveness of interviewees (and eventually quit interviewing more), but actually found theory saturation across all interviewees.

Grounded Theory

Process tracing was informed by Grounded Theory, in that the data, instead of being interpreted through the lens of received academic theories, were subjected to the Grounded Theory hermeneutic process, first intuitively in the field, then more rigorously in Oxford. The Grounded Theory method is uncommon in mainstream political science, but almost ideal for the purpose in hand. It is part of a movement critical of positivism and that pursues research not as a technical exercise so much as something that accounts for ethics and norms and the everyday practices of politics (Vromen 2010). The method was pioneered by sociologists (Glaser and Strauss 1967), yet the author, although trained in political science methods, found it easily adaptable to the facts of her cases, and reliable both operationally and theoretically. The beauty of it is to seamlessly integrate exploration into research – indeed, to give needed depth to the abstractions one succumbs to from existing paradigms such as Rational Choice or Social Constructivism. As it happens, both paradigms were corroborated by this method; indeed, nested conditions of constructivist influence like identity, which condition actors' preferences, are prerequisite to fully fathoming the 'Rational' Choices (Jupille et al. 2003). Grounded Theory starts with the concrete ontology of what in the literature is presented as abstract 'preferences'.

Methodical comparison at successive levels of inferential abstraction is key to this method. But what is to be compared? The short answer is everything found in the field relevant to the research question. The facts are important, of course, but more important are the conceptual categories suggested by their 'fitting together' as (characteristic) aggregates. The 'conceptual property' of these aggregates is an abstraction summing up the nature of the facts. Predictions can then be made on the basis of such conceptual categories, which survive until proved theoretically defunct for any class of data. The process preceding the interesting, testable level has two stages: the researcher first notes what informants say. She is looking for the meaning of events, but lets informants utter what they think it is. After that, the 'memos' or recordings instantiating their giving meaning are compared. This practice of 'free memoing' (free in the rough sense of free association in psychoanalysis) records 'intuitive preconscious thought' which arises in the course of research (Glaser 2013). There emerges, as if by itself, concepts on the level of abstraction of, for example, the Mississippi River. The Mississippi River is not a particular fact but an abstraction the human brain 'jumps to' almost involuntarily (Kang et al. 2017); an abductive inference in the lingo of Charles Sanders Peirce (see below). The investigator attending the River in person at many different times and places will experience it as fragmented and discrete and may not recognize 'the same river' without aids like maps and signs – if any have been elaborated by precursors. For that matter, we know the Mississippi is always in flux – the water constituting it is never the same from minute to minute. In short, it is directly perceived and scientifically known to be 'many' yet counted as one. In this formative stage, the observer is generating just an icon or rubric out of 'puzzle pieces'. In the second, synthesizing stage, she compares several icons like Mississippi and Amazon, seeking not abstraction (which she already has) but a *higher level* of it, running through them all like a golden thread. This would be 'river', in contrast to abstractions that might otherwise be confused with it, such as 'lake' or 'sea'.

Construction of concepts like Mississippi, then river 'in general' are prerequisite to non-trivial causal explanation, especially operationally. In social science above all, theory bears on awareness of *context*. An objective example from an unrelated study carried out by the founders of Grounded Theory is the category of 'social loss' (to family, to occupation) emergent from the care of dying patients, in the context of whether the patient is made aware or not that he is dying (Glaser and Strauss 1967: 24). The conceptual properties that emerged were: (i) the *cues* that led to awareness, and (ii) the *stakes* involved in various parties' becoming aware. But this was only the first stage; at the second, higher generalities about cues and stakes were discovered by comparing such disparate groups as building subcontractors and spies, bearing in mind that the choice of what to compare is important (Glaser and Strauss 1967). A sample of a conceptual property drawn from this research is: (i) 'EU dependency on the CoE' from the first stage, and (ii) 'dependency on expertise' from the second. Interview data that might or might not imply (i), by itself, was memoed and compared with all other memos exhibiting the same property, not so much (though also) for triangulation as for specifying the property of (ii).

Conceptual properties reflecting new viewpoints or interpretations were coded as soon as they transpired. Many codes logically integrated into an *ultimatum probandum* were theoretical inferences from the data. If a theory coalesced, further coding was halted to spare the author from contemplating the generalizability of existing codes (avoiding the 'bottleneck' of an unwieldy, stale coding). The author preferred to remain open-minded throughout the process lest incoming evidence be force-fitted into a premature mould. This created opportunity for original theorizing – one is not bound by codes created *en passant*. In Grounded Theory, the researcher continues to adapt and refit the coding long after she has left the field and is back home. This way of proceeding and the logic underlying it differs from mainstream comparative politics (King et al. 1994).

In thus formulating theories and doubting them, the author relied on abductive logic (Reichertz 2007), or 'inference to the best explanation [available]'. It is 'bottom-up' reasoning, yielding an 'iconic argument' in the words of its theorist, Charles Sanders Peirce, who discovered in it the mode of reasoning used in everyday life. It leaps directly to the best explanation from whatever data are available, not bound by formal premises arrayed in syllogistic hierarchy. Syllogism does not distinguish good, better, and best explanations, it only knows true and false; otherwise, abduction could be classified as a species of induction, as it moves from particular to general. A leap to the best explanation is a leap in the twilight if not in the dark; therefore, contextual reasoning calls for 'testing the best' to try and falsify it. Taking from political ethnography:

> When you skip a stone over a pond's surface, it leaves ripples; the stone may then be [gone], but we still track those ripples (at least for a little longer) . . . we can surmise that a stone had been there when we see the ripples, and we can look to clarify aspects of the conditions it created [and what produced it].
>
> (Yanow 2009: 35)

To apply this simple example to a paraphrase of Peirce's own words, the pattern of ripples and splashes 'is the very image of such a [stone skipping] . . . Here is an iconic argument, or abduction of it'. If rummaging about, we overhear boys passing nearby say that they are going as usual to Miller's Pond where we saw those ripples, '[h]ere at last is an indication that my theory is correct . . . although it would be inaccurate to say that there is any definite probability . . . since I do not know [who else or] how often' they go or what they do there. 'Peirce' inquires of local parents and finds out that all fourteen of their sons skip stones in the Pond, but no one else does, and one son was there yesterday morning, when we saw the ripples; hence we

> must think that the probability [is one in fourteen that Tommy made the ripples] . . . combining the arguments into one mixed argument, and considering, what is logically relevant, that I have no serious stake in the question, I am satisfied to consider the mixed argument as proof [that Tommy could have done it].
>
> (cf. Peirce 1902)

Though Peirce does not use the word, this is tantamount to 'logic triangulation', where multiple forms of logic are brought to bear in multiple ways to confirm the same inference. Peirce expounds at length criteria for double-checking one's abduction, many of which seem more ethical than logical for example, 'How much does it matter if you get it wrong, what is your interest in this?' The author scrupulously followed them all. To close Peirce's logic-triangulation circuit, the inferences the author drew from the sum of all her cases were deployed deductively to test not only the author's own theory, but also theories from the literature, for example, 'socio-legal research suggests that the legal professionals who drove the early stages of European integration implicitly assumed that law is morally superior to politics; the entrepreneurs who spearheaded the transformation of Judiciary institutions in CEE stem from the same background; therefore, they too believe law is superior to politics.' This conclusion was applied *inductively* to test data about Network Community beliefs. So the 'logic circuit' was run until 'saturation', meaning that no greater confidence was obtained by further 'mixed argument'. To avoid tedium for the reader, these circuits were not recorded in the main body of the monograph.

The data

At the risk of being labelled 'too empirical', the author deems it essential in a qualitative study to make transparent not only the chain of inference culminating in the *ultimum probandum*, but the empirical data supporting it (Anderson and Twining 1991; Moravcsik 2014). Data (if any) not fitting the author's theories were not to be excluded, to vitiate charges of cherry-picking data, and to exhibit the degree of saturation. Qualitative data as text obtained from elite interviews or written material, being critical to the causal picture, were generously excerpted. The very human voices of the informants were allowed to be heard and their own words to speak for themselves. They fell into predictable patterns of which the direct quotations herein are exemplars. The reader can see for himself if the inferences drawn from the interviewees' testimony are logically sound and indeed the best explanation.

By far the main source of primary data was interviews with the elites, and the database generated contributed to the originality of this research. Elites drove the institutional revisions studied here and thus were critical sources. Interviewing in social science is a robust way to: (i) corroborate other theories; (ii) find out what a sub-population believe; (iii) infer the beliefs and behaviour of the larger, embedding population; and/or (iv) reconstruct causal chains of events (Tansey 2007). In this study, interviewing of elites was used successfully for all four ends. A great number and variety of elites involved in basic decisions of Judiciary institutional design policy were interviewed across Europe between 2010 and 2014 (the Annexe exhibits a sample of interviewees). Interview length ranged from 40 to 240 minutes. Transcripts are available for scrutiny to those who may wish to replicate any of this research, except where anonymity was negotiated. The interviewees were not always asked the same questions, which were designed to follow up new leads and fill out the rich causal account. This project was an 'assembled jigsaw puzzle' and cast its data-net widely.

Interviewees were not sampled randomly or representatively, as the aim was to trace process one step at a time, not detect remote correlations. The author tried to interview all the most important political players who partook in the events studied, and fairly succeeded with a great many. Random sampling would have found none of the important informants. Selective and chain-referral sampling were the apt methods (Tansey 2007). The selection criterion was the interviewee's 'insiderhood' in the Network Community as it concerned Judiciary institutional revision. The author did not select interviewees for any other characteristic; certainly none were selected for their beliefs; it could not have been known in advance anyway what their beliefs would turn out to be, and the author was expecting more belief variance. It was not possible to know beforehand that most if not all interviewees turned out to have been transnational in their career path from early on. Most were empirically found networked-in, but in the few cases where their leading role furnished grounds for presuming them so, it was confirmed.

No claims of the interviewees being a 'representative' group of elites is made, or that the selection was balanced in terms of country, age, sex, level of governance; however, the activists or entrepreneurs of the Network may have been over-represented compared to the 'unsung' population of the Community. The latter group is part of the Community and apparently as committed to the same goals. As the entire Network is elite, it is a moot point whether their consensus paradigms were shared by the rank-and-file of the legal profession or not; what the latter might believe is of no practical importance. So little variation in the views of the interviewees was found that to carry out a large-N statistical study would have been, as well as logistically infeasible, superfluous, adding little to the qualitative data.

Mainstream political science too often dismisses interview evidence as 'anecdotal'. But interview data are more reliable than is generally conceded, if the evidence sought is what actors think, what makes them think so, and what motivates them to act. Interviews, of course, are always biased in a certain sense: elite interviewees are ordinarily ego-centric and not omniscient. They are wary of revealing too much of their motives and agendas to outsiders and a certain amount of prevarication is expected from all. For instance, rarely do they admit that they were motivated by dissatisfaction with the status quo; none actually said, 'I was dissatisfied with the workings of democracy.' The author had to infer the causes of dissatisfaction descriptively from their utterances. The Network Community shares a strong culture of consensus and solidarity, evident in the fact that they took pains to reveal little to the author about each other (and they often knew each other very well) that might be construed as a betrayal of trust. Sometimes, especially regarding internal dissent, some interviewees kept to a discreet 'speech code' in giving answers. Much was inferred circumstantially by comparing answers across many interviews and against other sources. Given a thick data set, prevarication is easily detected through triangulation. The sheer number of elites interviewed by the author (at least a hundred) was enough to offset this weakness and then some. One interviewee would let glimpse details that another kept veiled. To compare data of this kind is also triangulation. Doing so was a little like reconstructing a fossil genome by collating its overlapping remnants.

Elite thinking, for all that, substantially reflects reality in matters of both fact and norm most of the time, *or else the elites could not maintain their status.*

They won the competition for power, so who can say that their grasp of reality is precarious? Because the subject-matter is (socio-)legal reason and practice, it is not as difficult to draw out assumptions as with less rational discourse, especially as the questions were designed to encourage elite interviewees to reflect on their beliefs and what can justify them. The responses contributed enormously to constructing a story rich in empirical detail, such that the author need not shy away from attributing causality to the unobservable. This is an approach to inference familiar to those working in the 'realist tradition' of the social sciences (Gaventa 1980; Shapiro 2005).

Wherever possible, interview data were validated against documents: legal instruments, parliamentary minutes, policy papers produced within the Network, evidence from secondary or academic literature. The scholarly literature was a valuable source of corroboration. Judiciary power has been approached by multiple disciplines, viz. political science, socio-legal studies, law, law and politics, and international relations. Time and again, scholars presented sound evidence but overlooked its significance, blinded by their commitment to this theory or that method. Moravcsik is atypical only in his transparency. He meticulously assembled archival data of lawyers-*cum*-politicians driving the genesis of the European Convention on Human Rights (ECHR), but never made anything out of their career backgrounds, modus operandi, and deeper motivations, the origins of their beliefs, or their network connections, some of which he was aware of.[7] Elite transnational networks being 'off his radar screen', he tested neo-functionalist predictions by looking for evidence of 'civil society' influence on the origins of CoE's human rights regime, of which he finds precious little. This he construes as confirmation of his notable intergovernmentalism (Moravcsik 1995). Had he done more exploratory work – that is, not taking the meaning of 'civil society' for granted – it might have dawned that the

[7] As witness his commentary on the reaction of elite British dignitaries to the ECHR draft in 1950: 'The defense of British institutional idiosyncrasy elicited the most violent rhetoric from British politicians and officials. Lord Chancellor Jowitt's official paper criticized the draft convention, largely the work of two distinguished former British officials, as "so vague and woolly that it may mean almost anything. Our unhappy legal experts . . . have had to take their share in drawing up a code compared to which . . . the Ten Commandments . . . are comparatively insignificant . . . It completely passes the wit of man to guess what results would be arrived at by a tribunal composed of elected persons who need not even be lawyers, drawn from various European states possessing completely different systems of law, and whose deliberations take place behind closed doors . . . Any student of our legal institutions must recoil from this document with a feeling of horror"' (Moravcsik 2000: 240).

Network Community is the sort of 'civil society' quasi-'interest group' which acts through governments *from the inside* rather than petitioning them from the outside. Reinterpreting existing evidence in a new light is an essential part of science. Methods of assembly and validation do not alone matter; also essential is the level of 'metaphysical' awareness of one's own a priori analytic outfit one approaches interpreting the body of evidence with. (The cynosure is Copernicus, who had no 'special/extraordinary data'; it was how he *interpreted* the same data that made the difference.)

Normative-historical comparison

Normatively framing the empirical effort was a historical comparison, taken up once the author discovered that the USA had inspired the lion's share of the Template. The Original Intent of the Framers, in their own words and deeds, was set as a benchmark against which the Template and its makers were judged. The data sources were, in addition to secondary literature, original documents, for example, letters of US presidents. The cohort-like temporal trajectories of Judiciaries in CEE and Europe more generally were considered in their historical-spatial connectedness with older developments in the USA. Comparison to the role of the US Judiciary before the Civil War was coded after Grounded Theory methodology to illuminate the Network Community and its handiwork.

Overview of the book

Part I begins by methodically identifying and inquiring into the biography of individual actors, the interviewees whose witness formed the empirical ground on which at a higher level of abstraction the existence of a collective actor, a community of elite transnational networks, is theoretically premised. This Network Community is very real; it can give the impression of a beehive that 'hives off' groups and individuals to take concrete action, who are anything but insectile or robotic, however; but creative in forwarding the common agenda. The Network Community's internal makeup and nature is interrogated: who is involved in Judiciary revisionism in Europe? What are their agenda, deep motivations, common interests, and power resources? Chapter 1 explores the Network Community's historical antecedents and presents an inventory of its membership and key resources arising from networking, constituting the basis of their ambitious expansion. Chapter 2 examines the Network's boundaries on sharing the collective identities of legal professionals and transnational elites, as well as a culture of substantive decisional consensus; which serve to exclude outsiders, dampen internal conflict, and consolidate the power to affect the external world. The Community is rooted in the solidarity of like-minded transnational legal professional elites who coalesced to build world peace, first through international law, and latterly through the supranational organizations of European integration. Elite solidarity is necessary for elite collective agency, without which the Community cannot cause anything in public affairs. Chapter 3 shows the Network Community in action effecting its common agenda, the empowerment of the Judiciary and correlative disempowerment of the elected branches of democratic governments. This the Network pursue consistently in accord with the precept 'personnel is policy'. Their members coordinate each other through the deliberate cultivation of mutual interdependence, rendering the Community as a whole politically more successful than if its individual members (such as magistrates' associations) were acting alone.

Once the Network Community has empowered itself enough to both hang together and exert sway over the rest of society, the question becomes what to do with such power? But for the assumptions the Network Community holds, its effects on the ground would not be what they are. By evincing and cross-examining the assumptions built into their Template, Part II engages crucial normative-as-causative issues.

Chapter 4 analyses the Network Community's discourses, revealing key assumptions held by members about the qualities of their agenda. As a quasi-experimental control, the author deploys Anglo-Saxon constitutionalism's classical conceptions of the separation of powers and checks and balances, judicial independence and the rule of law, the justice and utility of which has stood the test of time. Comparison in theory and in practice with the transnational Template proved to be thought-provoking both causatively and normatively. It demonstrated that the Network think of these conceptions as emanating from the autonomy and supremacy of a Judiciary empowered to annihilate all other contestants in case of conflict with itself. The comparison with the British constitutions of Blackstone and the US Constitution as understood in 1787 is an attempt at X-raying the causal role of hegemonic norms in both the governance *and* the scholarship of Europe. The chapter ends with an empirical catalogue and critical examination of those acts of state which alone the Network Community conceives as legitimate checks and balances on its Judiciary. Chapter 5 evidences that judges and the Network Community 'sponsoring' them commonly assume themselves morally superior – in a peculiar way – to all other actors in a political context; and what the ramifications of this superiority are supposed to be. It is reasoned that the hegemonic power of this assumption constitutes a (possibly the) major cause of judicial power over the nation-states of Europe, and the normative basis of judicialization. Chapter 6 analyses the origins and evolution of the three organs that make up the transnational Template, which for better or worse have become settled public policy practically across Europe. It will profoundly impact the world beyond Europe. It disempowers all other political actors to make public policy in defiance of judicial preferences, even on issues that do not touch the guilt or innocence of subjects of state power. Majoritarian preferences lie defenceless before the legal professional elite's veto, at a minimum. The long-term goal is the anti-majoritarian reshaping of the majority.

As a final caveat, the reader should note that the author has used a legalist style of exposition: the logical conclusion and its meaning are presented first, before the evidence is given. Some advise that this order should be reversed to avoid the appearance of confirmation bias, but the author has found that this style of reasoning maximizes transparency. It is best if the reader is not left, possibly in confusion, waiting to find out where the argument is going.

Part I

The transnational Network Community

The academic literature on Judiciaries in CEE has noted the involvement of a manifold of actors in the revision of Judiciary institutions after the fall of Communism. Here is a typical example:

> [I]n the enlargement context, NGOs, experts, magistrates and civil servants actively took part in the process of definition and diffusion of norms and standards of judicial reforms addressing the attention of the governments of the Member States, both old and new . . . judges and prosecutors, domestic NGOs and journalists challenged politicians who attempted to subordinate the judiciary to the political. Supported by powerful international actors . . . they worked alongside opposition parties to promote judicial reforms and the independence of the judiciary . . . domestic reformers – following the recommendations of the European Commission – drew inspiration from the old Member States and from a series of international organizations such as the Council of Europe . . . and a series of American organizations.
>
> (Coman 2014b: 5)

This sketch of the manifold and others like it are quite accurate, very necessary, and valuable. And the analyses and case studies provided to specify their activity is generally good. Even so, descriptions are like the list of *dramatis personae* heading up a play by Shakespeare, and the case studies are like the scholarly introduction, glossary, and critical apparatus. What about the play itself? Is it not about what the *personae* themselves think they have attempted, and what that ultimately means? The power relations and dynamic conflict between them? Their passions and deep motives, clashing and converging interests, and stratagems? The story of Judiciary governance in Eastern Europe, dry as it may sound as an academic title, proves as absorbing and intriguing as Shakespeare. The one difference is that he wrote of individual protagonists acting on their own behalf, whereas today's *personae*, those, that is, who actually drive the action forward, are *teams* of players acting in disciplined concert with each other, reflecting the collectivist or solidary nature of contemporary governance.

Part I is about transnationally networked elite self-empowerment in the 'internal' sense of their own essentially self-made power resources, which are the causes of success of the Template in terms of sheer agency. This is foremost a story of the *dramatis personae* as such, who they are, what is the nature of their complex interrelations and interactions, and which are the causes of pan-European Judiciary empowerment. In all of this, the interviewees and informants are allowed to speak for themselves, sometimes at length. All Network Community attributes illustrated in this Part – the networking between individual and dividual members, their power resources, the sharing of collective identity and consensus, entrepreneurial agency – empower the Network to empower themselves enough to carry the day at the domestic level and thus empower Judiciaries against national governments, first in Eastern Europe, and then beyond. But for that to happen, the Network's inner powers to empower must have first sufficed.

1

The ambit of the Network Community

Networks are structures of personal and collective power resources, which include social and political capital, privileged access to information, 'nodality', and often other more tangible assets like money (cf. Hood 1983; Scharpf 1997); the selective availability of which influences individual behaviour and mediates individual agency. These resources must nevertheless be activated by the agency of individuals, as networks have no agency of their own (Dowding 1995). Networks also have no coercive force of their own. Network power is distinguishable from hierarchical power by its want of the latter's encompassing command and control system, under which the many obey the few for fear of the consequences of disobedience; thus so that the strengths and talents of many, each compensating for another's weaknesses and incapacities, may be directed to one goal. A network has a horizontal and quite voluntary bonding structure, hence it does not automatically have a common goal. What makes networking so powerful despite lacking the capabilities of hierarchy is how it can span laterally between and within organizational hierarchies, bypassing problematic hierarchs, reaching out beyond them *and* even itself to knit together for a common goal all interested parties, to the extent this can be agreed by consensus, rather than command as such.

Networks may encompass agents both individual and collective; analytically, their 'membership' may be conceived as a spectrum. At one end, the individual is the irreducible element, even if ensconced in institutions and rarely acting alone. At the other end of the spectrum, one may find whole government organs, if all staff of significance is networked-in and insofar as the organ can act to achieve the network's agenda(s). In between stands the gamut of formal and informal institutions and of course the individuals who partake in and of them.

Individual members

Individuals have always been the Network Community's most important resource. Writing of 'Euro-law associations', components of the Community, and their role in aid of the judge-made integration of Europe in the 1960s by the ECJ, socio-legal scholars have noted the centrality of individual member initiative or entrepreneurship:

> The success of Euro-law associations . . . was in large part a result of the political capital of association members. Inspired by the meetings, members . . . used their offices to help the European legal integration project – lawyers found test cases; judges promoted European arguments before national courts and referred cases to the ECJ; professors wrote supportive arguments, planned conferences and imparted ECJ doctrine to the next generation of academics and practitioners.
>
> (Madsen and Vauchez 2005: 19)

Who is who, then, in the Network Community? The core is formed by elite legal professionals of long standing, transnational in orientation, but other kinds of actors ought to be included who may not have legal training: functionaries in international and supranational organizations like the CoE or the EU, human rights groups, an elite minority of national officials and political dignitaries, officers of philanthropic organizations, and even elite media. Individuals are networked-in with organizations. Some hold office inside formal organizations, such as associations, supranational organs and national ministries; but many others are 'floating around' yet networked-in. They move in and out of institutions, and may or may not be learned in the law. Some are legal professionals in businesses related to law, others not. Some are more entrepreneurial than others.

National and supranational judges

Transnationally networked-in judges manning national Judiciaries form the core membership of the Network Community. Invariably, it is the apex courts of appeal they staff. CC judges make up a substantial proportion of the European Commission for Democracy through Law ('the Venice Commission'), especially those from the member states of CEE (Venice Commission 2014). Supreme and Appellate Court judges make up the entire staff of some networked-in supranational organs such as the

Consultative Council of European Judges (CCEJ) (Consultative Council of European Judges 2014c).

European judges from every level of the judicial hierarchy customarily organize themselves in national magistrates' associations, which in turn are members of transnational associations such as the European Judges Association (EJA); which itself is a regional member of the UN-sponsored International Association of Judges (IAJ). National judges make the membership of transnational associations such as *Magistrats Européens pour la Démocratie et les Libertés* (MEDEL) as well, which accepts both individuals and national associations.

Judges of supranational tribunals, too, belong to the Network Community. The ECJ alone has furnished many members right from the beginning of EU integration, as witness the solidarity of their agenda in the 1960s to constitutionalize European integration (Vauchez 2008, 2015). Most European Court of Human Rights (ECtHR) judges are recruited from the Network, quite openly. They, in turn, draw on its power resources, even when unnecessary, almost in the manner of Veblen's 'conspicuous (or status) consumption' (Veblen [1899] 1934); they reference CoE Recommendations or CCEJ Opinions in their decisions – for example, non-binding, standards-setting documents put out by the supranational organs – to reflect their identification with transnationalism and with the Network Community, more than to express anything logically necessary to the decision.

Law school academics

'Men of ideas' are the keystone of the arch in the global trend toward Judiciary empowerment and the judicialization of politics, prominently at the national level in the West – from the USA and Canada to France and Germany, and recently even Britain (Stone Sweet 1992; Morton and Knopff 2000; Rozenberg 2014; Parau 2015d). At the supranational level, too, law academicians have been the Network's brain trust, as in ECJ-driven integration (Madsen and Vauchez 2005).

Academics tend to be more entrepreneurial and more involved in the Network Community than judges. What motivates them? Humankind generally seeks money, power, sex, celebrity. In academe, however, the thirst for intellectual glory is overriding: the reward is kudos (the ancient Greek word for 'glory') paid in the coin of being widely cited (Blackmore and Kandiko 2011). Universal admiration is a key behavioural motivator, established by behaviourists no later than B. F. Skinner.[1] Transnational and supranational involvement burnishes academic kudos to a shine. Academics in both common and civil law systems collaborate with judges to develop the jurisprudence of apex courts, support legal professional networks materially and morally, disseminate the precepts of the judicializing community in publications and media briefs, and encode the Network's common agenda in public policy by offering their services to popular representatives who nowadays delegate duties that in the past they would have performed in person (Morton and Knopff 2000; Rich 2004; Merryman and Perez-Perdomo 2007; Leucht 2010).

Networked-in with various elements of the Community depending on specialism, academics are probably called on by government organs more than anyone else to draft legal opinions, constitutions and organic laws, and to set transnational standards governing the judicial power. Supranationally, they take part in policy making in Strasbourg, which relies on expert advisory groups. For instance, academics were involved in each of the successive revisions of the CoE Recommendations on Judicial Independence in the late 2000s that attempted to develop norms on the power relations between the Judiciary and the elected branches of government. Their contribution was significant enough to be cited by the Chairs of the expert groups who drafted the revisions: 'We were assisted by some very capable academics, Dutch and French . . . the academics . . . did most of the drafting work' (CoE Steering Committee member: Interviewee 3), and, referring to a German academic: 'She had worked on judiciary independence and gave advice to our group . . . She was very proud that some of her ideas were retained' (CoE Steering Committee member: Interviewee 1).

Some of the most important functions in politics, drafting constitutions and organic laws, are routinely delegated – in fact, wholly given

[1] Primates in general, and humans in particular, stand out in the animal kingdom for greater susceptibility to social (dis)approval than to any other reinforcements (even food): 'The human being's affinity for group membership may have had its origins in the behaviour of his phylogenetic ancestry. The human being is born into the family group . . . spends his life in various groups, seldom abiding outside of groups. Group membership and participation is a necessity for the human ego. The ego's worth is wholly dependent upon the admiration of others, first upon the admiration of the primary dependent-upon external agent – the parent – and later upon parentified object and cathected others . . . The group tends to become familified – modelled upon and related to as the family group of one's origins and early formative years' (Comfort 2003: 153; see also Harlow 1958).

over – to legal academics who are networked-in, or at a minimum, deferential to the Network; in that capacity, they have unilaterally swayed the fundamental choices of peoples and polities. The abdication of the representative function has gone the farthest in the new democracies of CEE, where human capital and political rectitude are scarce. Academicians effectively monopolize the critical early stages, agenda setting and policy formulation, of the drafting of constitutions and organic laws pertaining to Judiciary institutions, which once entrenched, set the balance of power between the Judiciary and the elected branches. This applies to the CCs above all, in the first post-Communist democratic constitutions, drafted after 1989, as witness Romania and Hungary:

> In our country, in the debates in the [1991] Constituent Assembly, it was hard to convince even the lawyers that we needed a distinct authority of this sort. They said, 'In 1923, the High Court of Cassation and Justice, which is similar to the Supreme Court today, was responsible for this, so let's go back to the way things used to be.' Then *we* [the academicians] explained that in Western Europe things were no longer the way they were in 1923. The present Constitutional Court was created out of these debates and discussions.
> (Ion Muraru, President of the Romanian Constitutional Court, in Mungiu-Pipidi 1997: 78; emphasis added)

It was a creation fraught with birth pangs. Bitter disputes arose at that time (1990–91) between the academic specialists in constitutional law and the politicians, all of whom were members of the parliamentary committee drafting Romania's constitution, which had been set up by the Constituent Assembly that took over after the overthrow of Ceauşescu. At a certain adversarial point in the proceedings, the legal academicians secretly formed what they later called a 'shock team', consisting of a handful of law professors serving on the committee, plus experts assigned to the committee but without voting rights, and other jurists who were not even committee members. The team took it upon themselves to re-draft, over a weekend in the offices of the Law Faculty of Bucharest, the provisions on Judiciary power already adopted by the committee, which they deemed 'too prudent and minimal', allowing more involvement by democratic representatives in Judiciary governance than the academics preferred (Iorgovan 1998: 74). A few MPs protested this move for introducing 'new elements' into the draft constitution that were never debated or approved, as well as for the usurping manner in which this had been done. In the words of the president of the committee (one of the academicians): 'When we went back [to the committee], a discharge of egos took place . . . the politicians . . . accused us of circumventing the committee' (Iorgovan 1998: 74). The MPs on the committee had been assuming something closer to a Westminster parliamentary model, but they did not resist the *'coup d'État'* with alacrity, and that option was precluded by the academicians. In a similar vein:

> The Hungarian Constitutional Court was founded by its [first] President, [law professor] László Sólyom . . . The Constitutional Court is not made of judges but of academics with no practical skills, but full of ideals – an ivory tower institution, and thus the best guarantee for ideals such as human rights. Sólyom was most effective in creating the Constitutional Court as a very privileged body.
>
> (Academician and political adviser: Interviewee 4)

Academics have continued to play a pivotal role in every constitutional revision since, further entrenching the Template of the Network Community. Again, in Romania, academicians who were already CC judges became the constitution-drafting experts for the 2003 revision. They took the opportunity to cement their own Court's supremacy over Parliament by expanding its jurisdiction to include even Standing Orders of Parliament, the rules of its internal governance:

> **Q:** Public Law Professor Antonie Iorgovan is considered to have been a great lover of the Constitutional Court. Was he influential in 2003, when the Constitutional Court's competences were greatly expanded?
>
> **A:** Yes, he was influential and he insisted a lot on [the inclusion of] Art 96, which establishes the competences of the Court, and which contains a provision that the Court shall have competences in other domains as established by organic law . . . Taking advantage of the Bill being drafted, a provision was introduced empowering the Constitutional Court to check the constitutionality of Parliament's decisions, whether the Chamber of Deputies or the Senate.
>
> (CC judge: Interviewee 5)

The academicians also abolished Parliament's right to overturn a decision of the CC by a two-thirds majority:

> **Q:** Where did the idea of abolishing Parliament's nullifying power come from in Romania in 2003?
>
> **A:** From those who used to be Constitutional Court judges and who were in the Constitution Drafting Committee . . . People who were able to weigh up the desirability of Constitutional Court decisions not being overturned by Parliament.
>
> (CC judge: Interviewee 5)

Academicians are amongst the most versatile members of the Network Community, moving in and out of academe into private legal practice, government service, Judiciary offices, and/or politics, where they act as legal advisers to political dignitaries, or as dignitaries themselves in charge of judicial affairs. Rodica Stănoiu was a member of both the Romanian Academy of Sciences and the Venice Commission before becoming Minister of Justice in Romania from 2000 to 2004. University of Michigan Law School graduate Siniša Rodin, the Jean Monnet Chair at the University of Zagreb Faculty of Law, was an expert on Croatia's Judiciary reform during EU accession negotiations, writing reports and evaluating his country for the benefit of EU organs. After Croatia's accession, he was appointed the Croatian judge to the ECJ. László Sólyom, who before 1989 held a number of academic positions in Hungary and East Germany, including Fellow at the Hungarian Academy of Sciences, after the 1989 revolution became the founder and president of the Hungarian CC (1990–98), vice president of the Venice Commission, and president of Hungary (2005–10).

Lawyers-cum-*politicians*

The Network Community includes legal professionals who engage in partisan politics, moving between the legal and political spheres according to the electoral fortunes of their parties. This practice has been in decline in Western countries (King 1981), but is ascendant in CEE, where lawyer-politicians comprise but a fraction of the mass of elected office-holders (most of whom *not* networked-in), yet were decisive leaders in the domestic politics of the Judiciary. They achieve positions in their parties' upper echelons far more often than ordinary politicians, and in government tend to occupy high office as State dignitaries: ministers of justice, prime ministers, and presidents. In Parliament, they disproportionately staff powerful Standing Committees – for example, Constitutional and Legal Matters, which assesses the constitutionality of bills, draft regulations in all fields of law, and attends to Judiciary organization.

In Hungary, for instance, most bills are submitted to the Constitutional and Legal Committee, in which the number of MPs with legal training is higher than average. The Constitutional and Legal Committee of the Czech Parliament is made up mostly of lawyer-politicians tasked with scrutinizing every bill that originates in the Ministry of Justice as concerning judicial matters, as well as the drafts of constitutional amendments.

The Moldovan Parliament's Committee for Legal Affairs, Appointments and Immunities is second only to the Committee for Budget and Finance in importance, being perceived as such not least because it reviews most bills before they reach the plenary (Roper 2002). As one native put it recently, 'Moldova is now run by lawyers' (OSCE officer: Interviewee 7).

By virtue of their real or perceived expertise, and their professional interest, lawyer-politicians are likelier than any others to serve on the expert committees that CEE parliaments rely on to draft constitutional and organic law, especially provisions concerning Judiciary power. A high official of the Venice Commission notes, 'It is of course natural that lawyers are drawn more to constitutional issues than teachers or trade unionists, or that the influence of lawyers there will be considerable' (Venice Commission official: Interviewee 8). It is a pattern that has been observed from Moldova to Romania and beyond:

> Who were those who drafted the judiciary provisions of the Moldovan constitution after Moldova became independent in 1992? Mr. Barbaneagra who is now Councillor on Security Matters to the Moldovan President . . . Mr. Susarenco, a lawyer who worked in the Ministry of Justice, having been judge at the Constitutional Court and at the Supreme Court, and Mr. Timofti, the current President of the Republic of Moldova . . . The MP who advocated that the judges are given full responsibility over the organization of the Judiciary is from the Liberal Party, Mr. Mihai Ghimpu, Speaker of Parliament [2009–10] and Acting President [2009–10]. He is a jurist.
>
> (MoJ civil servant: Interviewee 9)

Wherever in CEE the author inquired, the evidence was always monotonously uniform:

> Doru Taracila [Senator (1990–92; 1992–96; 2004–08); Vice-President of the Standing Juridical Committee (2004–06); Internal Affairs Minister (1994–96); professional lawyer; dean of the Calarasi County Bar], together with Antonie Iorgovan [Romanian jurist, law professor and politician; Senator (1990–92; 2000–07); Constitutional Court Judge (1992–96); lead author of the 1991 Constitution of Romania] were the most important actors in the 2003 Constitutional revision . . . Taracila was a key figure, though Iorgovan was the most vocal and persuasive . . . the one who was quietly drafting the text . . . was Taracila, also the spokesman of the governing Social Democratic Party . . . Iorgovan had been very important in 1990–91 . . . He had clear authority.
>
> (Jurist and MP: Interviewee 10)

Hungary was no different: 'The Hungarian Constitutional Court was founded by its President, László Sólyom . . . He was well-connected with the [Magyar Demokrata Fórum] leadership – this is why he was so influential in designing this institution' (Academician and political adviser: Interviewee 4). As Table 1.1 shows, the Fundamental Law of Hungary, which superseded the 1989 Constitution under the populist Fidesz government, was drafted in 2011 by a team of transnational lawyers-*cum*-politicians-*cum*-academicians, who were in this case, however, networked-in notably less, apparently due to their right-wing Christian orientation that assimilated them to the European conservatism epitomized in Britain by Edmund Burke and Roger Scruton (who with Fidesz founded the Windsor Club in Hungary, Poland, and the Czech Republic to promote Christian conservatism through publication and policy analysis) (Academician and political adviser: Interviewee 4).

Table 1.1 Professional profile of the drafters of the 2001 Fundamental Law of Hungary

Name	*Professional background*	*Education*	*National political involvement*	*Transnational political involvement*	*Academic involvement*
Dr József Szájer	Jurist	Eötvös Loránd University, Political Science and Law Department (1986) Lawyer's examination (1990–94) Visiting student, University of Oxford (1986–87) Research Fellow, University of Michigan (1988–89)	Deputy leader, Fidesz (1992–94) Vice Chair, European Integration Committee (1994–2002) Deputy Speaker, Hungarian Parliament (2002–04)	MEP and Vice Chair, European People's Party	Resident assistant, István Bibó College, Budapest (1985–90) Assistant Professor (1986–) and Assistant Lecturer (1996–2000), Roman Law Department, Eötvös Loránd University

Table 1.1 continued

Name	*Professional background*	*Education*	*National political involvement*	*Transnational political involvement*	*Academic involvement*
Dr Gergely Gulyás	Jurist and Attorney-at-law (2004–08) Lawyer, Goulash Gregory Law Firm	Law degree, Catholic University, Budapest (2004)	MP (2010–) and Deputy Chair, Committee for Human Rights, Minorities and Civic and Religious Affairs, Hungarian Parliament Member, National Executive of Fidesz (2006–) Deputy Speaker, Hungarian National Assembly (2014–)	Evidence of networking with other European Christian Democrats	Lecturer, Constitutional Law, Károli Gáspár University of the Reformed Church (2005–)
László Salamon	Jurist	Eötvös Loránd University, Faculty of Law (1972)	MP for MDF-Fidesz-Christian Democratic Party (1990–2013) Vice President, National Assembly (1994–96) Member, Committee on Constitution (1990–94; 1998–2013) Chair, Committee on the Constitution (1998–2002)	Desk research yielded no evidence of transnational activity.	Constitutional Law Lecturer and Professor, Law Faculty, Pázmány Péter Catholic University (1995–)

Name	*Professional background*	*Education*	*National political involvement*	*Transnational political involvement*	*Academic involvement*
			Member, Committee on Drafting of the Constitution (1995–98)		
			Chair, Committee on Drafting the Concept of the New Constitution (2010–11)		
			Judge, CC (2013–)		

Sources: Salamon 2015a, 2015b; Gulyás no date.

Transnational civil servants

National civil servants, whether legally trained or not, may prefer to migrate to the supranational level to make policy, to get out from under their national hierarchical superiors to the extent that opportunity presents itself. Politicians rely on them to represent their nations' interests and views in the supranational policy processes governing human rights and judicial institutions, most of which takes place in the CoE, not the EU. It is national civil servants who staff the Steering Committee undergrowth arrayed under the CoE's Committee of Ministers (the counterpart of the EU Council of Ministers). In a parallel arrangement, standing intergovernmental organs, which steer or superintend the proceedings of other committees in designated policy domains, stand at the apex of the CoE's comitology system, comprising over three hundred committees of 'various national officials and experts, normally imported for short visits from national capitals' (MacMullen 2004: 414). Comitology is now the 'standard working method' of the Committee of Ministers (EJA officer and CoE adviser: Interviewee 11).

The European Committee on Legal Co-operation (CDCJ – *Comité européen de coopération juridique*) is the Steering Committee in the domain of human rights and Judiciary institutions. CDCJ was set up in 1963 with responsibility for the 'standard-setting activities of the Council of Europe in the field of public and private law' (European Committee on Legal Co-operation 2014). The CDCJ is staffed with legally trained, senior civil servants working for the Ministries of Justice of their respective member states, who 'come together and cooperate over what they should do' at the supranational level (CoE Steering Committee member: Interviewee 1); that is, they set the agenda and formulate policy.

*Lawyers-*cum*-career civil servants in the supranational organs*

The legal professional background that Network members inside the supranational organs share with outside members facilitates the latter's access to policy makers. This makes the Strasbourg Network quite unique in Europe. Even the most powerful lobbies in Brussels, such as the agriculture lobby, are unlikely to enjoy the same access or pre-positioning inside the supranational organs. The European Commission is not staffed by farmers who identify with their fellow farmers.

Transnationally oriented lawyers dominate the CoE's main organs as well, not only the ECtHR, but also the General Secretariat, especially its Directorate on Human Rights and Legal Affairs. The Secretariat has been an active player in the supranational policy process as it pertains to human rights and Judiciary institutions. As one of its senior civil servants told the author:

> **Q:** Is legal training a condition for working in the Legal and Human Rights Directorate?
>
> **A:** No, it's not . . . *it is highly recommended* but I know *some* colleagues who are working . . . in the [Human Rights and Legal Affairs] Directorate who do not have legal background.
>
> **Q:** If you were to estimate how many of your colleagues have legal background in the General Secretariat as a whole, would you say that they are in the majority?
>
> **A:** *Yes*. But if you look at some other sectors in the Directorate, for instance, people dealing with prisons or with the police, they won't necessarily have a legal background. They would have an expert background really fitting to their profile but not necessarily a legal one.
>
> (CoE civil servant: Interviewee 12; emphasis added)

'Expertise' fitting to 'profile' implies that those labouring in human rights and Judiciary affairs would have the profile of a Network Community member. Even more likely is that they became networked-in, once hired, if they weren't already. They certainly network closely with the Venice Commission, as witness this senior civil servant in the Directorate-General (DG) of Political Affairs of the General Secretariat:

> We cooperate, of course, very closely . . . for example, we cooperate daily with the Venice Commission, implementing the programs together . . . we have an electoral assistance programme, which is managed by this DG, but the activities are implemented very closely with the Venice Commission and with the colleagues in the Media Department [of the General Secretariat].
>
> (CoE official: Interviewee 13)

The staffs of the EU supranational organs, too, must be included in this inventory, particularly if involved in negotiating EU Eastern Enlargement. It was legal professionals inside DG Enlargement who were in charge of negotiating Judiciary redesign and other juridical matters, and monitoring the results in the two accession waves – 2004 and 2007:

> Before the European Commission, I did a law degree at Edinburgh University for 4–5 years and then I did a Masters in Law at the *Collège d'Europe* in Bruges . . . As far as judicial reform [in CEE] was concerned . . . we [DG Enlargement] built a team . . . Yes, we were [all] lawyers.
>
> (EC official: Interviewee 14)

This pattern is being repeated with the Balkan accession candidates. Here, too, the senior civil servants in charge of judiciary revision are lawyers. According to one of the Heads of Unit:

> I am a lawyer, I am a member of the Italian Bar, and I used to work as an attorney at the law, but I spent the majority of the time at university, because I have a PhD in international law, which I did jointly between an Italian university and the US.
>
> (EC official: Interviewee 15)

The *Collège d'Europe* is a training academy not just for legal professionals, but for 'Eurocrats' more generally, who go on to staff the supranational organs of both the EU and the CoE:

> I am the General Director for . . . [anonymized] in the General Secretariat of the CoE, I have been working for this organization for nearly thirty-five years, so I have done all my career in this house. I am a lawyer by training. I have graduated in law in France and came from the *Collège d'Europe* in Bruges. The CoE was my first job and it will be my last one.
>
> (CoE official: Interviewee 13)

The *Collège d'Europe* in Bruges originated with the European Movement, whose 'first major achievement' was the creation of the Council of Europe in May 1949. It went on to bring forth the *Collège* and the European Centre of Culture in Geneva, both of which were parts of a Grand Design of European integration (European Movement International 2015; Centre Virtuel de la Connaissance sur l'Europe 2018). The *Collège* facilitates the type of socialization that lays a solid foundation for elite transnational networking. It is surely reinforced by the revolving door between *Collège*-trained Eurocrats working for the CoE and/or the EU, and quite likely other international organizations. In the words of a former Head of Unit of DG Enlargement:

> I am a lawyer. I used to work for the Council of Europe before I joined the European Commission. I worked for the European Court of Human Rights for one year, and then for the Legal Affairs Committee and the Political Affairs Committee [of the CoE General Secretariat].
>
> (EC official: Interviewee 16)

Networking-in through formative education or through revolving-door migration from one apex office to another means that *fonctionnaires* in the European Commission, like the legal professional accession negotiators, do indeed network with their counterparts in the CoE, and through them with the broader Network Community.

Collective members

The Network Community also includes collective members: associations, governmental organs, independent advisory bodies, which completes the progression along the spectrum of collectivity from individuals through civil society in the broad sense to hierarchical institutions; reflecting the Community's panoply of power resources from membership-as-power to resources the Community as a whole constitutes or can avail itself of.[2]

[2] In reality, no bright line separates these purely analytic distinctions between individual and dividual members qua resources compared with other power resources. Both individuals and organizations are both members and resources. A supranational organ is a member and a power resource of other types at the same time, even if one could argue that it constitutes the latter more than the former.

Supranational organs

The Network Community, through its networked-in supranational civil servants, reaches inside integrative organizations – not just regional ones like the CoE, the EU, or the Organization for Security and Co-operation in Europe (OSCE),[3] but other organizations of global reach like the UN and the International Monetary Fund (IMF) – the 'international community', in other words. The staff of such governing organs are usually networked-in but may be entrepreneurs in addition, a 'transnational' status that belies their officially delegated duties in subordination to these hierarchical organs. The mere fact of holding a post in which contact with the Network is inevitable does not automatically make one a member, however: the Venice Commission, for instance, comprises one commissar from each member state, chosen by its government – a mode of appointment not characteristic of, nor conducive to, networking. *If* a government dislikes the Venice Commission's current tendency, it possesses discretion to appoint a spoiler, who would presumably *not* be networked-in.

The organs of the EU and CoE constitute the most important ones for the Network Community. The sheer number of policy domains pre-empted or coordinated by Brussels means that interest groups seeking to impact domestic institutions must peddle influence inside EU organs. As the EU is *the* regional organization in Europe, the one most effective at altering the governance of the nation-states so our elite networks do reach deep into the EU organs. Indeed, they were in a real sense 'grandfathered' into them, having been involved in the EU's creation at a time when European elites were seeking supranational solutions to their collective problems. Even today, a sector of these networks continues to orbit Brussels, interconnecting lawyers who serve commercial consultancies and other corporate interests (Lahusen 2008).

It is the CoE organs, however, that have proved the most important for the Network Community as a whole. Legal professional networks have found them more accessible fora for developing pan-European norms on

[3] OSCE is a trans-Atlantic organization which traces its origins to the Conference on Security and Co-operation in Europe created in the '*détente* phase' of the Cold War in the 1970s to facilitate dialogue and negotiations between East and West. Its 'comprehensive approach' to security encompasses a very wide range of issues, including human rights. 'Human rights' are defined in a way that allows the OSCE to engage in reforms of national domestic institutions, as well as support the jurisdiction of supranational courts like the International Criminal Court (ICC) (OSCE 2016).

the Judiciary and judicial practice. The latest such project harmonizing norms and standards of judicial power is little more than 'industry self-regulation', resembling similar processes in the EU. These might be less technical than telecommunications standards, for example, but the legal professional networks aspire to the same self-governance:

> **Q:** What arrangements should be put in place so that judges have decisional independence, but are held accountable as well, when they overstep their competences?
>
> **A:** I begin with the social status of judges, which is a very special status. Judges should be judged only by their equals. Issues of . . . establishing their competences, the way in which they judge impartially, or not, disciplinary problems, can only be decided by . . . their equals.
>
> (Jurist and career politician: Interviewee 17)

The CoE General Secretariat is the Network Community's 'crown jewel'. It has nodality like no others, going between and joining up many far-flung power centres in the Network, keeping them in touch with each other and abreast of the supranational policy process. One Secretariat functionary described it thus:

> My task was to bring experts together, send them the relevant documents that would be the basis for discussion and then start the discussion . . . We had a first meeting where we agreed on the structure that [our project] would have. That was my first task: to put in writing what they have been discussing for three days.
>
> (CoE civil servant: Interviewee 12)

The Secretariat is involved in the policy process alongside with the transnational civil servants on the Steering Committees: 'The first draft is written within the Secretariat. This is the norm . . . The Secretariat is very important, especially the Human Rights and Legal Affairs Directorate' (CoE Steering Committee member: Interviewee 1), which is staffed by networked-in legal professionals. This empowers the Network Community to set the agenda on all juridical affairs for the CoE, and to inscribe it in pan-European standards. The common agenda of the Network Community then becomes the agenda of all Europe.

Access to these supranational organs is a major power resource for the Network Community, reaching well beyond nodality. This is illustrated by a political contest over the Serbian Judiciary in 2009. The Serbian government sacked large numbers of judges, a move the pan-European judges' association MEDEL felt themselves interested in and damaged by.

They had easy *entrée* via the Network Community inside the European Commission to lobby the European Commission for intervention:

> In the case of Serbia . . . we went . . . to DG Enlargement because they have a say, and we wrote to Mr Štefan Füle [the Enlargement Commissioner], and addressed the Members of the EP as well, and Mr Füle and the Commission were made aware of our position and tried to follow it.
>
> (MEDEL high official: Interviewee 2)

Evidently, MEDEL had an expectation of being sympathetically heard and heeded by European Commission heavyweights, an expectation resting on nothing observable but the Network Community itself and its common identity, agenda, and elite status – in short, its solidarity and *in situ* consensus.

Similar patterns have been documented before, but in other policy domains. Interest groups in EU member states and candidate countries have shown an ability to prevail over the national government and majority preferences by networking, then allying, with supranational officials of the European Commission and the European Parliament with whom they shared political interests and policy agendas. A very small 'new civil society' minority became 'the mouse that roared' only because it aligned with a transnational Network with superabundant political capital on offer, especially inside influence, and an elite contrarian agenda which spanned the local and the supranational (Fairbrass and Jordan 2001; Parau 2009, 2010).

Professional associations

The fall of Communism in 1989 and Eastern Enlargement beginning in the 1990s opened up a world of new opportunities to the Network Community and its Strasbourg operation. Since then, judicial and magistrates' organizations have mushroomed – typically transnational associations arising voluntarily and operating independently of the national governments in which their members are employed.[4] They 'share and discuss common

[4] These include: the Conference of European Constitutional Courts, the Association of the Councils of State and Supreme Administrative Jurisdictions of the European Union, the European Judicial Training Network, the Association of European Administrative Judges, the Network of the Presidents of the Supreme Judicial Courts of the EU, the European Network of Councils of the Judiciary, and the European Judges and Prosecutors Association. For a comprehensive overview, see de Visser and Claes (2013) and Dallara and Piana (2016).

problems', 'learn from foreign experiences', and 'tackle common challenges' (de Visser and Claes 2013: 77); however, they are not nearly so apolitical as that form of words might imply. Their *modus operandi* and *raison d'être* are agenda-driven, resembling the type of interest group, classically associated with the European Commission, that represents the interests of the more technical industry sectors. The companies in these sectors combine in membership associations (legal professionals do this too), and usually succeed in influencing EU regulations affecting themselves. The EU's dependence on industry expertise translates politically into industry self-regulation or capture of the regulatory regime (Reinke 2012). All developments toward creating supranational norms governing the national Judiciary in the last twenty-five years have been put on the CoE (hence EU) agenda by the transnational networks of legal professional associations upon which the CoE and hence the European Commission have come to rely.

Associations furnish power resources to the Network Community, lending moral and material support to members and to the whole Network, from tangibles like information and funding to intangibles like ideas and an aura of authority (see also Piana 2007a). Yet they are not command-and-control apparatuses in themselves, but 'parliaments' of elite consensus building and action coordination, facilitating non-hierarchical policy coordination across national boundaries. They have stacked up an impressive record of consequential policy formation and implementation: 'Euro-law associations coordinated the actions of individuals to propel [European] legal integration in a constitutional direction' (Madsen and Vauchez 2005: 19). Finally, they intervene in national politics to lessen domestic resistance to Judiciary empowerment. They matter to the story of Judiciary institutional revision in Europe because they have furnished such a panoply of ways and means to help legal professionals get out from under hierarchical domination in the national political order, inside and outside the Judiciary branch.[5]

MEDEL, an association on the political Left, is a prime example of this. It maintains close ties with the Socialist Group in the European Parliament

[5] In the court system, lawyers are subordinate to judges, for instance, and younger judges are subordinate to senior. Senior judges can make life difficult for their juniors. Interviews carried out by the author of the younger generation of judges in CEE revealed that they are dissatisfied with their subaltern status, often perceiving the hierarchs as abusive and authoritarian; as one former Romanian judge put it, they act like 'tribal chiefs' (ECJ clerk: Interviewee 18).

(MEDEL high official: Interviewee 2). Like all associations of its kind, it lobbies on behalf of the material self-interest of judges, viz. higher wages, better working conditions, etc. It considers its actions as a quasi-trade union to be part and parcel of its political action:

> we are going against the old structures inherited from the past . . . we are for the rule of law and independence of the judiciary, for the modern conception of the State . . . if judges have autonomy you can hope for a better salary . . . You cannot condemn a judge to hunger . . . In a CEE country like Romania, judges may earn 1,000–1,500 Euros a month . . . that's not enough.
>
> (MEDEL high official: Interviewee 2)

MEDEL was founded in 1965 by

> young judges from Germany, France, Italy, Spain and Portugal who were attending courses at the École nationale de la magistrature in Bordeaux and wanted to get free from under the strong political influence of the Christian Democrats and allegedly from the Socialists, too, and to connect with their neighbours.
>
> (MEDEL high official: Interviewee 2)

A kindred discovery was made by Vauchez: that Euro-lawyers preferred acting at the supranational level because it freed them from 'structural subordination to politicians in national parliamentary regimes', which then yielded 'unprecedented degrees of freedom in the promotion of their traditional professional agenda' (Vauchez 2008: 133).

MEDEL's 'rival', the EJA, was founded in 2003 by a Network Community entrepreneur and a member of its inner circle, Secretary General of the Italian Supreme Court of Cassation, and a Supreme Court judge in Rome (EJA officer and CoE adviser: Interviewee 11). The EJA is an association of national judges' associations that facilitates networking between judges across national boundaries in Europe: 'We are judges . . . we needed to have an arena, a forum to discuss the problems that we Europeans have. This is why we created a regional [European] group' within the IAJ (EJA officer and CoE adviser: Interviewee 11). The EJA and its members lobby for more than judges' material self-interest: it is freely admitted that they pursue agendas that are properly political, such as the 'structural independence' (*sc.* autonomy) of the Judiciary branch. In the words of one judge, the President of an EJA member association:

> There were ups and downs, some things have been accepted or have been listened to [by the Croatian government] . . . but mostly what happened in all these years is that we were under the monitoring of the EU and experts came here, that they always wanted to speak with the judges and the

> judiciary itself . . . And then we had . . . opportunities to speak with those experts, and we said, 'This is good and this is not, this should be changed. According to the Council of Europe or UN standards this is not right in Croatia and should be changed.' *And then* that *comes from abroad back home, and* then *it is accepted* . . . For example, the last thing we managed to fight was the immunity of judges, which was out of the question [for the Croatian government] . . . And we had a lot of possibility to contact our friends in other associations such as the Association of Judges in Europe . . . We also managed through that kind of co-operation with international partners to show to our government that the standards were international and it was the one that went through as we proposed. The last item [on our agenda] is the new constitutional changes which would put the Judiciary Council in a different position. We will become more independent structurally because judges will elect their members in the Council . . . The Executive has a hostile approach [to this], as everywhere else.
>
> (JC official: Interviewee 19; emphasis added)

The American Bar Association (ABA) was one of the first organizations to specifically target the legal profession in CEE for counter-hierarchical empowerment, that is, to train them how to resist hierarchical impositions, ultimately to organize them in an alternate hierarchy of their own, but not to aim for an impossible abolition of all hierarchy:

> The American Bar Association has tried to influence judiciary reforms through financing . . . [and] training . . . ABA does not get involved directly in politics, does not work with politicians. We do not lobby but empower others to do so . . . we have supported lawyers' associations, who then lobby politicians. The Lawyers Association in Moldova [for instance] is very weak. ABA supported them in their lobbying of government on the Legal Profession Act.
>
> (ABA officer: Interviewee 20)

The value of the Network Community and its association membership as power resources is not lost on newcomers, particularly legal professionals operating under severely constrained domestic opportunity structures (including but not limited to purely material scarcity), which can deny basics taken for granted in the West, such as court logistics and essential operating procedures:

> **Q:** Why is it important for the Moldovan judges to be part of the European Network of Judiciary Councils?
>
> **A:** We have obtained many documentary materials produced by the Annual General Meetings of the European Network of Judiciary Councils . . . [and] we try to take these materials on board . . . because they discuss many issues that are important to the Judiciary . . . Last year, issues discussed included

> the technical-material equipment necessary to courts, how to construct budgets, and disciplinary procedures.
>
> (SCt judge and JC official: Interviewee 21)

Legal professionals as far afield as Africa aspire to join the European Network Community. Probably the chief motive is that transnational networking *constitutes* the kind of power that will be to their advantage in domestic political contests, exerting leverage within the hierarchy of national political institutions. In the words of one of the most active of the EJA's members:

> The Algerian Association or the Congo Association are . . . extraordinary members of the European Judges Association . . . What's in it for them that membership in the European Judges Association is so important? What are they losing by not being part of it? . . . If in Italy you say, 'You are not a member of the European Judges Association', who cares? But in these countries it is very, very, very important . . . What do they gain from it? Do they stand to gain power? . . . Yes, of course . . . the international label gives them a stronger bargaining power *vis-à-vis* [their national] government, parliament, and even the press.
>
> (EJA officer and CoE adviser: Interviewee 11)

To conclude, transnational legal professional associations as multi-faceted lobbying groups aim to advance the personal and political interests of the legal professional faction they represent. On behalf of their members, they lobby political leaders, national and supranational, for specific private and public goods – higher salaries and intervention in favour of members in difficulty, as well as help to the judicial systems of poor countries – but also their policy agenda of judicial self-empowerment, which they believe is also a public good.

Independent advisory bodies

Other organizations belonging to the Network Community sit somewhere in between the non-governmental and governmental spheres. Foremost are the so-called 'independent advisory bodies' to international and regional intergovernmental organizations. At the international level, these include the UN-affiliated IAJ, with regional branches on several continents. In Europe, there are the CCEJ and the Venice Commission, both affiliated with the CoE. Their power originally stemmed from the exigencies of Eastern Enlargement and its aftermath, but now it has expanded far beyond this. In the beginning, they 'fell between the stools' of non-governmental interest group and intergovernmental organ, but with time they have been grafted onto the formal structure of the CoE General Secretariat. Since the fall of Communism, both have become major agenda setters acting through the CoE on matters judiciary.

The class of organizations differs from transnational legal professional associations in important ways. They are configured intergovernmentally as member states' forums. Often the representatives are given autonomy once appointed, and in formal terms enjoy their member states' imprimatur; at a minimum their acquiescence. Thus, for some political purposes they may be counted as a 'piece' of the government; and yet, like private legal professional associations, they endeavour to sidestep and outsmart their national governments, particularly the core Executive with whom the Network Community vies for policy-making power. At the same time, they lobby for the Network agenda and, transcending special interests, unlike the professional associations, they constitute its real power centres. They hold fast to a vision of governance by courts and judges, and deploy deep stratagems for making it a reality. Their relationship with intergovernmental organs proper is a quid pro quo: they trade off the use of their indispensable expertise for policy influence.

The Venice Commission specializes in matters of judicial review and CC design, as well as the relation of domestic to EU and international law. It was founded by Antonio La Pergola (1931–2007), the archetypal transnational legal professional elite. Italian lawyer and politician, and a committed European federalist (La Pergola 1993), he held senior offices in Italian and pan-European judicial and political institutions: member of the Italian Supreme Council of the Judiciary (1976–78); Justice and then President of the Italian Constitutional Court (1978–87); member of the European Parliament (1989–94); Advocate General then Judge of the European Court of Justice (1994–2006); member of the Committee of Wise Persons on the Restructuring of the Council of Europe. La Pergola had been educated not only in Italy, but also at Harvard Law School, America's and probably the world's foremost nursery for incubating the theory and practice of the judicialization of politics (see Tate and Vallinder 1995).

La Pergola almost certainly availed himself of political support from the CoE through the Italian Minister of Foreign Affairs, Giovanni (Gianni) De Michelis (1989–92), who represented Italy in the CoE at the time, and whom La Pergola knew when serving together under the De Mita government (1988–89), De Michelis as Deputy Prime Minister, and La Pergola as Minister for Coordination of Community Policies and *rapporteur* of the implementation of Italy's legal obligations arising from membership of the European Communities (Parlamento Italiano no date). As Italy's Foreign Affairs Minister at the relevant moment, and so an *ex officio* member of the CoE's Committee of Ministers, De Michelis was well positioned to influence the Committee to put on its agenda the proposal of an 'advisory body' to the CoE on constitutional matters. In the words of a senior official in the General Secretariat of the CoE:

> The origin of the Venice Commission is a very old one . . . I am old in this house and I have seen a lot of things . . . I have seen the genesis of the Venice Commission and at the time it was mainly an Italian initiative of the then Minister of Foreign Affairs Giovanni (Gianni) De Michelis . . . and it came from the fact that the CoE had bodies with expertise in all fields of legal activities: penal law, criminal law, family law, administrative law, international law, but it did not have any constitutional law body, probably because at the time, that is before 1989 . . . there was no such a feeling of a need of a constitutional body in Europe . . . But it was mainly an Italian initiative at the time, which the Secretariat of course supported, because there was a feeling that there was something, a piece missing in the network of legal bodies of the CoE.
>
> (CoE official: Interviewee 13)

The Venice Commission looms over the judicialization landscape of Europe like a promontory. As well as CC judges, it comprises academics and practitioners specializing in constitutional, public, and international law, who make their expertise available for member states' domestic constitutional issues. It enjoys authority in the international community: 'The Venice Commission has the best experts' (OSCE officer: Interviewee 22). Its greatest influence, however, is over the CoE's newest member states – those from CEE. It was involved in the post-Communist transition from the start, well before Eastern Enlargement, in advising, monitoring, and (informally) preconditioning accession to the CoE on the entrenchment in CEE constitutions of certain Judiciary institutions of interest to the judicializing community (Piana 2007b). According to a CC judge in Romania:

> The Venice Commission had been asked to help even in 1991: our experts went there, theirs came here; the collaboration was very good and has been kept over time. In 2003, when the Constitution was revised, four members of the Venice Commission came here and gave us their feedback and made suggestions, which the Constitution Drafting Committee liked. This connection with the Venice Commission is maintained now as well.
>
> (CC judge: Interviewee 5)

Since its creation, the Venice Commission has established a reputation even beyond CEE as the go-to authority on all constitutional matters, as witness the frequency with which governments turn to it for expert opinion when revising their fundamental charters. Its membership now reaches well beyond Europe to include seventy-six nations, including the USA, not too far short of half the world's total of 196.

Those who counsel resorting to it – the elite legal professionals to whom politicians hand off the drafting of revisions of constitutional and organic law – are almost always networked-in. Many are or have been members of the Venice Commission themselves:

> it is . . . specific to Central and Eastern European countries where . . . more frequently . . . members of the Venice Commission are . . . closer to the political process, and also involved in decision making at the national level, and of course bring this experience on to the Venice Commission, but also back to the national level.
>
> (Venice Commission official: Interviewee 8)

Networked-in academicians, especially, hold their peers in the Venice Commission (in essence, themselves) in high regard: 'One cannot neglect to take into account the scientific authority and expertise of the Venice Commission. Any collaboration of this kind can only be beneficial' (CC judge: Interviewee 5). In the words of Antonie Iorgovan, Professor of Public Law and the father of the Romanian Constitution: 'the Venice Commission is made of first-rate experts . . . It is the Holy Grail of European law' (Antonie Iorgovan, speech in Parlamentul României 2003).

The CCEJ is a council of judges as such rather than academicians or scholarly experts, and concerns itself with other judiciary matters than constitutional law. It was set up in Strasbourg in 2000 to be an 'advisory body of the Council of Europe on issues related to the independence, impartiality and competence of judges' (Consultative Council of European Judges 2014a). Although it was a Resolution of the Committee of Ministers of the CoE that formally established the CCEJ, the Ministers played little part in it; rather, it originated with Network entrepreneurs operating informally outside the CoE structures. As one of CCEJ's founders put it:

> I remember talking to my Polish 'opposite number' in some ante-room in the *Palais d'Europe* in Strasbourg and we were talking about . . . the mindset [of judges], and how we could best get judges, especially the more old-fashioned ones, to think in . . . a more modern way. He and I both simultaneously came up with the idea that it would be a good idea to have a CoE-sponsored group of judges so that judges can influence each other.
>
> (CoE Steering Committee member: Interviewee 3)

The Resolution that 'a consultative group made up of judges be set up within the Council of Europe' was put on the agenda of the CoE Ministers of Justice's annual meeting, which in 1999 was held in Moldova's capital, Chişinău (Committee of Ministers of the Council of Europe 1999; CoE Steering Committee member: Interviewee 3). The Resolution identifies its authors as 'the Ministers'; however, it is common knowledge amongst insiders that Ministers' meetings are not actually taken very seriously: 'In the EU, Ministers meet quite regularly, but in the CoE, Ministers of Justice meet once every year for one-and-a-half days, one day for social gathering [giggles] . . .' (MoJ senior official: Interviewee 27). Hence the attendees at these meetings are usually Deputy Ministers of Justice or lower – senior civil servants with legal background – not the Ministers themselves. Most importantly, their agenda is actually set by others, usually the General Secretariat in consultation with the host country. Who prevails over whom in case of disagreement over the agenda varies, depending on the host country's clarity of purpose and assertiveness (CoE Steering Committee member: Interviewee 1; CoE Steering Committee member: Interviewee 43). At this meeting, no such disagreement arose, as the Moldovans lacked any ideas of their own for an agenda; instead, they appealed to the General Secretariat and to the Steering Committee on Legal Co-operation (CoE Steering Committee member: Interviewee 3). This opened the door for networked-in CoE insiders to set the agenda they wanted, and they inserted the CCEJ. In the words of the Network entrepreneur in question, 'the Moldovans accepted the idea with great glee' (CoE Steering Committee member: Interviewee 3).

The CCEJ right away became much more than the advisory body it purported to be (see the section 'Personnel is policy' in Chapter 3). Its Opinions are now cited by judges of the ECtHR and even the UK Supreme Court (SCt). It has become *the* agenda setter de facto for Europe on matters of Judiciary governance and institutional design, exhibiting an evolution like that of the Venice Commission, as hinted at by career civil servants in the CoE, who themselves seem to be confused or ambivalent over the institutional role of the CCEJ:

> For the legal profession, what the CCEJ produces . . . are very important documents. The problem is that in our [CoE] institutional framework, we have clear definitions of committees and what their rules are, and a legal instrument to be adopted by the Committee of Ministers – and I highlight that, to be *adopted by the Committee of Ministers* – it can only be prepared by an intergovernmental [Steering] committee, that's clear. So then the CCEJ is providing opinions which are very useful, but I think when it's coming

> from such a committee, it is really a sectoral [interest group] angle, it is very sectoral because it will only represent the views and interests of that particular profession, whereas normally when there is something prepared by government representatives they have to ensure internal domestic coordination with other ministries, and what comes from the intergovernmental committee is much more balanced . . . I am myself not that clear where the CCEJ sits in relation to the formal structure of the CoE. If you at look its origins, and [compare that with] what it has now become, it grew really, really beyond the initial mandate. That is quite clear when you examine its evolution chronologically . . . Initially, it had an advisory role but then with so much expertise and competence, the advisory role transformed into setting guidelines for the profession, which is a standards-setting role that normally intergovernmental committees have . . . their mandate has extended beyond the original competence.
>
> (CoE civil servant: Interviewee 12; emphasis in original)

The CCEJ thus got itself accepted as another major agenda-setter on Judiciary issues in Europe. It works closely with transnational associations and the CoE, and has intervened well beyond CEE to empower elite judges and judges' associations to resist national political action against the judicial interest:

> **Q:** Do national magistrate associations lobby the European Commission and the CoE to put pressure on domestic politicians?
>
> **A:** Yes, this happens. I can give you an example in which I proceeded in this way. In 2001 . . . I was the Vice President of the [national] Association of Judges . . . we were already a member of the CCEJ . . . Government actions were foreseen to the disadvantage of judiciary . . . I wrote a letter to the ECtHR and the General Secretary of the CoE asking them to try and influence the leadership of the country . . . This led the CCEJ to examine this petition of mine . . . At that time, if the [national] Judiciary Council proposed a judge for a post, the President had the right to reject it and the Judiciary Council was able to do nothing about it. As a consequence [of my action], the legislation was amended so that . . . if the Judiciary Council proposes the same candidate again, the President does not have the right to reject him. This was passed by the government . . . and is still in place and observed. This is an example of how a non-governmental organ such as the Judges' Association as a member of the CCEJ had an indirect influence on the reaction of the CCEJ and of the CoE's Committee of Ministers to the national authorities.
>
> (ECtHR judge: Interviewee 23)

The CCEJ enjoys such a degree of autonomy that some of the most nationally minded member states are becoming concerned, as witness the Norwegians' ruefulness over their inability to check that body's influence over their own domestic public policy. Senior civil servants in the Justice Ministry tacitly have implied that they would do something about it if they could:

> At the very beginning, the first Norwegian member [of the CCEJ], who was a justice of the Supreme Court, was selected or nominated by the Minister of Justice, so certainly in the beginning the Ministry was involved in the nomination on a formal level. The name was passed on to the CoE by the Ministry of Justice, and we expected the Norwegian member to give a report to the Ministry of what happened during the [CCEJ] meetings. In the course of time, the membership became totally independent and rather *subject to self-recruitment*. I remember in particular his successor who . . . had no positive feelings about giving a report to the Ministry of Justice about what happened, and even less being nominated to those meetings by the Minister of Justice, and in the end there was no actual follow-up on the part of the Ministry, so little by little the Norwegian participation became totally independent from the Ministry, and this is certainly what it is like today . . . But it is the government that is involved in the administration of the courts, which is now governed by a semi-independent authority – the so-called 'Courts Administration' – and it can be useful to receive news of what has been discussed and what were the conclusions of the CCEJ . . . because if questions are to be discussed and solutions implemented in the Norwegian setting . . . the court administration and the government must also be involved.
>
> (CoE Steering Committee member: Interviewee 43; emphasis added)

To conclude, ad hoc agenda-setting organs were set up through Network entrepreneurship but then evolved to become part of the CoE array of supranational organs, or so closely affiliated with them that a distinction is hard to draw in practice. The member states at least nominally appoint the Venice Commission, rendering it contingently intergovernmental. This might bring some control over personnel, hence policy, yet these nominees can easily slip member states' control, once appointed. Having become 'autonomous', the appointees are likelier to be networked-in than if seconded by Ministries of Justice and remaining subordinate to the Minister.

Public and private funders

Political actors, no matter how gifted, can achieve nothing without material resources. Amongst the most powerful of 'behavioural reinforcements' is money, from whatever source, private or public (Skinner 1971). Material resources matter all the more because the Network Community is a minority of a larger elite class which is itself a minority in the larger society. Such an outnumbered cohort, even when faced with but minimal resistance, could not possibly transform power relations between the Judiciary and the elected branches across whole regions of Europe without adequate funding. Even comparatively small amounts matter if they outmatch what isolated, unorganized adversaries can afford or raise on their own, or if made available to first movers to make an indelible impact before opposition can start itself up from scratch. Transnational mobilization entails the highest (for most actors, insuperable) transaction costs, and can easily tip the balance of feasibility (Coase 1988).

No rival network, no 'Judges United Against Activism', could arise without comparable support. The deafening silence of anti-judicializing dissenters in transnational and supranational fora bespeaks the unlikelihood that any network hostile to judicialization could ever qualify for support from the private and public funders who have been underwriting judicialization. Even if, supported by member contributions, any arose, the least false step (like internal dissent) could prove fatal if it exhausted the precarious reserve.

Philanthropic foundations such as the Rockefeller Foundation and the Carnegie International Peace Endowment provided the funding that enabled the first transnational lawyers, after their emergence in the 1870s, to consolidate their influence in Europe in the aftermath of the First World War. Without this funding, these legal professional networks would have remained a dream:

> From before WWI, the reputation of the Hague as a key centre for international law studies had already been established, but the Dutch capital became even more the real 'Mecca of international law' after the Permanent Court of International Justice's headquarters were established there in 1923 . . . The sumptuous Peace Palace that immediately hosted the International Court, financed by the Carnegie International Peace Endowment, became the first and most prominent temple of this internationalist 'religion'. In The Hague, the promoters of the science of international law could rely on a dense network of supporters . . . an Academy of International Law had already been created in 1913 with the support of the Carnegie International Peace Endowment. Each summer the Academy (also hosted in the Peace Palace) brought together the leading academic specialists in international law to teach small groups of students from all over the [Western] world . . . Teaching and learning at the Academy thus gradually became one of the capital steps and one of the critical credentials required for entering the budding community of believers in an international rule of law. . . . The *Institut des Hautes Etudes Internationales de Genève* (the Geneva Graduate Institute of International Studies) was created in 1926 with the joint support of the Swiss

> government, the Geneva University, and last but not least, the *Rockefeller Foundation* . . . [These became] supranational venues for lawyers . . . [who] seemed to subscribe, regardless of their national origins and political linkages . . . [to the] belief in the superiority of the *judiciary* mode of settling conflicts over any other political technology when it comes to organized peaceful international relations.
>
> (Sacriste and Vauchez 2007: 89–93; emphasis added)

Nearly a century later, transnational legal professionals bearing gifts of funding for Judiciary revisions and the rule of law first arrived in CEE from the USA. The ABA may have been the first to engage with constitutional and Judiciary matters in the region: 'Foreign influence was . . . exercised by experts from abroad. The American Bar Association has organized a number of conferences to offer technical advice on how to write constitutions' (Elster 1995: 393). The ABA continued its engagement through the 1990s and early 2000s, aiding the establishment of networking between judges and prosecutors, as well as between sister bar associations, to teach them to lobby the government for favourable policy changes (ABA officers: Interviewees 20 and 24). The ABA itself is in part funded by private money. According to a Network entrepreneur:

> After the fall of the Berlin Wall, after the collapse of the Soviet Union, you had the . . . Central and Eastern Europe Law Initiative (ABA-CEELI) . . . which had behind it the American Bar Association, which has behind it the money . . . of enterprises, of American companies . . . they did a very good job and . . . according to . . . their interests . . . In each country they had a sort of embassy of the American Bar Association, but . . . far more than this an embassy of American interests, economical interests in each Eastern European country . . . ABA-CEELI was the first to act for many years.
>
> (EJA officer and CoE adviser: Interviewee 11)

The Soros Foundation was another private funder that became involved in Judiciary revisions in CEE in the 1990s (Piana 2007a). Soros funded NGOs promoting human rights, for example, Lawyers for Human Rights (Lawyers for Human Rights officer: Interviewee 25). The network of Open Society Institutes monitored and published evaluations of CEE Judiciaries in the early 2000s through its affiliate Transparency International (Open Society Institute 2001). This became an important reference for interested parties like the European Commission, which used it in its monitoring of CEE candidates and apparently as an internal justification for intervention in Judiciary institutional design. The Commission is careful to proportion any idea that non-governmental actors (perhaps especially transnational NGOs) have influenced its policies on the rule of law and judicial power. In the words of a senior official in Brussels who oversaw the revision of the Judiciaries of several CEE countries:

> **Q:** What are the European Commission's sources of information about a candidate country?
>
> **A:** It depends on the local people [EU officials on the ground] . . . that is something I can't really answer because only the [European Commission's] political desk in each country . . . are dealing with them every day, and they get to know the people [on the ground]. They would be the ones that receive reports from Transparency International, from the Council of Europe, from the European Commission Delegation and then the official contribution of the country authorities themselves. And then they put this together and try to find a median.
>
> (EC official: Interviewee 14)

The transnational NGOs operating in CEE, however, have demonstrated just how influential they really are with the European Commission. According to one senior official in DG Justice, formerly in the Commission's Delegation in Bucharest during accession negotiations, who was charged with monitoring Romania's pre-accession Judiciary revisions, it was her background as a founding member of Transparency International that got her hired by the Commission (EC official: Interviewee 26). This seems to be a pattern amongst transnational organizations generally. An OSCE officer in Moldova described to the author her career in the NGO sector, where she created an umbrella organization of which Open Society was a founding member. She was hired by the OSCE from this organization. Corroborative illustration is seen in the facile migration of high-level elites in Brussels, whether legally trained or not, from the European Commission to the elite philanthropic sector, and vice versa (Open Society Foundations 2017).

The ambit of the revolving door connecting transnational NGOs, supranational organs, and philanthropic foundations calls for further research. What is clear is that migration of elites from one sector to another seems an integral process of transnational elite networking. Transnational civil society routinely collaborate and may be funded by the same philanthropists. Their officers were very often found to be members of the Network Community and to be laterally mobile between Network organizations. This is certainly the pattern in CEE. A monitoring report of the Open Society Institute is for this reason likelier to be given attention and weight by the Commission than one issued by almost anyone else.

The consequences are predictable. In the words of the chief drafter of the Hungarian Fundamental Law and the Vice-Chair of the European People's Party Group in the European Parliament:

> I had been a Soros scholar [at Oxford] but now . . . What I see at the European level is that it's not any more [Soros's] money which matters. Philanthropists give money for noble ideas, and that's good . . . And, the Central European University, too . . . this is not so controversial. But what Soros is doing is buying influence . . . not any more what he can buy with his money, but his people are sitting in the European Commission in the decision-making bodies and they are using the European Union money for what he was giving [his own] money for before . . . the effect of that is not an organic way of doing things. It has a very strong, distorting influence on what is happening in the world, essentially.
>
> (Jurist and MEP: Interviewee 35)

All kinds of NGOs haunt Brussels, and struggle to survive. Billionaire philanthropic foundations are in a class by themselves. It is hard to believe that networks and agendas are not carried over in this process, with such consequences for public policy as hinted by the informant quoted above. Foundations which promote judicialization may be dependent on the Network Community for its legal expertise, but at the same time they must keep their distance lest their brand and public goodwill be implicated.

It was the Soros Foundation which paid for some of the first American policy entrepreneurs to penetrate CEE after 1989 to advise on constitutions and the Judiciary. It would be anomalous indeed if such philanthropic foundations did not pursue their own networking with each other. Here is the author of one of the first books written by an American academic extolling the establishment of CCs in CEE:

> I would . . . like to thank those who have supported and sponsored my work in Central and Eastern Europe these last twelve years: Aryeh Neier, president of the Open Society Institute [funded and chaired by George Soros], who first got me involved in East Europe affairs in 1987; Wendy Luers, who founded and organized the Foundation for a Civil Society [funded by the Rockefeller Brothers Fund] which supported much of my early activity.
>
> (Schwartz 2000: xx)

The continuing involvement of private funders is a pattern consistent with the historical record: in the 1960s and 1970s, the Ford Foundation teamed up with the United States Agency for International Development (USAID) and the World Bank to finance US Ivy League legal academics in carrying out rule-of-law dissemination programmes in developing and democratizing countries (Piana 2007a).

Corroboration that private funders are networked-in comes from the UK, a setting that could not be more different to CEE. Constitutional revision was put on the New Labour agenda by Charter 88, an organization unlikely to have managed such influence but for Trevor Smith, the chairman of the Joseph Rowntree Reform Trust (Smith 2008; Weir 2008). 'A New Magna Carta' (Political and Constitutional Reform Committee 2014), a blueprint for radical constitutional revision in Britain issued in 2014, likewise sprang from the collaboration of a coterie of MPs with certain legal-academic norm entrepreneurs who received philanthropic funding (the Rowntree and Nuffield Foundations being the most prominent) channelled through the Centre for Political and Constitutional Studies at King's College London. Private foundations supported previous bids for a written constitution as well, for example, Charter 88's, implying at least ideological consensus (King's College London 2015; Parau 2015d).

Supranational organs with control of the allocation of public revenue have also been a major source of funding for the Network Community. The EU has intervened with funding from the beginning of European integration; for example, the European Commission in the 1960s funded hosting organizations that catalysed transnational networking and collaboration to promote the ECJ's constitutionalization agenda:

> The WGE [*Wissenschaftliche Gesellschaft für Europarecht*], with its scholarly focus, put its energy into planning conferences where issues of European law were debated, and in writing analyses of the law . . . the AJE [*Association Française des Juristes Européens*] organized smaller meetings, lunches and seminars for national lawyers and judges . . . often bringing in high officials from the European legal system . . . The European Commission also helped develop the European legal field by establishing the *Fédération International pour le Droit Européen* (FIDE), an umbrella organization [which] sponsored conferences every two years in the 1960s, providing a means for pro-integration lawyers from different countries (including the United Kingdom) to get to know each other and to coordinate activities.
>
> (Alter 2007: 7)

Other regional and international bodies like the OSCE and the UN have been sources of funding for the Network Community's agenda in CEE and beyond (OSCE officer: Interviewee 22), speeding its success as *the* agenda-setter in Europe for Judiciary revisions. Even the shoestring budget that the CoE gives its 'missionaries' (CoE Steering Committee member: Interviewee 3) exceeds what competitors, had there been any, would have enjoyed; who if lacking equivalent funds of their own would have been obliged to spend their own time and social capital on raising funds from a general public whose interests judicialization (in its vulnerable formative stages) was causing too diffuse an impact. In any case, the panoply of networked-in funding bodies could always have supplied more funding had any such norm contestation actually arisen.

The CoE and EU have been the most consistent supporters of the Network Community in CEE:[6]

> In 1994 the memory of the fall of the Berlin Wall and everything that followed from it was very fresh and there was a great push towards helping former Communist countries modernize their legal system and equip them to comply with the requirements of the CoE in particular – the application of the principle of democracy and the rule of law. It was known that there were problems in the Judiciaries of some of those countries, really serious problems, and it was obviously a useful thing for the CoE to bring its expertise to bear on these issues . . . In those days, the CoE was much more effective than it is now . . . because it had much more money to actually invest in projects of this sort [before expansion of the ECtHR's jurisdiction siphoned it off]. It also did quite a bit of technical assistance, financial assistance programmes; they were forever setting up seminars, especially in Russia and some of the other Eastern bloc countries.
>
> (CoE Steering Committee member: Interviewee 3)

In the early 2000s, the CoE formally joined forces with the EU, after the latter had funded most of the CoE's Judiciary reform programmes in CEE (Piana 2007a). In practice, this meant funding for the Network Community's judicializing agenda was open-ended.

The media

As Walter Lippmann (1922) and others pointed out nearly a hundred years ago, the capacity of the public and their political representatives to know the world beyond their personal ken is very limited and dependent upon media of communication that rest firmly in the hands of others besides themselves. Absorbed in daily business, ordinary politicians (a fortiori the general public) lack both time and means to find out all that happens if the media do not inform them. It is significant, then, that a former General Secretary of the CoE has called his organization 'the best kept secret in Europe' (Davis 2010).

In politics, no one can keep secrets or prevent their significant impact on mass awareness and electoral politics unless media agree to omit or

[6] See Piana (2007a) for a comprehensive overview.

minimize them. Consistent omission of news about the CoE hints that media may be networked-in as well. Much of the media's power consists of the power to omit, in point of fact. Omission therefore constitutes an important power resource for the Network Community. It can disable Europe's ablest national politicians' efforts to keep track of and scrutinize developments at the transnational and supranational levels:

> what happens within the CoE . . . is not easily picked up either by the public or by the political environment in Norway. For MPs to know about it, they would have to be told about it. If they do not read about it in the newspapers, it has to be the government, or the Ministry of Justice, who informs Parliament about this [a policy development in the CoE], or it has to come through to their attention through the Parliamentary Assembly of the CoE . . . [In our] delegation to the Parliamentary Assembly there are very few representatives who are engaged in Judiciary institutional politics.
>
> (MoJ senior official: Interviewee 27)

Some claim that public uninterest makes the CoE not worth reporting. It might be best to take this *cum grano salis*, given the CoE's demonstrable impact on domestic policy making. An alternative explanation is that media owners and editors-in-chief are networked-in, or sympathetic to the Network Community agenda. As far back as the late 1960s, elite journalists covering European affairs had 'gone transnational', forming veritable 'networks of information exchange' resembling 'an advocacy coalition that actively promoted the European cause [of integration]' (Meyer-Sahling 2009: 121). Given the consolidation of media ownership that has culminated in and facilitates coordinated omissions, they are networked-in today a fortiori (Bagdikian 1983, 2004). As for their stance on integration, a pilot survey of transnational elite media (e.g. *Financial Times, Guardian, Daily Telegraph*) carried out by this author before the Brexit debacle found unswerving support for, at the very least systematic omission to criticize, supranational organs like the ECtHR, even in a country as strongly Eurosceptical as the UK.[7]

Of all the Network Community members, media may be the least critical and the most sympathetic to the supranational courts – and elite media support for the continued jurisdiction of the ECJ over Britain after Brexit may be some evidence of this.

[7] The systematic research project awaits being carried out which will inquire into how much the European media cover the CoE, and, if at all, how media portrayal affects public and elite reaction to it. Given the greater impact of negativity, it would matter more if media avoid a negative tone when they do cover the CoE and its Network than if they take a positive one.

Circumstantial evidence of media–Network interdependencies can also be found in some of the Law and Politics literature. In a recent article, Ran Hirschl noted:

> During . . . 'constitutional moments,' massive popular mobilization – often accompanied by international cheering by rights advocates, *Western media*, and democracy supporters – leads to mounting pressure on a despotic regime to relinquish power, democratize politics, and protect individual rights through constitutional reform.
>
> (Hirschl 2013: 361; emphasis added)

Stone Sweet, too, writing about the judicialization of politics in France, notes the role of media in promoting the ascendance of judicial power:

> Two constitutional revisions modified the [Constitutional] Council's jurisdiction. In a 1971 decision, the Council, prompted by a referral of the President of the Senate and publicly encouraged by law professors *and the media*, annulled a piece of government-sponsored legislation for the first time. In relying on a rights text, it effectively incorporated a bill of rights, partly unwritten and ill-defined, into the constitution.
>
> (Stone Sweet 2002: 81; emphasis added)

Research in the USA reveals close networked relationships between apex judges on the Supreme Court and metropolitan journalists, which has resulted less in media omission than in a positive tone and deferential approach in its coverage of the Supreme Court (Slotnik and Segal 1998; Davis 2011). The logic is that both media and courts are known for their counter-majoritarianism, and are often in fact conceived, and might even conceive themselves in their different ways, as 'checks and balances' on runaway majoritarianism. Thus they may be closer to each other, even before any networking takes place, in their policy preferences as well as in their modes of proceeding than either is with the elected branches of government.

This is corroborated by media collaboration with transnational elites in other countries and policy fields. Journalists reporting on economics and finance for vehicles such as *The Economist* and *Financial Times* are part of a transnational network of financial elites who have been promoting and disseminating their independent central bank Template. Their reportage and editorials represent this template to their readership as a *fait accompli* (McNamara 2003). Incidentally, this may also explain why apex financial institutions such as the IMF and the Bank of England intervened on the Remain side of the 2016 Brexit referendum. As noted by Lord Lamont, former Chancellor of the Exchequer (1990–93), 'all these great institutions . . . the Bank of England, OECD, the IMF have become increasingly politicized. There is a close interaction between the civil servants and all of them, interchanging, working together, and that is a consensus' (*BBC Newsnight*, 12 May 2016).

The experience that these varied groups of elites share is that they began by spontaneously networking with each other for plain self-empowerment; otherwise they never would have discovered how much their interests could converge if only they arrived at a consensus specific enough to constitute an agenda. The purpose of so many far-flung individuals inside and outside organizations continuing to network could hardly have been to advance the interests of individuals only. Network members are of course pursuing their individual interests that differ in detail, but are assimilated to each other in the aggregate or at a higher level of collective action. Thus for example, varied organs and individuals have varied motives, but if they find out through networking that their motives shore each other up, then networking is self-reinforced. MEDEL and the EJA operate as interest groups helping judges and national associations to more resources than the constraints imposed by domestic political forces would allow. The entire Network Community, however, would not have become involved that deeply in domestic issues; yet might be counted on to reinforce the efforts of such associations, which indirectly or ultimately benefit the Network. Even if the differences between individual members outnumber the similarities, if they all agree only on certain matters of supreme interest to all, whilst disagreeing on all other matters, they would constitute at least a latent community of interest. In fact, the Network do agree and are committed to a common agenda, empowering themselves collectively in the process. This is a motif to be apprehended and worked out in the remainder of this book. For now, it suffices to note that self-empowerment through networking is nothing new; indeed, it might be the 'ground state' of political action. As the American statesman and philosopher Benjamin Franklin vividly confessed in humbler (*ca.* 1730), yet essentially parallel circumstances:

> I had form'd most of my ingenious acquaintance into a club of mutual improvement, which we called the JUNTO . . . the Junto, was found so useful, and afforded such satisfaction to the members, that several were desirous of introducing their friends . . . [I] made in writing a proposal, that every member separately should endeavour to form a subordinate club . . . The advantages proposed were, the improvement of so many more young citizens by the use of our institutions; our better acquaintance with the general sentiments of the inhabitants on any occasion . . . *the promotion of our particular interests in business by more extensive recommendation, and the increase of our influence in public affairs,* and our power of doing good by spreading thro' the several clubs the sentiments of the Junto.
>
> (Franklin [1868] 1996: 45, 79; emphasis added)

2

Identity and solidarity

Networking between individuals who move amongst organizations across different fields of practice at different levels of governance facilitates the formation of collective identity, network consensus (decisional and substantive), both of which in turn facilitate elite political solidarity. That goes a long way toward explaining the Network Community's success at disseminating its Template across the world in a short time. The Network Community, although it spans impressive stretches of space and time, does have its limits, which are defined by the solidarity of identity and consensus.

Collective identities

The most important boundary is self-defined: its members share an identity, the awareness of having ideas, feelings, and interests similar to each other and distinct from others (Gurin et al. 1980). This collective identification is exclusive: 'who we are' sets 'us' apart from 'them'. One manifestation of this is the Network Community's interest in who is appointed to the governing institutions that they consider 'theirs', a theme that will be taken up at greater length below. There is no more enlightening encapsulation of the matter than Benjamin Franklin's recounting of his own network prototype:

> Our club, the Junto, was found so useful, and afforded such satisfaction to the members, that several were desirous of introducing their friends . . . We had from the beginning made it a rule to keep our institution secret, which was pretty well observ'd; the intention was to avoid applications of improper persons for admittance, some of whom, perhaps, we might find it difficult to refuse.
>
> (Franklin [1868] 1996: 79)

Collective identity to perdure must be nurtured, whence the members of a club feel themselves interested in who is permitted to join. Though not a 'secret' club – the Junto itself was not kept secret, either, for long – the

Network Community is private; in one sense, it is instituted by no public power, and in another sense, the mass media obligingly omit to publicize its existence or investigate its internal acts and communications. Yet its members are as self-interested in policing the boundaries of their collective identity, lest they are overrun by outsiders who are not 'us'. The Network Community, because at its core it is legal and professional, is able to exclude 'unsuitable persons' much more efficiently than the Junto. Thus, Bourdieu astutely remarks that

> the institution of a 'judicial space' implies the establishment of a borderline between actors. It divides those qualified to participate in the game and those who, though they may find themselves in the middle of it, are in fact excluded by their inability to accomplish the conversion of mental space – and particularly of linguistic stance – which is presumed by entry into this social space. The establishment of properly professional competence, the technical mastery of a sophisticated body of knowledge that often runs contrary to the simple counsels of common sense, entails the disqualification of the non-specialists' sense of fairness, and the revocation of their naive understanding of the facts, of their 'view of the case'.
>
> (Bourdieu 1987: 828)

Identity and identification are easily inferred from the discourses used by individual members all over Europe to describe their relationship with each other and with the Network Community as a whole. There abound pronouns indicative of collective identification such as 'we' and 'us', as well as nouns like 'friends', 'brother', 'relatives', and 'legal family'. Individuals employing such terms are casting in with chosen others, expressing a sense of belonging to a collective ego which is an affective, psychological fact. The same phenomenon has been observed by others in connection with sister networks; for example, the use of 'family' and 'community' constructs collective identification with the ECJ (Vauchez 2015), whilst it has been inferred that the transnational lawyers who crafted the European Civil Code were a 'united . . . European brotherhood' (Schepel 2007: 3–4).

As this chapter will illustrate, collective identification may be inferred not only from discourses but also from its members' acts, which preserve and advance its interests as a community. These included acts effecting and constituting solidarity and commitment, for example, through interventions that helped peers in distress, policed the boundaries of the Network, reached consensus in pursuit of a common agenda, disseminated that agenda, and defended it against opponents.

Legal professional identity

Collective identity is particularly tight amongst Network members who share a legal background. This is rooted in the legal profession and experience, and is implicit in the fact of having been educated in a certain way. The legal professional identity seems to begin at the national level, and afterwards is borne up to the transnational level. Lawyers have formed strong collectives in the European nation-states. In Germany, for instance, senior civil servants in the MoJ and Justice Ministers are almost invariably legal professionals, and previously some of them were judges. The collective identity is strong enough that Ministers and functionaries are not too proud to take lessons from their private peers, as all are part of an inner circle which encompasses the Ministry but would subsist very well without it. All are welcome to the 'Club of We':

> Lawyers play an important role in Germany. It's the legal family you might say . . . It's important what the lawyers say, what the judges say, what other parts of this legal profession are saying . . . We have a guild of lawyers which is more than a hundred years old.
>
> (CoE Steering Committee member: Interviewee 1)

Collective identity may also be inferred, indirectly, from acts of solidarity with the profession, both within and across national borders. Judges in many European countries (CEE included) are organized in trade unions and magistrates' associations whose *raison d'être* is to advance and defend their membership's self-interests. Unionization itself is a manifestation of collective identity. When French President Nicolas Sarkozy criticized judges for being 'too lax' (Chrisafis 2011), the Union of Magistrates – already antagonized by his reforms to the Judiciary – retaliated by, in effect, going on strike – that is, deigning to hear only the most urgent cases and mobilizing protests in the streets:

> Thousands of judges and lawyers have taken to the streets in unprecedented protests against Nicolas Sarkozy, paralysing the legal system and shutting down almost all France's courthouses . . . Judges took to the streets in dozens of French cities and towns, including Lyon, Bordeaux and Versailles. Outside the court of justice in Paris, more than a thousand judges and lawyers in robes gathered with placards and megaphones.
>
> (Chrisafis 2011)

In Romania, too, magistrates mobilized to protest their 'stress bonus' being cut, and even sued the State in its own courts to secure pecuniary benefits that the State was struggling to reduce, following its negotiations with the IMF (Coman and Dallara 2009).[1] Whether Sarkozy or PM Emil Boc of Romania were right or not is irrelevant. What matters is the astonishing solidarity of legal professionals that was put on display by these events.

Collective identity transgresses the boundaries of the nation-state, at least amongst elite jurists, and their organization in the transnational realm proves it. Transnational magistrates' networks care for the fate of their peers in every concerned nation. Here is the president of the Croatian Judges Association calling them his 'friends':

> we have a lot of . . . contact [with] our friends in other associations such as the European Association of Judges . . . [Concerning the membership of Moldovan judges] in the European Association of Judges, we feel that they are not allowed to . . . that they are prevented from making contact with the Association. They are not allowed to communicate by email . . . They did not come to the CoE meetings or the Association meetings . . . we think something is going on which is not acceptable.
>
> (JC official: Interviewee 19)

This sense of solidarity moves members to intervene across borders to succour their peers. Those in CEE can be so materially deprived that they cannot bear the ordinary cost of transnational networking. When certain transnational activities of the Network Community were too expensive for them to afford, networked-in, elite Romanian judges intervened to enable their Moldovan peers to participate, who experienced this help as a manifestation of brotherhood:

> We [Moldovan judiciary elites] have links [with Romania] and hope to improve our relations. We are acquainted with Ms Florica Bejenaru [President of the Judiciary Council] whom we know very well . . . with judges Horatiu Dumbrava and Cristi Danielet [MEDEL recruits in Romania] . . . We needed a lot of support and received their support. Because of their direct involvement . . . it was possible for two members of the Moldovan Judiciary Council to take part in the General Meeting of the European Judiciary Councils. We went to London in 2010 and to Vilnius in 2011, and this year we had an invitation again . . . and every time the organization and costs of travel were covered by the Romanian Judiciary Council. We believe that it is good to help your brother once or twice.
>
> (SCt judge and JC official: Interviewee 21)

[1] The stress bonus was worth 50 per cent of the net wage of US$1,650 a month. Without it, judges would have still earned bonuses totalling up to 85 per cent of the net wage. The average wage in the Romanian economy was approximately US$350 a month.

The Network Community does not hesitate to intervene in the domestic politics of established member states if they perceive their peers to be in need of support, not just for their own material well-being but also concerning the distribution of power. The IAJ hastened to second the French jurists' challenge to Sarkozy's 2009 constitutional reform, which sought to diminish the power of the French Judiciary:

> the main working group, within the European Judges Association, is the so-called Group on the Situation of the Member Associations . . . is currently working on both Eastern and Western Europe . . . In France . . . there have been recent reforms in which judges have become a minority in the Council of the Judiciary . . . The European Association issued recommendations . . . which [were] sent to the [French] House of Parliament.
>
> (EJA officer and CoE adviser: Interviewee 11)

The Venice Commission has intervened to obstruct the revision of Judiciary power in countries as remote from Europe as Kyrgyzstan, where it 'convinced the President not to abolish the Constitutional Court, although he had the intention to do so' (Venice Commission official: Interviewee 8). Venice was also the first to react to the Fidesz revision of the Hungarian Constitution, issuing its first Opinion on the constitutional change in 2011 (European Commission for Democracy through Law 2011a). Going beyond its remit from the Hungarian government to give its opinion only on certain designated specifics, it inserted an unsolicited admonition to the Hungarians against overhauling the CC's competence in budgetary matters:

> The Venice Commission regrets that the limitation of the competencies of the Constitutional Court as a result of the constitutional amendment adopted in November 2010 has not been repealed . . . As a result of [this] constitutional amendment . . . a serious limitation of the competences of the Constitutional Court was introduced . . . the Constitutional Court may assess the constitutionality of Acts related to the central budget, central taxes, stamp duties and contributions, custom duties and central requirements related to local taxes exclusively in connection with the rights to life and human dignity, the protection of personal data, the freedom of thought, conscience and religion or with rights related to the Hungarian citizenship. Also, the Court may only annul these Acts in case of violation of the above-mentioned rights.
>
> (European Commission for Democracy through Law 2011a: 2)

The Venice Commission's criticisms were observed generally to give priority to CCs over other judicial institutions like the JC. Its greater concern for the fate of that institution suggests that the Commission's members – current and former CC judges or constitutional law professors – identify with it, and therefore feel a threat to the Court's power as a threat to themselves. That the Commission is less outspoken on the design of the ordinary Judiciary suggests that the CC is more critical to the Network Community's supremacy over the other political powers of the nation-states.

Another manifestation of collective identity was found in the disappointed expectation of many Network entrepreneurs that other Network members will be equally committed. As a MEDEL leader exclaimed:

> Why the Czechs still don't have a Judiciary Council? Why are they so different from everybody else? They are like the Germans . . . they do not want to commit themselves . . . [but] in practice . . . they, too, are members of the International Association of Judges, and of MEDEL, so they dance at two weddings, and this is already very nice . . . That reassures you.
>
> (MEDEL high official: Interviewee 2)

The Network Community entrepreneurs can be vocal in their disapproval when the expected level of commitment is not forthcoming:

> Britain is one of the oldest members of our association. 'Member' if I can say so . . . two or three [British] jurists met and called themselves the British Association of Judges of the International Association of Judges. This was the British solution! And they always sent the same people . . . Lord Phillips [former President of the UK Supreme Court] . . . who has a very high position in the UK Judiciary, but he is not attending our meetings anymore.
>
> (EJA officer and CoE adviser: Interviewee 11)

It is a remarkable fact that lawyers who get involved in politics not only retain but prioritize their legal professional identity. Admittedly, they are bound to have multiple identities, yet identification and sympathy with the legal profession is so strong that they almost uniformly prefer judicial empowerment, and the corresponding disempowerment of the other branches, more than other politicians:

> During the term of this Judiciary Council, we had Minister of Justice Alexandru Tănase [2009–11], the current President of the Constitutional Court, under whom there was even more openness [to the demands of legal professional elites]. Mr Tănase . . . himself came with many initiatives which we judges accepted and desired . . . The current Moldovan President Nicolae Timofti used to be the President of the Judiciary Council . . . *All of us* . . . know the system and care about it.
>
> (SCt judge and JC official: Interviewee 21; emphasis added)

The sentiments of the Romanian jurists are no different at all from the Moldovan ones:

> Only in exceptional cases an institution [Parliament] acquiesces to the idea that its competences will be cut . . . It seems normal to me that Emil Boc [Romanian Prime Minister 2008–12], an academic with a solid juridical basis to come with such a proposal [enhancing the Constitutional Court's power], and here *we* too [lawyer-politicians in Parliament from across the political spectrum] have agreed with this measure to reduce the basis of Parliament's power to the benefit of the Constitutional Court.
>
> (Jurist and MP: Interviewee 10; emphasis added)

Lawyers-*cum*-politicians defend Judiciary empowerment designs against those who challenge them. One 'old school' Romanian jurist denounced the entrenchment into organic law of the mandate that the Judicial Council was to be the 'representative' of the Judiciary branch. He was immediately contradicted by ripostes from those committed to the Template. For example, a law professor, an MP, and a member of the Standing Juridical Committee of Parliament, went so far as to observe that the Judicial Council was analogous to a democratically elected Parliament, as if a body elected by no one but salaried civil servants, voting amongst themselves, had legitimacy equal with and parallel to a real parliament elected by the people:

> I want to clarify for my MP colleagues that this Judicial Council of Magistrates is the Parliament of the Magistracy in Romania. The Parliament of the Magistracy in Romania! Just as the Romanian Parliament represents the Romanian people in their relations with whomever, this Parliament of the Magistracy called the Judicial Council must be the representative of the magistracy.
>
> (Parlamentul României 2004a)

A sense of collective identity not only runs like a golden thread through the legal professional networks, it also bonds them with each other but also with a wider network far from all of whom are jurists. This is glimpsed in the following testimony of a British senior civil servant in the former UK Department of Constitutional Affairs who sat on the committee that drafted the 2010 CoE Recommendation on Judicial Independence. She, too, refers to a collective 'we' that includes jurists, although she had no legal background:

> Amongst the group [of experts who drafted the Recommendation] *we* had judges from very different backgrounds . . . and many of them were talking about exactly the same issues as being important to them. I actually felt that *we* were sharing that background, sharing that understanding . . . that's

> why I think the Consultative Council of European Judges is so important, because you get a very diverse background of judges all coming together to say what's important for the judges . . . what are the issues *we* need to talk about . . . . I think that's really important . . . the more you can actually share experience, the better.
>
> (MoJ official: Interviewee 28; emphasis added)

Note that she counted herself as if one of the judges, instead of speaking of things 'we [Executive bureaucrats]' need to discuss with 'them'. That collective identity is felt across the transnational judicializing community, reaching far beyond the legal profession, and is in evidence in words and deeds of solidarity and sympathy between not only the networks of Judiciary governance but throughout the whole Network Community, international organizations and metropolitan media included, which time and again was observed hastening to the defence of the transnational consensus in domestic political controversies.

This is very well illustrated by the controversy over Hungary's constitutional reform of 2011, when the Fidesz party moved to kerb the powers of the CC rather marginally in comparison with the alternatives extant amongst Western democracies. The whole Network Community – from the CoE to the European Commission to the IMF to the international and metropolitan media, and more – pressured Hungary to abandon the reform: 'At the end of last year [2010] the intention of the [national] authorities was to abolish [*sic*] the Constitutional Court. The Venice Commission intervened in Hungary . . . [It] would make a big fuss and then other international players would intervene' (Venice Commission official: Interviewee 8).

Likewise, MEDEL acted as if they were on the inside of the European Commission and could take for granted its intervention on the side of MEDEL's brothers the Serbian judges, a third of whom were to be dismissed by the government via a 'general re-appointment procedure' (Antonić 2008; MEDEL 2012). The mere fact that MEDEL could lobby the European Commission so confidently implies they had reason to believe they would have a good reception. How many people can write to the DG Enlargement with any expectation that they will even be noticed? The Commission is open to organizations like MEDEL in ways that are not available to just anyone. The deeper one burrows on the inside, the more privileged the access. Some are so embedded, they can end up being 'honorary Commissioners for life' (as it were):

> **Q:** Even now that you are no longer in the European Parliament, do you still have access to the EU officials?

> **A:** Yes, of course . . . I am not visibly on the lobbyist list because I don't need it because I have easy access, easier than any lobbyist would have.
>
> (MEDEL high official: Interviewee 2)

If ever there were anything like intra-Network access – the inside access of an accepted insider and confrère – this is it: some actors have more access than any lobbyist because they are already initiated into the 'mystery' and are one of 'us'.

The Network Community likewise intervened at the behest of the Croatian Judges Association to oppose proposed changes to the organic law of the Judiciary of which they disapproved:

> Constitutional amendments have been made which also brought changes to the law on courts and the law on the Judiciary Council. We, the Judges Association, asked for the help of the Council of Europe . . . there was a fact-finding commission which came to Croatia in parallel with a fact-finding mission of the International Association of Judges, and there was a judge . . . from Poland and [somebody] . . . from the Council of Europe, and one Spanish judge. They had a meeting with the Minister of Justice and with us, and they made a report which was secretly sent to the government and was never published. And the Spanish judge whom I know from other contacts told me that they in their reports, they accepted 90 per cent of our remarks.
>
> (JC official: Interviewee 19)

All these external interveners had precious little experience with Hungary, Serbia, or Croatia: they do not speak the languages and do not live under their governments. The EU may not have liked developments in Hungary or Serbia, but neither the Venice Commission nor the CoE are hierarchical subordinates of the European Commission or the Council of Ministers or the ECJ. Unless they had shared a collective identity with certain peers in the countries in question – who represent a very narrow slice of the domestic political spectrum – and a transnational consensus on what is 'appropriate' in relation to the Judiciary, why would they care?

Some countries in CEE and in Europe at large are less integrated into the Network Community (i.e., more 'insular') than others. Witness the discourse of one Moldovan jurist – a law professor and former CC judge – who is dismissive of the Venice Commission and Network intervention in domestic affairs to pursue harmonization of juridical culture and institutions:

> International conferences have been organized [in Moldova] with the participation of scientific societies, lawyers from the USA, from the CoE, the

> kids from the Venice Commission, who come and teach us, as if we have descended from a palm tree . . . It is our fault, because we listen to them. It is we who intone, 'Thus saith the Council of Europe.' But wait a minute – so what if the CoE has said it? There may be one thing that is good for Russia and another for Germany.
>
> (CC judge: Interviewee 29)

With the exception of a few isolated instances, none of the elite jurists and laity interviewed by the author expressed anything hinting of defensive or preponderant nationalism, even though she posed questions that should have piqued nationalists to express themselves, had there been any. In CEE, many expressions of transnational solidarity transpired, but few of nationalism. The conclusion must be that legal professional elites, even in the most marginally integrated countries, identify transnationally too.

The Network Community does not intervene in aiding only those already in its ranks. If it would maintain itself across borders and times, the feeling of collective identity must be spread over all suitable prospective members, spontaneously or by design. Evidence of deliberation is found in entrepreneurial acts to build up or reinforce identification with the Network Community (on the construction of collective identity within the ECJ, see Vauchez 2015).

Entrepreneurial acts of cross-fertilization and harmonization of juridical norms help solve problems and at the same time cement transnational identification. All judges, high and low, networked-in or not, have an interest, when confronted with difficult cases, in easing their workload by consulting others who may have already thought through the gnarliest issues. How wide the consultation ambit has become is hinted at by an official of a key transnational organization:

> If you have to decide a case and you distil the questions to be solved, and then you talk to your neighbour – for example, is this due diligence? is it not? What is due here in this case and what is not? – what is meant is to get more information about a case which is outside the knowledge of the judge, and even discuss what is the norm, what is the standard in this particular case, just to get more thinking about that . . . If you are a judge, you get the papers of the person suing and you think, 'What a good case, why does he refuse to follow this, etc.?' Then you get the paper of the defendant and you say, 'Oh, the other party is insolent; why bother this other person?' And . . . in the end you have to make up your mind . . . where do you find the right line here? That's a process and that needs some time. Sometimes you are very

> clear about it very soon, but sometimes you need a lot of time to think about it and that is made easier by [transnational] contact.
>
> (Venice Commission official: Interviewee 8)

It is not disputed that sound institutional reasons exist for cross-fertilization. It is true none the less that to facilitate the judicial practice of comparative case study is also to nudge cooperative judges toward the harmonization of constitutional jurisprudence. One manifestation is the effort to achieve a 'common legal culture', a goal that found a keenly receptive audience amongst elite legal academics in CEE. References to it are in the 2010 CoE Recommendations on Judicial Independence, which suggests a collective aspiration to achieve unity and solidarity on issues where diversity persists – for example, what constitutes 'appropriate' judicial conduct? In the same vein, one of the Venice Commission's missions is to network CC judges together to bring about a cross-fertilization and ultimately harmonization of constitutional case law across Europe. If this does not originate a collective identity in elements of the transnational legal professional networks, it must at least reinforce it. According to a Network mandarin, the founder and former President of the Hungarian CC:

> The third generation of Constitutional Courts [those of CEE] was born into a favourable international environment. The Courts had a world of flourishing international human rights jurisdiction around themselves . . . We have many examples of citing their judgments by Constitutional Courts of States, for which these judgments were or are still not binding . . . Although only the Constitutional Court of South Africa is obliged by the Constitution to consider foreign constitutional cases, the Constitutional Courts today usually work on a comparative law basis. A good example is the way of new ideas for abolishing capital punishment, which differ from the American argument. This way can be followed from Hungary to South Africa and then to the Baltic States, and then down to the Ukraine and Albania. On the other side, the new mechanism for international co-operation [extra-constitutional harmonization] should be mentioned: the Conference of the European Constitutional Courts, and the Commission for Democracy through Law, the 'Venice Commission'. The integrative impact of the Venice Commission has been momentous indeed and it serves the globalization of constitutional justice.
>
> (Sólyom 2003: 4)

Many legal professional networks are recruiting grounds for appointments to apex courts. According to one ECtHR judge, 'Before I came to the ECtHR I was the President of the Judges Association in my country . . . [Later] I left the Consultative Council of European Judges to come to the European

Court of Human Rights' (ECtHR judge: Interviewee 23). From there he was recruited to be the Chief Justice of the national SCt, once pro-European forces controlled the government. One often has the impression of the proverbial 'revolving door' that has been observed in regulatory politics (Salsich et al. 1980). Another Network insider, a founder and the former President of the CC in Hungary, had this to say: 'One has . . . to take notice of an interesting *personnel overlapping*. Many persons sit once in an international court, once in a domestic constitutional court, and serve another time in the Venice Commission' (Sólyom 2003: 4–5; emphasis added). Likewise with the two European supranational courts: 'four of the twenty-five current [as of 2007] ECJ judges previously served on the ECtHR, a career step that is nonobvious given that EU law is a vastly different field of expertise than human rights law' (Voeten 2007: 696).

Admittance through the revolving door is indicative of mutual recognition of activism and commitment to the supranational and international regimes. This in turn influences appointment to high office, given that 'personnel is policy' is a prime directive of the Network Community. The prior question to that is, which personnel and how shall they be identified? Appointing activists to the apex courts is characteristic of governments favourable to European integration. CEE governments in particular fall into this category due to their experience with Communism, and they feel under pressure to prove their commitment to international human rights (Voeten 2007).

Activism in the Network Community may be more than a 'recruiting ground'. It may also serve as a self-selective filter for those amongst elite jurists who actually feel a commitment to the Network Community consensus and thus 'aspire' to appointment to a supranational judicial organ in the first place. The organs that vet appointees are certainly staffed by transnationally active elites themselves:

> In some member states the [ECtHR] judge is nominated by the Minister of Justice. In my country . . . all candidates are interviewed by a [national] commission which secretly votes on the candidates. Three are chosen. The list is then sent to the CoE which organizes an exam for them at the Bureau of the CoE in Paris [the Advisory Panel of Experts on Candidates for Election as Judge to the European Court of Human Rights]. These three candidates are interviewed by deputies from different parliamentary groups of the [CoE] Parliamentary Assembly [e.g. the Standing Committee on Legal Affairs and Human Rights] *who are jurists of renown in Europe*. They vote secretly for one of the three candidates.
>
> (ECtHR judge: Interviewee 23; emphasis added)

An international body appointed by the CoE Committee of Ministers in consultation with the President of the ECtHR, the Advisory Panel was set up to 'offer . . . governments confidential advice on potential candidates before the final list of three is sent to the Assembly' (Parliamentary Assembly of the Council of Europe 2014). It is composed of seven

> personalities . . . chosen from among members of the highest national courts, former judges of international courts, including the European Court of Human Rights and other lawyers of recognised competence . . . [and] appointed by the Committee of Ministers [by simple majority] following consultations with the President of the European Court of Human Rights.
>
> (Committee of Ministers of the Council of Europe 2010)

The Advisory Panel's Secretariat is also the General Secretariat of the CoE – one of the nodes of the Network Community (see Chapter 1). The Network Community would of course be uniquely qualified – in more ways than one – to act in the capacity of 'international experts' on a panel advising member states and the Parliamentary Assembly on whom, finally, to appoint to the ECtHR (Table 2.1). This makes the Network a self-perpetuating filter of admission to the 'Junto'. Similar mechanisms control appointment to other supranational courts, one suspects. It is quite plausible to infer from the foregoing that membership of the Network Community is informally a mechanism screening 'improper persons for admittance, some of whom, perhaps, we might find it difficult to refuse' out of positions of influence over the common agenda, and ultimately over the power relations between the Judiciary and the elected branches. The member states of the CoE, however, have shown a persistent ambition to 'pack' the ECtHR with judges more to their own taste, a roadblock which the Network Community (e.g. President of the Advisory Panel) make no secret of being unhappy with (Lemmens 2015).

Table 2.1 Membership of the Advisory Panel (2015)

Name	*Position in the national Judiciary*	*Transnational involvement*
John Murray, Chair (Ireland)	Judge, Supreme Court of Ireland (1999–) Chief Justice of Ireland (2004–11)	Judge, ECJ (1992–99)
Nina Vajić, Vice Chair (Croatia)	Professor of Public International Law, Zagreb Law Faculty (1996–98)	Judge, ECtHR (1998–) President, First Section of the ECtHR (2011–)

Table 2.1 continued

Name	*Position in the national Judiciary*	*Transnational involvement*
Matti Pellonpää (Finland)	Justice, Supreme Administrative Court of Finland (2005–)	Member, European Commission of Human Rights (1990–98) Judge, ECtHR (1998–2006)
Jean-Paul Costa (France)	Member, Council of State (1966–68)	Expert, CoE working group on computing and the protection of privacy (1971–73) Chairman, 'Human rights and the role of public agencies' Group, International Institute of Administrative Sciences, Brussels (1993–96) Expert, Mission to Romania (1990) and Albania (1991) on behalf of the United Nations Centre for Human Rights Expert, Mission to Albania on behalf of the CoE (1995) Judge, ECtHR (1998–2011) President, ECtHR (2007–12)
Christoph Grabenwarter (Austria)	Judge, Austrian CC (2005–) President of Austrian Jurists' Association (ÖJT) (2015–) Substitute Judge, State Court of the Principality of Liechtenstein (2005–)	Ad hoc Judge, ECtHR (2002–05) Member, Venice Commission (2006–) Vice President, Venice Commission (2015–)
Michail Vilaras (Greece)	Member, Greek Council of State Associate Member, Superior Special Court of Greece Director, Legal Service of the Greek Government	National expert, Legal Service of the Commission of the European Communities (1988–90) Principal Administrator, DG V (Employment, Industrial Relations, Social Affairs) (1990–94) Judge, General Court of the European Union (1998–2010; President of Chamber 2004–10) Member of the Committee responsible for giving an Opinion on Candidates' Suitability to perform the Duties of Judge at the European Union Civil Service Tribunal (2012–15)

Sources: European Court of Justice 1998; Costa 2012; Directorate of Legal Advice and Public International Law 2015; European Council of the European Union 2015; Institute for European and International Law 2015a, 2015b; Grabenwarter no date.

Elite identity

Untypical of the masses it governs, an elite is a minority capable of initiating changes in society that may or may not be in the best interests of its broader segments (Wright Mills 1956; Lukes 1974, 1986; Connolly 1983). Its members are not necessarily government officials or elected representatives, as the latter may merely be 'carry[ing] out the policies decided by [some other] elite' (Dye 2008: 22). They think of themselves as destined and entitled to rule, and disregard the opinions of the masses, which they may even hold in contempt (Lasch 1995; Morton and Knopff 2000; Sowell 2010). They share a common social class origin in the upper socio-economic strata, fostering an awareness of their collective identity as elites (Dye 2008; Gurin et al. 1980). Their cathexis with each other may be stronger than any cathexes with their own birth countries (the 'denationalized globalizers', Rothkopf 2008). Ambitious *ab ovo*, they end up as the elite because they proactively take steps to empower themselves.

Nothing that the author discovered about the Network Community contradicts this description, although it should be noted that far from every feature of it was observed in every individual. It is they and not the mass of elected politicians who set the agenda and formulate the policies that empower the Judiciary. Few of them are subject to democratic scrutiny or accountability. Although governments do play a formal role in appointing some of them to supranational office, the concatenation of notional 'accountability' is so remote from popular choice that domestic voters cannot by any stretch of the political imagination be considered actual veto players in this game.

The Network Community comprises legal and political elites from every walk of life: lawyers in private practice, judges, academicians, officials of domestic and supranational governing institutions, as well as other state and non-state actors without legal training. Together they constitute a subset of the governing class in general. In one sense, all legal professionals are elites – of an intellectual sort. On the other hand, the Network Community does not include the entire legal profession (cf. Morton and Knopff 2000), the vast majority of whom are involved in little, if any, transnational networking. Most ordinary judges are in fact informally excluded from a voice in the network-driven changes affecting the branch of government they staff. This rank and file (who often require translators to communicate in English) may have no opinion at all on Judiciary institutional design. The elite consensus lies beyond their purview, and the issues with which the elite are preoccupied never cross their minds. They are more concerned about the quality of justice on the ground than about Network issues concerning the political power of the Judiciary:

> I used to be a member of the European Judges Association, I was even on the Board, but I have stepped down . . . They were dealing with issues that, in my opinion, aren't their job. My problem, and this is maybe due to the fact that I come from a different background: I come from the countryside and I have a different vision of courts and the way a judge has to behave. That is my daily problem. I am often surprised by the habitual approach of many judges to some crucial issues. You cannot allow the situation where a disabled child does not get a verdict for twelve years . . . And the parties suffer . . . If only those people would sit down and say, 'Let's do our job.' For instance, if you want to be the President of a court you have to take responsibility not just for your own work, but also for the work of all judges in that court.
>
> (Trial Court judge: Interviewee 30)[2]

Ordinary judges may even be hostile to their own transformation at the hands of the Network, to which their consent was never consulted:

> We have in the US a doctrine called 'inherent powers' which says that courts have certain powers to determine how they should be run and that that power cannot be delegated to the legislator . . . I gave a speech in France and a judge refused to speak to me afterwards. He was so outraged because in France that is the prerogative of the legislator and the Ministry of Justice.
>
> (ABA officer: Interviewee 31)

The Network Community pays no heed to this disaffection and may even dismiss it out of hand. On the recommendation of an expert commission dominated by legal academicians, the powers of the CC of Romania were expanded in 2003 to include arbitration of conflicts of a constitutional nature between all other public authorities. Insiders to the debates noted that most CC judges did not want this expansion of their jurisdiction:

[2] This interviewee, a judge at the municipal criminal court in Croatia, is clearly not a member of the elite transnational legal professional community:

> **Q:** Do you network, or are in contact with judges from other countries?
> **A:** The very fact that I am afraid to speak English tells you that I don't.
>
> (Trial Court judge: Interviewee 30)

> I saw the initial draft of the Constitution, and the proposal to empower the Constitutional Court to solve [inter-branch] conflicts was there . . . even the Constitutional Court, in its Opinion on the revised text of the Constitution, highlighted this amendment. They did not like it. And yet those who were revising the Constitution did not heed them.
>
> (Senior Presidential adviser: Interviewee 32)

In similar words in the same time frame, a European Commission official overseeing the revision autonomizing the Romanian Judiciary said, 'The reform of 2004 was pretty much a reform made without the Romanian Judiciary. The Judiciary was absent' (EC official, Interviewee 26).[3]

Some members of the Network Community, especially those in leadership positions in nodal organizations, may well be conscious of being elites networked-in and socialized in a particular way of thinking, to form a unique class. Supranational forums like the CoE have purposefully acted to encourage a consciousness amongst national European elites as belonging to a larger transnational elite (e.g. Checkel 2001). This surpasses processes like socialization and transnationalism, however, and perhaps even consciousness. It is initiation into an inner circle without which it might be more difficult to reach the 'top'. Certainly this is the case in CEE:

> We speak very often about the 'Strasbourg promotion' of political leaders, because many, many Prime Ministers, Presidents of 'new democracies' to use that terminology, have been members of the Parliamentary Assembly of the CoE, and that creates a certain solidarity between these political actors. So it is quite clear that Strasbourg has been important in the formation of the political elite in the new democracies . . . What do . . . these elites learn when they come here? . . . They learn about the others by exchange of experience, they learn about standards, values, norms, and . . . how these . . . are being implemented in other countries. It is comparative law in action, if you want.
>
> (CoE official: Interviewee 13)

[3] A parallel phenomenon may be discerned in evidence drawn from the context of South America, where national judges were found to be 'reluctant interlocutors' with the Andean Tribunal of Justice, which was modelled on the ECJ in hopes of reversing the failure of a 'struggling regional integration project' through top-down regional integration (Alter and Helfer 2017: 220). Further corroboration comes from Kosař (2016: 402) who notes that in Slovakia, 'court presidents had little influence on the design of the JCSR [Judicial Council] and were not among the major supporters of the Judicial Council Euro-model. On the contrary, incumbent court presidents at the moment of the introduction of the JCSR felt threatened by the new model and vigorously opposed it.'

Even entrepreneurs in MEDEL, a transnational association of judges reputed to be left-wing in their political orientation, are self-consciously elitist and feel little kinship with the 'Old Guard' Left that was populist in orientation (at least in principle). This can be read between the lines of the testimony of one of the founders and leaders of MEDEL:

> **Q:** Is there any difference between the centre-right and the centre-left when it comes to the institutional design of the Judiciary? For example, is the left generally more supportive of the idea of judicial autonomy compared to the right, in your view?
>
> **A:** The left – certainly in the CEE countries, from top to bottom, from Estonia down to Bulgaria – are still of the 'old crowd' [Old Guard Left] . . . [MEDEL are] for the rule of law and independence of the judiciary, for the modern conception of the State. That's what we appreciate . . . Clinging on to the old . . . categories of 'go with the trade unions' and 'go with the parties' . . . that's not resurgency [*sc. Risorgimento*].
>
> (MEDEL high official: Interviewee 2)

Having the elite mentality, Network Community members naturally think they ought to lead. It may be taken as evidence of class consciousness that they take for granted the subordination of society as intellectual inferiors assumed, expressly or not, to be incompetent (see Chapter 5). Certainly, the Network Community thinks of the peoples of CEE, in particular, in these terms, even in a country like Moldova, where elites are far less remote from the people because of the small population in a country where 'everybody knows everybody':

> **Q:** If keeping judges in check is an issue of morality, why not allow ordinary people to be members of the Judiciary Council?
>
> **A:** What do you mean by 'ordinary people'?
>
> **Q:** Ordinary people who might be selected by lot [like a jury].
>
> **A:** No, no, no. No state in the world can afford to engage ordinary people to decide certain things.
>
> **Q:** Ordinary persons, too, have a sense of morality, of right and wrong.
>
> **A:** Can you guarantee that the one who wins the lottery is the most moral and ethical person?
>
> (Jurist and academician: Interviewee 33)

Instead of Parliament and its constituents wielding a veto on the Judiciary, Network elites think that if any outside intervention is ever justified, it could only be by some other elite body:

> **Q:** How is Judiciary power to be checked and balanced?
>
> **A:** It all comes down to the . . . [judge-dominated] Judiciary Council of Magistrates . . . the check and balance . . . is simple: change the modality of nominating the members of the Judiciary Council . . . there should be seven journalists from seven media, television and radio in the Council, from all the major media . . . and leave in only one or two judges who would assess the legal part but not the ethical and moral part [of a judge's conduct], because in the situation where a court proceeds to investigate a judge, judges always seek what they seek; they look at whether the law is respected or not at a formal level . . . they should not preside over the morality and ethical standing of the institution they lead . . . Whether the media are distanced from the issue does not matter. The presumption of innocence exists everywhere . . . Why journalists? And why NGOs? Because at the end of the day, they are the exponents of a certain social group who has a particular social interest . . . they want to change, to improve things . . . the journalists are the fourth estate . . . when the judge sees the camera and the journalists, he is very afraid . . . afraid like the devil is of incense.
>
> (Jurist and academician: Interviewee 33)

Media and NGOs are, of course, themselves elites. Implicit is that elites may be checked only by other elites. This raises the question why the political elites in parliaments, who are a social elite, too, should be excluded from checking and balancing the Judiciary. It might be inferred that, unlike the media, MPs are electorally answerable to the masses. Perhaps they are not to be trusted precisely because they are democratically beholden.

The involvement of the masses in any decisions involving the Judiciary is regarded with horror by the Network Community. Mention of referendums and other modes of popular self-government is almost taken as an insult:

> **Q:** Some have proposed an alternative design to that of the Constitutional Court in the Czech Republic. These proposals say, 'the Constitutional Court should merely pronounce that the law is unconstitutional, and then let Parliament take six months to prepare a new law. If the law is not amended by Parliament within this period, the issue raised by that law should be put to a referendum.'
>
> **A:** This is a really old way of thinking, [this is] how the Communists think . . . the thinking that referendum will [ful]fill everything . . . it is not right, is not right.
>
> (CC judge: Interviewee 34)

The fact that judges of countries outside the West attribute extraordinary importance to being admitted to the 'club' of the European Network

Community is evidence of the elite status and normative soft power of this network:

> When the European Judges Association rejected the membership application of the Algerian Judges Association, the Algerians were crying. What's in it for them that membership into the European Judges Association is so important? . . . In those countries it is very, very, very important . . . They feel that everything which is international, it is a sort of endorsement of their position. It is this desire for international recognition.
>
> (EJA officer and CoE adviser: Interviewee 11)

The Network Community is in a certain sense 'above the law', since it is the king-maker, if not the formal lawgiver in all things judiciary. This privileged status is a double-edged sword, that can be legitimate in political settings where advocates of the rule of law are exposed to the lawlessness of those in command of means of material coercion. Transnational solidarity is of the essence in these circumstances. Elite solidarity is an 'offensive' weapon in the politics of mass democracy; but much more profoundly it may be felt to be a bulwark of self-defence in the struggle for power with potent and not always ethical foes such as the core Executive of the nation-state. This explains the otherwise puzzling weight of importance that national jurists like the Algerians impute to 'mere' membership of a transnational organization. It remains to be explained what all maintains elite solidarity through thick and thin, giving it the resilience to withstand assault by materially superior forces.

The culture of consensus

One manifestation of collective identity is consensus – that is, 'how we see and do things' (cf. Risse and Sikkink 1999; Johnston 2001). Consensus is a modus operandi for dealing with internal conflict and the threat thereof – by forestalling it. A network's members are all potentially veto players to each other when networking spills over into political agency. Internecine dissension over 'network goals' would paralyse them all and constitute self-disempowerment (Allen and Levine 1969; Morris and Miller 1975). This more than any other observable cause explains why, in the rare case when a contest over norms did arise in our Network Community, it was always muted and moderated. Anything more pointed or fundamental immediately threatens the transnational networking strategy of power-through-elite-solidarity.[4] Ramifying dissension if left unchecked could 'break the spell' of even the most carefully cultivated network consensus.

The Network Community has therefore made the culture of consensus its mode of decision making, so that all decisions may reinforce rather than undermine network solidarity respecting the rest of the world, dampening internal dissent and forestalling 'veto bombs'. Such a culture must either have been adopted with purposeful foresight, or else have emerged fortuitously as an adaptation to the 'selection pressures' at work on all political configurations. Internecine rivalry once interdicted, the Network (Community) can turn resolutely toward conserving, expanding, and consolidating their power over external rivals. An elite is by definition a minority; if it would rule, it will do best to unite, as the general public is always divided. Confronting the divided world with a united front, Network consensus may be the most potent mode of elite self-empowerment for overreaching the lagging, disorganized resistance of the majority. The cultivation of consensus may be sustained by nothing more than a shared awareness that elite power depends on maintaining solidarity.

In the absence of a deliberately cultivated consensus of the kind that typifies 'secret societies' like Franklin's, it would be rather the diversity of viewpoints that would be expected to prevail; this includes, in our case, divergence over the power relations between the Judiciary and elected representatives in an area as ethnographically diverse as Europe. The point that division of opinion is after all the default state of affairs in human society was eloquently made by James Madison in *The Federalist*, no. 10:

> As long as the reason of man continues fallible, and he is at liberty to exercise it, different opinions will be formed. As long as the connection subsists between his reason and his self-love, his opinions and his passions will have a reciprocal influence on each other; and the former will be objects to which the latter will attach themselves. The diversity in the faculties of men . . . is not less an insuperable obstacle to a uniformity of interests . . . The latent causes of faction are . . . sown in the nature of man; and we see them everywhere brought into different degrees of activity, according to the different circumstances of civil society. A zeal for different opinions concerning religion, concerning government, and many other points, as well of speculation as of practice; an attachment to different leaders ambitiously contending for

[4] This incidentally also raises the question of how does the EU and the CoE avoid the fate that has befallen so many non-Western regional organizations (cf. Alter and Helfer 2010).

> pre-eminence and power; or to persons of other descriptions whose fortunes have been interesting to the human passions, have, in turn, divided mankind into parties, inflamed them with mutual animosity, and rendered them much more disposed to vex and oppress each other than to co-operate for their common good.
>
> (Madison 1787)

The French National Assembly during the Revolution is one illustration that may serve to define with greater precision what elite consensus is *not*. It was the National Assembly that spawned the left-right ideological divide that to this day bedevils the politics of the Western world. But the Assembly was also fractured along other, less well-known fault-lines – for example, the Mountain vs the Plain – and eventually the whole Revolution self-destructed in factional infighting. It was the *lack* of consensus amongst the elites that drove both the Terror and the equally disastrous (from some viewpoints) Thermidor reaction and the accession of Napoleon. These two calamities sum up the elite dilemma, commending by bad example what European revolutionary parties finally realized the solution must be instead.

Anyone sharing in a consensus is empowered by it, in particular the entrepreneurs arising from our Network Community. They disseminate the Network consensus by setting the public policy agenda for outsiders to the Network – the rest of civil society who only with the greatest difficulty might possibly organize and co-ordinate their efforts from scratch to generate counter-entrepreneurs enjoying the unconditional backing of a solidary transnational front. What is more, transnational networking was often observed to be conducive to harmonizing the domestic and supranational levels, not just conserving but expanding and reinforcing consensus by winning domestic veto players over to 'the team'.

The origins of our Network Community suggest that it had settled on strong consensual norms as early as the nineteenth century, proceeding on the basis of 'a series of gentlemen's agreements' (Sacriste and Vauchez 2007: 95). The International Law Institute, founded in 1870 to promote international law and courts, had strong rules of consensus building, conceived as

> a circle bringing together Statesmen, teachers, specialists in public law, lawyers, voluntarily mingled together, removed from their own activities in the impartial, serene atmosphere of the Academy whose methods were honoured for being based only on scientific discussion procedures . . . this great doctrinal body destined to include the most qualified public law specialists

> of the Permanent Court of International Justice [the International Court of Justice since 1946] could lean upon to find in their doctrine 'an auxiliary means of determining the rules of law' . . . under the condition that it firmly maintained the . . . entrance requirements [of] (universalism and apoliticism), and that disagreements within the group would only be brought up in the form of a learned and courteous debate mingling legal technique and great principles of law.
>
> (Sacriste and Vauchez 2007: 95)

This way of proceeding is redolent of the rules of procedure that Benjamin Franklin describes in his *Autobiography*, implying that it was used as a mode of deliberation common to learned societies even two centuries ago:

> Our debates were to be under the direction of a president and to be conducted in the sincere spirit of inquiry after truth, without fondness for dispute or desire for victory; and to prevent warmth [i.e., 'hot temper' or 'zeal'], all expressions of positiveness in opinions, or direct contradiction, were after some time made contraband, and prohibited under small pecuniary penalties.
>
> (Franklin [1868] 1996: 45)

Benjamin Franklin and company were trying to craft a pure search for truth, unencumbered, they hoped, by the motive forces of the reptilian and mammalian layers of the brain. Dissension was kept within bounds by a ban on emotionalism, and the fear and anger it causes which so damages any tendency to unanimity. The debating society strove for consensus, a procedure very like the Socratic Method with its *telos* of unanimity (the political form of truth). Socrates was never content to agree to disagree; if dialogue had led to an impasse, he always sought universal common ground at some deeper level of inquiry. Unanimity differs from consensus in that it includes everyone (or excludes no one in particular, as in the way a jury is randomly selected). Consensus, by contrast – that is, *network* consensus – is ideological solidarity practised by an astute faction, and ought to be understood as such in a political context.

No network consensus is perfect. Slippage must sometimes occur, and when it does, it forebodes the peril of an ethical catastrophe. The Network Community does undergo internal dissent from time to time, but it tends to be marginal in the first place. For example, a hint of rivalry was detected between interest groups in Strasbourg: the European Judges Association perceived MEDEL as too left-wing, for instance, whilst MEDEL tends to look down on the EJA: 'The European Judges Association has been established about ten years after MEDEL and in a way they follow our path, only that they are a bit more conservative than us' (MEDEL high official: Interviewee 2). This has not lead to strife between the two interest groups, however: 'We are in a way all competitors, but we compete very peacefully' (MEDEL high official: Interviewee 2).

Marginal opposition may exist within the Consultative Council of European Judges, too, over the desirability of pan-European norms of Judiciary institutional design affecting democracy, but it is essentially negligible, and it is almost never openly expressed in public sources. Quite likely it would never have come to light but for the author's private interviews under anonymity. A former member of the Council and newly appointed judge from CEE to the ECtHR, who has not moved in transnational circles enough, having held only national posts before the CCEJ appointment, to have internalized the Network consensus as being off limits to controversy, employed the words 'trend' and 'in *my* opinion' spontaneously in the following:

> **Q:** What happens if a CEE State decides not to pay fines for refusing to enforce the decisions of the ECtHR?
>
> **A:** [I]n *my* opinion, we must not trend towards unifying European traditions, customs and values. The values . . . in each country should be determined by the spirit of the people of that country. Diversity is what makes the world beautiful, and in *my* opinion this diversity must be preserved . . . even when we, the Court, examine a case through the prism of a norm of law in the ECHR that binds all the member states, we must take into account the values of each country . . . its traditions, [and] spirit . . . so that we do not harm the national dignity of its people. In this sense I am partisan, so to speak . . . I don't think it's correct for Europe to trend towards creating a unique European citizen . . . The Soviet Union tried to create the Soviet citizen without taking into account the culture of each people. The consequences were disastrous.
>
> **Q:** Is this what is happening in the CoE? The Venice Commission talks about a common European legal culture and constitutional heritage.
>
> **A:** Yes, yes, this is true . . . if we harmonize . . . then what is left of diversity?
> (ECtHR judge: Interviewee 23; emphasis added)

If this insider to the Network Community detects a trend under way but censures it, yet qualifies that as being just '*my* opinion' instead of 'our opinion', then this implies that some internal dissent against the common agenda does exist but is personally managed.

The revision of the 1994 CoE Recommendations on Judicial Independence evidences not only that opposition within the Network is marginal, but that it is kept under wraps when it emerges. The revision was made by a small group of Network entrepreneurs in 2007 (CJ-S-JUST), but when presented for approval to the relevant intergovernmental Steering Committee (CDCJ), it was vetoed by appointee insiders to the Network Community from Germany, Norway, Britain, and Greece, which the CoE but for their veto would have pressurized to adapt their institutions, arising from a different tradition, to conform to the revised Recommendations. This small opposition was dissatisfied with the consequences at a 'fundamental constitutional level' (Bureau of the European Committee on Legal Co-operation 2008). Preferring the status quo of the weak and ignored 1994 Recommendations, the dissenters could have agreed amongst themselves to let that text lie, but the imperative to keep solidarity with the Network Community nudged them toward a compromise that continued to stress the importance of a Judiciary Council, as the activist committee members demanded, but sidelined national tradition to an opt-out, as their maximum concession to the dissent (CoE Steering Committee members: Interviewees 1 and 3).

The Network Community, aware of the importance of consensus in its own ranks, takes pains to avoid dissent, or tones it down. To resort to a formal, non-negotiable veto is frowned upon, and the steps taken in case of disagreement are always discreet, lest other members are antagonized. Recounting the revision of the Recommendations:

> We came to a specific point on [judge] liability in our debates on the Recommendations. The Scandinavians, in particular Sweden and Finland, have no disciplinary system for judges, which means that they have a very strict, far-reaching regime on the liability of judges . . . a judge can be tried, can get into a criminal investigation if he is not careful, if he is careless in his judgment. That's completely inadmissible for the rest of the forty-five member states. But now you have the problem of consensus, the Scandinavians will fight against this resolution . . . and the only way out . . . was to say 'please make a reservation, a sort of opt-out'. It is not a formal reservation as you have in a Convention, but you may say . . . paragraph X will not be applied by Sweden since Sweden's system is quite different. And that was the solution-out, and you find consensus by excluding an issue.
>
> (CoE Steering Committee member: Interviewee 1)

When national governments upset proceedings with a veto, Networkers take great pains to reconcile the factions and re-establish consensus. Four CoE member states vetoed the CJ-S-JUST revised Recommendation, and the Chair of that Committee, who had been the CDCJ's Chair in 2007, confronted in 2008 a CDCJ under a different Chair at member state insistence. The new Chair did everything in his power to avoid conflict with personnel from the 2007 group:

> We had an [expert] . . . in our group who had been in the first [2007] expert group . . . it was difficult in the beginning [to deal with] these persons from the older group. Not only did they feel scolded, but to tell them 'we cannot go on as you did, with promoting Judicial Councils' . . . [Nevertheless in the end] we had an excellent atmosphere . . . we came to an agreement on the text. There was no fight . . . We tried to be very polite to the first group in evaluating their work.
>
> (CoE Steering Committee member: Interviewee 1)

The culture of consensus is a general elite phenomenon and not unique to the Network. A transnational legal professional network of a very similar membership profile to the European one has also been identified in Canada. The Canadian network is engaged across the border with legal professional networks active in the USA (Morton and Knopff 2000). This in itself suggests a consensus similar to that reached in Europe. In Europe, the signal example is the EU, whose consensus-style decision making is the same stratagem that proved very successful in integrating Europe. The CoE, too, has been described as a 'tight-knit consensual community' (MacMullen 2004: 419), held together by shared norms and decisional arrangements purposely designed to facilitate consensus:

> the small size of the national representations, usually only two or three diplomats plus support clerical staff . . . facilitate[s] discussion and agreement in the Committee of Ministers acting through . . . Deputies, since individuals are well known to each other, and relationships of trust and ad hoc personal alliances may be established . . . There is a strong feeling among the participants that agreement and consensus should be achieved on a 'business as normal' basis.
>
> (MacMullen 2004: 418–419)

The General Secretariat is the chief institution facilitating consensus between the CoE member states:

> We [the Secretariat] are arbiters, we always try to find consensus, a solution which most countries, all countries can accept. This is our role. It's a go-between role . . . When you have to adopt a Convention, there you have different views, and you have to find a compromise which means that a Convention requires consensus in order to be adopted . . . You have to find a solution where everyone feels happy or able to be comfortable with. Or, for example, when you want the Committee of Ministers to adopt a declaration which requires consensus, which is one of the rare occasions where you

> need absolute unanimity . . . you have to find a language which is acceptable by all, because in all of the forty-seven member states you have different sensitivities, different interests, different views, which means that the Secretariat is a facilitator doing the fine language where everyone can join.
>
> (CoE official: Interviewee 13)

In stark contrast to the US Supreme Court, the consensual norm of both supranational Courts – the ECJ and the ECtHR – forbids dissenting opinions being published, which draws a veil over the scope of and reasons for dissent amongst the legal professionals of the Network Community. It is a lack of transparency that compounds the appearance of arbitrariness which the Courts create when they legislate from the bench. Some European political actors describe the ECJ as 'a black box':

> What [the European Commission] do is to try to use the European law . . . When we [Hungarian government] introduced the tax on the telecoms they said there is a rule in the European law which is saying that . . . [in regards to] telephone taxation . . . every levy should be . . . invested back into the telecom area, which is a crazy thing . . . They are doing it on the basis of and on the background of an EU regulation [that did not specifically address the tax issue] . . . Finally, the Court interprets, and the ECJ is even worse than the [Hungarian] 'invisible constitution' because they are completely . . . it's a black box. Nobody knows what comes out of that [ECJ] because there are no rules there . . . They are speaking about the *acquis communautaire* and so on.
>
> (Jurist and MEP: Interviewee 35)[5]

Yet so strong is the compulsion toward consensus that the transnational legal professionals who staff the Courts would rather risk profoundly alienating their member-state constituents (who are only subordinates to their jurisdiction after all) than break ranks with each other.

The drive to consolidate awareness of the importance of transnational elite consensus is also evidenced by the EU's option to accede to the ECHR, as provided in the Lisbon Treaty. Networked-in legal academics refer to the eventuality of open conflict between the ECJ and the ECtHR over the interpretation of the Convention as 'the nuclear option', as if dissension

[5] The 'invisible constitution' is nearly another name for the 'living constitution' (see Part II). It conceives of 'a constitution of the constitution' which is made up of principles that can be derived from any sources, including external ones – for example, European law, international treaties, the US Constitution (e.g. Schwartz 2000).

would impact the Network Community like a weapon of mass destruction which they must do everything in their power to deter.[6]

As the Community is one of global reach, it cultivates consensus well beyond the confines of Europe. For instance, the Venice Commission was intended to facilitate 'dialogue' between Europe and Latin America on Judiciary and constitutional matters (Venice Commission official: Interviewee 8). Transnational consensus is also facilitated by informal networking between local and European legal professionals, either directly or through global institutions like the IAJ:

> [This] has many regional branches. One . . . is called the Ibero-American Group, which means all the Spanish and Portuguese parts of America plus Portugal and Spain, [who] are currently in the process of negotiating . . . a Latin American Convention on the minimum standards for Judicial independence.
>
> (EJA officer and CoE adviser: Interviewee 11)

To conclude, the Network Community has the objective common interest of any elite minority in self-empowerment in a democratic context in which it is outnumbered. It cannot pursue self-empowerment autocratically with any hope of success, but must realize it through collective solidarity amid a deeply divided wider society. This is objectively what drives their networking for consensus.

Substantive policy consensus and its genesis

Consensus may be sought over anything, from theology to company policy. The consensus of the Network Community, however, stands out as incomparable and incommensurable with those of other communities of interest, because of implicating universal consequences. The Network Community's *self-interest* impacts on the grandest of scales the interests of everyone else in society. The Community pretends to solve social and political problems that transcend what is commonly thought of as 'mere'

[6] Participant observation by the author in the 'Politics of Judicial Independence and Judicial Accountability' workshop, Supreme Administrative Court, Brno (Czech Republic), 30–31 May 2014.

self-interest; *its* interest implicates everybody's, not only its own. Moreover, it has assumed responsibility to solve central societal problems in the way it deems most fit, not leaving it up to representative democracy to deliberate. This makes it notably different from any ordinary community of interest. The self-interest of the dairy lobby, in contrast, however selfish it may be, is so narrow that the pursuit of it harms society only marginally (cf. Hazlitt [1946] 1979). The Network consensus targets governance per se, instead of taking it for granted, as the dairy lobby does. Consequently, the societal damage that the Network Community is capable of inflicting is far and away greater than virtually any other interest group, as those on the receiving end of it can testify:

> Yes, there is a transnational community of interest. They have a kind of cosmopolitan approach to doing things – the national or concrete legislation, they want to change in their direction in order to limit them. If you have to go to the Constitutional Court in certain areas, then your business might not be so secure . . . Hungary is regaining her sphere of interest because after the transition Hungary was colonized – all the new post-Communist countries, their markets, everything . . . If you want to get back some sphere of interest, you cannot do it because our laws will protect them against you. And somehow you have to find ways of undoing that. And they are not happy about it. This is a fight of interests, but they are covering it with noble, universally acceptable principles which are far away from that.
>
> (Jurist and MEP: Interviewee 35)

Foremost, it is a self-interested consensus on the role of the Judiciary in a democratic society: what sort of majoritarian-to-non-majoritarian power relations *will* subsist between the democratic representation and the Judiciary? The fight of interests implicates the Network's common policy agenda to expand judicial power across Europe (see Part II). Judicial empowerment is the Network Community's self-interest, that which enables the judicialization of public policy contests.

Elite transnationalism was necessary to seed Europe with a judicializing trend, which presupposes a networked consensus and the agency of those having positioned themselves transnationally to overreach national governments. This would be our legal professional networks and the judicializing community backing them. The author could find no evidence anywhere to support the opposite inference: that such a trend sprang from the bottom up spontaneously and independently in each and every European nation (a causality so redundant as to defy Ockham's razor).

The genesis of the substantive consensus

Strasbourg is the seat of both the CoE and the ECtHR. These supranational institutions have always been a magnet for contemporary legal professionals whose utmost concerns have been human rights and Judiciary institutions. The Network Community's attraction to the CoE is partly explained by the former's entanglement in the origins of the CoE and ECHR, and the ECtHR in particular. It is a striking fact that the Network Community did not spring from CoE circles, as one might be tempted to infer from its members' close involvement in contemporary policy making in Strasbourg; the Network Community, rather, founded and so pre-existed them.

In the aftermath of the Second World War, the CoE was the earliest attempt at European integration; European elites created it to bring about 'closer unity between all like-minded countries of Europe' (Council of Europe 1949). Their grand strategic vision of integration came to nothing at that time: the CoE's member states rejected the European Constitution and, later on, the European Defence Community (Madsen and Vauchez 2005). The movers of these two projects were transnationally networked-in American and European jurists who also (most of them) held high political office. They belonged to and had the 'infrastructural' support of the post-war European Movement, an elite organization endorsed and presided over by Winston Churchill himself, and funded by the Ford Foundation and the American Committee on United Europe. The American lawyers-*cum*-politicians included, for example, George Ball, a member of the US Foreign Economic Administration, and founder of US law firm Cleary, Gotlieb, Steen, and Hamilton. Ball became legal adviser to Jean Monnet and was involved in the drafting of the European Coal and Steel Community (Madsen and Vauchez 2005). These jurists played a pivotal role in setting the agenda for creating the CoE and drafting the European Constitution (Madsen and Vauchez 2005). European integration, however, never took hold until the EU brought big business on board, with the prospect of a common market and industrial integration, which the national governments resisted less, too, because of the tangible benefits (Ludlow 2010).

The CoE might have been disbanded but for the ECHR. This treaty, which on its face affirms many of the basic tenets of democracy and the rule of law, did manage to make a start in integrating Europe through legal harmonization. The British elite supported this vision; indeed, Churchill had a hand in devising and drafting the Convention text (Ball 1959).[7] British lawyers:

> played a leading role in the preparation of the Convention in the Council of Europe: notably, Sir David Maxwell-Fyfe (later Lord Chancellor Kilmuir) as chairman of the [CoE] Assembly's Legal Committee, and Sir Oscar Dowson, former senior legal adviser in the Home Office, as the main drafter of the text of the Convention eventually approved by the Committee of Experts.
> (Lester 1984: 957)

It was these lawyers-*cum*-politicians within the European Movement who were the 'core of the lobby' for some kind of European Bill of Rights (Madsen and Vauchez 2005: 183). The purpose of the Bill, which entered into force in 1953 as the ECHR, was to 'establish . . . the foundations of a common legal space across Europe' (Council of Europe 2010c), to be achieved through the influence and case law of a European Court of Human Rights, a supranational body of transnational legal professionals:

> Legal entrepreneurs . . . came with the idea of . . . a European Political Community with its own Constitution. This had had the full support of the European Movement . . . some thirty lawyers and law professors were brought together for the purpose of studying comparative models of federalism . . . and transfer[ring] this specifically crafted knowledge to a European federation . . . legal entrepreneurs played a decisive role . . . the high profile professor of international law at the University of Paris, George Scelle . . . [took] part in the Committee of Lawyers drafting a European Constitution on behalf of the European Movement . . . the Rector of the University of Frankfurt, Walter Hallstein . . . became chairman of the German delegation to the negotiation of the Schuman Plan (and later President of the European Commission) . . . some of the most prominent political figures of the national delegations were in fact lawyers, for example François de Menthon and Pierre-Henri Teitgen . . . [They] were soon to take up central roles in the drafting and definition of the major documents

[7] Britain favoured the ECHR but not the ECtHR and certainly not individual petition to such a court in cases concerning alleged violations of the Convention and the jurisdiction of that court in such cases (Lester 1984). The British government's position reflected its preference for intergovernmentalism over supranationalism. A supranational court of the kind envisaged by the legal professional elites who drafted the Convention had clear implications for British governing institutions, which did not escape the attention of the Foreign Office at the time they were drafting it. Supranationalism is a direct challenge to the supremacy of both Parliament and the common law, the twin pillars upon which the British constitution rests. Britain supported an ECHR, but one that was enforced by national courts alone as part of the body of international law (Simpson 2004).

> of the institutions that arose from this mobilisation: the Statute of the CoE, the ECHR, the Schuman Plan, the European Constitution . . . key lawyer-politicians such as Pierre-Henri Teitgen, Sir David Maxwell Fyfe [British barrister and Conservative politician] and Belgian law professor Fernand Dehousse . . . became key players in the drafting of the European Bill of Rights . . . [Included were] a significant number of distinguished academic jurists (for example the eminent Scandinavian law professors Alf Ross and Frede Castberg) as well as a considerable number of what we might name 'the international legal repeat players', the set of internationalized jurists gathering at the central international legal associations . . . the Constitution ultimately failed . . . and the 'constitutionalization' and legalization of Europe was in many ways left to the two Courts set up under the auspices of the Council of Europe and the European Coal and Steel Community
>
> (Madsen and Vauchez 2005: 181–190)

All the high-profile lawyers-*cum*-politicians involved in these attempts straddled law, politics, and academe, and were characterized by a high degree of mobility between institutions and sectors of legal-political practice. They continued to exert influence long after they had created the EU institutions by dint of succeeding to high office in the structures they created (Vauchez 2008). Before ever attempting integration, they had forged a consensus that unified and motivated them in deciding how Europe was to be rehabilitated. This movement was strikingly similar to our Network Community, which has been active across Europe for two decades. Then, as now, their consensus transcended partisan differences (as suggested by their ideological affiliations), just like our contemporary Network Community. It is a robust inference that the two transnational network communities were and are one and the same. Both the historical and the present-day communities show a continuity over time not in individuals, of course, but in ideas, membership types (elites, legal professionals crossing national and official boundaries), institutional connections and affiliations, and ambitions. The contemporary Network Community is not even geographically confined to Europe, though it is particularly dense here. It has operated across continents from the beginning of its existence, and appears to be expanding; hinting that it is a Community of global reach, or at the very least has ambitions to become so.

The Network Community is therefore senior to and more foundational than the supranational structures of contemporary Europe. Its origins reach farther back in time than the founding of the CoE, the post-war situation of Europe, or the openness to integration that has become such a window of opportunity for the Network to pursue their forbears' inter-war agenda

(Koskenniemi 2001). The spread of transnationalism across the legal profession pre-dated its supranational institutionalization. As early as the nineteenth century, a hard core of entrepreneurial American and European lawyers was already actively promoting international law as the key to world peace (Abrams 1957). Also in the 1800s, prominent German lawyers were working to enact a civil code for the whole of Germany as a way of unifying it (Schepel 2007), with the ultimate end of bringing peace at last to the German-speaking world. The founding lawyers' transnational grand strategy seems to have been an idea inspired by Kant's essay 'Perpetual Peace', a 'Philosophical Sketch' in which he proposed three 'Definitive Articles for Perpetual Peace': (1) the civil constitution of every state should be republican (by which he meant, essentially, democratic); (2) the law of nations shall be founded on a federation of free states (a *foedus pacificum* that seeks an end of all wars forever); and (3) the law of world citizenship shall be limited to conditions of universal hospitality (a human rights groundwork) (Kant 1795). The underlying practicality of this seemingly high-flown ideal is reflected in one of the few empirically verified truths in the field of international relations: that democracies rarely or never go to war with each other. Our 'law missionaries' apparently took this to heart, and ever since have held that peace is too important to be left to diplomats and politicians.

Well before the Second World War, then, the proto-Network were striving to establish the supremacy of international law and international courts and their power to superintend national acts. During the inter-war period, European jurists seeking to persuade their reluctant governments to cede the power to codify international law to the League of Nations profited from transatlantic networking with their American colleagues. In fact, they borrowed from them the idea of codification itself, which had been developed in the context of pan-American conferences and the Organization of American States – on which jurists had exerted considerable influence (Sacriste and Vauchez 2007). Acting through the League of Nations, where they held influential positions, the proto-Network's entrepreneurs had managed by the 1920s to institute the International Court of Justice (or 'World Court'), destined to become the Judiciary branch of the UN (Sacriste and Vauchez 2007).

From its origins as a 'loose elite group of internationalist legal professionals', the Network Community of today has long been planning supranational political projects overarching its contemporary Judiciary Template in Europe. It has been endeavouring to convert its cosmopolitan idealism into positive legal obligations through supranational institutions (Koskenniemi 2001). Hence its pivotal role in founding the CoE and EU and in the consolidation of European integration through supranational law. The inferred continuity of an elite networked community of interest which once promoted the League of Nations and which today constitutes our Network Community is also expressly acknowledged by its members, who take pride in their ancestry. In the words of the founder of the Venice Commission:

> the principle of the direct effect of the law of European Union and of its supremacy over incompatible national legislation . . . have been formulated by the Community Court of Justice, and it has with perhaps a touch of rhetorical flourish been labelled by some commentators as judge-made federalism. We can read it, however, more simply, as a new formulation of the long-standing principle, according to which international law is part of the law of the land, and is directly applicable and enforced by national judges. The novelty is that international law has developed into the law of the Union established by the Treaty. And this law is in each member state part not just of the law of the land, but of the supreme law of the land. But the origin of such an impressive evolution still lies in the principle that relates to the direct application of international law . . . This widespread tradition of internationalism in European constitution law goes back, if we want to trace the point in time when it was acknowledged by constitution-makers as a common tenet of legal civilisation, to that Indian summer of peace between the world wars, which was the *esprit de Genève* and of the world around the League of Nations. It was only a transient season, true, before the aggressive mood of nationalism set in to sow the seeds of conflict. Who could deny, however, that the legalism of the *esprit de Genève* has with the help of hindsight been revisited and improved by the new *esprit de Strasbourg* after World War II? The road that leads to limitation of sovereignty and collective decision making among or over and above nation states was paved by the relationship between international law and municipal law, as established by several of the present-day basic charters.
>
> (La Pergola 1997: 10–12)

Stripping away the beautiful poetry, the 'spirit' La Pergola speaks of dwells not in heaven but in the heart and mind of man the political animal, and if its agenda had the pervasive influence claimed for it by such an authority, it must have been shared by multitudes of change agents in a realm not in the ether but in a political 'space' that has always been over and above the nation-state and its discontents. Historically, this is the space (or vacuum) left behind by the downfall, with the Peace of Westphalia in 1648, of the mediaeval Papacy's erstwhile superintending role in the European political economy (Eckhardt 1937; Croxton 2013).

The same spirit of utopian universalism still endures today, inspiring its entrepreneurs. The observer cannot fail to be struck by their contemporary policy goals, such as the one of interest herein – to harmonize judicial institutions and legal cultures across Europe. It is striking that those who have spearheaded the Network's transnational Template in the remoter parts of Europe are known within the Community as 'missionaries' – individuals propagating ideas that are not necessarily their own invention and spreading them to other lands.[8] All this hints that the contemporary Network consensus for world peace spills over into ambitions for power – to attain peace, of course, but more than just peace. World peace continues to be the wellspring of self-empowerment, but other goals are now deemed necessary to the purpose. Their exacting vision of governance features their own leading role in the scheme of things, suggesting they believe peace cannot be achieved without comprehensive judicial control of the political, drawing them into advocating a transnationally disseminated world order to cure humanity's ills which goes well beyond the absence of particular wars to embrace also the sub-agendas of 'human rights' and the judicial constitutionalization of politics, apparently following Kant (but ignoring the republican dimension). This has led them to their common master agenda of empowering the Judiciary via transnationally disseminated institutional templates (see Chapter 6).

[8] Two types of 'change agents' are distinguished for theoretical completeness' sake: entrepreneurs and missionaries (although no bright line exists in the raw and this monograph will not try to observe the distinction everywhere). 'Network entrepreneurs', known as norm or policy entrepreneurs in political science and international relations (Keck and Sikkink 1998; Checkel 2012), are the Network's biggest thinkers, 'people who are committed, who talk a lot' (CoE Steering Committee member: Interviewee 1); who 'have the courage to go against the status quo' even under adverse political conditions (MEDEL high official: Interviewee 2). Entrepreneurs are individuals who invent something for their own gain (if in terms of money, then power or prestige). They are ready to exploit, when they do not create opportunities to bring about the change they prefer. 'Missionaries' are non-State actors, like entrepreneurs; unlike entrepreneurs, they are more dogmatic but less self-seeking. Dissatisfaction with the status quo does not mean that they originate ideas radically different from the 'alternative status quo' of the group, organizational, or network perspective they spring from. Their contribution is to spread the gospel to other lands. Missionaries are likelier satisfied to be anonymous and act behind the scenes. They are keen to win converts at the top of organizational hierarchies. Future research on this topic might investigate the analytic distinction on the level of agent stratagems.

3

The Network Community in action

The common agenda

Network consensus has led to an agenda that is not some accidental, transient like-mindedness, or serendipitous convergence of opinion arising from truth itself (cf. Scruton 2010, 2011). It is a plan long deliberated, of the greatest political consequence. In setting the agenda for Judiciary institutions and their power relations with the elected branches, the Community is in fact largely setting the agenda about how Europe shall be governed, and by whom – whether through the judicialization of politics, or by ordinary democratic means (cf. Stone Sweet 2000, 2004, 2010). A power shift of the magnitude contemplated, now essentially accomplished, bears implications that go to the very heart of what democracy shall be and whether it shall even exist.

It is known that the supranational judicialization regimes (the ECJ and the ECtHR) were created in part as a transnational legal professional strategy to escape the confines of the Continental civil law tradition, where the Judiciary is firmly subordinate to the core Executive. Domestic Judiciaries across Europe might therefore have been left out of supranational developments. Instead they are being nudged toward one design, and enlisted to the ends of the new supranational elite. This implies that the Template empowers neither domestic judges nor supranational judges alone, but the whole Network Community for whom judicialization is the generally preferred means to its ends.

The European Commission, the ECtHR, and the CoE General Secretariat have a built-in incentive to revise national Judiciaries to foster fealty to the supranational regime. The national judges' own transnational networking and their self-interest in being empowered over other domestic actors make them more likely to uphold supranational law. This might explain why the European Commission has funded and promoted the creation of some of the transnational judicial networks that have sprung up in

Strasbourg, especially in the last twenty years (Piana 2010); and why it has funded training that teaches national judges to side with supranational law (see Chapter 6). Without indoctrination, they would have been far more likely to defer to national law, as witness, for instance, the rulings of CEE courts in the 1990s, which ignored the ECHR and the jurisprudence of the Strasbourg Court even after their countries ratified the Convention (ECtHR judge: Interviewee 23). According to Commission officials in DG Enlargement:

> I was keeping an eye on judicial reform [in CEE] . . . because so much of the [problems with implementing the] *acquis* kept coming back to a malfunctioning judiciary . . . we are advising the member states whether a candidate is in position to join the club and a huge part of that is whether they can implement the *acquis*, and they cannot implement the *acquis* if their judicial system is not working . . . for whatever reasons, whether historical, budgetary . . . we don't really care academically why, but if the end result is that the *acquis* is not going to be implemented appropriately, then we have to step in.
> (EC official: Interviewee 14)

The admitted main concern of the supranational organs is that national judges uphold EU law and ECtHR case law if these come into conflict with national law. This legitimate concern is not comprehensively enough framed. It is being used to justify the Network Community's preference for a supremacist, autonomous national Judiciary, not so much for fear that supranational law will be utterly neglected as because those bodies of law lend themselves to activism and supremacy per se. The Template is imposed on grounds which tend to obscure the bigger picture in domestic political debates; that is, that the entire supranational order is the creature and construct of the same Network Community. This is what has enabled the common agenda to thrive and consolidate itself over time.

It appears from the totality of the evidence that this European integrationist agenda was always intended to be achieved through the judicialization of politics. The legal professional elites at the Network Community apex are deliberately in pursuit of it, as observed by Antonio La Pergola, founder and first President of the Venice Commission:

> the [European] Union is not destined to become any kind of federal superstate, where the principles of constitutionalism could be enthroned in their plenitude, even when the powers of the European Parliament will not [*sic*] be perfected. The more perfect Union we may aspire to is a generalised system of co-decision, a balance between parliamentary and the intergovernmental bodies, with the Commission in between as a peculiar executive . . . The one

> area where constitutional heritage is relied upon as a powerful catalyst of integration is, in sum, that of judicial guarantees. The thrust of the great European experiment is the creation of an open space as seedbed of individual rights and of emerging common citizenship side by side with national citizenship in the State of origin. The rights flowing from the Treaty and from secondary European legislation tie in with the root-rights, the basic human rights any person must enjoy to be a user of the market and a citizen of the Union . . . It is the rule of law, then, more than any factor of homogeneity, that becomes the energizing principle of integration as a new dimension of constitutionalism.
>
> (La Pergola 1997: 12–13)

The human rights agenda, regardless of its abstract merits or demerits, is not the issue. It is whether the judicialization of politics is necessary to carry it out, and whether its merits can offset the chief demerit of judicialization, its violation of what will herein be called the 'ground' due process of law. It will be seen in Chapters 4 and 5 how the Template encodes elite minority rule over the majority through the peculiarly labile way the concept of 'rights' has been re-defined and re-deployed. It is a twist on 'right' in the antique sense of Blackstone and akin to the Continental *Recht* or *droit*; a sense which predates 'human rights' and does not involve the same ironic tension with ordinary justice. To trade off the liberty or the justice of whole peoples in exchange for an elite agenda is a fool's bargain. The risk of judicialization is if it quashes along with abuses the people's right to make (or break) such a bargain in the first place.

Legal professional elites at the apex of the Network Community are dissatisfied with what they perceive as the insufficiency of contemporary European integration through the EU. Giving the EU more power is unlikely to work; it is clear that Europe does not want to be a federal state like the USA. The integration the elite desire cannot be attained through either parliamentarism or intergovernmentalism (i.e., the political branches), as this would empower the member states to resist; hence, *faut de mieux* it must be perfected not through the Judiciary alone, whose power is limited, but through the judicialization of *all* politics. In this, the Network Community appears to be succeeding:

> [A] new mechanism for international co-operation should be mentioned: the Conference of the European Constitutional Courts, and the Commission for Democracy through Law, the 'Venice Commission'. The integrative impact of the Venice Commission has been momentous indeed, and it serves the globalization of constitutional justice. Besides the official collection of court decisions a new body of authoritative opinions in constitutional matters is

> emerging . . . the opinions of the Venice Commission . . . extend beyond justicable [*sic*] problems and . . . cover all fields of human rights *and democracy*.
> (Sólyom 2003; emphasis added)

By imposing an '*acquis* Plus' through both Brussels and Strasbourg – the places where they in fact rule – the Network Community is substituting its own vision of Europe for any one of a diversity of alternatives that member states would surely have considered by now, had they been left to themselves; as witness not only the enforcement problems at the domestic level of both the EU *acquis* and the decisions of the supranational courts, but also especially the popular rejection of further integration (on those infrequent occasions when referendums are conceded).

The Network Community, or elements of it, can react violently when confronted with defiance of its agenda, especially by those considered 'outsiders'. József Szájer, Fidesz leader, constitution drafter, and Vice Chair of the European People's Party Group in the European Parliament is an eyewitness:

> My big debate was in the European Parliament . . . even Stalin had given more time for the defence of the short trials for their own enemies than what I had . . . I do not say that everything we did was the best. I have my own criticism, there were difficult choices to make, it is not that everything is clear white, but I can defend every single decision: why we were doing it, how we were doing, and also can say that what we did is not even a little bit that different from what Germany, France, Italy, and Britain are doing . . . [Hungarian PM] Orban spoke about 'illiberal democracy'. Maybe the choice of words was wrong but what he meant by this is that democracy can be Christian Democracy, Social Democracy, and Liberal Democracy, and since he is a Christian Democrat he wants Hungary to be a Christian Democracy . . . that was the essence, that's what he said. That we want some liberalism but that the under-regulation of the financial markets and other things failed in the front of our eyes. It collapsed. And they are still fighting for liberal lack of regulation over banks, bankers, and other things?
> (Jurist and MEP: Interviewee 35)

No disagreement over the common agenda on Judiciary institutional design was found between the CoE and the various interest-group judicial networks, either:

> [T]he principle that at least fifty per cent of the Judicial Council members should be judges elected by their peers [comes] from . . . international treaties . . . The European Charter concerning the Status of Judge [drafted by Network entrepreneurs], the Recommendations of the Council of Europe . . . the Venice Commission recommends the same thing.
> (MoJ civil servant: Interviewee 9)

Nor was any disagreement over the transnational Template observed between the European Commission and the other parts of the Network Community: 'The European Commission thought that Judicial Councils would be a way to eliminate political interference and strengthen judicial independence. The Council was put in place to establish separation of powers and independence' (EC career civil servant: Interviewee 36; see also Coman 2014b). The JC is what the legal professionals in the Network have pursued across Europe, implying that their common agenda is the European Commission's as well. And even more persuasively,

> what is the main guiding light in this field [Judiciary reform]? It is the European Court of Human Rights and the work of the Venice Commission and other CoE formations and study groups and associations . . . there is a lot of work going on in this field, it is all going in the same direction, so of course, we encourage you [candidate governments] to follow the recommendations that have already been made. Why reinvent the wheel?
>
> (EC official: Interviewee 14)

Very little or no disagreement could be detected between various other supra- and international organizations and the rest of the Network Community:

> Any norms or laws that the Venice Commission does not like are perceived unfavourably by the EU . . . There are other organizations and committees that have a lot of influence [on CEE]. The European Judges Association . . . the UN . . . all these organizations work together . . . The OSCE is also very important here.
>
> (EC career civil servant: Interviewee 37)

The finding, that a common agenda knits together the far-flung constituent parts of the Network Community, is confirmed by the scant literature on the Judiciary design agenda promoted by the Network Community, which found other international organizations, even those quite remote from politics and law, to be behind the same agenda:

> [T]he World Bank and other multilateral donor agencies have made Judicial Councils part of the standard package of institutions associated with judicial reform and rule of law programming . . . Efforts to produce model 'best practices' have ensured much replication and refinement of the Judicial Council model. For example, the Association of European Magistrates for Democracy and Freedom (MEDEL) produced a Draft Additional Protocol to the European Convention on Human Rights, called the Elements of European Statute on the Judiciary (known as the 'Palermo Declaration'). This model statute states that there shall be a supreme council of magistracy, at least

> half of whom are judges and also including appointees of the parliament . . . the supreme council will produce a budget for the courts, manage the administration, and control recruitment, assignment and discipline of judges . . . The Council of Europe made a similar recommendation in a document published in 1994 . . . Other international organizations have followed suit.
>
> (Garoupa and Ginsburg 2009: 109)

The most recent members of the Network, the elite jurists of CEE, also profess the common agenda. Academics in particular are amongst its most zealous advocates. The law professors who drafted one of the many revisions of the Romanian Code of Civil Procedure in the late 2000s fully agree with their peers in the ECtHR that the national courts can and ought to settle public policy disputes on the basis of vague constitutional or international law principles (see Chapter 5).

Evidence that academics are key players in sharing the Network agenda and enacting the agenda abounds throughout both East and West. Transnational legal academics' collaboration in the 1960s with the ECJ to transform the EU Treaty into a quasi-constitution is well documented (Alter 2007; Vauchez 2015). Across the Atlantic, a now stale joke in legal academic circles in the USA gloats that the nation's sovereignty rests with Harvard Law School (Morton and Knopff 2000). Others have noted the 'powerful synergy' (*sc.* network consensus) in the USA between the appellate Judiciary and the legal professoriate, who are the judges' main constituency (Glendon 1996). In Canada, too, law school academe is said to subsist in a 'symbiotic' relationship with the transnational legal professional networks (Morton and Knopff 2000); a 'phalanx of academics' is credited with playing a key role in mobilizing support for the Charter of Rights and Freedoms in the early 1980s (Russell 1983). In France and Germany, the legal academies have routinely collaborated with judges so as to influence jurisprudence and bolster the legitimacy of CCs (Stone Sweet 1994).

In Norway, Judiciary revisions which, contrary to Norwegian tradition, gave courts autonomy of the kind embodied in the Template (see Chapter 6) were spearheaded by an expert committee set up by the MoJ and chaired by President of the Supreme Court Carsten Smith, a former law professor and former Dean of the Faculty of Law, University of Oslo, known by his colleagues as 'extremely enthusiastic about human rights and [the idea] that we [Norwegians] should ratify conventions and make them binding on a higher level than ordinary laws . . . [and] about the ideas from the CoE' (SCt judge and academician: Interviewee 46). In Britain, the Constitution Unit at University College London is known as a tireless lobbyist for constitutional and Judiciary revision, and some of its leaders take the utmost pride in providing judicial elites a platform from which to call for a UK Supreme Court (which has now been realized), without always considering the remote consequences. More recently, law school professors at the Centre for Political and Constitutional Studies at King's College London single-handedly drafted the 2014 'New Magna Carta', a blueprint featuring three alternative pathways to codifying a UK constitution (Political and Constitutional Reform Committee 2014).

Elite lawyers-*cum*-politicians at the domestic level are one with academics (who trained them) in pursuing the common agenda of Judiciary empowerment, quite regardless of partisan loyalties. Here is the testimony of one elite judge, until recently President of the Template's Judicial Council in Moldova (bearing in mind that the Juridical Committee is a standing committee in many CEE parliaments and is almost invariably staffed by lawyers affiliated with all political parties):

> **Q:** Did anybody in Parliament oppose this reform which empowered the Judicial Council at the expense of the Moldovan Parliament and the Executive?
>
> **A:** In the current Parliament [2010–14] . . . we [elite judges] collaborated a lot with the Juridical Committee . . . When there are proposals concerning laws that affect us or the Judiciary system or the modification of the Codes we [elite judges] are invited. At every meeting we are invited. They ask us to issue a consultative opinion for any law project concerning us [the Judicial Council] or the Judiciary. We work a lot in the spirit of collaboration [not separation] of powers. In the meetings of this Committee there have been many times where we had full backing from them.
>
> (SCt judge and JC official: Interviewee 21)

Even lawyers belonging to the Communist Party, who are classically amongst the most outspoken opponents of Judiciary empowerment (Kühn 2004), seem now to share the Network consensus behind the common agenda:

> **Q:** Was there any opposition from the Communists in Parliament to the Judiciary reform that transferred power from Parliament to the Judicial Council?
>
> **A:** No, categorically not. When it comes to this aspect of politics, at those meetings in Parliament in the Juridical Commission in which I took part, I did not see this partisan aspect play a role, whether you are talking about the left or the right or the centre or anything else.
>
> (SCt judge and JC official: Interviewee 21)

And the situation in Croatia was found to be exactly the same:

> **Q:** Would the Judicial Council have been strengthened in 2010 without pressure from the European Commission? Did Croatian politicians feel obliged to follow a certain template?
>
> **A:** It would have happened anyway . . . there have been large-scale expert debates at various levels concerning this issue . . . They were mostly professors from law schools . . . Politicians too, but only those who at the same time also had a legal background . . . Political positions [party affiliations] were completely irrelevant.
>
> (Jurist and MP: Interviewee 47)

Private funding for the Network agenda supports Judiciary empowerment, hinting at just such a consensus between philanthropic foundations and the Community. The subveners of Judiciary (re)designs are not 'equal opportunity' funders. Herman Schwartz, an American law professor funded by the Soros Foundation to advise CEE countries on constitutional design, authored one of the first academic books touting the benefits of CCs in the region. He was not just any lawyer but one who in his own words had 'a New Deal perspective' (Schwartz 2000: 10). It is doubtful that anyone promoting a conservative agenda, an Antonin Scalia, would be funded. A New Deal lawyer will be biased toward promoting judicial review by CCs in its most activist mode:

> If they [Constitutional Courts in CEE] are to survive and if their actions are to command respect and obedience, they must somehow persuade their respective society, both its people and its leaders, that their decisions are based not on partisan political considerations but on neutral, objective law, *even when the issue in dispute obviously has very contentious political origins and consequences. They must do what U.S. Chief Justice Marshall is credited with having done: transform public policy disputes into questions of constitutional interpretation that can be decided by texts, procedures, principals, and rules that are generally accepted as legal and not political* . . . by a means that former Hungarian Constitutional Court president László Sólyom has called 'legal argumentation'.
>
> (Schwartz 2000: 4–5; emphasis added)

In principle, the issue is whether one believes tax-exempt philanthropic foundations vet funding applicants ideologically or are purely philanthropic without ambitions of their own.

Britain's recent constitutional and Judiciary revisions corroborate the inference that funding is conditional upon pursuing an agenda in consensus with the Network Community. Charter 88, an elite intellectual movement that arose in the late 1980s but might have failed without funding from the Rowntree Trust, made entrenchment of a written bill of rights the top item of its agenda for constitutional change, an agenda which influenced the New Labour manifesto of Tony Blair in the 1990s, particularly the Human Rights Act (Unlock Democracy 2013; Parau 2015b). Bills of rights are known to have the effect of empowering judges (Hirschl 2004). Intention is not observable, but foundation owners and staff steadfastly refused to be interviewed, which raises at least a rebuttable presumption that they mean to omit from the public sphere, as a matter of corporate policy, the existence and nature of any agendas they do have. In any case, private funders cannot be unaware of the implications of what they fund.

The Joseph Rowntree Charitable Trust underwrote the forerunners of the Liberal Democrat Party in the UK – those at the forefront of advocating a written constitution. Both the Rowntree Trust and the Nuffield Foundation sponsored the Centre for Political and Constitutional Studies at King's College London, led by Robert Blackburn, to draft the *New Magna Carta*. Professor Vernon Bogdanor, another of the Centre's Directors, sat on the Joint Commission of the Social Democrat and Liberal Parties, set up in the 1980s to make recommendations for constitutional revision (Joint Liberal/SDP Alliance Commission on Constitutional Reform 1983). Not by sheer chance, one may presume, did Rowntree and Nuffield favour with funding just those elite jurists who promoted judicialization, whose expansive bills of rights are prone to precipitate, in preference to other jurists who would have stood by parliamentary supremacy.

Finally, elite transnational media have a stake in the common agenda. By campaigning for or against a policy issue, the media implicitly take sides for one elite group against another (or for what they claim is the 'popular faction' against 'the elites' and vice versa). It has been noted already that the media in the USA and Canada side with apex courts, depicting them as neutral arbiters, not activist policy makers in their own right (LaRowe 2010). Evidence from Canada also shows that the media pick and choose law school academics to be their authoritative sources of information, selection of whom is often observed to lean heavily in favour of positive portrayals of activist courts and their decisions (Morton and Knopff 2000). Such portrayals affect public perception, subtly conditioning support for judicialization (Baird and Gangl 2006). More consequentially, media are likely to tip the balance of power between the main elite factions; the contenders in question in the case of judicialization of politics being the Network Community on one side, and on the other the resistance to that agenda, who in Europe are nationalist elites and their constituents.

The elite international media are a power resource which the Network are entitled with priority to resort to, with or without reference to 'Strasbourg', to disseminate their message transnationally and inhibit domestic political moves undoing their common agenda. The media were observed mobilizing audiences in favour of apex courts in CEE, as elsewhere. For instance, media leapt to relay the censure by legal professional and academic opponents of the Hungarian Fidesz and Romanian Ponta governments when the latter moved to revise the Judiciary power in 2011 and 2013, respectively, which included trimming the powers of their respective CCs; omitting from the coverage that the CCs had assumed prerogatives surpassing anything Western countries had ever tolerated. For example, a statute of the Government previous to Ponta had empowered the CC to police Parliament's internal political proceedings, which it was misusing to obstruct the agenda of Ponta's PSD, the judges' partisan *bête noir*. Ponta moved to repeal the statute by emergency decree, as the Romanian constitution allows subject to parliamentary ratification. The Romanian CC proceeded to rule it *unconstitutional* for Parliament to repeal its own (admittedly organic) statute, as if the CC was the only legitimate government whose power, once delegated, may never be recalled.

An enraged reaction erupted from Brussels and Strasbourg; heads of state such as Angela Merkel, none of whose business it was, denounced Romania; but most remarkable of all was how elite international media weighed into their astonished readership. The *New York Times* published incendiary denunciations of the Hungarian Fidesz and Romanian Ponta governments by American jurists and their collaborators, some of whom are legal professionals of Hungarian or Romanian origin who oppose Fidesz or Ponta, respectively, and who were amongst those who petitioned the Network Community for intervention (Scheppele 2011, 2013; Bánkuti et al. 2012; Bánkuti, Dombos et al. 2012; Scheppele and Perju 2012).[1] These articles were unapologetically partial to the interests of the 'CC party', even though its domestic American readership could hardly so much as comprehend, let alone be expected to care about Hungarian or Romanian judicial affairs:

> The actions of the Ponta government combine polarized party politics with a constitution-smashing revolution . . . Ponta and his allies have been so

[1] Scheppele is Laurence S. Rockefeller Professor of Sociology and International Affairs at Princeton University. She is renowned amongst her peers for her access to the metropolitan media, a privilege available to very few academics (even elite ones).

> intent on removing Băsescu that they have stopped at nothing to achieve this result . . . They threatened to remove justices of the Constitutional Court who had sided with [President] Băsescu in the past and – when international criticism roared about the threats to the judges – instead cut the jurisdiction of the Constitutional Court . . . In this climate, all eyes are on the Constitutional Court. What . . . is the Court doing to stave off constitutional crisis in Romania? The Court has been sidelined by both a statute and an executive decree which have removed its jurisdiction, but it has nonetheless made decisions over the last week that have tried to sort law from politics . . . A close reading of the Court's reasons published Thursday (12 July) shows that its strategy is to claim jurisdiction over the decisions of parliament after striking down as unconstitutional attempts to limit its own powers, while at the same time voluntarily limiting its review to only those decisions that, in its narrow interpretation, 'impact on constitutional values and principles' . . . On the legal side, while the recent decisions both on the referendum and on attempts at limiting its jurisdiction show a certain amount of bravery on the part of the Constitutional Court, one also sees effects of the extraordinary pressures on the Court . . . [It] is probably doing the best it can to preserve itself while still fulfilling its responsibilities to keep politics within constitutional boundaries. This survival strategy is likely a reaction to the enormous political pressure on the Court in recent days . . . [T]he recent decisions . . . on attempts at limiting its jurisdiction show a certain amount of bravery on the part of the Constitutional Court.
>
> (Scheppele and Perju 2012)

Radio Free Europe reported the affair from the same one-sided perspective, whilst clearly trying to undermine the government's credibility with *ad hominem* memes such as 'ex-communist' or 'plagiarism':

> Romania's Constitutional Court has accused leftist Prime Minister Victor Ponta of trying to dismantle it and said it has notified EU authorities of threats to its independence . . . Ponta, who is facing calls to resign over accusations of plagiarism, ignored a court ruling last week . . . Ponta's ex-communist Social Democratic Party (PSD) has since threatened to replace some judges, accusing them of political bias. The court said in a statement on July 3 that its judges 'have noted the virulent attacks the court was subjected to by the government and other public institutions as well as propositions made to dismantle the court'.
>
> (Tomiuc 2012)

The media consumer is presented nothing from the other side of the controversy, not even basic facts such as what exactly either government intended. Yet to anyone who takes the trouble to drill down into the data, the bona fides of both governments are hard to dispute. Neither sought any drastic revision of the Template that would have 'dismantled' either

CC. The most significant fact of all, that Parliament had delegated the power in question just a few years before, plus the whole paradox of *any* court assuming the jurisdiction to strike down organic statutes and even constitutional amendments, was crucially omitted by the international media, which painted a heroic image of a victim-Court suffering the persecution of cartoon villains. Here is a clear instance of the transnational media taking sides in concert, regardless of the merits (indeed, actively suppressing the merits of the opposing side), in a domestic power struggle which did not contest the judicialization of politics per se, but merely *any* retrenchment of Judiciary power, no matter how minimal.

Transnational media coverage was transparently one-sided.[2] Its sheer vitriol was so shocking that Fidesz politicians experienced it as

> a conscious . . . orchestrated attack against Hungary . . . which started when the [Socialist] Luxembourgian Foreign Minister . . . said that 'the media law in Hungary is horrible because it violates rights.' He did not say anything as to why – nothing. This started the whole political attack, and then it spread over in the whole European and the world press, and . . . after you created this framework – 'they are not good, and they are doing something very dirty . . .' – then you don't need to argue anymore . . . It's as if the debates in the *Bundestag* would be reported . . . only from the Greens' point of view, which is the tiniest party which has no influence on things.
>
> (Jurist and MEP: Interviewee 35)

It will be said that it is Fidesz who is biased, but parallel data from the Romanian case point to a relatively minor difference in governing philosophy. Indeed, Romanian elite jurists who, unlike Fidesz or the PSD, neither held a stake in party politics nor bore the brunt of media outrage, nevertheless deplored the coverage. They are well known, moreover, for their sympathy with CCs – 'I am a fervent supporter of constitutional

[2] When researching these episodes at the time of the controversy, the author found page after Google page of search results of nearly identical news stories about the situation in Hungary. Not one of them presented factual information about that government's legislative agenda, nor analysed why they were pursuing it. The mystery agenda was none the less cast by one and all in a highly emotional, negative tone, apparently aimed at enraging (at a minimum prejudicing) the media consumer against Hungary's elected politicians. The author could not fail to notice the effect this coverage had on her Oxford University colleagues at the time, even those working in disciplines as remote as Tibetan Studies. Nobody knew a thing about Hungarian politics, but all were strongly opinionated about the 'appalling events' in Hungary. Yet when prompted to state reasons for their indignation, or just facts about what was going on, no one could do either.

review [said one of the few in-depth researchers in that field in Romania] and of the Kelsenian model of Constitutional Courts, and . . . would never agree with the elimination of the Court from the . . . constitutional system' (Selejan-Guţan 2012) – yet this jurist disapproved of the Western reaction as extreme and unreasonable. Another opined that strictures against limitless jurisdiction are not Romanian doctrine only; that any foreign constitutional law doctrine will teach that Standing Orders of Parliament are political acts and do not properly form an object of CC jurisdiction; that in Hungary, too, something similar happened – that is, the tone of the coverage was such that 'one got the impression the Communist dictatorship was being reinstated, and that the rule of law was collapsing.' These jurists were very critical: 'any conclusions of this kind must be premised on exact investigation of the context. You cannot simply accept political propaganda published in the Western press' (Academician: Interviewee 48).

The Romanian case may be an outlier, but the ferocity with which the media in the judicializing community, even more than the legal professional networks, resisted any diminution of power, no matter how minimal, constitutional, or reasonable, implies that the Network's self-empowerment for their own sake is an integral part of the common agenda. This seems what, at bottom, binds the members of the Network Community to a consensus agenda, perhaps even more so if the ego-centrism is partly *un*conscious. The conduct of the media is what, above all, has exposed the Network Community as at bottom an exclusive (for the 'right people', semi-permeable) club for members' mutual benefit and, given the scope of its common agenda, for the general public's benefit too, one tries to hope. The sharing of collective identities and Network consensus enables coordination and interdependence, which in turn empower the Network over the nation-states of Europe (so long as domestic veto-players remain dormant). And as the Romanian and Hungarian cases show, nations that have submitted to its Template may find it harder than anticipated to escape, if it proves detrimental.

At all events, the elite transnational media were everywhere observed to propagate and justify the consensus, and to support the Network Community implicitly in the pursuit of its common agenda; all of which implies that media systemically partake in the Network Community and share its ultimate goals without caring a fig for the details of public policy as such. Media are not a power resource that 'belongs' to our Network Community or to any other. They are big-business enterprises firmly under the control of their owners, and have reasons of their own for supporting the Network – or not (always). It follows that international media would have reacted aggressively to Fidesz not principally to defend the Community's interests, but their owners' interests, which were also hit by the Fidesz Party reforms. As one of the designers of Hungary's new Fundamental Law observed:

> Media is a business, which means that companies whose interests, and very important direct shares, have been hurt here in Hungary – banks, utility companies – also the international human rights community, which is a business in itself with their own interest. If there is no fascism, you cannot be anti-fascist. If you cannot get money for fighting fascism, then you have to close down your business.
>
> (Jurist and MEP: Interviewee 35)

Further research is needed to discover more about how, why, and with what effect media contribute. The question would be how much, if at all, the success of the Network depends on concentration of media ownership and cartelization, and with it the consolidation of viewpoint.[3] In any case, the transnational media were observed to propagate and justify the consensus, and to support the Network Community implicitly in the pursuit of its agenda.

Personnel is policy

The Network consensus is the solidary basis for effectuating a common agenda which is based on it. An agenda is effectuated by agents; these must be loyal to the principals and their principles and not stray from them – hence the importance of personnel. Supranational organs involved in CEE Judiciary affairs invariably rely on outside experts for their advice to these countries, and for monitoring and assessing the state of their institutions. The choice of experts becomes 'key', as their views influence what these organs recommend (even coerce) CEE governments to do.

[3] The experience of Italy in the early 1990s might be archetypal. It strongly hints that the left-oriented press favours courts. According to a Network entrepreneur who witnessed the 'Clean Hands' campaign in Italy: 'During the Clean Hands period from 1992 to 1994 . . . no journalist dared to write a strong line against judges. Things have changed completely . . . because part of the press now belongs to the other party. It belongs to the President and to the Prime Minister [Berlusconi]. It belongs to the right. Your remark that the media in Central and Eastern Europe is friendly towards the Constitutional Court though not towards the ordinary Judiciary is just like the situation in Italy' (EJA officer and CoE adviser: Interviewee 11; see also Magalhães et al. 2006).

European Commission officials are particularly quick to deny any suggestion that they may be politically selective in their choice of experts, portraying their experts' opinions as merely their own, amongst many others:

> **Q:** How do you choose your experts? There are all kinds of experts out there.
>
> **A:** When they are saying, on the Croatian side, 'the experts say this, or the Commission says this', the experts are, of course, free to have any opinion they want, and write their opinion as to how things should be, or identify problems with their Judiciary, but that is their opinion, and we always make that very clear to the candidates . . . that 'this is the experts' opinion and this is not representative of the Commission's opinion.'
>
> (EC official: Interviewee 14)

The evidence, however, supports an inference that the Commission does rely on their experts' views probably more than they are prepared to admit:

> The assessments are not binding in any way, but . . . they did some work in Turkey, which . . . was appreciated *or at least it was not questioned* here in the Commission. They did something in Serbia. They will be going to Montenegro.
>
> (EC official: Interviewee 39; emphasis added)

The same dependency may also be read between the lines of this expert deployed by the European Commission to a country in the Balkans:

> The government . . . ignored the [Network Community] standards . . . it is very clearly stated in the Opinion I wrote that members of the Judicial Council cannot be active politicians, they cannot be MPs . . . These recommendations were ignored [by the domestic government] even though they have been written in the reports [I wrote], and I assume the Commission, too, insisted on that . . . that this institutional arrangement is against the standard . . . the representative of the Commission discussed with me this issue many times. Do I think my report had an influence on the 2010 constitutional revision [of the country in question] that changed the terms of the Judiciary with the elected branches of government? . . . our reports can have an impact . . . they have an impact on reforms, but only as long as the Commission insists on that . . . we give our input but it has to be taken up by the Commission.
>
> (Judge and EC adviser: Interviewee 40)

In other words, the Commission provides the 'muscle' which exacts from accession candidates compliance with the opinions of the experts chosen by the Commission. Determining the exact extent to which the Commission relies on these experts is beyond the scope of this monograph. What matters is that the experts who were observed were change agents networked-into or aligned with the Network, or known to them for their 'reliability'; from which it may be inferred, taking all the other evidence into account, that this is the usual practice. Non-activists and un-networked activists face the disheartening and daunting task of challenging the vast power resources and personnel depth of the Network Community, a disincentive to get involved. No interview or documentary evidence of dissent from the common agenda was ever found by the author amongst actors know to be Network members. Even if the EU or CoE did not select experts for their political orientation, practically by default they would have lit on the 'usual suspects'; unless they had been prepared to expend considerable time and resources (for which no evidence was found) to identify a broad spectrum of expert points of view to painstakingly balance the mix. The information of the interviewees implied quite the opposite, that the Commission knows already who they want:

> Why did the European Commission decide to send me to CEE? There was a tender and I was selected by the Council . . . After that I took part in bilateral or Twinning projects, and I also spoke at conferences in many countries, both on behalf of the Italian Ministry of Justice and of the European Commission under the TAIEX service . . . I did not apply [to go on missions to CEE] . . . I was selected by the European Commission, so they had their own sources of information. And they came to me.
>
> (Judge and EC adviser: Interviewee 40)

Although the interviewee claimed not to know why the European Commission picked him, one might surmise motive from his further testimony. The reader should remember that the interviewee's tone of voice, its animation and zeal, cannot be conveyed in cold print:

> Many Italian judges, not only me, feel that we are no longer Italian judges or prosecutors, but we are European judges and prosecutors because we work in a European system . . . The European law [of both the EU and the CoE] is part of our system, and very often we have to decide what law to apply in case there is a conflict between the two, which means that in that situation we are European judges.
>
> (Judge and EC adviser: Interviewee 40)

The ethos of being a European and not a national judge invokes Haas's concept of a cultivated spillover from the supranational level, and the transfer of loyalty from national to supranational institutions (Haas 1958, 1961). This is something the forerunners of the Network Community have been encouraging since at least the 1920s:

> The *Institut des Hautes Études Internationales de Genève* [the Geneva Graduate Institute of International Studies] was created in 1926 . . . The initial purpose

> of the institution was really and primarily to train administrators who would be truly detached from loyalties to the great powers . . . This became . . . [a] supranational venue for lawyers . . . [who] seemed to subscribe, regardless of their national origins and political linkages, . . . [to the] belief in the superiority of the judiciary.
>
> (Sacriste and Vauchez 2007: 89–93)

Here is the origin of the enthusiastic evangelization of European integration through law by so many transnational legal professionals, and their desire to win 'converts' even beyond Europe. It argues an alignment with today's Network Community and its common agenda, as is attested by experts sent by the European Commission to CEE, some of whom were independent in the sense of not being appointed (and not necessarily vetted, either) by the CoE. This is evidence that 'reliability' is something quite independent of formal membership of, or affiliation with, any given association or institution, but originates directly from the (proto-)Network.

Alignment with the Network Community cannot but contribute to the determination of whom to select as an expert. It is unlikely that the supranational organs would select one critical of the common agenda, like this elite Moldovan jurist: 'International conferences have been organized with the participation of scientific societies, [of] lawyers . . . from the CoE, the kids from the Venice Commission, who come and teach us . . .' (CC judge: Interviewee 29).

Experts from countries generally sceptical of interfering in domestic policy making on a scale approved by the Network are also unlikely to be chosen as experts. Norway is a case in point, having scarcely been involved in the supranational and international intervention in Judiciary governance in CEE. Norway is not a member of the EU, but is a member of the CoE. Since the EU and CoE share a common agenda and collaborate on judicial affairs, Norwegian experts could in theory be called upon. Norway sponsors NORLAM, its own programme on the rule of law and Judiciary rehabilitation in Eastern Europe. They are known to be less aligned with the Network agenda and generally reluctant to intervene in aspects of national institutions that touch upon the power relations between the Judiciary and the elected branches of government:

> Norway has been involved in Judiciary reforms in some CEE countries. What is Norway trying to do? Are we trying to export our own Judiciary institutional models? Definitely not. What we are doing is to send teams with practical experience in legal affairs – judges, prosecutors, police, lawyers, prison officers, and defence attorneys – to CEE . . . These are practitioners

> who stay one or two years on the spot and . . . share [their] experience with individual judges and judges' associations . . . One of the main topics has been 'single main hearings' . . . to teach . . . the usefulness of having a single court hearing in a case instead of the system they have today, where you listen to one witness one day and next month you hear another witness so a case drags out for months and years. We taught Georgia to make one single hearing that would take one to three days and then that's it, you have the verdict. What about the European Commission? We are not member of this club. We have one expert in Northern Iraq seconded by the European Commission, but that is outside the EU . . . Our kind of assistance differs much from other kinds of assistance to CEE . . . Very often . . . I had seen the work of the OSCE, which is much more about monitoring [CEE countries] and sticking up your finger, and then the EU [experts] come with a lot of money . . . and stay for a very short time, put up a list of demands, and then leave again . . . [Our approach] has given us credibility . . . also because we have no hidden agenda . . . Advising countries on the organization of the Judiciary is outside the scope of what we are doing . . . we are practitioners focusing on practical work . . . We have never thought about and we were never asked to do [institutional redesign] . . . we have a mission but we have no missionaries.
>
> (MoJ senior official: Interviewee 27)

The Norwegians echo some British legal professionals. Britain, too, has exported a great deal of lore about judicial administration and its everyday workings to CEE and beyond, rather than the whole formal institutional structure of it. Of those who do get involved with the Network Community (concerning the correct extent of intervention in other countries' constitutional affairs beyond practical experience):

> we [British] are not evangelical . . . we tend to get much more directly involved in terms of sharing ideas and experience concerning court administration . . . if we are doing exchanges with particular jurisdictions, they will very often be both administratively and judge-led. It is about, 'How can we do such-and-such?' . . . 'How do you make your justice system work?' . . . our judges have been very much involved in saying, 'This is our experience, and this is how you can get involved in court administration without compromising your independence.' It tends to be much more practical about effective court operation. That's where Britain's influence tends to be most.
>
> (MoJ official: Interviewee 28)

Nevertheless, the pattern of selection of British experts by the supranational organs (as Britain is a major member state) for deployment to CEE suggests that it may be motivated by their propensity to make recommendations favourable to the expansion of Judiciary power. One British expert selected by the European Commission was a High Court judge and Labour ex-politician well known in Britain for supporting the 2005 revision of the Judiciary branch under the Blair Government, which brought it more in line with the Template (Parau 2015d). There were plenty of experts in the UK of the first calibre who had vehemently opposed this revision. Even if a minority (which is far from certain), it was one substantial enough to be visible from Brussels and Strasbourg, had the European Commission or the CoE wanted to cast their 'net' wide enough. Conspicuous examples include Lord Hoffmann and the staffs of think tanks such as Policy Exchange, who are vociferously sceptical of judicial empowerment (Pinto-Duschinsky 2011). The Commission cannot predict the behaviour of each expert; they can be ideologically selective across the board, however, to make it more likely for judicialization to prevail overall.

In Romania in 2004, it was an expert from Germany, funded by the European Commission via the PHARE project, who consolidated the transnational Template. His sway was shored up by the intransigence of the Commission and its threats to delay or adjourn Romania's accession. The Romanian Ministry of Justice had chosen as its expert a French jurist who was more sceptical of maximal Judiciary empowerment. The Government's Bill for the organic law of the Judiciary did empower it but stopped just shy of the maximal. The Government and its expert lost (Parau 2015b). It was shelved in Parliament for the Commission-funded one. Evidently, this was not by chance:

> When the Judicial Council was being drafted, under an EU-PHARE project, I and other judges went to many EU countries where the Judicial Council exists to find out what the arrangements were and what the problems and disadvantages . . . The German expert . . . helped . . . by making available materials about Judicial Councils, especially the Spanish one, which Romania took inspiration from, and the Dutch one [whose Judicial Council is weaker]. The European Commission was more sympathetic to the [Spanish] version because this [the Bill embodying it] came out of an EU-funded project.
>
> (JC high official: Interviewee 41)

The Commission favoured the 'home team' but not likely out of simple institutional loyalty as this interviewee could be read as suggesting, but because the Network Community's common agenda is preferred by it (Parau 2015b).

Unless no jurist in the whole of Europe disagrees with this agenda, which is demonstrably not the case, the inference must stand that the supranational organizations have selected the experts on whom they rely

– for their . . . reliability in pursuing that agenda. The experts would have been known to be part of the Network Community that the supranational functionaries are themselves networked into.

The Network Community's judicializing standards are the default for assessing national judicial institutions, as no other standards exist. No one but the Network Community has undertaken to develop any standards in the first place, let alone develop them in a transnational/supranational framework. Few even question this state of affairs:

> [In my report for the European Commission] there are thousands of references to the Croatian law, and then there are references to European standards . . . used for assessing a [country's Judiciary] system. I justify each affirmation I make with reference to European standards. I never give my personal opinion . . . I use my culture and my perspective in order to assess the local system in the light of European standards.
>
> (Judge and EC adviser: Interviewee 40)

The testimony of a British judge who partook in a handful of missions to CEE on behalf of the European Commission, but who has not seemed particularly active in the Network Community otherwise, acknowledges the force of a ubiquitous benchmark in spite of a hint of scepticism on his own part:

> What kind of standards do we use to evaluate a country's Judiciary? That's a difficulty, and therefore in some cases I'd say 'Look, really it's up to the Romanians or it's up to the Turks to decide', but there are European standards in the sense that the Council of Europe has . . . Recommendations about the independence of the Judiciary, for example. In the EU itself, the Court of Justice has said in certain cases, they've made comments about things like the independence of the Judiciary, so you can draw that out.
>
> (High Court judge: Interviewee 42)

Experts of this kind end up looking consensual with the Network, except it is not by preference, but by default. Corroboration of the lack of alternatives to the Network consensus comes from an Italian judge whose transnational involvement and missionary zeal for European integration through law identified him as a Network entrepreneur:

> [In] Europe . . . we have standards about independence . . . One might not accept that the CoE Recommendations or the Opinions of the Consultative Council of European Judges are sources of law . . . because they are not issued by . . . legislators [and therefore] . . . they are not binding . . . [but] those standards are applied only because they are convincing. They are not imposed by the European Commission . . . but those Opinions and

> Recommendations are references which are taken into account when discussing how to change the system and how to improve it and have, for sure, an impact on the reforms.
>
> (Judge and EC adviser: Interviewee 40)

Lack of an alternative to standards that inherently judicialize politics is not a stable equilibrium; it must be cultivated and maintained. This inference is a corollary of the choosiness with which the supranational organs approach the matter of expert selection, as if it were not enough that the Network's standards are now defaults. The selectivity of experts and lack of alternatives together constitute a case of mutually reinforcing, reciprocal causation, holding each other in place interdependently where neither might have been able to subsist on its own.

Interdependence and coordination

Far more is at stake than the experts who advise the supranational organs over judicial institutions. The Network do not transact expert selection only, they also coordinate other change agents, along with groups and organizations across national boundaries (cf. Rhodes 1996). Coordination of agency is necessary to the pursuit of a common agenda; it renders the whole Network Community politically powerful and more than the sum of its components. Coordination is 'enforced' or upheld over time by interdependence; the groups and organs that the Network Community joins up, relying on each other on a regular basis, learn to trust their 'comrades (in arms)'. Coordination and interdependence are particularly thick between the supranational organs and the larger Network Community. This symbiotic relationship reshapes both sides' opportunity structures, enabling the supranational hierarchies to expand the scope and reach of their power through the breadth of the expertise of the various networked-in legal professional and other networks; whilst these and the whole Network get to set domestic agendas, inter alia on Judiciary institutional design, by 'hitching a ride' on the supranational organs' intergovernmentally derived authority. What is more, transnational coordination and interdependence subsisting between the Network Community and national governments are also a means to the Community's self-empowerment.

The EU's interdependence on the CoE

The supranational organs and the transnational Network Community have escaped the formal hierarchies of the Westphalian nation-state; even so, power relations between them are not perfectly horizontal, notwithstanding the interdependency of network and nodality, or the co-equality in principle of coordinate 'branches' of supranational government. The empirical evidence tells that the CoE is the driver of European integration through law, whilst the EU ox pulls the cart. There is evidence of some rivalry between the two supranational organizations, but in the last reckoning, it is the CoE that holds the reins in what matters most to the CoE. But it is the legal professional networks, in turn, that hold the reins of the CoE in what matters most to themselves and to the wider judicializing community.

To begin with the EU lacks the expertise to know what institutional designs to pursue that would judicialize politics in the member states. The European Commission is too leanly budgeted to keep their own juridical experts in house. It employs very few legally trained experts in comparison with other types of professionals (Georgakakis 2012), and whoever the Commission does employ are not experts in Judiciary institutional design; which has therefore to be outsourced.[4] All kinds of experts exist outside the EU organs, but the Commission relies on those only who have the Network Community's imprimatur:

> The European Commission has relied on the Venice Commission and CoE. What in particular has inspired the Commission to follow them? How do we know that they are the best experts, or that they have the best ideas? . . . these have the seal of the CoE.
>
> (EC official: Interviewee 39)

The insularity and self-referentiality of this reasoning and the consequent selectivity of experts is a fact confirmed by the CoE itself:

> [The European Commission] use very often, in their own assessment of the performance of the candidate countries or of the member-state

[4] '[W]e were faced with problems [in CEE], so we organized projects, and then it was left to the project implementers . . . administrators and consultants [which] CEE governments hired to decide what was best for themselves – and we had the Twinning exercise as well' (EC official: Interviewee 16). This testimony of a Head of Unit who negotiated accession with Romania makes it sound as if CEE governments had the freedom to choose these experts; however, the empirical data suggest otherwise, or at least they suggest a more ambiguous picture.

> countries . . . the results of the CoE Conventional monitoring, be it the judgments of the ECtHR, be it the report of the Committee for the Convention of Torture, be it the report of the European Commission Against Racism and Intolerance, the Framework Convention on National Minorities, etc., etc.
>
> (CoE official: Interviewee 13)

The Venice Commission is often cited by a European Commission eager to boost its own image of authority. An appearance of the supremacy of its expertise has been cultivated; a supremacy which implies (always taking care to avoid formally invoking) an obligation to obey:

> The Copenhagen Criteria are not very precise . . . in that, very often, it is quite difficult for the European Commission to take a position . . . it is quite convenient for the[m] . . . to have . . . outside bodies as a reference, so as to be able to say, 'The Venice Commission has said so and so', and then they can simply refer to it . . . Countries are aware, that *if they ever want to join the EU*, they have to be in line of our [Venice Commission] standards because EU attaches a lot of importance to what the Venice Commission says . . . The Venice Commission has been playing a role in defining the EU Copenhagen Criteria . . . *though certainly not a formal one.*
>
> (Venice Commission official: Interviewee 8; emphasis added)

Alternatives to this discretionary mode of governance do exist. The European Commission could make better use of the expert-pool databases such as TAIEX, upon which some supranational organs already rely (European Commission 2015). Open to whoever can document contributable training or experience, experts could be selected at random from it. Or the Commission could set up its own advisory bodies, staffed by member states seconding their civil servants or MPs, and rely on them. It would not be prohibitively costly as member states will surely believe they benefit from uploading influence supranationally. But instead, everything comes from the top down, as the Commission would be constrained in the agenda it could pursue if member-state preferences, and their potential divergence, were given priority, particularly on issues as critical as Judiciary-elected branch power relations. The exclusion of alternatives is itself some evidence that the supranational organs default only to those who set agendas they prefer anyway. As the European Commission has vetted candidate countries' fitness to accede to the EU in terms of their alignment with the common (Network) agenda, candidate governments have taken note, aware of where the agenda is actually being set. According to a Venice Commission official:

> At the present moment . . . there's the Serbian application [for EU membership], and there we have several issues on Serbia . . . which is on our

> agenda now, because the Serb government . . . wants . . . to have our [Venice Commission] opinion before the [European] Commission issues its . . . Report on their application, to be able to refer to it [on] any concerns with the Judiciary . . . With Montenegro the European Commission has been discussing the Judiciary . . . it doesn't like what it sees, but it doesn't quite know what to propose.
>
> (Venice Commission official: Interviewee 8)

Such an inference to the Venice Commission's agenda-setting power is not misplaced: business as usual is harmony with the European Commission; conflict is the exception, given that the two Commissions need each other to consolidate a shared authority over countries that aspire to EU membership, but might resist Network influence: 'Why do Moldovan politicians consult the CoE and the Venice Commission so often? Because the authorities . . . think it will help them integrate into the EU and get the financial support that comes with it' (EC career civil servant: Interviewee 37). The European Commission will sometimes even 'sell' the Venice Commission to prospective accession candidates:

> Turkey is a main area of cooperation between the EU and the Venice Commission . . . the EU convinced Turkey to work with the Venice Commission . . . the [Turkish] Prime Minister . . . was not very interested in this, so it was thanks to the contact established by the European Commission with the Ministry of Justice that we have now been quite involved in judicial reforms in Turkey.
>
> (Venice Commission official: Interviewee 8)

The CoE, though it has clearly assumed the role of driver of European integration through law, is still dependent on the EU for 'muscle' and for funds. This is critical (see also Dallara and Piana 2016). Network entrepreneurs are well aware of this dependency:

> There is a sort of joke . . . we complain about the CoE . . . we have to go to CEE with very little money . . . each time I go on a mission, I lose money . . . The EU pays better . . . we are the heart of Europe, and EU is the wallet.
>
> (EJA officer and CoE adviser: Interviewee 11)

The CoE itself depends on the EU even in its own bailiwick: 'In Strasbourg there is no money at all . . . if you spend your time there trying to find money, is a waste of time. The money is in Brussels' (MEDEL high official: Interviewee 2). Interdependency and a need for mutual collaboration is implied by a CoE senior official:

> What is new – and we are very, very happy – is that after a very, very long process, finally the EU has opened a delegation in Strasbourg, a

> fully-fledged delegation . . . Why is this desirable? Because the EU is an important partner . . . [who] fund[s] many, many of our cooperation joint programmes . . . the EU is a strategic partner of the CoE.
>
> (CoE official: Interviewee 13)

CoE officials do not deny that Europe is governed in most domains more by the EU than by the CoE, but insist that the EU depends heavily on the CoE in all juridical matters, and would find it much more difficult to pursue integration without the CoE. As a senior civil servant with years of experience in the policy-making process inside the CoE put it:

> The European Commission make use a lot of the CoE. They copy all they want. They are thieves . . . The CoE is a much older structure . . . The European Commission are standing on their own, they are very proud and don't look to their poor brother in Strasbourg, their poor relatives.
>
> (CoE Steering Committee member: Interviewee 1)

CoE career civil servants were likewise found to 'look down' on the EU – witness the implication that the European Commission prevaricates if it denies how clueless it is about the Judiciary and human rights (cf. MacMullen 1997). The contempt is heartily reciprocated. In the words of a high official in the Commission:

> I used to work for the CoE, and I see the difference between the two organisations . . . We [the European Commission] do not follow the CoE very much. The strength of the Commission, the amount of information it could have, the amount of advice, the amount of technical assistance that it could get through consultants, it is much more than what the CoE could deliver, so we do not listen very much to the CoE.
>
> (EC official: Interviewee 16)

Undoubtedly, the Commission could engage the best legal experts in the world without reference to the CoE. Its dependence is thus as striking as it is undeniable. Lower-ranking officials in the Commission have admitted as much to the author:

> The question of whether we openly cite the basis of our recommendations as being CoE Recommendations . . . here the field becomes a bit more grey, and I think there is resistance to go that way because there is institutional pride. I don't think this is something we publicize [out of] pride, but . . . we are working . . . closely with the CoE.
>
> (EC official: Interviewee 14)

This touchiness about its dependence is itself evidence of it. The simplest explanation is that the Network Community, reaching into both organizations, maintains their interdependence as the institutional basis of its consensus and common agenda; this implies that the European Commission and the CoE are both informally subordinate to the Network Community as a whole (and as an overarching global project) in all that concerns the latter. This knowledge is not esoteric to Network insiders. According to MEDEL:

> They [European Commission officials] sometimes seem to have forgotten the origin of their [own] EU activities. These originate in the CoE, in the Protocols . . . major civil law and criminal law provisions have their source in the CoE. The CoE . . . paves the way, it tests the views . . . it asks member states, and the representatives of national parliaments, who make up the Parliamentary Assembly of the CoE . . . there are some governments who really want to go for something [policy-wise], and then they formally leave it to the CoE's General Secretariat.
>
> (MEDEL high official: Interviewee 2)

The EU's subordination to the CoE in the project of European integration *through law* is further illustrated by the latest developments. The EU already requires accession to the ECHR as a precondition of accession to the EU. Now the Lisbon Treaty provides for the EU itself to accede to the ECHR:

> the entry into force of Protocol No. 14 represents a crucial step in improving the effectiveness of the Court and the protection of human rights in Europe . . . Protocol No. 14 provides the legal basis for the possibility of EU accession to the Convention, to which the EU is committed under the Lisbon Treaty. EU accession will further strengthen the protection of human rights in Europe by submitting the EU's legal system to independent external control with regard to the rights protected by the Convention, as interpreted by the Court in its case law.
>
> (Council of Europe 2010c)[5]

The EU has in effect accepted a default 'submissive' role which would hardly be forthcoming but for a pre-existing policy consensus uniting both sides of the relation. Brussels has not conceded to Strasbourg *faut de mieux* as some interviewees seem to imply; it must expect the CoE to set the agenda that the Commission prefers. Whatever rivalry persists is less over what should be done than over who should do it (and garner the *kudos*).

[5] As of the date of going to press, the ECJ had ruled against the scheduled accession to the ECHR.

This is mirrored in their respective charters of rights: 'the EU Charter on Fundamental Rights basically repeats, [and] to a large extent overlaps with the European Convention on Human Rights' (EC official: Interviewee 39). Put even more poignantly by another Commission official:

> In the past, there have been institutional jealousies between the European Commission and the CoE concerning judicial reform, but a bigger power struggle was going on between the two. Enlargement was just one of the most visible and high-profile fields where the two institutions were active . . . the Commission . . . and also the CoE w[ere] very active, but this is part of a bigger picture . . . when they were drafting the Constitutional Treaty . . . a lot of the discussion was over whether the EU should join the CoE or whether the CoE should perhaps [thought left unfinished] . . . I think at a certain point in the discussion there were powers in the EU who wanted to replace the CoE altogether and the EU to have the power, and also the power struggle between the Luxembourg Court, our Court of Justice, and the ECtHR in Strasbourg and whether the ECJ should enhance its competence to start dealing with these issues and whether then there will be a clash of jurisdictions and so on, so there is a whole, bigger struggle that we [DG Enlargement] in a way have nothing to do with, but are . . . almost on the cutting edge of it because we are one of the chess pieces.
>
> (EC official: Interviewee 14)

Jockeying for ownership of the 'action plan' is evidence rather of motives like professional jealousy than a contest over substance. It may fairly be said that the EU and CoE pursue through and with each other a common agenda transcendent to European integration both politically and geographically, if one considers the nature of the 'ever closer' policy coordination between them:

> We [the CoE] have had a liaison office in Brussels since the late 1960s . . . finally the EU has opened up a delegation in Strasbourg . . . institutionally [it] is very good that both institutions have their representations at their headquarters. Why is this desirable? Because the EU is an important partner . . . the majority of our member states are EU member states . . . we have interaction with the EU in many, many sectors . . . and very extensive cooperation . . . and consultation with the European Commission in particular in its Enlargement policy *and its neighbourhood policy* [both of which implicate the Judiciary], and of course, [the] *constant coordination and exchange of notes*.
>
> (CoE official: Interviewee 13; emphasis added)

For its part, the European Commission is ever more mutually accommodating: 'it is my policy, and this is filtering upwards in the hierarchy, to always have an understanding of the need to have desk-to-desk contacts with the Council of Europe' (EC official: Interviewee 14).[6] 'Desk-to-desk contact' means direct lateral communication and networking, instead of the 'diplomatic' protocol of addressing one's hierarchical superiors who address the other organization's superiors who address their subordinates, and back again. This implies the administrative 'fusion' that Wolfgang Wessels had noted was happening by the mid-1990s between the national administrations of EU member states (Wessels 1997, 1998). Thus it is that the integration of the elites themselves has since before the European Coal and Steel Community and all along, preceded and undergirded the integration of 'Europe' – and may in reality constitute the lion's share of it (over and above the Single Market).

The CoE's interdependence on the Network Community

Sometimes the supranational organs depend almost entirely on outside expertise, especially on industrial regulatory questions that call for knowledge that does not exist outside the industry itself. Whenever this is the case, whether in a classic branch of industry such as telecommunications or in judicial affairs, the industry ends up shaping the regulatory regime to govern itself (Reinke 2010, 2012). In the last twenty-five years, a supranational Judiciary design regime has likewise come from the same legal professional 'industry' on which the CoE has come to rely for so much else. In fact, the very idea of pan-European Judiciary institutional norms has been put on the agenda of the CoE and the EU by this industry.

And this is not the half of it. The Committee of Ministers, the CoE analogue of the European Council, has delegated considerable policy-making power to a series of Steering Committees that are nominally intergovernmental in that they are formally composed of senior civil servants appointed by the member states' Ministries of Justice. But they meet infrequently and in practice do little. Most of the time, policy development (certainly the agenda setting, at a minimum) is not carried out by the 48 member states in

[6] An informal interdependency and coordination between the EU and other intergovernmental organizations has also been advancing. According to a European Commission official: 'We have some contacts with the World Bank . . . because they also have assistance projects. They have their indicators; they do rule of law; so we have a dialogue . . . it's mostly exchange of information . . . we listen to their findings and they listen to ours, so we can use [each other's] things . . . but there is no formal mechanism' (EC official: Interviewee 39). See also Coman (2016).

intergovernmental sessions, but re-delegated to the Bureaux of the Steering Committees, sub-units or 'secretariats' consisting of a select few civil servants from the Steering Committees, who steer policy de facto.

In the domain of human rights and Judiciary institutions, the Steering Committee that matters is the European Committee on Legal Co-operation (CDCJ). The CDCJ meets too infrequently, as usual, to get anything done. According to one of its most experienced members:

> As the Steering Committee now meets only once a year . . . [it] would [n]ever be in position to do any kind of steering . . . meeting only once a year [means that] . . . by then everybody has forgotten what happened last time and you, as a Steering Committee, have no chance in taking the initiative and following it in an efficient manner. Compared to thirty or forty years ago, over the last ten years there has been considerably less scope for the Steering Committee itself to decide on its future working items [agenda].
>
> (CoE Steering Committee member: Interviewee 43)

The CDCJ Bureau comprises just six member-state representatives elected by secret ballot from amongst the CDCJ committee members. They are the ones who do the actual steering:

> The Bureau does the groundwork, including preparing the plenary meetings of the CDCJ . . . It adopts Opinions to be suggested to the [CoE] Parliamentary Assembly . . . examines texts adopted by the expert subcommittees or specialist groups. Suppose you have a draft text of a CoE recommendation. First, CDCJ adopts it, then it sends it to the Bureau who discuss and critique it, pointing out areas of concern that need to be reworked . . . The Bureau makes the policy decisions . . . they give a political flavour to the expert work, e.g. that certain provisions can be adopted . . . or that such things cannot be adopted . . . The most important task of the Bureau is to prepare the next meeting of the CDCJ.
>
> (CoE Steering Committee member: Interviewee 1)

However, the Bureau itself only meets two or three times a year, which is still not all that frequently (CoE Steering Committee member: Interviewee 1). Its protocols are generally insufficient for transacting the business in hand. Only a fraction of its members take the important decisions. If the Bureau would make policy, then it, too, must rely on 'outsiders' to the member states' Ministries of Justice. Business is actually effected in collaboration with (i.e., in heavy reliance on) the legal professional networks, either independent individuals or representatives of interest groups, who are inside the Network Community.

When a Steering Committee calls upon a group of outside experts, its personnel is selected by just a few in the Bureau, sometimes only the Chair, who has discretion about whom to rely on; that is, the Chair's entrepreneurialism will determine whether the choice will rest entirely within their discretion. The Chair may or may not enlist the counsel of the Human Rights and Legal Affairs Directorate of the General Secretariat (itself networked-in):

> How much the Chair of a Steering Committee decides to rely on the Secretariat? This certainly comes into play. Some Chairs will be more active than others, some would be really pushing the Secretariat. It can really vary from one Chair to another.
>
> (CoE civil servant: Interviewee 12)

A Chair who is not a Network entrepreneur might seek to balance out the composition of the group somewhat to better represent the full spectrum of opinion amongst legal professionals. Otherwise, he or she will be prone to rely on the legal professionals most active in pursuing the common agenda. This may lead to an expert group that is 'packed' with other Network entrepreneurs. Table 3.1. illustrates this point clearly: all of the experts who were selected to revise the 1994 CoE Recommendations on Judicial Independence were transnationally networked judges engaged in policy making in the most active circles of the Network Community – CCEJ, IAJ, EJA , experts to the CoE – and known within it to have promoted the idea of judicial self-governance at least since 1994 (CoE Steering Committee member: Interviewee 1).

The net result in either case is more or less reliance on the Network Community, not the member-state governments. Inevitably, the more active elements of the legal professional networks are the transnational jurists staffing interest groups in Strasbourg, for example, or the networks that originated as 'advisory bodies' to the CoE, including but not limited to the Venice Commission and the Consultative Council of European Judges (see Table 3.2).

Come what may, the legal professional networks constitutive of the Network Community play a crucial role in CoE agenda setting and policy development, not least by deciding who amongst them will take part in the process that formulates the Judiciary's power relations to the elected branches. There is much confusion on this point, as the formal expert-recruiting process gives the appearance of engaging the member states: 'when setting up a group . . . the member state delegations are asked to nominate candidates and submit their CVs to the Secretariat. The Secretariat together with the Bureau then tries to find some kind of balanced composition' (CoE Steering Committee member: Interviewee 43). What the CoE means by balance was clearly articulated to the author by a career functionary in the CoE Secretariat, who was charged by a CDCJ Chair to put

Table 3.1 Profiles of the 2007 Group of Specialists on the Independence, Efficiency and Role of Judges (CJ-S-JUST), who drafted the first revision of the 1994 CoE Recommendations on Judicial Independence

Name	*Evidence of Network identity*
Edwin Kilby (UK), Chair	Barrister Head of European Strategy and Institutions, Law, Rights and International Directorate, Justice Policy Group, Ministry of Justice Involved in international affairs as a lawyer since 1994
Giacomo Oberto (Italy)	Judge, Court of Appeal, Turin Deputy Secretary General, International Association of Judges (2012–) Expert adviser to the CoE since 1995 Expert adviser to the CCEJ European Judges Association Member of CEPEJ
Maja Tratnik (Slovenia)	Judge, Supreme Court (2004–) President and member of the JC (1999–2004) Member, Board of the Slovene Judicial Training Centre (1999–2004) President, European Judges Association (2002–06) President, International Association of Judges (2006–08) Member, Advisory Board of the International Association for Court Administration (2012–) Member, Board of Trustees, the Academy of European Law, Trier (2003–06) Expert for the CoE, EC, and OECD on judicial independence
Alain Lacabarats (France)	Deputy public prosecutor (1975–84) Vice President, *Tribunal de grande instance*, Paris (1988–99) Judge, Court of Cassation, Paris (2004–) President, CCEJ (2004–05) Member, CCEJ Bureau (2007–)
Gerhard Reissner (Austria)	Judge, District Court, Hainburg (1982) Vice President, Association of Austrian Judges (1994–) Member, CCEJ and its working party (2000–) Vice President, International Association of Judges (2003–07) President, International Association of Judges (2007–09) Vice President, International Association of Judges (2008) President, European Association of Judges (2009–12) Vice President, CCEJ (2009–12) President, International Association of Judges (2012–) President, CCEJ (2012–14) Expert on projects of international cooperation in the framework of International Association of Judges, of the CoE, of the European Commission (e.g. Albania, Egypt, Brazil, Bulgaria, Hungary, Moldova, Serbia, Slovakia, Slovenia, and Turkey)

Sources: Compiled by the author from the following: European Commission for the Efficiency of Justice 2013; Consultative Council of European Judges 2014a, 2014b; International Association for Court Administration 2014; International Association of Judges 2014; CoE Steering Committee member: Interviewee 3; EJA officer and CoE adviser: Interviewee 11.

Table 3.2 Profiles of the 2009 Group of Specialists on the Judiciary (CJ-S-JUD)

Name	*Position and transnational involvement*
Eberhard Desch (Germany)	Head of Division of International Law, Ministry of Justice President CDCJ, CoE: 'one of the most experienced civil servants in Europe within a serving member state, one with the greatest experience [of the CoE policy process] at the time' (CoE Steering Committee member: Interviewee 43)
Gabriele Bajons (Austria)	Head of Department, Ministry of Justice Participant in Annual Meetings of the Ministers of Justice of the CoE member states GRECO member, CoE
Diana Kovačević-Remenarić (Croatia)	Head, Department of Human and Organization Resources, Ministry of Justice
Maris Järv (Estonia)	Head of Legislative Drafting and Development Division, Department of Justice Administration Policy, Ministry of Justice
Philip James Fitzpatrick (Ireland)	Former Chief Executive Officer of the Irish Courts Services
Inge Lorange Backer (Norway)	Director of International Affairs, Ministry of Justice Long-standing participant in the Steering Committee on Legal Co-operation (CDCJ), an intergovernmental committee of the Committee of Ministers, CoE
Tatu Leppänen (Finland)	Counsellor of Legislation, Ministry of Justice
Włodzimierz Wróbel (Poland)	Professor of Law
Bogdan Zimnenko (Russian Federation)	Chair of the international private law department, Foreign Affairs Ministry
Kay Birch (Britain)	Senior civil servant (non-lawyer) Head of Constitution and Judiciary Division, Ministry of Justice
Andrei Chiriac (Moldova)	Lawyer
Maja Tratnik (Slovenia)	Judge, Supreme Court
Giacomo Oberto (Italy)	Judge, Court of Appeal, Turin Deputy Secretary General of the International Association of Judges
Daniel Ludet (France)	Conseiller, Court of Cassation, Paris
Egidijus Bieliūnas (Lithuania)	Judge, Supreme Court, Vilnius
René Verschuur (The Netherlands)	Vice President, Court of Appeal, Leeuwarden
Carlos Gómez Martinez (Spain)	President, Court of Appeal, Palma de Mallorca

Table 3.2 continued

Name	*Position and transnational involvement*
Sophie Kwasny (CJ-S-JUD Secretary)	Civil servant, CoE General Secretariat, non-jurist
Orlando Afonso (Consultative Council of European Judges)	Judge, Court of Appeal, d'Evora, Almada, Portugal Vice President, Consultative Council of European Judges
Jean-Paul Sudre (CEPEJ)	Avocat Général, Court of Appeal, Paris CEPEJ
Thomas Markert (Venice Commission)	German Ministry of the Economy Secretary General, Venice Commission
M. Drzemczewski (Parliamentary Assembly)	Parliamentary Assembly, CoE
Gerhard Reissner (European Judges Association – NGO)	Vice President, Austrian Judges Association, and President, District Court of Floridsdorf, Vienna, Austria European Judges Association International Association of Judges
Pierre Vincent (European Federation of Administrative Judges – NGO)	Chamber President, Administrative Court of Appeal, Nancy, France European Federation of Administrative Judges – NGO

Sources: Directorate General of Human Rights and Legal Affairs 2009; Group of Specialists on the Judiciary (CJ-S-JUD) 2009.

together an expert group to help draft one of the CoE Recommendations. No hint of sensitivity to or awareness of judicialization as the issue standing in need of balance was observable:

> My first role as a Secretariat civil servant was to try to achieve balance and a high-quality participation of experts . . . *by balance I mean gender and geographical* balance . . . That was my first task: to come up with a good group of people. We could not include every member state . . . I knew nothing about the topic . . . My knowledge was really minimal . . . I contacted colleagues . . . particularly my colleagues in the European Commission for the Efficiency of Justice [CEPEJ] . . . Because they knew most of the persons that were recommended by the member states, I checked with them if the persons had the right level of the language we needed, *if they had a good record of cooperation with them.*
>
> (CoE civil servant: Interviewee 12; emphasis added)

However sincere in seeking balance of one kind or another, the Bureau and General Secretariat have no real choice but to rely on the Network Community's constituents to vet an expert.

Every supranational organ, even the ECtHR, has been enmeshed in a similar web of interdependency. The ECtHR has no enforcement power over the CoE member states. It depends on the CoE as a regime and on other supranational organs to arrange compliance. The European Commission, usually in concert with the General Secretariat, comes to its aid often: 'Any[thing] . . . that raises issues which the Venice Commission does not like will not be perceived favourably by the EU. An indication is that we [Moldova] always execute the decisions of the ECtHR' (EC career civil servant: Interviewee 37). The Romanian Government disobeyed ECtHR rulings against itself over *recurs in anulare* for a decade from 1993 to 2003 (Minister of Justice: Interviewee 44). It would surely have continued to do so had the European Commission not muscled in, exploiting EU accession conditionality to coerce the Romanians to abolish it (Parau 2012).

The ECtHR's reliance base is remarkably broad; it even includes the IMF and quite likely other international bodies. According to one judge on that Court:

> Some international treaties are declaratory. Others are obligatory. The ECHR is an obligatory treaty, the enforcement of which is ensured by the ECtHR decisions and by the compulsory power of these decisions. A member state cannot refuse to enforce the decisions of the ECtHR . . . If a country does not respect the status of the CoE and its obligations towards the CoE, there will be a vote in the Parliamentary Assembly, and sanctions will follow, such as the suspension of the vote, damage to the image of the country, problems with grants and financial allocations by the CoE, the IMF and the EU and the European Commission, because they are all connected with each other.
> (ECtHR judge: Interviewee 23)

The Network Community, in turn, can rely on the ECtHR to help consolidate their Judiciary design norms at the domestic level as concrete issues arise. For example, transnational entrepreneurs told the author, 'The ECtHR occasionally makes references to these Recommendations [on Judiciary Independence]. Its judgments cannot use them as the law, but it can refer to them to resolve ambiguities' (CoE Steering Committee member: Interviewee 3). Recommendations, after being cited as authority in the case law of a supranational court with jurisdiction over the CoE's members – essentially all the nations of Europe – do not remain mere recommendations. What is more, citation of the Network's norms feeds back into the discourses of the transnational entrepreneurs who created them, a ubiquity and self-referentiality that is apt to make them hegemonic (see Part II below). According to one Network entrepreneur: 'You have to consider that the principle of judicial independence of judges [as the Network defines it] has been asserted many times by the ECtHR . . . [whose] case law . . . is a source of law which has to be respected' (Judge and EC adviser: Interviewee 40; see also Dallara and Piana 2016).

A similar pattern is in evidence respecting other international legal forums such as the ICC (see also Dallara and Piana 2016). According to an elite Croatian jurist, 'The Organisation for Security and Cooperation in Europe and others were complaining about the war trials and how the domestic government handled the demands of the International Criminal Court' (MTA official: Interviewee 45). The Network Community rode to the rescue of this Court too, having already drawn together national and supranational legal professionals who collaboratively pressurized reluctant national governments to submit to the ICC jurisdiction. This is corroborated, for example, by an EC official:

> Croatia must deliver results on the ground, which is not always the case and which evidences a lack of political will in some areas, like prosecution of war crimes; a patriotic government does not want to be seen to pick on its heroes in the homeland war.
>
> (EC official: Interviewee 39)

Elite self-empowerment by transnational networking and network consensus, plus a critical opportunity (EU accession), is again the key unlocking the mystery – in this case, how a few remote bureaucrats should be capable of overriding even so passionate and unifying a current as patriotism in war.

Synergy: the invisible ascendancy of the Network Community

The political branches in any State would naturally be reluctant to give away their own power to other political actors. The Network Community, for its part, is well aware that its agenda depends in the end on coercion in some form, even if it is only to suppress veto players. It needs them to give their power away to, or least permanently lease it back from the Judiciary. Nowhere is this more evident than in post-Communist CEE, where steep socio-political hierarchies almost guarantee the legal professional networks are easily ignored. In the words of an ECtHR judge and the former president of a national judges' association:

> We express our opinions, send letters . . . [and] make proposals to the government, the Parliament, and President but we have no decisional power . . . *as*

> *a rule [we] are opposed to the government and the legislature in the State* . . . and try to influence . . . them. To what extent we reach our scope depends on the State.
>
> (ECtHR judge: Interviewee 23; emphasis added)

Networks lack hierarchical command and control within themselves, and rely on those who do have it; whence the Network turn to the *supranational* organs, as they are intergovernmental first, supranational only after. They whisper into sympathetic ears on the inside who will insert the common agenda into member state governmental proceedings, advancing it farther and faster than the Network could ever have done by themselves. And the European Commission has not hesitated to open up windows of opportunity for the Network Community to be involved in domestic public policy making if it affects judicial institutions, including removing resistance to the Template. Moving the common agenda can entail using all the coercive leverage of EU accession conditionality if prospective candidates prove reluctant to cede to unelected courts the competences of elected bodies. In this, the Commission has facilitated consolidation of the proto-Template entrenched in the first post-Communist constitutions, but had not translated into as much judicial activism as hoped for (Parau 2012, 2015b).

Romania, once again, is a case in point. For years during accession negotiations, the Romanian Government neglected or refused to comply with the Network Community standards on judicial power, such as elected politicians' exclusion from involvement in Judiciary governance. Finally, in 2004, the Network Community via the European Commission threatened Romania with delayed accession to the EU. As this happened in a year with multiple elections to be fought, the governing party had no choice but to yield (Parau 2015a). Croatia too resisted until very close to the end of negotiations with the EU. According to one Italian judge active as a CoE and European Commission expert on Judiciary institutions in the Balkans:

> [I]n Croatia the government decided . . . to keep members of Parliament in the Judicial Council, which means that they ignored the standards . . . it is very clearly stated in the opinion I wrote [for the Commission] that members cannot be active politicians, they cannot be members of Parliament . . . these recommendations have been ignored even though I have written [about them] in the reports.
>
> (Judge and EC adviser: Interviewee 40)

This triggered EU intervention to nudge the government toward the Network Community norm:

> The most difficult Chapter has been Judiciary and Fundamental Rights . . . the Croatians would have liked to close that Chapter, but there were about 23 benchmarks in [it] . . . there were frequent high-level contacts between the [Croatian] President and the Prime Minister, and our [European Commission] Vice-President [Viviane] Reading and our [DG Justice] Commissioner on those benchmarks . . . the Commission has high leverage . . . [consequently] members of the [Croatian] Judiciary Council have been elected from among their peers for the first time, just as the [CoE's] recommendations say. But that was very late in the process . . . we made references to the Opinion of the Consultative Council of European Judges, saying that there should be a substantial majority of judges in the Judiciary Council.
>
> (EC official: Interviewee 39)

The European Commission involves itself in national Judiciary affairs in any way the Network Community 'programmes' it to do. On the basis, partly, of her own observation, the author has concluded that the EU will follow the Network paradigm blindly, but will depend on the CoE only insofar as the CoE proves itself 'reliable' respecting the paradigm. For example, the Hungarian Fidesz Party in 2011 undertook constitutional revisions consisting of an ethical alloy of robustly justifiable reforms curbing the heedless, over-empowered Hungarian Constitutional Court and Judiciary Council, immixed with the usual notorious court-packing: lowering the retirement age for judges and other magistrates from 70 to 62 years of age. The Commission's extraordinarily violent reaction to this event corroborates the inference of an overriding Network influence over the EU. The Venice Commission, on the other hand, was milder in its criticism of the revisions (which were minor adjustments to the powers of the CC compared to other member states) until the European Commission took the unprecedented step of threatening to withhold the Venice Commission's funding unless it publicly condemned the Fidesz reforms in the strongest terms. The sin of defying the Network may not go unpunished. In the words of József Szájer, Vice Chair of the European People's Party in the European Parliament and chief architect of the Fundamental Law of Hungary:

> Sure, they [the international bodies] are networked with each other. The same people are moving from one place [office] to another. The financing comes all from the European Commission. I argued before the Venice Commission when I represented the Hungarian government and defended the Hungarian constitution. I said, 'I am not disputing the points of opinion. There is a dispute between ours and your opinion. You can have your opinion. But I am disputing factual mistakes', and I had a long list of things on

> certain laws . . . I don't think the Venice Commission authority is good if they are putting in false things . . . I asked them to change them. That would have taken one week. They said, 'No we cannot do that, because the European Commission demanded us to do it for the debate already which is going to be in the European Parliament in July. So, we have to do it now. We cannot delay, wait for the next meeting.' And then over the dinner they added, 'We do not want to lose our financing because they blackmailed us.' And this is not a made-up story. It wasn't a lie because I [also] spoke with Viviene Reading and she confirmed, 'Yes, yes, we [the European Commission] we didn't find anything against you [Hungary], but we are using the Council of Europe and the Venice Commission against you.' She explicitly said, 'We are doing that.' They were really blackmailing them: 'You [representatives of the poorer member states of the Venice Commission] are getting all your money from us. How will you travel to Venice next time if we are not giving you the money?' It is as base as that.

The 'extraordinary rendition' measures on behalf of the Network did not stop there. The Hungarian Constitutional Court teamed up with opposition parties to prevail on the European Commission to exploit its powers to issue so-called 'Country Specific Recommendations' under the European Semester – a supranational mechanism intended to coordinate *economic* governance across member states – in order to 'flag up' that Hungary had supposedly undercut the independence of its Judiciary (whence the latter's contestation of the Recommendations all the way to the Council of Ministers), and thereby to discursively sanction and humiliate the Hungarian Government before other member states for its Judiciary reforms, notwithstanding that (as the Hungarian Government argued) internal Judiciary change of the kind pursued had little nexus with the economic surveillance and coordination of the European Semester (European Commission 2013; Mahieux 2014).

None of the supranational organs have any legitimate jurisdiction to set and then enforce pan-European norms of Judiciary institutional design for their respective member states. They were not even designed for it: the EU is oriented toward governing the Single Market, having begun life as a coal and steel community. Its member states have never delegated to it any competence to regulate national judicial institutions:

> ['Judiciary and Fundamental Rights'] is the only Chapter where we don't have a predetermined *acquis* and say, 'adopt all of this please, and make sure you have the administrative capacity to implement it.' It's just the opposite . . . *We don't have any powers within the Treaties to do that.*
>
> (EC official: Interviewee 14; emphasis added)

Those who are outside the European Commission agree. A legal professional involved with both the CoE and the EU over the last two decades as an outside expert in judiciary design had this to say:

> On one side you have the CoE, which has very refined, good, technically reliable documents, but which are not binding, not enforceable, but which could be taken as a sort of framework, legally binding, for all the European countries as minimum standards . . . but the CoE does not have the strength to say about these technical tools 'these are binding'. On the other side you have the EU, which theoretically speaking does have the power, the tools . . . Directives, Regulations . . . but, of course, according to the general principles of the Treaties, this [the Judiciary] is a question that cannot be addressed . . . because you cannot have a[n] EU Regulation . . . concerning Judiciary institutions.
>
> (EJA officer and CoE adviser: Interviewee 11)

As if in compensation, there emerged from the European Commission an extraordinary feat of coordinative improvisation: in tandem with the CoE, the Commission created its own informal leverage over domestic Judiciary institutions, a unilateral assumption of competence which was facilitated by the EU's Eastern Enlargement. The sad state of the Judiciary in CEE – especially from the standpoint of the EU's dependency on national Judiciaries to effectively implement the *acquis* – is what prompted the European Commission, in the first instance, to intervene in the Judiciary affairs of accession candidates. Up through 2004 with Romania's and Bulgaria's accession, the Commission circumvented its lack of proper, delegated competence by constructing extra conditions of accession (and new competences for itself) out of the indeterminate Copenhagen and Madrid Criteria, which merely obligated candidates to commit to 'the rule of law' and have administrative capacity sufficient to implement the *acquis*. Out of such an aspirational mandate the Commission crafted and imposed detailed, punctiliously enforced conditions for Judiciary revision and redesign which the EU member states themselves never legislated nor even debated (Parau 2010, 2015b). Here is a senior official in DG Enlargement coming close to admitting the European Commission has made a practice of assuming a limitless, and contestable, authority to impose whatever conditions it sees fit, if it calculates it can get away with it. It often does get away with it, with all except the well-established member states:

> All of the member states and all of the candidates are members of the CoE, so we are not doing anything that is outside the . . . competence . . . We do not strain away from the EU ideal to force a candidate country as one of the preconditions . . . We can set whatever preconditions we want for joining

> this club . . . so it's not out of this world to say, according to the Treaty you have to be a country which respects fundamental rights and has a functioning Judiciary.
>
> (EC official: Interviewee 14)

As Part II shows, in practical institutional design terms, a 'functioning Judiciary' has come to mean one empowered to the point of potential autocracy. This means the Template, which was presumed coterminous with CoE standards, even though the latter were bespoke to accommodate member states whose Judiciaries diverge from the Template significantly. By the time the Balkan accession processes began in 2005, the Commission had formalized its punctilios by non-majoritarian fiat, decreeing the Judiciary to be a component of its accession negotiation protocol.

The European Commission depended almost entirely on the Network Community to formalize its specification of national Judiciary institutions. It is probably no exaggeration to say that, under the impetus of Eastern Enlargement, the Network Community is the one that has been in power *de facto*, not the European Commission or the CoE (let alone their respective member states), on matters of Judiciary-elected branch power relations. In the words of a senior civil servant in DG Enlargement:

> A new Chapter was created that the Commission negotiates [Chapter 23 'Judiciary and Fundamental Rights'], and it was empty . . . How important has the Venice Commission been? . . . The CoE, the ECtHR and its case law, the various recommendations of the CoE including, but not only, the Venice Commission . . . *that's it*, that's our *acquis* replacement! That's everything! . . . I spent six months on the website of the CoE, and reading the case law of the ECtHR . . . I had meetings with the CoE to try and improve institutional cooperation between us . . . and we invited them from Strasbourg, from the ECtHR for a seminar for all of the people [in the European Commission] working in this field, because many people [in DG Enlargement] . . . and in the new units created under DG Justice were facing this . . . to learn about what to demand, and what to advise, and what to recommend, and what benchmarks to set in this field where we don't have any *acquis*, and we didn't really have a DG to rely on . . . The work of the CoE is so hugely important . . . and we encourage you [the accession candidate] to follow the Recommendations that have already been made by the CoE.
>
> (EC official: Interviewee 14; emphasis added)

This is confirmed by a senior civil servant in DG Justice:

> There is a very clear Recommendation of the CoE which comes from the Consultative Council of European Judges . . . we [the Commission] have a negotiation job to do – Judiciary and fundamental rights – based on the *acquis*.

> And this is the *acquis* with which candidate countries have to align. . . . what exactly is the *acquis*? . . . we have to distinguish between hard *acquis* and soft *acquis* . . . in the area of fundamental rights we have the European Convention [on Human Rights] . . . and now we have the Charter [of Fundamental Rights of the European Union], which is its hard *acquis* and its EU *acquis* in the sense that it's not CoE any more. But for the candidate countries we also have the European Convention on Human Rights. We consider that hard *acquis*, which means they have to implement it properly in all areas . . . then we have the case law from Strasbourg, which is also hard *acquis*, you could argue. And then you have all the other instruments, the Recommendations . . . that is where the Consultative Council of European Judges comes in, and the Venice Commission *et cetera*. So we rely on them . . . [Otherwise,] there is not a lot going on here in the Commission . . . we are not a fundamental rights agency . . . The CoE has the expertise on Judiciaries, they developed it . . . we are just tagging along with them . . . our basis is what the CoE has, simply because they developed the basis and we don't have one.
>
> (EC official: Interviewee 39)

Neither the ECHR nor the case law of the ECtHR actually make any part of the EU *acquis*; nor did the Copenhagen European Council, when enacting its Criteria, even so much as reference the ECHR or the ECtHR, nor would it have had any jurisdiction to do so, absent its ratification as EU law by the European Council and Parliament. Thus, styling them hard *acquis* or soft is breathtaking once the full implications are understood: 'the rule of law for thee but not for me'. The Commission is treating as an integral part of the *acquis* that which has not even the colour of democratic consent. To top it off, the ECHR vests neither in the ECtHR nor in the Committee of Ministers nor in the Parliamentary Assembly any jurisdiction to impose terms and conditions on the Judiciary institutions of CoE member states. What the Commission has done, therefore, is to shrewdly sidestep their plenary lack of jurisdiction in this sovereign matter by joining arms with all who likewise lack jurisdiction. This confronts accession candidates with a united front, whilst at the same time diffusing blame in case of backlash. This bold manner of proceeding also informally empowers non-state actors as a by-product, and strictly speaking *ultra vires*, with the panoply of the EU's coercive conditioning as leverage. In none of this was any effectual objection heard from the memberships of either the EU or the CoE. The author found that this 'dormancy' and omission to sanction acts that are illegal *sensu stricto* is what has enabled the Commission and its mentors in the Network Community to impose, on the basis of phantom jurisdiction, this 'extra-conditionality' on the accession candidates of the East.

Part II

The judicializing paradigm and its Template

Part I investigated the basis of the Network Community's immense internal potential to cause changes in Judiciary governance in Europe, viz. transnational networking and pooling of power resources, the sharing of collective identity, and a policy consensus which ensures their political solidarity. Having been observed in action pursuing its common agenda through a strategy of 'personnel is policy' and intra-Network interdependence and coordination, Part II shifts the focus to self-empowerment qua networked elite agency and its extra-Network causative potential, especially in its power relations with Europe's democratic governments and their governing structures.

As norms constitute often unrecognized causes, attention is given to the Network Community's construction of universal (hegemonic) norms of Judiciary governance, beginning with paradigmatic assumptions about the role of courts in democracy. The purpose of revealing these assumptions and their political and ethical consequences is, firstly, because they causally explain the Template – without them, some other Template would have been made, or none at all – and secondly, in order to cross-examine them normatively. The underlying assumptions are never mentioned by either the Template's disseminators or its receivers, or by researchers, not even after the *fait accompli* of their realization through their spreading across Europe and now globally. Proximately, they implicate the power relations between non-majoritarian courts and the majoritarian organs of government; ultimately, however, they are about how Europe's democracies shall be governed and by whom. Part II rounds out, if it cannot absolutely complete, the causal nexus explaining why this Template exists and has prevailed in CEE. Its paradigmatic assumptions are causes in themselves not only of its genesis in the Network Community but also of its reception by the larger society.

The Network Community's paradigmatic assumptions are rooted in classic hegemonic norms (Foucault 2000; Hirschl 2008). They are socially constructed, not guided by any single (party of) mastermind(s), or not necessarily, or wholly; though entrepreneurs may well mastermind their dissemination and reception by those farther afield. The society constructing these assumptions includes not only Network insiders but also outside political actors who may not be benefited by them nearly as much but find that it 'costs' less to acquiesce, or be recruited, or lie dormant. That the judicialization paradigm has developed in a linear way over generations of time stretching back to Civil War America, as evidenced in the next chapter, argues a phenomenon larger than a conspiracy, and thus evolutionary. In this, the Network Community and its members are themselves prisoners of their own discourses. Their stratagems are in the service of the normality that they, too, take for granted and do not know how (in a sense) to question. And the unconscious ego-centrism of their faith in self-empowerment to make that normality prevail is likewise a prisoner of it.

This is the key to understanding the paradox of an unconscious or semi-conscious evolution which is yet very much the handiwork of interested parties. As any reasonably disinterested normative critique of the discourses of the Network Community cannot but discover, the Network paradigms are not moral absolutes which are 'just given'. It is not a moral absolute that judicial supremacy and autonomy are prerequisite to (or constitute) judicial independence and the rule of law, and this is exposed by a historical comparison of the Network Community's paradigmatic assumptions concerning the separation of powers and checks and balances (the ground of Judiciary institutional design) with those of the classical models of Whiggish Westminster and Antebellum America.

So likewise are all of its normative assumptions vulnerable to refutation. Both the Network's revision of the classical model and its drive to self-empowerment rest on another normative assumption which may be the unique ground of the whole judicialization phenomenon, if anything is – an observable cause to be constantly at work throughout the history of the Network Community and its forerunners from their nineteenth-century origins to the present. This is that their peers on the bench are morally superior in a political context to other actors, insofar as judges rely on sheer intellect, without resort to material coercion or material incentives in order to prevail in political contests.

The consequence of this is the conviction of the elite corps of legal professionals (qua networked) that they are entitled to superintend democracy, over and above their independence from its political processes. The conviction of superiority is not bound by any higher law (such as Natural Law), but spills over jurisdictional and other political bounds as an assumed moral duty and a corresponding prerogative to reconstruct society out of the norms and values of the Network Community. Reconstruction is a step beyond even superintendence, but both are supposed achievable through the living-constitution interpretative paradigm, a classic hegemonic discourse which the public does not know how to veto or renegotiate. Some further reasons why this rather incredible assertion of judicial power has been accepted by the public are also broached.

Finally, Part II gives evidence of the Template's implementation on the ground at the national level, mostly in CEE, but increasingly in Europe as a whole. It has been far from power-neutral or in a normative sense Pareto-optimal, but is extensively power-redistributive by rendering judges, and by implication the Network Community behind them, autonomous and supreme.

4

Thesis and antithesis: To check or not to check the Judiciary

In our contemporary epoch of judicialization, the separation of powers has become a shibboleth of constitutional design. It was observed that the Network Community has strongly influenced the constitution-designers of CEE to entrench this principle, discursively, and thus programmatically at first, then in those constitutions they were newly drafting. It emerged as an issue in Romania, for instance, only hours after Ceauşescu fled: the revolutionary junta, appearing on the balcony of the Central Committee building where Ceauşescu had just made his final speech, outlined a blueprint for Romania which featured a 'separation of powers' between Legislative, Executive, and Judiciary branches. The principle was put atop the public agenda at a time when Romanians were still being shot at and great uncertainty loomed over the direction in which the Revolution was going (Parau 2013c). The Network Community's conception of the separation of powers has been deployed ever since to urge its Judiciary Template not only upon CEE but all Europe. It has become one of the key principles animating the most recent trend toward pan-European norms on judicial independence.

Even Western nations such as Britain, where the rule of law was born and the Judiciary has indisputably functioned independently for centuries, have been nudged toward that concept of separation of powers which is peculiar to the Network Community. The Westminster model troubles the Network: 'We [the Network Community in Britain] used to have firm issues about the separation of powers because of the Lord Chancellor' (CoE Steering Committee member: Interviewee 3), who straddled the pretended separation between 'branches' (although the British separation differed from the American one essentially). The entrepreneurship of certain elite jurists prevailed on the Labour Government of Tony Blair to sever the British Constitution from its traditional moorings and let it drift with no definite destination (Parau 2015c). The more than millennium-old institution of the Lord Chancellor, and the Appellate Committee of the House of Lords, though neither had ever failed, were jettisoned for elements of the Template – and justified in terms of the Network's monomaniacal separation-of-powers model.[1] In the words of the Government minister who introduced the Constitutional Reform Bill in the House of Commons:

> The ultimate court of appeal is doing something different from the legislature; it should be doing it separately, and should be clearly seen to be doing it separately. Functional separation of the judiciary at all levels from the legislature and the Executive is a cardinal feature of any modern, liberal and democratic state governed by the rule of law . . . They [the Law Lords] are there as judges and it is no longer tenable to see those judges act in the legislative role.
>
> (House of Commons 2005)

Parliamentary sovereignty was conserved for now, but such a separation lays the groundwork for illimitable judicial review and eventual supremacy over Parliament. This revolution excited no controversy and proceeded despite the dearth of evidence of any difficulties with the rule of law or judicial independence in the UK:

> **Q:** Why was separation of powers needed in Britain?
>
> **A:** The arrangement that existed worked very well . . . It was very much a sort of philosophy. The Lord Chancellor at the time . . . was very much looking at constitutional reform. For example . . . the role of the Lord Chancellor . . . which had been both Head of the Judiciary and a member

[1] The relegation of the Lord Chancellorship illustrates the ambivalence of Network influence, which may better or worsen the Judiciary depending on a nation's idiosyncrasies. The Lord Chancellor was simultaneously answerable to three distinct bodies of high political actors: (1) the Government in the House of Commons, (2) the House of Lords, of which he was the Head, and (3) the Bar (that is, the corps of barristers who set the tone and trend of the English Judiciary); whilst also presiding over the Court of Chancery, the ultimate authority of the Equity branch of common law. So many competences combined in one man could have constituted despotic power, but for his clear accountability as an agent of multiple principals, any one of whom, if displeased, might end his tenure. Naturally, the Prime Minister has a 'shorter leash' than the Bar to keep the Lord Chancellor on, but the Bar's disaffection too could be enough at length to defy or oust him. Hemmed in on all sides, he must do a tolerable job of pleasing everybody, whether everybody is 'on the same page' or not. The end-all of the separation of powers is to opportune the erection of checks and balances where none existed before. But if they exist already, what is the use?

> of the legislature and a member of the government, was a very unique UK institution, and he was concerned that effectively you could not wear all three hats. If you remove the role of the Lord Chancellor, who then is the head of the Judiciary? Well, the Lord Chief Justice needs to be head of the Judiciary. . . . it was very much a political will . . . there was no question or issue around the quality of the judgments of the Law Lords. It was the wish to have the separation more firmly established.
>
> (MoJ official: Interviewee 28)

It will be made clear how the paradigm of the Network Community (including its British chapter) has diverged from the classical conception of the separation of powers. Its very justification has been changed from the end-purpose of dividing a ruling elite against itself by facilitating mutual defection, so as to limit the power of *all* branches of government, including the Judiciary; to the opposite end of uniting and empowering the elite in and through the establishment of the Judiciary as supreme and autonomous. The interconnection between the separation of powers, checks and balances, and the freedom of ordinary folks from the will of any corps (or network) of elites has been *ignored, or suppressed.*

However reverently they may refer to the separation of powers, many in the Network seem to have thought only cursorily about what it is or what it is for, beyond serving as a springboard for one's own agenda. Time and again, the author observed in the field that hardly anyone could give a coherent account of it. When those in the Network Community do theorize about separation of powers, they dogmatize it in a form ostensibly assimilated to the traditional 'pure doctrine' of jurists in continental Europe going back to Montesquieu and the eighteenth century, which affirms the same ulterior purpose as in Westminster or the early USA, to prevent abuses of power, but takes for granted whether and how it works:

> A 'pure doctrine' of the separation of powers [teaches that] it is essential for . . . political liberty that the government be divided into three branches or departments, the legislature, the executive, and the judiciary. To each . . . there is a corresponding identifiable function of government . . . Each . . . must be confined to the exercise of its own function and not allowed to encroach upon the [others] . . . The final element in the doctrine is the idea that if the recommendations with regard to agencies, functions, and persons are followed, then each branch . . . will be unable to exercise an undue control or influence over the others. Thus there will be a check to the exercise of the power of government over 'the people' because attempts . . . to exercise an undue degree of power will be bound to fail . . . The pure doctrine [is] a 'negative' approach . . . The mere existence of several autonomous

> decision-taking bodies is . . . a sufficient brake upon the concentration of power . . . They do not actively exercise checks upon each other, for to do so would be to 'interfere' in the functions of another branch. However, the theory does not indicate how an agency . . . [is] to be restrained if [it encroaches] upon the functions of another branch.
>
> (Vile 1998: 14–18)

It was just this 'veto vacuity' which led James Madison, the Father of the US Constitution, to supplement the pure doctrine in the American Constitution with a 'theory of positive checks and balances' whereby

> each branch was given the power to exercise a degree of direct control over the others by authorizing it to play a part, although only a limited part, in the exercise of the other's functions. Thus the executive branch was given a veto power over legislation, or the legislative branch was given the power of impeachment. The important point is that this power to 'interfere' was only a limited one, so that the basic idea of a division of functions remained, modified by the view that each of the branches could exercise some authority in the field of all three functions.
>
> (Vile 1998: 18)

Our elite transnational Network Community has been promoting Judiciary revisions in CEE in the name of judicial independence, the rule of law, and human rights for at least the last twenty-five years. A comparison with the classical constitutional traditions of the USA and Britain reveals that the Network have understood these assumptions and institutionally encoded them in ways that far exceed what is necessary simply to put their professed goals into practice. Classical separation of powers homed in exclusively on shielding the individual from material State (including Judiciary) coercion. It was strife over political liberty that gave birth to the constitutional legacy of Britain and the USA. The Network Community's motives, however, are strikingly different: it is to normalize the judicialization of politics and to empower judges to make public policy often but not always in the name of human rights.[2] It is this peculiarly labile concept of

[2] Take, for example, the decision of the ECtHR in *Lautsi v. Italy* imposing laicization on Italian state schools unilaterally (without consulting the Committee of Ministers or the Parliamentary Assembly of the CoE). The Italian state had placed crucifixes in its classrooms, but had not obligated children to do or believe anything, like attend Mass or profess the Catholic faith. None the less, to bring the suit within the appearance of the individual versus state power, it was claimed that the crucifixes coerced non-Christian children. The Court accepted the plaintiff's implicit theory of motivation in the teeth of everyday experience that inanimate objects do not coerce (people do), and even though no evidence showed any child to have been

rights that can be remoulded to justify coercing some individuals in favour of others in policy disputes; instead of letting the lawgiver decree then reasonably protect all individuals without favouritism – not from each other's abuses (which is the Legislative remit) but *only* from the State. Yet unilateral condemnation by judges of any other political actors is of the essence of judicialization. This Network Community agenda has been progressing gradually but steadily all across Europe since the Second World War at the latest. The Judiciary revisions of recent years, from CEE to the UK, can be fully understood only in this broad political context.

The classical meaning of the separation of powers and checks and balances

A normative comparison of the transnational Template with classical constitutionalism produces an 'x-ray' of the underlying assumptions of both, exposing the kind of government that must rest upon them. The latter straightforwardly divided State power into multiple, separate, independent, latently adversarial 'departments', or singly ineffectual particles. The ulterior purpose of this device was to take all subjects who stood accused (or otherwise liable before State power) and entitle them to a 'ground due process' which by default exempts him as a free citizen from the State's coercion unless and until its particular departments *all concur* in finding him guilty (Bains 2011; Parau and Bains 2012). This unanimity, and only this, reuniting the particles of State power into one, has any right to nullify the subject's ordinary exemption, exposing his life, liberty, and property to the privations of punishment. Any one particle of the State defecting from the concurrence trumps all the others by interdicting their unanimity, so that the accused is found

coerced by any agent. What is more, the Court ignored the same logic as applied to Christian children, who might well have been coerced actually (not just virtually) into deifying laicism by the real agency of real persons: the plaintiff and allies who would police compliance with a Court threatening sanctions. Thus in the name of human rights, a supremacist Judiciary (itself an organ of the State or supranational regime) coerces some humans in favour of others in an ideological dispute, to settle which the only alternative to majority rule is *elite minority* rule. A rights discourse is not a bona fide solution, since all children are coerced to attend the same schools, and it is a zero-sum trade-off whose ideology shall prevail there. It is beyond the scope of this study to survey the ideologies of the Network Community, but its commitment to laicism is not in serious dispute.

innocent/held harmless by default, and retains life, liberty, and property intact. In theoretical terms, each particle of State power is a *veto player* interdicting legal condemnation – except if none of the players vetoes it. Every stage of ground due process, running from enactment to prosecution, to conviction through to pardon, offers the possibility of veto.

Classical checks and balances are mechanisms amending, nullifying, or demurring to enforce any unilateral determination of guilt by any branch, even the Judiciary (Paulsen 1993). These mechanisms apply to single cases, not only to the letter of general law (as by parliamentary re-enactment qua check and balance). No check or balance is forbidden because it is applied *ex ante* or *ex post*, in the case or out of it. A check and balance *ex ante* takes place prior to any judicial ruling that might be corrected, but one *ex post* takes place afterwards and so is capable (in principle) of righting the balance of political forces in the case in favour of liberty. A check and balance that is 'in the case' affects its disposition, but one 'outside the case' cannot alter a case outcome, but it can alter with checking and balancing intent, the overall operation of the Judiciary. Any branch's powerlessness to condemn unilaterally, combined with its plenary power to exonerate unilaterally, sets up a structural asymmetry in the adjudication of guilt and innocence. Simply by making it harder to attain guilt, it formalizes the presumption of innocence, rendering it more than an empty promise. A system structurally biased toward finding innocent with finality must entail guilty defendants being sometimes ruled innocent. All rules are 'mechanical' and may fail to deliver justice. The evil is excused on the grounds that worse still are the evils of governmental, including judicial, discretion. *In fine*, the accused or the responsible enjoy multiple chances of keeping possession of their life, liberty, and property – the *political* consequence of legal acquittal – because any one branch can find innocent, but only all three can find guilty. Concretely, a judge may pronounce 'X is guilty', yet be properly and constitutionally overridden by another branch pronouncing (retroactively, even) 'X is not guilty', without damage to judicial independence or the rule of law.

The purpose of separation of powers was never to taxonomize insular spheres of action for each branch for its own sake, or for the sake of any goal unrelated to personal freedom *from* the State. Nor was it the purpose to insulate a select few to rule all others from the bench. It was to potentiate the ordinary exemption of free men from ready abuses of State power, whether from the bench or from another co-equal authority:

> separation of powers does not operate alone as a canonical principle of our constitutionalism. It is one of a close knit set of principles that work both separately and together as touch stones of political legitimacy . . . The [related] principle of checks and balances . . . requires the ordinary concurrence of one government entity in the actions of another (and thus permits the first entity to veto the actions of the other) . . . We may divide power because we want there to be multiple centres of recourse – many places to which citizens can appeal when they are not receiving satisfaction from other centres of government.
>
> (Waldron 2012: 6–7)

The US Constitution, as originally drafted, epitomized the classical separation of powers in the functional (not the social class) sense. The Framers considered it an 'essential precaution in favour of liberty', as each 'branch' of the separation was far less dangerous than all combined (Madison 1788a). Usurpation or, in effect, re-incorporation of the powers of one branch by another was hindered, as 'no one could transcend their legal limits, without being effectually checked and restrained by the others' (Madison 1788b). Classical checks and balances were manifold and did not necessarily involve the Judiciary at all. Congress and the President might check each other and the States might check the Federal Government. The partitioning and commingling of the separated functions to constitute mutual checks and balances meant that no practically impermeable barrier separated branches of government (Manning 2011). A too-absolute separation, by which the acts of one branch are totally ensconced from intervention and thus correction by all the others, was rejected. A separation that left all adjudication solely in the hands of judges risked over-empowering them to *define* guilt and liability unilaterally without recourse to veto players. As Jefferson (1784) put it in 'Notes on the State of Virginia' (*mutatis mutandis* substituting a supremacist Judiciary for the legislature of the Republic of Venice):

> All the powers of government, legislative, executive, and judiciary, result to the legislative body. The concentrating these in the same hands is precisely the definition of despotic government. It will be no alleviation that these powers will be exercised by a plurality of hands, and not by a single one. One hundred seventy-three despots would surely be as oppressive as one. Let those who doubt it turn their eyes on the republic of Venice. As little will it avail us that they are chosen by ourselves. An elective despotism was not the government we fought for, but one which should not only be founded upon free principles, but in which the powers of government should be so divided and balanced among several bodies of magistracy, as that no one could transcend their legal limits, without being effectually checked and

> restrained by the others. For this reason that convention which passed the ordinance of government, laid its foundation on this basis, that the legislative, executive, and judiciary departments should be separate and distinct, so that no person should exercise the powers of more than one of them at the same time. But no barrier [at all] was provided between these several powers [in the Republic of Venice].
>
> (Jefferson 1784)

Checks and balances on each other by the branches of the State can be and have been arranged through alternate institutional designs. Britain has never followed the US model of a functional separation of powers. The British constitutions are senior in time and concept to the US, and feature a more ancient and historical separation of powers between three social classes. This is something quite different but equally (some say more) effective (Bagehot [1867] 1963). The Monarch, the Lords, and the Commons each could veto the Acts of one or both of the others, stopping encroachments pernicious to its own interests and liberties. As Blackstone expressed it:

> [As t]he executive power of the laws is lodged in a single person, they have all the advantages of strength and dispatch that are to be found in the most absolute monarchy: and as the legislature of the kingdom is entrusted to three distinct powers, entirely independent of each other; first, the king; secondly the lords spiritual and temporal which is an aristocratic assembly of persons selected for their piety, their birth, their wisdom, their valour and their property; and thirdly the house of commons, freely chosen by the people from among themselves, which makes it a kind of democracy; as this aggregated body, actuated by different springs and attentive to different interests, composes the British parliament, and has the supreme disposal of everything; there can no inconvenience be attempted by either of the three branches, but will be withstood by one of the other two; each branch being armed with a negative power, sufficient to repel any innovation which it shall think inexpedient or dangerous. Here then is lodged the sovereignty of the British constitution . . . in no other shape could we be so certain of finding the three great qualities of government so well and so happily united. If the supreme power were lodged in any one of the three branches separately, we must be exposed to the inconvenience of either absolute monarchy, aristocracy, or democracy . . . If it were lodged in any two of the branches: for instance, in the king and house of lords; our laws might be providently made, and well executed, but they might not always have the good of the people in view; if lodged in the king and commons, we should want that circumspection and mediatory caution, which the wisdom of the peers is to afford; if the supreme rights of legislature were lodged in the two houses only, and

> the king had no negative upon their proceedings, they might be tempted to encroach upon the royal prerogative, or perhaps to abolish the kingly office, and thereby weaken (if not totally destroy) the strength of executive power. But the constitutional government of this island is so admirably tempered and compounded, that nothing can endanger or hurt it, but destroying the equilibrium of power between one branch of the legislature and the rest. For if ever it should happen that the independence of any of the three should be lost, or that it should become subservient to the views of either of the other two, there would soon be an end of our constitution.
>
> (Blackstone [1765] 1809: 50–51)

Political functionality has been more broadly, informally conceived in the British tradition than in the American. The Lord Chancellor, for instance, was a singular institution from an American standpoint; the incumbent was accountable to three rival constituencies at once: the Cabinet, the House of Lords, and the Bar. This last 'interest group' stands wholly outside Parliament or public office, or anything which might be conceived as a 'branch of government'. Yet Britain's elite community of jurists and barristers facilitated the consolidation of individual liberty, the independence of the Judiciary, and the rule of law in the seventeenth (England's revolutionary) century, by defending them against the absolutist claims of the Stuart dynasty – see Sir Edward Coke's Petition of Right (Coke 1628; White 1979). Nowadays, Britain is the country with the longest tradition and experience of judicial independence and the rule of law in Europe, notwithstanding that they have not that separation of powers which derives from the American Constitution.

Classical checks and balances on Judiciary decisional output

Checks and balances on the Judiciary classically consisted of powers to correct or curtail the effect of (prospective) judicial condemnations in actual cases (see Table 4.1). The Executive could directly intervene through pardons individual or collective, prospective or retrospective; likewise, through the 'Executive discretion' to omit to arrest and prosecute known violators; or a positive command to law enforcement to 'stand down', provided this has the effect of omitting to detect or receive knowledge of guilt or liability, precluding the consequent jeopardy. Prosecutorial discretion is a check on the Legislative making draconian laws: an Executive that omits to prosecute a law will not be haling its alleged violators into court. But this can check the Judiciary, too, if the Executive is anticipating judges will 'hang 'em high' (Lafave 1970). An order to stand down does not encroach on judicial independence, as it is addressed to lower-ranking officers of the Executive branch only, and not to the officers of other branches. Even though Executive inaction in these instances is not usually memorialized to name and define the 'third-party beneficiaries' of inter-branch mutual checks, as with pardons, a political decision taken by an Executive superior exonerates legally, in that all criminal and some civil cases cannot come to judicial process.

Non-enforcement of actual or prospective condemnations (not exonerations) is tantamount to legal nullification. The Executive may stop short of that by using discretion to 'commute' the penalty or to prosecute only the worst offences. Therefore, Executive inaction is legally and politically significant, and may not be presumed culpable neglect. Non-enforcement becomes more definitely nullification of judicial acts when it is formalized in a pardon, which unlike simple inaction or order to stand down is a document legally binding on the Judiciary branch. Classically, the pardon was a check on judicial power of uncontested legitimacy. It was used by American presidents to check the Supreme Court, whose powers and discretion nowadays unconstitutionally resemble a European constitutional court (or vice versa).[3] Pardon differs from Executive discretion or stand down in that, in addition to naming or defining defendants, it permanently alters their legal status and rights (Easterbrook 1989; Paulsen 1993).

Private laws are also legal instruments, addressed by the Legislative to named defendants or defined classes of persons, beneficially affecting their legal rights in judicial and administrative proceedings, and not only in legislative and prosecutorial ones. The Legislative power to nullify acts of adjudication through what is also known as 'bills of indemnity' and 'parliamentary amnesties', is less well known as a check and balance. Private laws may be proactive or retroactive, and work just like Executive pardons in exonerating nominated private parties from judicial condemnation or administrative action. They are legitimate checks on judicial power, provided they relieve persons judicially condemned, including prospectively. They may not work as a condemnation, however, to nullify a judicial order like habeas corpus to release a prisoner, if the polity is one of divided

[3] President Jefferson conceived he was nullifying the Alien and Sedition Acts prospectively as well as retrospectively when pardoning all who had been convicted under them, and he said so. The rest of the country evidently agreed since the Acts were never enforced again.

government where the Judiciary *can* have the last word by likewise 'relieving' the accused (by quashing the accusation).

Parliaments, comprising many more veto players than one Executive head of State, face higher decisional transaction costs; therefore, one would expect Legislative checks on the Judiciary to be rarer than Executive ones, and to inure to the benefit of VIPs only, such as ambassadors, army generals, ministers, and royalty. This expectation is not always borne out. Prefacing its private legislation with the formula 'For the *relief* of [name of private party]', the US Congress included five of them amongst the first 108 laws it ever enacted in 1789–91, and by the late 1800s had actually passed more private than public laws. But since around the time of the Second World War the practice has been in decline (Dwyer 2009). In Great Britain, the *locus classicus* of Parliamentary nullification of the judicial power to impose liability – but without amending any constitution or repealing any statute or overturning any case law *precedent* – would be the Act of Free and General Pardon, Indemnity and Oblivion of 1660 (12 Cha. II ch. 11). It exonerated whole classes of persons who had committed crimes during the English Civil War and the Interregnum but for enumerated exceptions (murder, piracy, buggery, rape, and witchcraft), plus nominated individuals who had partaken in the regicide.

Private laws need not be reserved for once-in-a-lifetime events, as their history in the USA and Britain shows. The power to nullify judicial condemnations *ex post* and *ex ante* is as timely and as topical as today's newspaper headline. In CEE, the need for limits to judicial power was felt keenly enough very soon after 1989. The Romanian restitution cases of the 1990s made the issue salient. In the early post-Communist period, the courts began to hear complaints of landed property confiscated without compensation decades before by the defunct Communist regime when it swept into power after the Second World War. In the ensuing forty years, generations had been born, lived, and died in quarters assigned them by the State, who had had no part in the injustice. Innocently relying, to their detriment, on these assignments as the only surrogate for property rights under Communism, these tenants were suddenly stripped of it all, when activist judges unilaterally condemned them to eviction with no provision of relief, merely in order to vindicate (arguably) stale claims by absentee heirs of the previous owners. Parliament had enacted no laws defining the rights and obligations of the parties to this novel class of actions. The courts took jurisdiction anyway on the basis of a constitutional declaration of principle: 'The right of property, as well as the debts incurred by the

State, are guaranteed' (Article 41-1).[4] The Article goes on, however, to state that 'the content and limitations of these rights shall be established by law.' Ignoring that qualification, the activists rushed to judgment.

The suffering of the evictees became infamous, galvanizing Romanian President Iliescu to stop the evictions by bidding the Executive to demur to enforce those judgments. Iliescu's intervention, though formally only a recommendation, was tantamount to nullification because the legal uncertainty it introduced (about enforcement) sufficed to inhibit ongoing or prospective cases from being litigated any farther until Parliament enacted a general solution years later (Parau 2012). This illustrates how judges too can be arbitrary and unjust to the point that the people cry out for relief, and that the elected branches' power to check and balance the Judiciary is essential to prevent (activist) abuses even today. It matters supremely, then, whether the judicial act to be nullified has found innocent or guilty.

This is why classical checks and balances are *ex post* and may be brought to bear inside the case. They are applicable retroactively to release persons in jeopardy from legal guilt. As the Romanian cases illustrate, a holding harmless or a finding innocent has political implications, too, for it leaves matters as they currently stand: the status quo is found innocent, as it were, even if ambitious elites disagree.

Table 4.1 Classical checks and balances on the Judiciary

	Ex ante	*Ex post*
In the case	Legislative inaction Prosecutorial discretion (Executive pardon) (Private legislation)	Non-enforcement Executive pardon Private legislation
Out of the case	Court packing Defining jurisdiction	Impeachment Revision of jurisdiction (rare)

Like any tool, checks and balances may be misused – for example, to mitigate some condemnations (of cronies and bundlers) but not others. The Socialist government in Romania moved to 'ease overcrowding in

[4] There was also an equally vague Civil Code provision (Art. 481: 'private property rights are inviolable'), which some courts claimed jurisdiction on the basis of. It too was a statement of principle addressed to Parliament and the Executive ministries as much as to the judicial power, if not more so, and would probably have been found 'unconstitutionally vague' (for restitution purposes) by the US Supreme Court.

prisons' – for which Romania was condemned by the ECtHR – through pardoning first and foremost elites convicted of corruption (Council of Europe 2012; Boffey 2017). Nullifying judgment can be an act of tyranny too, as if Parliament repealed all laws or the President pardoned all criminals. Systematic omission to protect the innocent is morally equivalent to persecuting them, as when Nazi police stood down whilst rioters ran rampant on *Kristallnacht*. Divided government only works when the normative or moral basis for it is not thoroughly corrupt.

That moral basis was articulated very well by the American Framer Alexander Hamilton, who was able to assume human nature, because of the condition he found it in in early America and Great Britain, more confidently to be a melee of good and evil in which good never fails to co-exist:

> Th[e] supposition of universal venality in human nature is little less an error in political reasoning, than the supposition of universal rectitude. The institution of delegated power implies, that there is a portion of virtue and honor among mankind, which may be a reasonable foundation of confidence; and experience justifies the theory. It has been found to exist in the most corrupt periods of the most corrupt governments. The venality of the British House of Commons has been long a topic of accusation against that body, in the country to which they belong as well as in this; and it cannot be doubted that the charge is, to a considerable extent, well founded. But it is as little to be doubted, that there is always a large proportion of the body, which consists of independent and public-spirited men, who have an influential weight in the councils of the nation.
>
> (Hamilton 1788a)

Competition and independence in a system with checks and balances

Mutual checks and balances are possible only if the other branches are as independent of the Judiciary in the interpretation of constitutional law as the Judiciary is of them. The meaning of constitutions, especially, must be contested by multiple, competing authorities, between multiple levels and branches of government, governing elites, and the people qua political electors (or jurymen), if they are to have any meaning at all independent of a privileged body of interpreters (Gant 1997; Kramer 2004). A text must be contested to have any objective meaning, or it will not exist (but for its bare facticity), apart from the preferences of those empowered to override all other preferences. 'The constitution is whatever the judges [or a designated corps] say it is' is little short of '2 + 2 = whatever the mathematicians say it is'. It is *not* – if words and numbers are to mean anything besides say-so. By the nature of meaning – 'a mean' in between two or more persons – meaning cannot be fixed by a special caste of arbiters. It dissolves the shed between their own personal discretion and *universal meaning* – a boundary only maintained by the push-back of other actors.

Nobody articulated the idea of elite competition as cogently as Thomas Jefferson. As president, he unilaterally nullified the Alien and Sedition Acts of President Adams, his predecessor, which had criminalized political dissent, notwithstanding that the Federal Judiciary had ruled them constitutional (Lash and Harrison 2007). It was a blanket pardon of everyone the Judiciary had condemned which reached into the future to nullify the Acts, so that no one could be prosecuted under them ever again. In words Jefferson addressed to John Adams's wife Abigail:

> You seem to think it devolved on the judges to decide on the validity of the sedition law. but nothing in the constitution has given them a right to decide for the executive, more than to the Executive to decide for them. both magistracies are equally independent in the sphere of action assigned to them. the judges, believing the law constitutional, had a right to pass a sentence of fine and imprisonment; because that power was placed in their hands by the constitution. but the Executive, believing the law to be unconstitutional, was bound to remit the execution of it; because that power has been confided to him by the constitution. that instrument meant that it's [*sic*] co-ordinate branches should be checks on each other. but the opinion which gives to the judges the right to decide what laws are constitutional, and what not, not only for themselves in their own sphere of action, but for the legislature & executive also in their spheres, would make the judiciary a despotic branch.
>
> (Jefferson 1804)

Likewise, President Andrew Jackson in his message vetoing Congress's renewal of the National Bank's charter – an institution which the Supreme Court had ruled constitutional – re-asserted the President's equal right to interpret the Constitution:

> If the opinion of the Supreme Court covered the whole ground of this act, it ought not to control the co-ordinate authorities of this Government. The Congress, the executive and the court, must each for itself be guided by its own opinion of the Constitution. Each public officer, who takes an oath to support the Constitution, swears that he will support it as he understands it, and not as it is understood by others.
>
> (Jackson 1832)

Classically, all branches not only might but also ought to partake in constitutional interpretation, but none is supreme over the others (Paulsen 1994).

Jefferson's Rule *for cases of a political nature* (where the harmlessness/innocence of no person with liability/in jeopardy is being decided) is that it lies in the power of any branch to interpret the Constitution, without any duty to obey the putative superiority of another branch (Engdahl 1992). This arrangement never led to interpretive anarchy – the argument frequently preferred to justify judicial supremacy (Alexander and Schauer 1997). In the two cases just cited, both Jefferson and Jackson prevailed – they had the last word, inasmuch as the power to act or to omit to act had been placed in their hands by the Constitution itself.

The right of independent interpretation rests on the principle of competition between branches of government and the elites who staff them. This classical democratic theory holds the key to sustainable democracy, for elite competition qua division of powers and likelihood of defection from one another constitutes a form of 'circulation of elites' (Pareto 1916), in that the power of final decision circulates from branch to branch, forestalling the domination of any elite group for any length of time (Dahl 1971; Etzioni-Halevy 1993; Diamond et al. 1995).

It is in this broader political context of the desirability of and provision for elite competition that judicial independence must be understood. Decisional (as distinct from structural) independence had political and historical priority: judges must make their rulings 'in accordance with their [own] determinations of the evidence, the law and justice', without alien determinations being imposed on them by the 'coercion, blandishments, interference, or threats' of others (Rosenn 1987: 7). The English Judiciary is the *locus classicus* of decisional independence without more, who have been exempt from undue influence for centuries. Yet given the settled doctrine of parliamentary sovereignty in English constitutional law, judges are not even co-equal to Parliament or the Crown, let alone supreme over them (Blackstone [1765] 1809). Nor has the rule ever existed in the English constitutions requiring the Crown or Parliament to obey any or all judicial decisions, though Executive officers of the Crown may be obligated to do so. The judge's role is simply to weigh in with an independent determination of guilt or innocence. Independent adjudication is thus a means to a specific end; it is the last ordinary chance for the accused or respondent to be acquitted.[5]

[5] This might suffice for those scholars in the field of political science who are seeking to develop a general theory of judicial independence, for whom the purpose of independence must be one of the elements of such a theory: 'A second requirement of a general theory is

The classical model might also help explain the relationship between judicial independence and the rule of law, which constitution framers and academic scholars tend to take for granted. It is commonly assumed that judges are the causes of the rule of law, when in reality it may well be the other way around. The causal direction is not in fact clear. If causation ran the other way, then the independence of the Judiciary would depend on the prior existence of the rule of law (Rios-Figueroa and Staton 2009). History tends to support the latter. In the common-law tradition, the rule of law can be traced at least as far back as Magna Carta. But Magna Carta was not made because judges were independent (at that time they were the King's servants), but because many interested parties, elite competitors to the King, from barons to bishops, forced him to submit to the rule of law both in and out of court. It is likely, then, that the rule of law was the cause of judicial independence; considering also that judges were not immunized from dismissal at the King's displeasure until 1701. The independence of judges enhances the rule of law already in place; absent which rule, judges can do little. The constructive agency of the rest of society stands revealed as precursor and prerequisite; just as the agency of the Network Community was prerequisite to legal professionals' exerting so much leverage over the member states of European supranational organizations.

The constitutional paradigm of the Network Community

The Network Community, especially in the context of CEE, dismisses the classical conception as antiquated if not contemptible, with stock phrases that gesture to the 'very different situation' of contemporary Europe as grounds for invalidity. The Network's entrepreneurs have seeded Eastern Europe with this meme: 'In 2003 the Constitution [of Romania] was amended. The principle of separation of powers was explicitly stated in Art. 1 . . . [although it is] qualified by legal doctrine as "scientific regress" because in the entire world the principle is

to have some coherent idea of the purpose or rationale of judicial independence. Judicial independence is not an end in itself . . . a theory of judicial independence must be based on some idea of what that end is' (Russell 2001: 4). Here is that end in its primordial essence.

considered passé' (CC judge: Interviewee 38); and 'Yes, well, that was two hundred years ago' (SCt judge: Interviewee 6).[6]

The author observed that essentially all her informants in the field were oblivious; none were able to recognize amnesties and pardons as *checks and balances* on the Judiciary. These, especially when exercised by the Executive, are even supposed – in the teeth of the classical model – to stultify the separation of powers. The Executive role is just to 'nominate judges, execute judicial decisions, and originate norms concerning the organization of the judiciary, and the competence and procedure of courts' (CC judge: Interviewee 38) – *if* that much. Acts of the Executive that might hinder rather than serve judicial power, such as nullifying, ameliorating, or demurring to enforce judicial decisions, are universally held in the Network to be 'attempts to thwart the principle of separation of powers' (CC judge: Interviewee 38).

Logically, an illegitimate Executive intervention *ex ante* would be necessary to 'interfere' with purely decisional independence, whereas, Executive non-enforcement *after* a decision has been rendered and put on record is strictly *ex post* and does not affect the independence with which it was made. Networked-in legal professionals none the less condemn any Executive check and balance inside the case. Non-enforcement qua 'innocence verdict' is invariably deemed illegitimate interference with the Judiciary. When they were queried if the Romanian President was right to deny enforcement of the restitution decrees, a typical response was: 'The President was wrong. His intervention was interference with the courts. A President cannot say "I won't respect the judgement of the courts"' (SCt judge: Interviewee 6). Illogically, Executive 'amnesty' is accepted as legitimate by the same elites:

> Of course, a President has the competence to pardon a defendant and that would be OK, the end of the game; and of course, the court cannot say 'I am

[6] This is a typical answer given by legal professionals when asked in interview to comment on Jefferson's nullification of the Alien and Sedition Acts by pardon, even after it was indicated that this was not the only time the Supreme Court's claim of a monopoly right to interpret the Constitution was refuted. It is redolent of Christopher Lasch's lamentation of contemporary man in an 'age of diminishing expectations', the pastless man who holds history and tradition in contempt, in 'The Waning of the Sense of Historical Time' – the first section in *The Culture of Narcissism* (1978). Lasch comes from a psychoanalytic and humanist-sociological background, and his book is more of an interpretative framework than an empirical study. None the less, he arrived at roughly the same conclusions as I have by a quite contrasting path.

> sorry, Mr President, you have no competence to pardon'; the President has the general competence of amnesty.
>
> (SCt judge: Interviewee 6)

But this is conceived as somehow no part of the rule of law, hence it is not recognized as a check and balance in the case *ex post*, competent to settle *constitutional meaning* like Jefferson's pardon.

Pardon is conceived solely as an act of mercy and a sometimes necessary exception to the rule of law:

> [Concerning the Executive using his power of general pardon as a check and balance on judicial decisions] there was some discussion of this issue when the last [Croatian] President pardoned somebody, a petty drug dealer . . . and the public didn't want that person to be pardoned . . . Presidential pardon is a way of showing a human face to somebody who behaved well, but who was rightly sentenced by the judiciary.
>
> (Academician: Interviewee 49)

Also deplored is any idea that an Executive pardon might be used conditionally, like judges use suspension of sentences, to exact good behaviour from defendants in exchange for continued possession of life, liberty, or property, even though the equivalence of a pardon to an acquittal or a conditional suspension of sentence is evident:

> It is unacceptable that the President pardoned a woman and that he set conditions under which she would be pardoned, that she should behave in a certain way . . . That is something which courts do when they find you innocent and release you from jail . . . they will set conditions under which you will not go back to jail. But these are the courts . . . whereas the President does not have any power basis anywhere . . . he just decides on the basis of his free will.
>
> (CC clerk and academician: Interviewee 50)

Executive pardon is admitted on one side and condemned on the other, on the fuzzy basis that the Executive should not 'just use its free will' – though courts do just that. Precedent (in the common law tradition only) may at times constrain their free will, but then apex courts overturn their own precedents at will, too, as in the USA (Kelsen 1942; Blaustein and Field 1958); but also increasingly in civil law jurisdictions, where an expectation has lately crystallized that CCs ought to defer to precedent, if not as an 'expressly recognized source of law' then as a 'judicial tool' that helps avoid legal anarchy (Selejan-Guțan 2016: Chapter 5, Section F, para. 10).

Checks and balances by Parliament are likewise rejected out of hand. Bills of indemnity, also known as 'parliamentary amnesties', are known, of course, but not in a way that admits of use as checks on the Judiciary. According to a legal professional regarding the Czech CC:

> Bills of Indemnity would not be a legitimate check and balance. I like to think that it is not a person who is deciding about my freedom, but there are always some rules, and that these rules are made in a process in which I took part. Of course, it is a fiction . . . because I do not know what is going on in our Parliament, but I am more ready to accept this than the idea that some people [MPs] just vote about me [not even if they find him innocent, apparently, after everyone else has found him guilty], if they want to . . . I would not want Parliament to vote on me, because parliaments [unlike courts] usually don't need to give reasons about what they are doing.
>
> (CC clerk and academician: Interviewee 50)

The assumption that bills of indemnity and legislative amnesties are 'outside the rules' implies a grave loss of comprehension of the separation of powers. The last thing separation is for is to forbid a defendant to be found innocent; tipping due process toward innocence is the whole point. A parliamentary act *or* inaction that prospectively finds innocent is at least as good as (in fact it is better than) a judicial ruling to the same effect (as it spares the accused ever being accused in the first place), and it is a radically different step, both legally and politically, from *any* act holding guilty. Yet the legitimacy of the judicial act is never doubted by the same persons who frown on too regular and 'political' use of amnesty, pardon, and indemnity as ways of giving meaning to rights and constitutions.

The political, not just legal, gulf between guilty and innocent is what the Network Community understands least, although it is the whole meaning of the classical system of government. The structural tilt in favour of innocence is not understood, or if it is, it is not duly salient in Network thinking or in their Template. Some transnational jurists come near to articulating its import in the context of criminal law, but only insofar as judges are correcting themselves; representatives need not apply. Articulation of a clear rule ('he perfects interpretation who holds innocent') is debarred by the assumption that courts have not so much the final as the *only* word on the law:

> Our [Czech] President . . . has the right to pardon. . . . there is also amnesty . . . where the President can say, 'Those who committed so-and-so should be set free' . . . or that '[against] those who should be convicted for such an act, the proceeding may not be started'. It is normal. But I cannot imagine . . . in Europe . . . that the President . . . can say, 'the law is not applicable' . . . It is not possible . . . It is also not good [for the President to interpret

> the Constitution with finality] . . . because in such a case the President will actually be over the Constitutional Court. And that is not possible, because the function of the Constitutional Court is to control every act of every organ of the State.
>
> (CC judge: Interviewee 34)

What is even more remarkable, networked-in legal elites in CEE exhibit a patent psychological resistance to knowing more about classical arrangements such as those in the USA before the Civil War, or in Britain. Even when these arrangements are not misunderstood as government-functional 'taxonomy', comprehension of how checks and balances work is still notably deficient. In the Network Community's understanding, no mutuality is possible: judges must be empowered to check and balance elected representatives, and the latter disempowered to act vice versa. Above all, classical *ex post* checks on the Judiciary are universally censured as contributing nothing to the cause of justice. Reciprocating or correlational checks and balances in the mildest form are forbidden now. A typical example was the fate meted out to the procedure of *recurs in anulare* ['recourse in annulment'], a modest check on the Judiciary by the General Prosecutor which in a few CEE countries was available up until the 2000s. In Romania it was summarily abolished in 2003.[7] The case was likewise in other countries as different from each other as Poland and Moldova. Strikingly, Poland's recent constitutional reforms have reinstated an equivalent of *recurs*, likely because of specific dysfunctionalities in the actual delivery of justice after all external checks on the Judiciary had been abolished; as distinct from sheer malice or corruption, as the case of Romania will evidence in Chapter 6. The 2017 reform 'includes a new mechanism for "extraordinary appeal", whereby almost any case adjudicated since Poland's present constitution was adopted in 1997 can be reopened if the prosecutor-general, who is also the justice minister, supports it' (Davies 2017).

[7] That it was beneficial is admitted by native jurists, but it was abolished anyway, because 'judicial power' out of their own hands is intolerable to the Network. In the words of one Romanian ex-Minister of Justice: '*Recurs in anulare* was not a bad institution. It was discredited by the fact that the General Prosecutor was a member of the Executive' (Minister of Justice: Interviewee 44). The abolitionists' pretext was an ECtHR ruling that faulted *recurs* for introducing legal uncertainty into adjudication; a stunning irony considering how much legal uncertainty the Court's own jurisprudence has introduced into all the courts of Europe.

Monopoly and 'cooperation' instead of checks and balances

The Network's conception of constitutionalism inverts elite competition. Cooperation and consensus amongst elites in lieu of competition is what one hears in the Network Community's discourses, as witness the nearly identical 'shop talk' of legal professionals as widely divergent from one another as are the Romanians:

> Art. 1 paragraph 4 of the Constitution specifies that the State is organized according to the principle of separation of powers, legislative, executive, and judicial, within the constitutional democracy. For many years, even in Romania, nobody conceives of a strict separation of powers, but of collaboration between them.
>
> (CC judge: Interviewee 38)

divergent from the British:

> the discussions that have taken place [in Britain] about judicial independence have been . . . that you can only have an effective justice system if the executive and the Judiciary work in partnership . . . judicial independence has very much been seen in the context of, the judges very much want to work positively with the administration, but recognize that they need to be careful in how they do that, so they are not seen by those who come in through the doors of the court as somehow colluding with the executive, for example about how much money might be available or very long cases have to wait . . . precisely because the principle of judicial independence is so strong . . . particularly when resources are tight, we nevertheless need to work in partnership. The question is how do you achieve that balance between independence and partnership?
>
> (MoJ official: Interviewee 28)

Reforms, therefore, pursued in the name of separation of powers are likely to be a formality only. For public consumption, the Network Community touts its discourses, justifying judicial independence. Once the public in the person of ordinary MPs is quiet (or dormant), networked-in judicial and political elites proceed to reunite behind the separation just formalized. Here is evidence of a tacit agreement to consolidate power in the hands of a united elite. When the elite forms a hegemonic class, it both impairs democracy and perturbs the elite in its power relations with each other (Pareto 1916; Mosca 1939). Collusion is collaboration which is not transparent to the public; in the context of a bona fide policy dispute, it implies debilitation of the workings of democracy. When elites quit competing to negotiate amongst themselves a 'peace pact', the separation-of-powers mechanism is stultified, as its counterbalancing function relies on checkers and balancers acting independently of each other. The co-operation testified to above may or may not have reached that level yet, but it is inherently prone to abuse.

When it comes to their own legal interpretations however, the pervasive thinking of the Network Community in Europe is anything but collaborative or even corelational. Instead it echoes the US Supreme Court's assertion of unilateral prerogative in *Cooper v. Aaron* – that courts have a monopoly over interpreting the Constitution:

> Article VI of the Constitution makes the Constitution the 'supreme Law of the Land.' In 1803, Chief Justice Marshall, speaking for a unanimous Court, referring to the Constitution as 'the fundamental and paramount law of the nation,' declared in the notable case of *Marbury v. Madison* . . . that 'It is emphatically the province and duty of the judicial department to say what the law is.' This decision declared the basic principle that the federal judiciary is supreme in the exposition of the law of the Constitution, and that principle has ever since been respected by this Court and the Country as a permanent and indispensable feature of our constitutional system.
>
> (*Cooper v. Aaron* (1958) 358 U.S. 1)

This dismisses without refuting the example of the early Presidents and their vindication of all branches' right, indeed duty to interpret the Constitution independently of each other, according to a calculus of finality based on the legal and political divide between the guilty and the innocent; and that inter-branch disputes about the distribution of power is to be settled inter se,[8] or *in extremis* by their democratic constituents, if not in nonce conventions then in ordinary elections. Instead of that subtle and effective design, the author heard the same argument time and again, that the lack of a single arbiter will lead to interpretative anarchy, as illustrated for instance by this typical response:

> If the President [Executive] refuses to enforce the law because he claims it is unconstitutional despite of the fact the Constitutional Court said it is constitutional . . . then the President does not obey the law. Everyone in this country must obey the law . . . The only, *the other possibility is anarchy*. For instance, in our Supreme Court, we think that some laws are unconstitutional and if the Constitutional Court rejected our motion saying that the laws are perfectly constitutional, and we decided that the laws are unconstitutional anyway and we will not follow that . . . that's anarchy . . . if the Constitutional Court says, 'This is constitutional' then we have to obey the law . . . the President

[8] In a bargaining process the outcome of which is known in game theory as a Nash equilibrium.

> can veto a Bill . . . [but] cannot simply say, I ignore them . . . they are stupid, they don't know what the Constitution is . . . of course, the power to interpret the Constitution is not a unique power of the Constitutional Court, of course, but this is a different issue from that of . . . who is the final arbiter . . . You can do nothing against a possible reading of the Constitution [by a judge] . . . the Executive branch cannot *sanction* our judges only because they think that theirs is not the best reading of the Constitution or that it is the wrong reading of the Constitution . . . nothing can be done against this because if you open this issue, if you open [Pandora's] box . . . there will be eternal discussion, and then you are creating the state of anarchy. There must be always someone who decides, who decides with finality.
>
> (SCt judge: Interviewee 6; emphasis added)

Confusion lurks in the word 'sanction' to describe how the Executive would check and balance the courts, as it rather demurs to enforce the courts' sanctions upon *itself*. Also confused is the assumption that a court with final say over all brings the 'right' kind of stability, or that stability is more desirable than what is lost: accountability and participation (Whittington 2002). The stability of an interpretive monopoly may destabilize politics in the long run, not just by exacerbating the democratic deficit, but by erasing the boundary between the men with the monopoly and any objective, impersonal meaning a Constitution might have. Equally stable alternatives (from the standpoint of legal certainty and predictability) are more compatible with democracy and the rule of law *not men*: parliamentary supremacy, for example (Ward 2006).[9]

The Network Community, in particular, is unable to recognize that a ruling is not properly judicial which purports to command coordinate powers to do any positive act over and above respecting the judge's adjudicatory findings between parties subordinate to the powers that be. This is surely one of the root causes of why confusion reigns over the status of CCs, whether judicial or not. In fact, CCs proceed in judicial fashion, but do what no one body of men, judicial or not, ought to be allowed to do. This is not separation of powers, but their reintegration in the manner of administrative bureaucracies, which also command and control whatever

[9] It is plausibly objected that parliamentary supremacy is morally equivalent to judicial supremacy, and the UK Parliament has been characterized as an 'elective dictatorship' (Hailsham of St Marylebone 1990). It is true that Parliament no longer has the internal separation of powers Blackstone described above, which made of it a world of its own, institutionally, but elective is still elective. If Parliament is an elective, then a supremacist Judiciary is a non-elective dictatorship.

department of life and of the law is assigned them. Courts as the Network has designed them may be styled along with the Regulatory State as so many mini-dictatorships, because their power is all or mostly unchecked; but this is deemed tolerable because none of them dictate over the whole of life. To this piecemeal regression to autocracy the judicialization of politics and the self-expansive jurisdiction of courts bears all too much likeness. Yet when queried, the Network Community shows little awareness that such an 'unseparation of powers' might be problematic.

The illimitable power to say what the law means once for all has begun to foment unrest in CEE. A few Presidents have challenged the judicial interpretative monopoly imposed by the Template. Czech President Václav Klaus refused to yield to the CC in a dispute over the power he assumed by inference from the Constitution to refuse to appoint judicial candidates who were too young. Romanian President Ion Iliescu bade the Executive to decline to enforce judicial rulings in the restitution cases. Wittingly or not, both were following Jefferson's Rule that the power to decline to obey within their own jurisdiction is an act of constitutional interpretation per se. The question seems not to have been settled once for all time. It is accepted more widely inside the Network than outside.

The alternative to anarchy hysteria is to let the contest over the meaning of the Constitution run its course until a thoroughly deliberated solution emerges, rather than assuming that all disputes must reach closure as soon as possible because anarchy (or gridlock) is bad. Undoubtedly closure is desirable in disputes over guilt versus innocence; however, in cases of a political nature, as over the lawful powers of the elected branches, gridlock may actually be good in that it prioritizes democratic deliberation over closure. The pressure to negotiate and compromise weighs upon the parties to any conflict, lest their donnybrooks discredit them before the voters, and is always subtly at work. But even if the parties gridlock, that at least means that the State will do less and stay small.[10] The partisans of liberty approve: if government interferes less, then liberty will abound more (Hazlitt [1946] 1979). This desideratum is seconded by the public choice literature, where gridlock is praised because it 'mak[es] actions that are not desirable more difficult to undertake[,] . . . increases the role of deliberation in the

[10] A classic case of letting conflict run its course is the President's War Powers, to settle which the US Supreme Court has declined to intervene. Anarchy did not ensue. The President hammered out a modus vivendi with Congress.

political process', and improves the overall quality of decisions; as it 'makes the political decision process more rational and in line with the public interest' (Berggren and Karlson 2003: 100, 107). If inter-branch negotiations permanently fail the power to settle defaults to the constituents, who can vote out incumbents if dissatisfied, or if satisfied, re-elect them (Madison 1788c). A practical example of this is the 'judicial recall' election in the USA.

What would change if this classical reasoning were applied to the supranational regime of the ECHR? Things would work very differently because the separation of powers implied in the CoE's institutional structure would function to introduce elite competition, instead of bypassing it in favour of the unilateral powers given to the ECtHR, which are so typical of judicial supremacy.[11] Conspicuous examples of the lack of elite competition include *Lautsi v. Italy*, where crucifixes in state school classrooms were unpredictably 'discovered' to have been violating the ECHR, presumably since 1955, and *Hirst v. UK* (No. 2), where a national law depriving convicts of the right to vote was found to breach the principle of universal suffrage in ECHR, Art. 3 (European Court of Human Rights 2005, 2009). The UK Parliament defied the ruling, censuring the ECtHR for reading into the Convention norms that the States parties never contracted for. It is not so much that the Court's particular rulings could not be defended in principle, as that it has annihilated any pretence of due process on that ground-most level effected by real checks and balances.

If the CoE were ever to observe its own, classically configured separation of powers, the Parliamentary Assembly would have to enact a general interpretation of the ECHR mandating laicity, before a judgment so overriding of subsidiarity as banning crucifixes could be decreed; likewise, that its universal suffrage mandate extends to outlaws (in the extreme case, to illegal residents). The Committee of Ministers qua Executive would concur independently, or not: had they 'vetoed ' the Assembly's enactment, the matter would end there; but if concurring, they would proceed to cite violating member states before the ECtHR. Private litigants could be countenanced only if the Assembly enacted enabling interpretations which the Ministers did not veto. Only if the Ministers and Assembly concurred first would the ECtHR have any jurisdiction.

[11] And resemble in so many ways the 14th Amendment jurisprudence of the US Supreme Court, post-Civil War. See 'The political-historical origin of Constitutional Courts' in Chapter 6.

People are inured to modern courts playing judge, jury, and executioner, yet the classical model thrust them into the role of 'exonerator of last resort', offering defendant member states, in the instance of the CoE, the last chance to be found not in violation. The judges' professional duty would be to prospect for rational grounds (if any) for dissenting from the political branches' condemnatory concurrence. For balancing the rights of subsidiarity with ECHR rights in the setting of a supranational polity, the classical model is superior. It is not only more compatible with a democratic rule of law, but is less susceptible, to boot, to transnationally networked legal elites inserting their agendas into the Conventional jurisprudence without the fully debated and informed consent of the States parties.

The presumption that the last word in both guilt and innocence belongs to courts and all others must obey is rooted in the Network Community's distrust of post-Westphalian power politics, which is blamed for failing to keep the World Wars and totalitarianism from engulfing Europe (cf. Murray 2017). The tacit premise is that judges could have prevented these calamities, a premise which itself rests on the assumption that judges are morally superior to politicians, and disobeying them is unthinkable. This sentiment is doubly strong in parts of Europe with recent experience of Communism. Here is the anxious remark of an East European jurist: 'If the Executive does not enforce judicial decisions, you create a . . . dangerous precedent; we grant yet again [as under Communism], illegally, a right to the Executive not to execute a judicial decision, at his choice, at his discretion' (CC judge: Interviewee 29).

The uniform assumption of the Network Community is that evil ever rests with the Executive (and Legislative) and never with the Judiciary (and by extension, themselves). When presented with examples of mechanisms classically available for the Executive or Parliament to exercise *ex post* in the case – even if only to find innocent – legal professionals in CEE immediately concluded that politicians will exploit them to subvert justice. Wittingly or not, they presume political actors will never find an innocent man innocent, only a guilty one; whilst a court would never find a guilty man innocent, but only an innocent one. In the words of one Croatian jurist:

> **Q:** Should the power of pardon be in the hands of the President?
>
> **A:** No . . . We still fear the cult of the personality . . . I don't think that the solution would be to concentrate the power in the hands of one person again, but . . . to ensure that one [branch of government] can control the other. We shouldn't go back to the rule where one person makes all the decisions.

> In the USA, that functions in a very different way. The President has the power, but all the mechanisms of check and balance are so old that the whole system functions without many problems. It is hard to imagine that they will have a dictatorship.
>
> (Academician: Interviewee 51)

It is certainly plausible that corruption in CEE is so universal that essentially all politicians can be counted on to abuse whatever instruments they have at hand, including checks and balances, applying the law selectively to 'get' their enemies and equally selectively to let off their cronies, whilst caring nothing for righting real miscarriages of justice. The exercise of checks and balances is not automated but discretionary, and discretion is by its very nature prone to abuse. But it stretches common sense to deny that judges in such a society cannot be far behind. The judicial regalia may give the appearance of uprightness, but confers no immunity from a universal venality. According to one Moldovan judge:

> When there is corruption in the whole country, one branch of power cannot be corruption-free . . . there have been talks about bringing to Moldova French and German judges. These might be good ideas, but this does not mean that they will change the society. They might be able to correct moments, but not society.
>
> (ECtHR judge: Interviewee 23)

Past trauma does influence the rejection of the status quo, that is, the classical separation of powers (cf. Erdos 2010); but it is a precarious faith in their own collective moral superiority to 'politics' that informs legal professionals' interpretation of the past.

Judicial independence as structural autonomy

The trend to autonomize and supremacize Judiciary output, the goal of those who judicialize European politics, has been matched by a parallel, equally important trend to autonomize input as well in the last twenty-five years – 'input' meaning who is permitted to become and remain a judge: their recruitment, training, appointment, career, and discipline. The Network Community now hinges both the input and output legitimacy of the Judiciary on its autonomy from the rest of society and the State.

It insists that the entire autonomy of the Judiciary as a whole is mandated by the separation of powers. In the words of an expert sent by the European Commission to assess the state of Judiciaries in the Balkans: 'The trend to insulate the Judiciary from the elected branches of government is very good. It is only respecting the principle of separation of powers' (Judge and EC adviser: Interviewee 40). According to a senior civil servant in the European Commission's DG Justice, who is also a legal professional and has been involved in Eastern Enlargement, judicial autonomy is essential to checks and balances:

> If you have an autonomous Judiciary you are more likely to achieve a higher degree of protection against undue influence coming from the Executive or political circles, which means that you can operate checks and balances between the branches of the State.
>
> (EC official: Interviewee 39)

The Network have neglected the more fundamental matter of decisional independence, which controls the quality of ordinary justice on the ground, by focusing on the 'structural independence' of the Judiciary (*sc.* institutional autonomy). It is assumed that structural independence brings about decisional independence.

Insulating judges from politicians and the games they play will of course often be very desirable if not unproblematic. Structural constraints for accountability's sake can be abused. Lowering judges' salaries may shock them into submission or render them more venal; yet not all structural constraints threaten decisional independence to the same degree (Russell 2001). Salaries might have to be cut in an economic crisis, and this might on occasion be a legitimate sanction in terms of democratic accountability. The US Judiciary has a measure of structural independence distinct from insulated autonomy, according to an American legal professional working in the CEE region:

> we have in the US a doctrine called inherent powers which says that courts have certain powers to determine how courts should be run and that cannot be delegated to the legislator. . . . I worked with CEE judges on a mediation project . . . and I suggested to the group that was over here for training . . . to set up a pilot for mediation to see how it worked. In the USA if a court wants to do that, they would not go to a legislator to ask permission. They just do it. This is an example of inherent power . . . But the Eastern Europeans said, 'We cannot do that; we need to have permission from the legislator.' This is an example of how the overall structure of government would affect judicial independence. We had a lot of judges from Russia and Eastern Europe coming over [to the USA]. And the problem that we kept running into is that the courts are run by the Ministry of Justice, and this seems to paralyse them.
>
> (ABA officer: Interviewee 31)

Inherent powers are believed by some observers to underlie or constitute judicial independence, even if this does imply a circumscribed autonomy.

Plenary judicial autonomy calling itself judicial independence is reacted against when belatedly seen through. It was probably the main determinant of Hungary's controversial reforms. Fidesz's chief constitutional draftsman and reformer had this to say:

> How important was the Judiciary reform to Fidesz's constitutional reform? The Judiciary has been the only sector of the society which hasn't been touched during the post-Communist transition. No one touched it because no one conceived of it as a power. Now we do. Now we can see that because the boards [Judicial Council] are deciding . . . but at the time the combined effect – that we did not see it as a power, and that everyone was speaking of judicial independence, the wrong concept of judicial independence . . . complete judicial self-government for judges is a complete violation of separation of powers and checks and balances. If judges are regulating themselves, they are collapsing the system economically with their decisions and there is a complete lack of reform of their house . . . In Europe Justice Ministers are appointing court presidents. Obama is appointing Supreme Court judges with parliamentary control. This is part of the normal power separation everywhere. Here [in CEE] we left it to the courts . . . The ivory tower arrangement was reproduced but without responsibility. Power is responsibility. You have to be accountable to the public and the public is partly the Parliament.
>
> (Jurist and MEP: Interviewee 35)

The Network Community seeks not just the type of independence for the Judiciary that allows the Judiciary a reasonable modicum of freedom in handling its affairs. Legal supremacy atop plenary autonomy is the policy goal which the Consultative Council of European Judges and its sister judicial networks have been endeavouring to enact via the CoE:

> The authority taking the decision on the selection and career of judges should be independent of the government and administration. In order to safeguard its independence, rules should ensure that, for instance, its members are selected by the Judiciary and that the authority decides itself on its procedural rules.
>
> (Consultative Council of European Judges 2001)

In practical design terms, this means a system of governance of the magistrates by the magistrates and for the magistrates (see Chapter 6) (cf. Kosař 2016). Autonomy on this scale insulates the Judiciary from the people, not just their representatives. This is an autonomy over and above what history shows is required for decisional independence – a maximalism characteristic of self-perpetuating institutions like the French Academy and the Harvard Corporation, institutions 'not formally accountable to anyone nor subject to anyone's direction' (Levinson 2006: 1303).

The cause of plenary autonomy has found a receptive audience in regions that have but recently emerged from tyranny, only to be swept up in the trend to judicial empowerment. Romania is a case in point. The legal academician who headed its first Constitutional Drafting Committee candidly instructed the Constituent Assembly that 'the Judiciary power has been conceived as an autonomous power . . . To this end we have moved the setting up of the Supreme Council of Magistrates [JC]' (Adunarea Constituantă 1991: 13). The merest involvement of elected representatives in the most marginal aspect of Judiciary governance is condemned as interference with the Judiciary:

> We were told that the Judicial Council has been created to guarantee the independence of the Judiciary from the politic. If the Council is presided by the President of the country, an Executive actor, you already have an interference of the Executive with the judicial power. It is possible, from respect for the President of the country to say that he presides honorifically but he cannot preside efficiently.
>
> (Jurist and career politician: Interviewee 17)

Even the repeal of a jurisdiction created *by statutory enactment* is construed as an interference with judicial independence. To try and hold a fragile governing coalition together, in 2010, a minority Government vested the Romanian CC with jurisdiction of Parliament's internal governing procedures, no less. But when the successor government of the opposition, which did not need the Court to keep order, proceeded in 2012 to recall Parliament's prerogatives, the Court denounced it as 'a threat to its independence' and an attempt to 'dismantle it' (Constitutional Court of Romania 2012). What was striking was to see the Network Community stand in stern solidarity with an absurd exaggeration.

The Network Community's actual paradigm of checks and balances

The paradigm that the separation of powers has for its end the autonomy and supremacy of the Judiciary goes hand in hand with the taboo on any check or balance which might encroach on judges' policy-making discretion. Following the lead of its legal professionals, the Network Community assumes certain procedures are checks and balances which are nothing of the sort. This error has fed the illusion of continuity with the classical political heritage of Western modernity that is rapidly being supplanted by a very different kind of governance of superficially formal similarity.

Ex ante *checks outside the case: appointments*

The Network Community assumes the vetting of magistrates by the political branches prior to appointment is a check and balance, because judges with a history of constitutional adventurism can be sifted out (or in):

> The first thing that should be done in the appointment of Constitutional Court judges must be to prove the adherence of the candidate to the Constitution. The candidates must bring proof. How would he prove that? Through his decisions, if a judge, through his or her publications, if a professor, and so on.
>
> (CC judge: Interviewee 34)

Appointment is supposed capable of checking judicial discretion *ex ante*. According to an influential legal professional in the Czech Republic:

> Judicial appointment . . . is a kind of check and balance . . . the question is who makes this appointment? If judicial appointment is made by the Judiciary itself, then, of course, there is no check and balance and that is dangerous. Imagine that parliamentarians will elect themselves or that the President will appoint his successor. This is exactly what has exist[ed] in Hungary [until the 2011 Fundamental Law] and [what still exists] in Romania. But if the Executive branch appoints them, which is the case here [Czech Republic] and in the USA, and in some other European countries . . . that is the exercise of checks and balances: one power cannot reproduce itself.
>
> (SCt judge: Interviewee 6)

Appointment vetting does prevent power from reproducing itself; however, this does not mean that pernicious errors of constitutional significance could be sifted out on the individual case level. Appointment vetting is *ex ante* and out of the case; it cannot home in on exact injustices. It can, however, influence the balance of judicial ideology on a court. In the words of a Czech Supreme Administrative Court judge:

> More self-restrained judges were appointed to the bench [in the Czech Republic] after 2003, when the first term of most judges expired. This was an important factor in recreating the jurisprudence of the court . . . One can check and balance the political opinions of the judges through

> appointments . . . at the Constitutional Court level . . . It is not true that the Judiciary cannot be controlled through appointments.
>
> (SCt judge: Interviewee 6)

The power to vet appointments is not the power to determine the policy content of output. The power of appointments to achieve ideological balance is fuzzy, glacially slow, and not steerable; as witness the many US Supreme Court appointees who have disappointed their appointers by ruling inconsistently with their pre-appointment histories; for example, Blackmun, Souter, O'Connor (Epstein et al. 2007). One most recent instance of this is the decision over the Affordable Care Act (Obamacare) in 2012, which saw Republican-appointed Chief Justice John Roberts, having written the erstwhile-majority opinion holding it unconstitutional, swing over to side with Democratic appointees to write the revised-majority opinion finding constitutional, inexplicably, the same thing he had just argued was unconstitutional.

Modulating judicial ideology is no check and balance in the classical sense. Controlling judges through appointment is as adequate qua democratic accountability as electing MPs for life: there is no apprehension of retribution *ex post*. Nothing guarantees either class of official will refrain or desist from corruption in the exercise of power. Even term limits cannot guarantee that. Ideologues err. Ideological bias on a court will be experienced as miscarriage of justice by those not sharing it. However much one may sympathize with a cause, those who reject it have a right to the benefit of ground due process – a right the abuse of which appointment vetting cannot be relied upon to prevent.

The reproduction of both ideology and personnel is likelier when legal professionals play the key role in the appointment process. Elected representatives are not always in full control even in traditional processes like the American one. Evidence from proceedings for appointments to the European supranational courts shows that member states do not always have entire discretion: they may depend on the Network Community's referrals and recommendations. Appointment to the ECtHR is a case in point. The transnational legal professional networks staffing the supranational organs make the choice in fact, once the process reaches the supranational stage (or before). The number of candidates is culled to one by the lawyers on the relevant Parliamentary Assembly Standing Committee:

> A list of candidates is sent to the CoE [by a member state] . . . These are interviewed by deputies from different parliamentary groups of the CoE Parliamentary Assembly [viz. the Standing Committee on Legal Affairs and

> Human Rights] *who are jurists of renown in Europe*. They vote secretly one of the three candidates.
>
> (ECtHR judge: Interviewee 23; emphasis added)

In some political settings, appointment vetting is used by politicians to *purge* the Judiciary when their preferences or ideologies and the judges' diverge too far. The appointment power may then effect a change so massive that it becomes checks and balances with a vengeance. Fidesz in 2011 lowered the mandatory retirement age for Hungarian judges, to oust more than two hundred of them in order to unpack and repack the courts *en masse* with their own creatures (Halmai 2017). (This law was eventually watered down under Network Community pressure.) Fidesz enlarged the CC to repack it as well. Conflict erupted between the Romanian government and CC and peaked in 2012 with PM Ponta threatening to replace all the judges on the grounds of bias. Court-packing has happened since the beginning of modern government. In 1801 in early America, the Federalist Party packed the Federal courts, including the last-minute appointment of John Marshall; in 1937, President Roosevelt tried (but failed) to expand the Supreme Court from nine to fifteen so he could tip the balance of opinion with his own loyalists (Turner 1961; Caldeira 1987).

Given this history of disappointment and vengeance, it is surprising to hear members of the Network Community claim that appointment vetting is at least a potential check and balance, even as they show full awareness that it rarely works as such. Networked-in legal professionals in CEE (by inference elsewhere) were observed acknowledging that appointment vetting usually breaks down in practice, yet at the same time insisting it was one of the preferred checks and balances. According to a leading light of the Czech judiciary:

> If judges are too activist, if there is too much activism, that becomes unjust . . . The Judiciary would lose entire credibility and support from politicians, and the extreme reaction would be what happened in Hungary: they intentionally nominated justices who will be self-restraining . . . Some are saying that the way to control activist judges is to rely on exit . . . judges exit the Judiciary if they abuse their power, for instance. But what it matters more, I think, it's the entry. Entry into the Judiciary *is* the exercise of checks and balances. Of course, we should not appoint someone who is super-activist and would like to change the law by being a judge. But you can find out . . . or you cannot, it depends . . . If you appoint someone at the age of 40 you can look at his background . . . Does this mean leaving judicial activism to chance? What if their ideology changes? If you see what the judge did in the last fifteen years professionally, it would provide you

> with some hint about how he might behave . . . It is true, it is true he may end up in an activist court . . . That is why you have to send there a strong personality. For instance, there is a lot of discussion why the European Court of Justice is so activist. The ECJ has been the force behind European integration, it has always been the force behind European integration . . . There is a specificity in the ECJ, in that judges are appointed for a short period of time . . . although they can be reappointed. One reason is that national governments would like to exercise some control over those judges at the ECJ. And you can see repeated attempts by member-state governments to change the Court by sending more Eurosceptic people there. Those attempts have so far failed. I met a Slovenian judge, a current [ECJ] judge at a conference, and he told me, 'You know, I was quite Eurosceptic before I came to the Court, but the Court has changed my mind.' So yes, it is possible [for peer pressure to co-opt self-restraining judges].
>
> (SCt judge: Interviewee 6)[12]

Other networked-in elites were even more candid about the ineffectiveness of appointment vetting: 'The system in the US is so much more developed, and still they are not able to control the future good behaviour of judges, so how can you make something like this work here [in CEE]?' (CC clerk and academician: Interviewee 50). If even legal professionals in the backwater CEE know this, who in the Network Community does not? One is tempted to conclude from the foregoing that the Network are deploying appointment vetting as an 'alibi' that allows them to claim to be 'checked and balanced'; that the Community had never bothered until just recently to abolish political participation in judicial appointment vetting, unlike how it has jealously targeted 'political' checks and balances that do work, precisely because it is a paper tiger that negligibly threatens the judicial empowerment agenda.

Appointment vetting may not be negligible, but the question is whether it suffices to the end of holding the Judiciary democratically accountable. Appointment vetting is not specific to any case in which justice miscarried, and happens before the candidate has done anything to be held accountable for. It confines the elected branches to *ex ante* mechanisms outside the case, which except for (attempted) ideology purges are but stabs in the dark. Appointments matter to the general quality of justice, but qua checks and balances are blunt instruments that scarcely touch judicial errors or restrain trespasses of jurisdiction. They cannot restrain legally unjust or politically tyrannical decisions, which is what checks and balances

[12] See also Chekel (2003).

are for.[13] Moreover, regardless what democratic accountability may subsist through elected-branch participation in judicial appointments, the Network Community has been trying to get the CoE's member states to abolish it (see Chapter 6).

Ex post *checks inside the case: internal appeals*

The Network Community has been steadfast in maintaining the only acceptable *ex post* checks inside the case to be those internal to the Judiciary, or to the Network Community itself through judicial transnational networking. Internal appeals to higher courts or another judicial hierarchy are uncontroversial; however, these are not checks and balances that arise from the separation of powers.

Elite lawyers practising in the apex courts of CEE aver 'The only challenge to a final decision by the top national court can be before the European Court of Human Rights' (CC judge: Interviewee 5). Or:

> Errors of adjudication must be remedied through procedural means internal to the Judiciary and not by multiplying checks and balances [in the hands of the elected branches]. Errors can be committed by the elected branches, too. Against those errors, what checks and balances can be introduced?
>
> (CC judge: Interviewee 38)

Finally, in the words of an officer of MEDEL, one of the pan-European associations of judges most actively involved in CEE: 'Does judicial insulation undermine democracy? No. There are ways of judges being held to account through the appeal mechanisms' (MEDEL high official: Interviewee 2).

The consensus of the Network Community is that only legal professionals have a right to pass judgment on other legal professionals:

> our accountability has to be a professional accountability in the sense that we have to demonstrate that we are able to perform our job professionally and to do that we have to be officially evaluated . . . impartiality . . . [It] is a precondition to be a judge . . . and there is accountability as well, and this is disciplinary accountability, so if we have a good system of professional evaluation in place, a good system of disciplinary responsibility of judges, accountability is ensured.
>
> (Judge and EC adviser: Interviewee 40)

[13] Impeachment is sometimes claimed as a check and balance, and in theory this is so. However, impeachment is a blunt instrument that costs so much to organize as to discourage the attempt. If not so costly, it might also be misused to threaten judges' decisional independence.

The belief that only judges know how to check and balance each other reveals a tacit conviction of the Network Community that judges (and by extension itself) are morally superior in any political milieu (see Chapter 5); hence, outsiders are unworthy to wield external checks and balances to bring errant judges in line.

Ex post *checks outside the case*

The Network Community holds *ex post* checks and balances illegitimate unless they are outside the case – that is, after the case is closed and its disposition final. These measures include enacting novating laws, revisiting the Judiciary budget, amending the constitution, criticizing judges in the media, and the judges' own moral virtue. None are classical checks and balances, and some may be abused by politicians to undermine judges' decisional independence. Yet little criticism of such measures is found amongst Network members.

Passing new legislation
The Network Community admits representative democracies may pass new laws superseding court decisions, or re-enact a statute found unconstitutional by the courts as reaffirmation of their stake. In the property restitution cases in Romania:

> Parliament could have stopped the Romanian courts from restituting property . . . Parliament could have immediately reacted if they did not want judges to restitute. They could have adopted a law to the contrary but they did not . . . if Parliament does not like the judge-made public policy, they can change it.
>
> (Academician: Interviewee 49)

Re-enactment might be a 'second-opinion mechanism', providing the courts with an opportunity for 'sober second thought' (Nagel 1993: 13). It is no check and balance per se, however, because the decision in the case remains exclusively in the hands of the courts.

Controlling the Judiciary's budget
The Network Community was observed sometimes to mistake for checks and balances political interventions of the kind which easily degenerate into manipulation of judges and intimidation over future decisions. A legitimate check and balance reverses a judicial decision after the fact,

but leaves judges free to decide how they will. It confines itself to the case, not impacting the Judiciary systemically, unless in response to a systemic evil like corruption, which can taint all cases. The Judiciary budget presents the perils and temptations of just such a wrong, yet some in the Network consider it an *ex post* check:

> The Executive and Legislative power have the right to adopt norms which regulate the activity of the Judiciary, including wages. The Legislative initiative must be used every time it is necessary to put a stop to the slippage of the Judiciary. In addition, *the administering of the budget* of the Judiciary power continues to be made by the Justice Ministry which *constitutes an element of the system of check and balance*.
>
> (Minister of Justice: Interviewee 52; emphasis added)

Indeed, budget control is one of the few remaining 'checks and balances' on the Judiciary that the elected branches still have. And it is one of the few potential accountability mechanisms the Network Community still complains of:

> I took part in a conference of the Constitutional Courts and the greatest majority of all were complaining that there is a governmental mechanism through which the government *controls* the budget of the Courts and through this, one can *constrain* the institution a little bit when you find it inconvenient. This is the only argument that the Constitutional Courts were able to find to explain their incomplete independence.
>
> (Senior Presidential adviser: Interviewee 32; emphasis added)

Some politicians in CEE are now becoming aware of the negative potential of insulating the Judiciary, which may explain why they have held onto the power to control the Judiciary budget in most of their countries (see Chapter 6). According to a political adviser to Romania's President:

> If power over the budget of all the courts . . . is given to the Judiciary as well, practically no control exists over the Judiciary because one cannot intervene with judicial decisions, one cannot intervene with the budget, on the career of judges you cannot intervene because they are life-tenured, so the Judiciary would escape completely and the risk is that the Judiciary is a power that under no form is overseen.
>
> (Senior Presidential adviser: Interviewee 32)

Political control of the budget protects the people from activist overreach only very imperfectly; it leaves the defendants' disposition untouched. Equally important, budget manipulation is used to pressurize courts and compromise their independence (just as it is used in CEE to incentivize post-election 'political migration' by politicians from losing to winning parties). According to a Czech Supreme Court judge: 'Politicians use the budget to control the Judiciary; those judges or courts which comply get rewarded financially' (SCt judge: Interviewee 6). But a legitimate mechanism targets the harm judicial acts do to ordinary people. A presidential pardon addresses wrongs which the public may know something about. Budgeteering is completely opaque.

Constitutional amendment

Amongst the few *ex post* checks and balances after case closure which the Network Community regards as legitimate is constitutional amendment: 'What happens if politicians are not happy about a Constitutional Court decision? They can only change the Constitution' (ECJ judge and academician: Interviewee 53). It is the same in the supranational context: amending the ECHR is claimed to be the only legitimate check and balance on ECtHR judicial activism. According to a senior official in the European Commission:

> If the political majority considers that the line [taken by a court] is wrong, they can change that by changing the law. [In the case of the ECHR] the answer would be that one has to change the Convention. Next time they rework it, if the Brits aren't happy about voting rights for prisoners, then they specify a reservation in the text.
>
> (EC official: Interviewee 39)

The unrealistic nature of such a remedy in practical politics is something the Network Community is content to ignore. The 'next time' the forty-eight CoE member states rework the ECHR is likely to be decades or generations in the future (or never). Far likelier is that the transactions cost of revisiting the Convention and the political costs of obeying the ECtHR's whims will cause member states to abandon the ECHR.

In the meantime, the Strasbourg Court's jurisdiction is discretionary. Even networked-in elites admit this when probed:

> The European jurisdiction of the Strasbourg court is binding upon the member states . . . at the national level you can change the law, but here they cannot do it, because they cannot change the Convention, which is really an interpretation of a very vague provision.
>
> (EC official: Interviewee 39)

Even if cost-free, amending constitutions and Conventions to check and balance an apex court would festoon them with petty reservations to statements of principle which were never meant to bear the 'creative' meaning activists vest in them. The transaction cost of switching paths causes path dependency and the 'stickiness' of institutions, guaranteeing the ineffectuality of checking and balancing through organic revisions.

The media

Network Community members sometimes claim media effectually restrain judicial discretion: 'Once judges become openly more creative, more law creative . . . they do have a certain responsibility to the public . . . once the judges are all the time in the newspaper, this would have an influence on them' (Academician: Interviewee 49). The presumed restraint depends on judges' presumed concern for their reputations (or that a 'bad' reputation in the media is undesirable):

> A body elected by judges [to govern the Judiciary] would be the best place to take action [against misbehaving judges], because that reflects badly on all judges. There is no reason why they would tolerate that . . . if there is strong evidence against a judge, then there is a trial and his peers might be in his favour . . . but if you have an open society with media freedom . . . there is a limit to how much one can protect one's colleagues.
>
> (EC official: Interviewee 39)

What is assumed is that the media control reputation. Even if true, to check and balance or hold to account, the media must be impartial and not activists themselves, which, as argued in Part I, cannot be taken for granted, even where media freedom *from State control* (the control of the elected branches) is undisputed. But even in the most ideal conditions of freedom and impartiality, no media can overcome the public's sheer cluelessness or hold to account in the teeth of its apathy. According to a Czech CC judge:

> Who should control the Constitutional Court? The people . . . through the media . . . through their saying that they are satisfied with our decision making or that they are disappointed. But ordinary people take little interest in Constitutional Court decisions, do not read the Court's opinions, and do not really understand what is going on.
>
> (CC judge: Interviewee 34)

Elite legal professionals take media impartiality for granted, disregarding that they are political actors who may have an interest in 'gate-keeping' what the people know about judicial affairs. Here is one of the very few jurists in CEE to point out this reality, a former CC judge:

> The journalists will promote the interests of the mass media. [Checks and balances by the media will work] until the moment someone will appear

> who is more or less Mussolini, Hitler, or Stalin and we will be back to square one [dictatorship].
>
> (CC judge: Interviewee 29)

The Network Community also assumes media biases mutually cancel out; editorial collusion across all outlets is off their radar screen. In CEE, the media are better known for being just as corrupt as the rest of society, including the judges whom they supposedly keep in check. Neither can media freedom be presumed in CEE, as witness ownership by party bosses, and other influences.

'Self-accountability'

The Network Community frequently claims that judges are 'self-checking'. Its entrepreneurs insist that judicial review must transcend the letter of the law and take 'higher' considerations into account, 'constrained' only by the principle *ex aequo et bono* ('from the equal and good'). Judicial discretion will be checked by the judges' 'in-built responsibility':

> Constitutional Courts are more a political institution than the regular courts, because they are interpreting an act [the Constitution] which is very, very vague, so they can actually impose their own values upon this very easily . . . which makes it even more important that they should internalize the consciousness that there is a limit to this, that they are not doing it for themselves, that they have to have a certain responsibility . . . All the checks and balances that judges need is for them to be moral. It is true that if you are moral in the beginning, you might become corrupt . . . That is all true. That is the risk . . . What we miss now in CEE is for judges to realize that they are judges, that they are doing a law-creating function, that there are limits to this function, but that we cannot define the limits, so they have to 'feel' the limits.
>
> (Academician: Interviewee 49)

Or consider another networked-in legal professional high up in the judicial hierarchy in a CEE country:

> The good functioning of checks and balances depends on the honesty and competence of judges . . . a justice of quality is not achieved by multiplying the checks and balances but through the careful selection of judges who must be of very good quality . . . Of course, Constitutional Courts can abuse their power . . . This is ultimately a matter of perfecting the activity of judges and of regulation following mainly feedback from judicial doctrine [that is, the tutelage of legal academics] . . . The judge must cultivate an inner independence from drives, passions, or ideological affinities which would taint his decision . . . This is foremost a problem of character. . . . The moral

> dimension of the judge is what permits him to impose his own independence, remain impartial, and respect the principle of equity, of justice . . . only people of character can maintain their independence intact despite threats or soliciting.
>
> (CC judge: Interviewee 38)

This belief in the inherent morality of legal professionals and its efficacy as a check and balance runs against the universal truth that human nature is corruptible. As Madison (1788d) said, 'If men were angels, government would not be necessary.' It is the deficiencies of human nature that checks and balances are needed to control. The Network Community nevertheless insists that its own caution and sensitivity to political reality will weigh in on its self-restraint and constitute a sufficient check and balance:

> Judges cannot decide . . . whatever they want . . . They are restrained by political reality . . . They will restrain themselves . . . We [Czech Supreme Court judges] . . . will say the pension system in the Czech Republic is unconstitutional . . . but we will not be able to say how the law shall be drafted . . . Even if [judges] . . . were too activist, still, they know that the reality controls them . . . They have no control over budget and they cannot enforce their judgment . . . As claimed in the Federalist papers . . . the Judiciary is 'the least dangerous branch'.
>
> (SCt judge: Interviewee 6)

Political reality constrains judges only if they go to such an extreme as to provoke a reaction. Many a usurpation of the public power to make policy causes no backlash, yet is illegitimately decided by judges, pension policy being an exemplary case. Essentially none of what the Network Community recognizes as a check and balance is such in any realistic sense (i.e., *ex post*); except for impeachment, the 'nuclear option' that is Mutually Assured Destruction politically, none put judicial discretion in check or subject judicial conduct to democratic discipline (see Tables 4.2 and 4.3).

Table 4.2 External checks and balances on the Judiciary per Network Community

	Ex ante	*Ex post*
In the case	Prosecutorial discretion	n/a
Out of the case	Appointment vetting (only of apex court judges)	Impeachment Lowering wages and manipulating the budget of courts

Table 4.3 Internal checks and balances on the Judiciary per Network Community

In the case	Appeal to a higher court
Out of the case	Appointment vetting
	Disciplinary proceedings
	Formation/training of judges

Judicial independence as it is conceived in CEE is pursued not as emancipation but as empowerment of judges. All of the proceedings which the Network Community acknowledges as checks and balances and legitimate fall outside the case, whether *ex ante* or *ex post*, rendering judicial decisions not only independent but autonomous. But checks and balances working in the case *ex post* is where the action is in a robust libertarian popular system of government (i.e., a democracy). Autonomy, meaning 'self-law', is exemption from the law of another; this would seem the opposite of autocracy, which is 'rule by self [over others]'; except that when the domain of autonomy is no longer limitable by another's boundary on self's jurisdiction, then autonomy will expand to occupy the political space of autocracy. If autonomy is exemption from accountability, then it becomes autocracy when combined with supremacy of decisional output.

The Judiciary becomes a state within the state, the boss of all other political actors. In this Olympian ensconcement, the judicial Self instrumentally deploys a legal style of reasoning to craft rationales *ex post* for getting what the Self wills, as the American lawyer Herman Schwartz candidly admitted (see Chapter 3). The discredit in which the transnational legal professional networks hold classical checks and balances hints at their dream of a Judiciary that disposes not only guilt and innocence, but any issue of public import; a Judiciary that 'writes its own ticket'.

The Network Community members the author observed seemed unaware of the contradictions involved in their assumptions about the Judiciary, as separation of powers is not understood by anyone; even the learned apparently think as they do by default. But if the matter rested there, it would be hard to see how abstract ideas could have inspired such zeal to proselytize across Europe. Why not stay home and practise law? Something about these default assumptions must incite political ambition: they fit together so conveniently, forming a behavioural reinforcement feedback loop. By deliberate or inadvertent confusion of ideas, judicial autonomy, especially as self-defined jurisdiction, has been empowering a creeping autocracy, enabled, in turn, by the Network Community's solidarity behind it. The motive and commitments on which this trend rests are explored in the next chapter.

5

The assumption of intellectual-moral superiority

The sea-change reconceptualization of the classical model by the Network Community, which underlies the Judiciary Template – that is, of an unchecked and unbalanced Judiciary to have monopoly over public policy conflicts that come before it – would not be taken seriously unless the rest of society were predisposed to it by political norms which they share with (and had constructed for them by) the Network Community. One shared norm is one of the fundamental assumptions at the heart of the Network Community agenda. It is widely accepted or rarely questioned that judges are intellectually and thus also morally superior, not as a superior race but as keepers of superior norms for interpreting the law upon which many social and economic relations depend. The Network Community encompasses the shared identity of the legal professionals; by default, they assume themselves to have a share in the moral superiority.

The assumption of moral superiority exceeds that of intellectual superiority rooted in professional training. Expertise would not suffice for the Network Community to succeed. Experts perform when called upon. They may or may not be positioned to impose their preferences on the issues submitted to their arbitration, but always they are servants, not masters. Those whom the Network Community has judicially disempowered might have objected to mere expertise, but when ensconced in its own branch of government and its interpretative supremacy normalized; when judges across Europe network transnationally to harmonize their jurisprudence, bonding through a shared identity and assumptions of governance; then that is more consequential, politically, than an expert body, or even an epistemic community. It becomes a new form of government.

To the Network Community, it seems self-evident that moral superiority entitles it to power. The Judiciaries of Europe now superintend society through judicial action according to their own norms and values routinely, by default, without any representative authority specially having to call upon them to do so; and, as reconstruction is the logical sequel to superintendence, to reconstruct any society they deem reprobate. This set of ideas, at first accepted only in part but latterly wholly embraced by the democracy itself, is what forms the basis of the Network's power, and what justifies their Template.

The public now accept as normal, even expect, that the corps of judges are superior to the State, and the Network Community has further convinced them that judges own the constitution and laws, and may edit them without democratic consent if necessary. These prerogatives are spearheaded by the 'living constitution', a style of legal interpretation according to which the letter of the law is no constraint on interpretation, as it was under classical separation of powers, but a pretext the auguries of which judges are uniquely qualified to divine. Once it is understood that it makes the corps of judges master of the master-control document of the whole system of laws, the living constitution stands exposed as a hegemonic discourse *par excellence*. It is everywhere propagated by the Network, and everywhere accepted by the public (until very recently), hence the transnational Template is never vetoed at all, let alone as much as one might expect.

The assumption

The assumption of better than political motives goes to the heart of the Network Community's approach to politics. In the USA, the *fons et origo*, the ethical superiority line of reasoning is a commonplace. Keith Whittington sums up the argument of leading constitutional lawyers, such as Henry Melvin Hart, Jr., Herbert Wechsler, Alexander Bickel, Ronald Dworkin, thus:

> Principled reasoning . . . is the exclusive preserve of the courts. It is worth calling attention to three separate features of this argument. First, it assumes the Court does in fact engage in principled reasoning . . . Second, it assumes that other political actors do not engage in principled reasoning. The elected branches of government are understood to be disinterested [*sic*] in and incapable of reasoning about constitutional meaning . . . Third, it is understood

> that constitutionalism is centrally about matters of principled reasoning, morality, and justice. Constitutions are about removing some decisions of principle from the hands of political majorities who merely seek to assert their will . . . The value of judicial reasoning is that it converts questions of naked power and occurrent preferences into questions of justice.
>
> (Whittington 2000: 516–517)

Jeremy Waldron, too, notes the assumption of superiority that 'rights foundationalists' hold of judges:

> our respect for . . . democratic rights is called seriously into question when proposals are made to shift decisions about the conception and revision of basic rights from the legislature to the courtroom, from the people and their admittedly imperfect representative institutions to a handful of men and women, supposedly of wisdom, learning, virtue and high principle, who, it is thought, alone can be trusted to take seriously the great issues that they raise.
>
> (Waldron 1993: 20)

In Europe, Richard Bellamy has critiqued judicial supremacy (or 'legal constitutionalism' in his lingo) for making the untenable normative and empirical assumption that judges are morally superior to, and independent of, politics. He points out that this assumption derives from the 'idealization of US constitutional arrangements and the role of the Supreme Court' by scholars such as Rawls and Dworkin (Bellamy 2007: 10). A similar observation has been made in Canada by Morton and Knopff about the powerful influence toward the judicialization of politics and the reconstruction of society exerted since the 1960s by an activist, postmodern legal academy:

> Convinced of their own unique virtue and the corruption of all who disagree and question, postmodernism fuels the new reign of political correctness that has stifled intellectual freedom at Canadian universities for the past decade . . . Constructing one-sided and self-serving accounts of conflict is what common-law lawyers are trained to do . . . minority, multicultural, native, feminist, and gay rights advocates have deconstructed such traditional legal norms as judicial independence, judicial impartiality and the rule of law as nothing but disguises for class privilege, racism, sexism, and heterosexism . . . [It is this legal professional community who] form the shock troops of today's Court Party.
>
> (Morton and Knopff 2000: 131–132)

Like their counterparts in North America, the transnational legal professionals in the Network Community assume that they are superior in their own persons in consequential ways (viz. intellectually) to all other political actors of significance. The assumption does not stop with superiority over politicians, but spills over to the rest of society and becomes an assumption of superiority over it as well. Their political influence stems essentially from this superiority alone. It is imputed that intellect is the only 'weapon' of the Judiciary branch, and that this dependence on reason alone gives rise to the claim of a special kind of moral superiority, in that reason as such is morally superior to 'brute force' and 'naked self-interest' in political contests. On this basis, it is assumed that the whole of the Network Community, and networked-in judges in particular, are the most capable to save democracy from itself – for example, from a 'populist dictatorship'.

Legal professionals and the judicializing community supporting them, if they utter this assumption in public at all, are never heard to claim a comprehensive superiority to others, as an aristocracy might, for example.[1] It is *only* by virtue of being obliged by the separation of powers to fight political contests with no force but sheer intellect. It is that exclusive reliance and their otherwise all-round disarmedness which circumstantially thrusts them into such a position where coercion by neither the sword nor the purse is available to them as it is to other political actors.

Intellectual-moral superiority is essential to how Judiciary power is conceived by the Network Community who idealizes it as the weakest branch of government following the classic analysis of Hamilton, even whilst studiously ignoring his explicit stricture limiting judicial power to 'neither Force nor Will, but merely judgment' (Hamilton 1788b). Elite legal professionals typically try to reconcile their own views and Hamilton's, echoing him rhetorically whether in earnest or not:

> Judges are restrained by reality . . . even if they were too activist, still they know that the reality controls them . . . they have no control over budget and cannot really enforce their judgments [yet would insist that the Executive has no choice but to enforce them – ed.] . . . so it always – it has been famously proclaimed by the Federalist papers . . . the Judiciary is the least dangerous branch . . . The only 'force' of judges is reason.
>
> (SCt judge: Interviewee 6)

The assumption of superiority engenders the idealized archetype of judges as upholders of civil and human rights in opposition to crushing State

[1] It is an assumption not critically received in light of empirical or historical or contemporary experience. If asked point-blank if they are superior, most legal professionals would surely disclaim the suggestion (for public relations' sake if for no other motive), yet their reasoning, as evinced in this chapter, is often hard to fathom, absent such an assumption.

power. This archetype is a powerful yet puzzling one, as real judges are officers of the very State which is so dangerous.

Where is the source of this archetype's subversive power? One clue may be gleaned from Stone Sweet, who remarks that judges occupy the apex of an irreducibly simple social relation called a 'triad'. This is distinct from the 'dyad', which is the a-tomic kernel, Self and Other, of the social relations of cooperation and conflict. Conflict *resolution* is enabled by a third party; thus, it is *triadic* by nature (Stone Sweet 2000). People stuck in disputes 'instinctively' turn to judges for 'salvation' from relentless conflict with powerful and dangerous adversaries, rather as they turn to priests for confession and absolution from their own sins.

The judge-as-saviour archetype has persisted over vast stretches of time and space. Even today, it is apparently generally upheld: many surveys show that people trust courts more than they trust politicians (Schwartz 2000; Boulanger 2006; Voeten 2013). In the words of a Network elite jurist:

> When I was a Supreme Court judge . . . I used to hold public audiences. One day a lady came to me to talk about the behaviour of judges. She was trying to tell me that we judges must be angels in some way, and she was right.
>
> (ECtHR judge: Interviewee 23)

The same superhumanly righteous ideal is found in antiquity: the judges were the *only* permanent officials in Israel. A striking fact is that the Hebrew word *elohim* (plural 'lords') meant God – (as the monarch is styled 'We' and 'Ourself' in Magna Carta) – or it meant judges or else angels![2]

This persistence has deep evolutionary roots. Cognitive science and evolutionary psychology both find that the sense of justice is innate, whence arises a universal human need for a morally pure arbiter (Pinker 2002; Atran and Henrich 2010). Yet nature as usual is found to depend on nurture: experiments show that high trust in judges depends on what people (do not) know about the inner workings of courts – which media rarely broadcast for public consumption; in contrast to their broadcast of the messy personal details of partisan political wrangling (Baird and Gangl 2006).

The archetype is tenacious and tacitly subserves the thinking of legal elites. In CEE, those networked-in have been particularly susceptible,

[2] Judgment was enforced by the *posse comitatus* of men voluntarily assembling. In the end, the judges waxed corrupt, and the Israelites in desperation abandoned their primordial and unique libertarian theocratic constitution for the absolutism of King David (Samuel I: 8).

likely because of a psychological need to start afresh after Communism. Typical is Public Law Professor Antonie Iorgovan, a senator in Romania's first post-Revolution Constituent Assembly, who played a leading role in writing its first democratic constitution, in which he entrenched the transnational Template. He betrays his assumption that legal professionals like himself are superior to the rest of the Constituent Assembly in the following discourse:

> Among the members of Parliament [on the Constitution Drafting Committee] I was the only specialist in public law, a very necessary specialism at the time, as the Constitution was being drafted, not the Family Code. Plus, I was the only member of Parliament not elected from a party list . . . the debates of a Constituent Assembly cannot be led by a man who has no juridical logic . . . In order to come to the rescue of the members of Parliament's documentation and to create an atmosphere of a scientific seminar, not a political arena, I briefed the [Constitution Drafting] Committee at one of its first meetings with [two talks titled] 'Constitution – matters of content' and 'Separation of powers in contemporary political regimes' . . . Our [experts'] only chance was to ensure that the scientific spirit and not the allergy of political wrangling dominated the Drafting Committee.
>
> (Iorgovan 1998: 23, 46)

The Network Community's conviction of its intellectual-moral superiority is no mere point of vanity: it believes it deserves power because of it, and it has managed to convince other political actors of significance. Arguments from superiority have actually been deployed by network entrepreneurs to justify the transfer of power to legal professionals like themselves. To take but one telling detail, the legal academicians who drafted the (only proposed) Romanian constitutional revisions of 2008 enlarged the number of 'civil society' members of the JC – who are invariably legal academicians. They moved to 'forbid the nomination of Constitutional Court judges from amongst experienced politicians who have served as elected representatives in the past' in favour of experts of 'recognised professional reputation' – like themselves (Comisia Prezidenţiala de Analiză a Regimului Politic şi Constituţional din România 2009: 64).

Elite jurists in CEE look with envy upon the German Constitutional Tribunal, which they dream their own countries would emulate, as inter alia it would empower themselves. In the words of one CEE jurist:

> There are few Constitutional Courts in Europe which are professional. This is the German Tribunal which combines professionals and politicians. This is probably why so many courts around the world often cite the decisions of the German Court. Because they are very well argued . . . I researched this

> matter . . . the utilization of a Constitutional Court's jurisprudence by other Constitutional Courts . . . the other courts have no professionals, but politicians who try to 'save the situation' so to speak and issue a decision the aim of which is to get out of an impasse.
>
> (Senior Presidential adviser: Interviewee 32)

CEE judges also admire the power of Western courts and aspire to it, but act with circumspection for fear of domestic political backlash. One Czech jurist observed:

> We give Parliament limits, constitutional limits . . . we tell Parliament what [it can] do within certain limits. We . . . cannot tell them exactly what to do . . . The German Constitutional Court is very, very explicit in telling Parliament what it must do . . . and when the law should be considered to be 'the right law'.
>
> (CC judge: Interviewee 34)

Superintendent of democracy is an alluring paradigm for a legal professional on the outside looking in. Admiration and aspiration are plainly grounded on the same assumption of intellectual-moral superiority.

The local elites who had become networked-in reformulated the organic law of the Judiciary to immunize judges as if it were unthinkable that they might pervert the law or swerve from that reason which is transcendent to personal beliefs and political sympathies. A signal example was the abolition of the sole remaining check and balance on the Romanian Judiciary *ex post* under pressure from the ECtHR, whose intervention was taken for granted as following an apolitical reasoning, not its own *liberum arbitrium*:

> In 2003 the Romanian government abolished *recurs in anulare*. What explains this move? It was European Court of Human Rights which imposed the abolition of *recurs* through its decisions. The Court's decisions were based on principles and not on political influences.
>
> (Minister of Justice: Interviewee 52)

The ECtHR had been exacting abolition with frequent rulings against Romania in cases reheard by a second panel of judges at the instance of the General Prosecutor. In the words of a leading academic in charge of drafting the organic laws wherein *recurs* might have been reinstated:

> The 1995 decision of the [Romanian] Supreme Court – [that judges may not restitute private property confiscated under Communism absent an Act of Parliament regulating the rights and duties of tenants in possession versus heirs] – even if we accept that it was a correct decision, was no longer

> opportune given the ratification of the ECHR in 1994 . . . There have been discussions [recently] about the necessity of reintroducing *recurs in anulare*, but the idea was not retained in the Code of Civil Procedure because the [academic drafting] Commission, whose President I was, believed that a justice of quality cannot be achieved by multiplying checks and balances.
>
> (CC judge: Interviewee 38)

Networked-in legal professionals in CEE rarely question the ECtHR. Like all things Western, it is superior for that reason as well, and, because not openly partisan like Easterners, is supposed never to act out of political or class preferences. The fact remains that the ECtHR could easily have ruled *recurs* needed reform instead of abolition, just as in *Hirst* it did not hamfistedly quash the UK prisoner voting ban, but only ruled that it be softened. Proposals to reform *recurs* were in circulation already in Bucharest, which demonstrated the possibility (Parau 2012).

Courts, as legal professionals in CEE also follow the West in claiming, depend on reason alone whilst politicians make decisions ad hoc without system or principles:

> Courts have procedures and must decide on the basis of some legal reasons, or at least must pretend they are deciding on the basis of some legal norms; a President does not have to justify his decision at all. He just pardons.
>
> (CC clerk and academician: Interviewee 50)

Likewise the self-seeking constituents who vote in politicians who are all-too-representative are no less driven by passions and lacking in the intellectual-moral means of rising above them. (Yet when pressed on the issue, the networked-in admit paradoxically that the face of superior rationality is often a façade; that a rationalized decision is not necessarily a morally *or* intellectually superior one.)

Similar views were found again and again to be held of *all* judges, not just the ECtHR:

> it is necessary for the constitutional judge, as well as for the ordinary judge, to cultivate an interior independence towards his own drives, passions, and ideological inclinations which would taint his decisions. After all, independence is most of all an issue of character, a principle that matters as much as the person himself. The moral character of the judge enables him to impose his own independence, to remain impartial, and fair.
>
> (CC judge: Interviewee 38)

Idealization of judges suggests that legal professionals idealize themselves and their class. The corollary assumption is that 'politics' is, if not immoral, then certainly morally inferior. Judges are above politics, therefore they deserve power to command the elected branches, who have a corresponding duty to obey:

> In the State with the rule of law, the judge depends on the other branches of government, but he must also control them because the Judiciary power is less dangerous in what concerns the abuse of power; its scope does not consist in taking over political power, but in the double-checking and verification of the application and respect for the law, including by the other branches of government that pretend to have legitimacy because of being elected . . . Subordinate only to law, the judge cannot be the representative of a partisan ideology or movement.
>
> (CC judge: Interviewee 38)

If only it were true, judges would indeed be subordinate to law. But judges deliberately position themselves as superordinate who improvise the law under the pretence of interpreting a constitutional text, even when it says nothing about the issue at stake. It may be instructive to compare the ideal type with judicial reality. Important elements of the governance of the Italian Judiciary were adopted into the transnational Template because the Italian model empowers judges more than other models to govern themselves as an autonomous corps. Consider the following encapsulated history of the influence of politics in that assembly:

> It was not until the early 1960s that a gradual process began substantially to alter the traditional set-up of the Judiciary, and a number of related factors contributed to this evolution. First, the Higher Council of the Judiciary (*Consiglio superiore della magistratura*), which was formally established by the Constitution of 1948, finally began to operate in 1959. The National Association of Magistrates (*ANM*), a union-like association divided into several political factions (*correnti*) became the main player in Higher Council decisions . . . From right to left on the ideological spectrum, the most important [factions] are: *Magistratura democratica, Movimento per la giustizia, Unita per la costituzione*, and *Magistratura indipendente*.
>
> (Guarnieri and Pederzoli 2002: 54–55)

It is a state of affairs well-known in CEE, where the Italian model has been introduced:

> The Italian system . . . now when everybody is trying to introduce it . . . [it can be] foresee[n] that there will be political factions in the Judiciary, where you have the black, the blue, and the green judges and they put forward their candidates.
>
> (Academician: Interviewee 54)

A senior civil servant in DG Justice corroborates the fact that, behind the façade, judges are as partisan as the rest of society:

> the Judicial Council is almost like a trade union, because judges elect other judges. Obviously, if they organize themselves along such lines, there must be a political dimension, because trade unions have a . . . political colour to them, although it is not always obvious. But there will be clusters or groups of people, and they will of course intrigue against each other.
>
> (EC official: Interviewee 39)

The claim of 'least harmful branch', which networked-in jurists in CEE often voice, evidences a prior commitment to an ideal unswervingly held in the teeth of historical and contemporary counter-examples exposing it as unreal. This blinds them to the harm caused not only to losing parties, but to third parties foreseen and unforeseen, by judges who impose their policy preferences on the pretence of 'finding' them in the law.

The harm judges can cause has been put on display by the recent juridical history of CEE. The restitution cases precipitated an ethical debacle that gripped the nation as tenants were evicted from the homes in which they had been born. These judgments were affirmed by the Supreme Court. The Judiciary proved itself incapable of rectifying its own injustice. Likewise, the Hungarian CC struck down the Bokros austerity package in 1995 to protect certain social services favoured by the Court at the price of a runaway public debt (Sajó 1996). And in 2013, the newly supremacist Romanian CC ruled that expansions of its jurisdiction that Parliament enacts in its own discretion according to the letter of the Constitution may not be repealed.

The Eastern Europeans at least did not do more harm than their cynosure across the Atlantic. The US Supreme Court has handed down some notorious rulings, such as *Dred Scott* (1856), which held that neither slaves nor free blacks could be American citizens with standing to sue in Federal court as 'beings of an inferior order, altogether unfit to associate with the white race, either in social or political relations, and so far inferior that they had no rights which the white man was bound to respect, and that the negro might justly and lawfully be reduced to slavery for his benefit'. Another was *Plessy* (1896) that found segregation (apartheid) laws mandating the 'separate but equal' accommodation of blacks in public facilities, constitutional. In the contemporary era, the US Federal Courts have struck down legislation and even plebiscites of States of the Union on issues such as gay marriage and abortion upon which all constitutions are silent, and society, far from enjoying the consensus due for ratifying changes to a constitution, is bitterly polarized. Such rulings are enforced through contempt of court proceedings upon people without guilt except for having policy preferences the activist judges dislike; thus, the losers do in fact have reason to believe that harm has been caused to themselves and others (Bork 2003). The consequences for 'invisible' third parties are moral, too, transcending the material costs of being found in contempt.

The right of self-government is harmed when courts are ceded prerogatives to superintend the people's delegates – the more powerful branches of government, in theory – in whatever cases and at whatever level of micromanagement judges themselves choose to rationalize. Judge-made public policy overrides democracy, 'usurp[ing] a decision that should properly have been taken by the people or their representatives' (Waldron 1998: 345). It entails a loss of participation even when the quality of the output is high (Waldron 1998; Bellamy 2007). How justificatory even high quality may be (and how high it really is), is a matter for empirical inquiry and ethical cross-examination; research to date suggests that the output that is universally desired – for example, civic liberties, protection of human rights, the rule of law, rests already on solid ground in jurisdictions such as the Scandinavian countries, which have traditionally eschewed judicial supremacy (Hirschl 2013). Transplanted to Europe from America, such a system only deepens the Continent's already severe democratic deficit.

The consequence: the superintendence of democracy

The assumption of moral superiority has been a key Network justification for disseminating Judiciary supremacy since the Second World War. Rightly or wrongly, the elite transnational consensus at the minimum blames parliamentary democracy for doing nothing to prevent the pan-European (world) wars of the twentieth century, and is responsible, if anything is, for the destructive dynamism of the whole Westphalian system. The legal professional networks and their entrepreneurs actively participated in hammering out the post-war consensus in Europe. Political elites, too, were able to make themselves heard, arguing that parliamentary democracy cannot be depended on to prevent future wars. This allowed them to hold out their Judiciary norms as solutions.

This universally received interpretation of the Second World War gives way under scrutiny. It took a calamity of the dimensions of the First World

War, and then the immediately ensuing hyperinflation and Great Depression to drive the nations of Europe to desperate measures like the elections of Hitler and Mussolini (and even then, Hitler only won a third of the vote in 1933). No polity, nor branch of it, could have withstood the pressures put on Germany during the period from 1914 until 1945; just as none in CEE withstood the Communist Party. It is not denied that Hitler's only consistent opponents were the Conservatives, who in his cultural and historical context were anti-democratic monarchists. In that narrow sense, one might lend the transnational elite the benefit of the doubt and concede *arguendo* that Fascism might be classified a 'democratic' phenomenon, but this ignores once again the exogeneity of the causes that drove 'populist' politics in the inter-war period.

The Network Community even to this day ritually denounces 'populism' as rogue government. The proto-Network's preferred solution was to institute its own elite consensus dating back to before the First World War (see Chapter 2). Its entrepreneurs who drafted the new legal regime in Europe argued that the empowerment of a supranational Judiciary over the States of Europe created an essential check on untrammelled democracy. Discussing the origin of the ECHR, Andrew Moravcsik states:

> By far the most consistent public justification for the ECHR, to judge from the debates in the Council of Europe Constituent Assembly, was that it might help combat domestic threats from the totalitarian right and left, thereby stabilizing domestic democracy and preventing international aggression. (It is helpful to remember that both Hitler and Mussolini came to power, at least initially, by constitutional means.) [Pierre-Henri] Teitgen [lawyer, major figure in the French *Résistance*, Minister of Justice 1945–46], the chief French advocate of the ECHR in the Assembly, considered 'Fascism, Hitlerism, and Communism' as the major postwar threats to democracy. Governments, Teitgen argued, should seek to 'prevent – before it is too late – any new member who might be threatened by a rebirth of totalitarianism from succumbing to the influence of evil, as has already happened in conditions of general apathy. It is not enough to possess freedom; positive action must be taken to defend it . . . Would Fascism have triumphed in Italy if, after the assassination of Matteoti, this crime had been subjected to an international trial?'
>
> (Moravcsik 2000: 237)

Teitgen and colleagues have a point: it is not humanly possible to foresee and prevent nations falling on desperate times. A democratic reaction to hard times is so unpredictable that it is understandable how the whole Network Community views national political institutions with visceral mistrust. The fact remains that national courts did equally little to stop

Fascism, a fact which the Network Community scants in its discourse. The Austrian CC – the progenitor itself – crumpled when conflict flared with the Imperial bureaux, despite its powers being augmented between 1925 and 1929. After the authoritarian coup in 1933, it was dissolved and the successor 'High Federal Court' packed with partisan loyalists (Kelsen 1942; Constitutional Court of Austria 2015). If Kelsen's own handiwork could be hollowed out by ordinary domestic forces, it would have fared worse under Hitler. Yet the Network Community carries on professing the superintendence of the Judiciary over 'politics', the CC *über alles* (as it were). Typical is Hans Kelsen himself, who noticed no irony in his complaint that his invention's exclusion from meaningful decision making 'was the beginning of a political evolution which inevitably had to lead to Fascism and was responsible for the fact that the annexation of Austria by the Nazis did not encounter any resistance' (Kelsen 1942: 188). Putting aside the point that Fascist parties can pack courts just like unaccountable transnational elites, surely judicial resistance, had there been any for real, would have been steamrolled with the greatest of ease.

The Network Community has realized the vulnerability of the national Judiciary and has tried to go around the national courts to empower its superintendence of democracy. This history explains in part why many Network Community schemes have aimed at the supranational level, whilst neglecting national Judiciaries, relatively speaking. The Network went supranational first and from that superior position created a Template to be downloaded onto the national level. Budgetary limitations on lateral transnational networking may also have figured into the equation. Yet the obvious vulnerabilities of national Judiciaries could not have failed to suggest that consolidation at the supranational level and transnational collaboration and harmonization could ensconce the Network Community and its institutions in a fortified position. National Judiciaries are trusted only insofar as they have been reformed – that is, supranationally or transnationally socialized to follow the Network Community consensus.

What convinced transnational legal elites that supranational courts and international law could achieve world peace? One can hardly fail to discern the universal unconscious ego-centrism of man that assumes self-empowerment to be the natural solution. Moral superiority to politicians is taken for granted; the Network need never or rarely promote it as such. Why else do they trust themselves to superintend democracy? In the words of a former Deputy Chief Justice of the Czech CC:

> The phenomenon of judicial empowerment is quite recent. You can see it as a reaction to World War II. The individual is the sacrifice and the basic element in a State. Her or his rights must be protected. Courts are there to protect these rights.
>
> (CC judge: Interviewee 34)

'State' here implies an organ powerful enough to crush the individual, which political science calls the 'core Executive'. Parliament is a mere debating society; somewhere else, there must exist force enough to enforce the acts of Parliament, which will be capable of enforcing its own will instead. The presumption must be that this coercive organ cannot be trusted to respect individuals. But the Network Community lumps the political branches together, despite their vast differences: *neither* Parliament *nor* the core Executive can be trusted; and yet judges (by affective extension the Network Community) can be. They alone are reliable; they are more independent of 'the State' than parliaments, let alone bureaux; are more at arm's length from the core Executive than any other politically significant actors, etc.

The Template was widely disseminated to institute the assumption of moral superiority over politics, and to be the vehicle of Network superintendence. Once attributed a political neutrality others lack, the Network Community then instituted the 'appropriate' authority to solve conflict between the political branches: 'In theory there is no organ other than the Constitutional Court which can solve conflict between public authorities under conditions of independence and impartiality' (CC judge: Interviewee 38). Not only that, but 'one needs a neutral arbiter that could resolve certain divergences that can appear between the three branches of government' (CC judge: Interviewee 5). It is universally assumed in the Community that only 'we' legal professionals can be neutral. This harks back to the hopeful assumption of the dyad that the third party who completes the triad will be neutral and not self-interested in the dyadic conflict that it is resolving (Stone Sweet 2000).

To the peoples on the ground in CEE, Constitutional (and other 'apex') Courts were specifically expected to prevent backsliding after the exit from (Communist) dictatorship. Uncritically, they have received the opinion of legal professional superiority. Britain, the Nordic countries, and others have a settled tradition of democracy, a public habit or custom of it; in the East, by contrast, the Judiciary is held out as a compensatory substitute for the lack of democratic culture and robust democratic institutions. According to one high official of the Venice Commission:

> It is true that many traditional democracies do not have a Constitutional Court. There is in effect a link between the history of the country and the fact of . . . where you have a Constitutional Court. In countries [with a] . . . history of democracy, like United Kingdom, Netherlands, Scandinavia, the need for a Constitutional Court was not felt very much; while in countries having gone through dictatorship . . . first kind of dictatorship – Germany, Italy, Spain – and then dictatorship, Eastern Europe – in these countries, the need for a Constitutional Court was felt more strongly, and it is no coincidence that these are pretty much the countries having Constitutional Courts with varying powers.
>
> (Venice Commission official: Interviewee 8)

The veneration of CCs in CEE can be so extreme that some even appear to believe they can substitute for the (lack of) national morality. This attitude is then corroborated by a corresponding assumption of (intellectual-)moral superiority, encoded in how the Network Community, rooted in the West, thinks of itself in relation to Eastern Europe. Whilst having an idealized image of itself, it holds as inferior, if not clueless, the electorates and representatives of the new democracies; the solution lying in the Network's own superintendence of them. East Europeans are, for the duration, not competent yet, so the transnational legal professional elite must step into that role as if *in loco parentis*:

> In CEE . . . it was rightly felt . . . that to give to the Executive or to Parliament the highest role in the appointment of judges would lead to a very dependent Judiciary, very dependent on the Executive; to give it to Parliament would lead to excessive particization [*sic*] . . . With the old regime [in Germany] it was better to have some political influence, so the Executive [there] plays the major role in appointing judges. But to do this in Eastern Europe would be quite disastrous. There was a need to find something else, and the Judicial Council model [the Template] was considered the best.
>
> (Venice Commission official: Interviewee 8)

As noted above, national Judiciaries are vulnerable; the Network consider themselves justified in not relying on them even in the West, as some were compromised by Fascism. They mistrust national Judiciaries in the East *a fortiori* with their notorious telephone justice. In the words of the Venice Commission: 'To compare Eastern Europe with Germany after the war, there was a feeling that the Judiciary had compromised itself' (Venice Commission official: Interviewee 8). Why, then, is the Network Community so keen to empower the Judiciary and CCs in every CEE country? One reason is that the Network have been husbanding their resources to expand into 'virgin territory' like CEE to recruit and network-in national legal elites, especially apex judges, on the gamble that they will digest their consensus and their assumptions, and implement the common agenda. Those socialized into the Network's ways may be counted on to act accordingly in high judicial office. Through recruitment and training, they are recreating the CEE's national Judiciaries in their own image.

Many legal academics who became networked-in and went on to inscribe CCs in the legal instruments of the post-1989 transition, ended up being appointed CC judges themselves. Over time, as a class they lost influence over such Courts, supplanted by politicians who, although mostly legally trained, were still politicians. This is not what the Network Community prefers:

> If one looks at the [CEE] Constitutional Court from a general perspective, more and more it can be observed that the Constitutional Court judges are former politicians, ministers, and MPs . . . let's . . . have only professional judges control the constitutionality of acts, because we trust ordinary judges more than Constitutional Court judges who are political nominees.
>
> (Senior Presidential adviser: Interviewee 32)

That judges are trusted so implicitly betrays a belief that the legal professional class is indeed considered intellectually-morally superior. The Network Community therefore strongly disfavours lay members, notwithstanding its theory that CCs are a 'politico-juridical body' (CC judge: Interviewee 38).

Another reason for placing a guarded trust in national Judiciaries, if and as reformed by the Network Community, is that the Network Community's search for safety and self-empowerment in transnational solidarity and supranational institutionalization has vantaged it to nudge-along the harmonization of CC jurisprudence across the whole European space. It fortifies the spine of each nation's judges to have norms of 'universal' (elite) consent to rely on.[3]

The Venice Commission, which spearheads this harmonization, assumes that it knows what CC judges in Europe actually want. More importantly, the transnational legal professionals who make up the Commission see no problem in their own influence (see Chapter 2), whilst everybody else's influence threatens to violate judicial independence. If a judge's discussion of a case with a non-judge compatriot constitutes 'undue influence', that

[3] It is true that some CCs in CEE have followed the German CC in defying the ECJ on one point or another (Sadurski 2012). However, the phenomenon investigated here is not a characteristic of the EU regime. It is centred on the CoE, which predates the EU, and is more fundamental to Europe than German CC jurisprudence.

reasoning ought to apply to the influence of a foreign judge of the Venice Commission. (It is true that a powerful, unscrupulous enough compatriot could threaten the judge's independence, but so long as it remains in the public arena, the decision could be made in consultation with many different compatriots, whereas the transnational patrons of a judicial elite are also hidden from public view and evade public discipline.) The discourse of key actors in the transnational networks reflects an assumption that is unconsciously egocentric – or 'ethnocentric', if one suspects judges of displacing ego onto a 'judicial nation' (see Chapter 6 where the JCs are cited in the legal professional discourse as 'parliaments of magistrates').

To a thesis of a Network Community scheme to download to the national level a judicial superintendence of democracy forged at the supranational level, the national Judiciaries being the chosen vehicles of Community ambition, it is a corroborating fact that CCs in CEE have been so networked-in from the beginning, that in face of national political pressures, they have invariably turned for moral and political succour to their transnational confrères (Curtea Constitutionala a României 2012; Mahieux 2014).

Reconstructing society: the 'living constitution'

Although kudos is the medium of exchange of the elite intelligentsia, it is equally true that the Network's ambition is not to be superintendents of democracy for glory's sake. Intellectual-moral superiority entitles them to social-engineer or reconstruct society. The prerogatives they have won for the new Judiciary would have been otiose had they not believed democracy needed guidance from themselves. Integral to such an agenda must be a programme of superintendence, and then an apparatus, which is the Template. A superintendence which is accepted as normal by the society only prospectively, contingent upon performance and accountability, and subject to reopening, is no superintendence at all in the eyes of the Network Community. What is needed to ensconce the superintendence is a universal reason justifying intervention into any part of life deemed subject to legal control, giving the Network control over that control. They have found such a reason in democratic constitutions, radically reinterpreted by themselves as the 'living constitution' (aka the 'flexible document', both terms originating in America). The living constitution hermeneutic means in essence that courts can overwrite or inscribe constitutional texts with 'their own' (really, the Network Community's) agenda.

People without any legal background can grasp the *problematique* of the living constitution and its logic via a simple thought experiment. Suppose the President issued a '*Marbury*-moment' Executive Order vesting in himself power to interpret the Constitution with absolute finality, in lieu of the Constitutional/Supreme Court, on the grounds that Presidents are uniquely qualified as the only official actor elected by all of the people, hence the only one whose legitimacy suffices to protect and defend the Constitution. On what grounds would legal professionals object to this revolution? If they invoked the 'living constitution', the President could retort that that is precisely what justifies him: it is living indeed. But if they took their stand on original intent, how could they justify their own resort to the living constitution? If they denied that the document's 'flexibility' reaches their own powers, then they are exposed as privileging themselves: 'living for me but not for thee'. If they foist a 'general interpretive theory' of constitutional law, the President could rejoin, in the way of all academics, 'That's one theory.' It follows that the legal professional networks and their judicializing constituencies rely on the living constitution only insofar as it empowers themselves.

As early as early America, legal professionals did discover that a master legal document like a constitution can be invoked not just to hold persons innocent, but as the trump card in a power struggle inside the bowels of the state, over matters of state. Here is the genesis of US Supreme Court Chief Justice John Marshall's supremacy claim in *Marbury v. Madison*: hingeing on the constitutional rights of no man, but on a voted-out party's ambitious manoeuvre – in which Marshall himself was both an instigator and the chief beneficiary – to impose its partisans on the new government; in particular Marbury, who claimed a 'right' under a last-minute statute to take up a post inside a Department of State now headed by James Madison, as a hostile agent of the opposition (Goldstone 2008; Glickstein 2013). The remote consequence of *Marbury* in the contemporary epoch has been to uninhibit judicial interventionism in politics on the precept or pretext of a 'living constitution' which judges 'should read . . . as a broad statement of principle rather than as a detailed code' (Manning 2011: 1947). The 'living' conceit rationalizes discretionary judicial editing of apex instruments such as constitutions and international conventions.[4]

[4] A US example is the Supreme Court's striking-down the Line Item Veto Act of 1996, Pub.L. 104-130, 110 Stat. 1200, in *Clinton v. City of New York* 524 U.S. 417 (1998); an Act which empowered the President to veto the Federal budget line by line, and did not touch the rights,

This actually makes a dead letter of them: they can be moulded at will by a self-appointed elite in their own policy-seeking interest without a thought given to the consent of the governed (it may even be considered desirable in some quarters so long as the public understand nothing). Worded summarily and silent on most issues, constitutions and conventions opportune 'creative' interpretations that tacitly transform the rule of law not men into the rule of men not law.

In the supranational context, the ECJ has interpreted the Treaties, and the ECtHR the Convention as 'living constitutions', contributing much to the legitimacy crisis discreetly called the 'democratic deficit'. Granted, it stems from more than one governing arrangement (such as the rule that the European Commission originates all legislative proposals). The non-majoritarian ascendancy is epitomized in the ECJ doctrines of Supremacy and Direct Effect, neither of which are spelled out in the Treaty, and both of which empower the Court to proceed, in the manner of *Marbury*, to assert a limitless policy-making jurisdiction.

In every polity in the history of the West, whether civil or common-law, or under a codified or customary constitution, the jurisdiction of courts has been delegated by political authority as from principals to agents. The Template radically asserts agents' autonomy from principals in a way surpassing the independence necessary to the delegation, as will be seen below. Former Chief Justice of the Israeli Supreme Court Aharon Barak apotheosized the new dispensation in a single tenet: 'everything is justiciable' (quoted in Hirschl 2004: 196) – meaning the jurisdiction of courts (impliedly the Network Community) can be limited by no one. No longer confined to adjudicating guilt or innocence under laws made by popular consent, courts become cures for all that judges deem wrong. They do not merely superintend democracy in a reactive way but proactively intervene to remould its policy. This is why the Network insist on autonomy, not just independence.

The activist mentality is gradually creeping into Eastern Europe where the networked-in legal professionals are notably uncritical of the living constitution, as may be surmised from the behaviour and discourses of apex courts. According to an insider of the CC in the Czech Republic:

liberties, or immunities of persons in jeopardy to Federal power, but only the powers of the co-equal political branches, Congress and the President, as between themselves; and the self-interest of recipients of federal spending.

> This Court does not really care much about [the limits to] its jurisdiction . . . In the US they don't have a problem to say 'there are provisions in the Constitution which simply do not get before the Supreme Court' . . . while here, for example, when the President refused to nominate judges . . . a legal case was made before the Supreme Administrative Court . . . The judges treated the President's act as an ordinary administrative decision of an ordinary administrative body . . . Although I agree with the [decision's] substance . . . it is . . . contrary to the law that the case was decided by the Supreme Administrative Court . . . the same happened with the Chief Justice who was dismissed by President Klaus. She made a constitutional complaint that as Chief Justice she has the right to have a position at the Supreme Court, which is nonsense . . . The problem is that this [Constitutional] Court does not care much about whether they have jurisdiction or not. As long as they want to decide, they just do it.
>
> (CC clerk and academician: Interviewee 50; corroborated by Kosař 2017: 107)

And according to another leading Czech jurist, speaking in the context of the restitution cases in Romania:

> **Q:** The courts protected the rights of the original owners, but the tenants were being evicted so their rights were breached. What is to be done in a case like that?
>
> **A:** There are cases when it is legitimate for judges to apply the Constitution directly, to create law when there is a lacuna . . . when human rights are involved it is legitimate to do that . . . in the case of restitution of property in Romania, the tenants they could have tried to get a compensation for such a decision . . . A tenant can look for another flat. There is no human right to stay in one flat for the whole of your life . . . If judges decline to hear the case for lack of jurisdiction that means their right to justice is violated . . . When human rights are involved, judges cannot hesitate to create the law when there is none. The right to ownership of property is created first through the act of State. When the State will reject to give back this property . . . if courts say 'Yes, this property must be returned', that creates the right of ownership.
>
> (CC judge: Interviewee 34)

A slippery implication of limitless jurisdiction is what might be called 'vacuum jurisdiction'. If a given case is one in which the transnational legal professionals and Network Community want to intervene, jurisdiction is improvised; often predicated on interpreting the inaction of the political branches *not* as what it ought to be conclusively presumed – a determination that the classes of prospective defendants targeted by activists are not guilty – but as culpable neglect or a miscarriage of justice; that is, a *vacuum* of jurisdiction and responsibility which the Judiciary is entitled unilaterally to enter and occupy. This interpretation is deployed to justify cutting remedies from the whole cloth using the living constitution as pretext. If parliament will not legislate, courts must (at least, may) step into the vacuum and 'solve the problem'. It is then asserted that the Executive has 'no choice' but to bring its (not so harmless) will and force to bear enforcing it. Limitless jurisdiction is decoupled from legislative action or inaction; herein resides enormous power to colonize the 'virgin land' that is any vacuum of legislation or public policy. The transnational Template ensconces judges in just such a vantage point. Note how the interviewee CC judge (above) assimilates applying 'the constitution' to 'creating law', then concludes that the Court's fiat *creates* the right. It is a hallmark of judicial activism that one does not deny that the right in question was just that . . . in question, nor that improvising it prejudiced important interests, like tenants' reliance on prior acts of State. This interviewee is typical in giving no inkling of the ground due process stemming from the separation of powers (see Chapter 4), or its limits on the jurisdiction of courts.

This juridical stance is implicitly totalitarian and a classic slippery slope. In CEE many post-Communist constitutions have included (under whose influence is not certain) a litany of 'socio-economic rights' that open the door to endless judicial interventions with clear budgetary and redistributive consequences, with the taxpayer lacking representation in the lawsuit or the courtroom. If the constitutional revisions in CEE have not had this effect yet (*if* they have not), it is only because CEE countries are so poor, they have had no choice but to defy the courts, or else revise the Network revision of judicial power.

Separation of powers was invented to provide to parties to controversies, especially if unprecedented, multiple chances of being held harmless inter alia to save the harmless from eviction onto the street by unilateral fiat. It is not disputed that in the case of property restitution, the Romanian Parliament did nothing for years, or that its inaction might (or might not) be interpreted as negligence. However, given the economic state of Romania in those days, the likelihood is that the State was too poor to afford the compensation that would have been due to either the evicted tenants or the absentee heirs. Parliament, responsible for state finances, would have deliberately opted to take no action and to let the claimants to property confiscated by the Communists fifty years before wait a bit longer. Inaction is not necessarily culpable and may even be a positive benefit.

The alternative to activism is courts which respect the right of parliaments to delimit their jurisdiction by both action and inaction. When the

Romanian Parliament did get around to legislating on the issue of property restitution in the mid-1990s, it strongly favoured the tenants – in stark contrast to the lawyers' reasoning. The Act of 2001 settled the claims of the original owners, extended restitution rights to non-citizens, and allowed compensation in shares or equivalent property in kind (Dawidson 2004). Let the justice or wisdom of inaction be essentially contestable; the facts are incontestable that Parliament's inaction and the President's non-enforcement spared those who were being harmed by restitution-at-all-costs driven by a tunnel-visioned focus on 'rights'. The importance of these considerations is hardly confined to Romania: a debacle of like kind took place in the former GDR. Evicted tenants suffered as if undergoing 'forced displacement' (Blacksell and Born 2002). Transition from Communism is hardly the only social injustice that the legal doctrine of rights cannot properly remedy. Inaction did little to worsen the position of the original owners, whose harm under Communism had been incurred decades before, but avoided a far worse and very present harm to those without fault.

Yet the assumption that inaction is culpable and creates jurisdiction if the Network Community agenda calls for action was found everywhere. A legal academician-*cum*-supranational judge typically said:

> I don't see this is a danger . . . If parliament is silent someone has to act . . . In the absence of regulation . . . you can't leave things unsolved. Even if courts make a mistake, then parliament would be prompted to react. Imagine they make a terrible mistake in the absence of parliamentary regulation. I wouldn't initially be against such judicial initiative.
>
> (ECJ judge and academician: Interviewee 53)

There is claimed a judicial duty to 'fight injustice', but omitted is that this means to find persons guilty *unilaterally*, whether states or people or both.

Jurisdiction in a vacuum subtly assumes judges are uniquely qualified to cure the ills of society. This 'professionals-know-best' stance ends up entitling judges to presume legislative inaction is not liberal, when in fact inaction may be the one prudent, pro-social, principled decision for liberty that declines to criminalize conduct. Or when the political branches are divided, it is at least the best default state of affairs, analogous and morally equivalent to the presumption of innocence in law. 'Failure to act' leaves the people free to do as they think fit, whilst judicial activism rushes into the vacuum because they believe in the guilt of the accused. Such proceedings violate and override ground due process, the most fundamental of the processes that are due; investing judges with discretion to deny (to defendant member states, especially, in a supranational context) their rightful chances of being found innocent by any who stand outside the consensus of the day. In democratic politics, this is the majority faction, protection from the alleged tyranny of which has (deservedly or not) lent the Judiciary its sterling reputation. But in the international and supranational realm, the consensus is wholly an elite one.

Activism versus formalism

The Network Community assumes the judges promoting the living constitution to be morally superior to 'formalists', the label given to judges who refrain from improvising the law, because they are fulfilling the Network's morally superior agenda. Formalism, or judicial restraint, is the nemesis of activism insofar as it continues the tradition of a constitutionally limited Judiciary, whilst reminding both judges and society of how that used to work and how it was politically accountable. The contrast that a limited Judiciary sets before the public risks tarnishing the reputation of the judicializers, who conform more imperfectly than the formalists to the ideal archetype the public holds of judges as neutral arbiters. The Template is therefore designed to supersede, or better yet convert, as many self-restraining judges as may be left over from the past. Internal discord within the elite networks of legal professionals would expose their agenda to the many veto points a democratic polity offers, the dormancy of which the Network Community depends on to advance judicialization. A public revolt against activism has already happened in the USA, where public trust has been disappointed by the judicial activists' lack of disinterestedness (Paulsen 1994; Kramer 2004). Although not a case of crass self-interest such as a pecuniary stake in the outcome, when judges lack disinterestedness in momentous controversies, it means they have shed their inhibitions about partaking in the violence of factionalism as denounced by Madison (1787); who did not specifically foresee factionalism in the form of judicialization and an elite ideology of law. Judicial activism is essential to the ambitions of the Network Community, which cannot therefore give way to a contrary preference in the public for traditional jurisprudence. If in the end, the public will not give way either, then a world-historical conflict must eventually ensue.

To ensconce itself in legal supremacy, the Network Community takes pains to propagate its consensus on both ends and means; viz. judicial empowerment and judicialization via the living constitution, in order to get it socially accepted as normal. It is revision of the normative-as-causative which is the Network Community's irresistible inroad. It spares no one's feelings in the tactics it deploys to effect this leverage. Resistance is perceived as ill-intentioned; opposition to its common agenda is condemned as regressive, illiberal, possibly dangerous – in a word, illegitimate. An aspiring young judge in CEE will soon discover what he is supposed to abhor, as witness the following lines published in a reputable American law journal by a judge of the Czech Supreme Administrative Court – new and splendid and staffed by bright young things:

> Adherence to the letter of the law was discredited by the realization that the law might sometimes be grossly unjust, as happened under the Nazi era. Some influential legal scholars, such as Gustav Radbruch, even associated positivism with the horrors of the Nazi machinery. The growth in the role of the Judiciary, 'the least dangerous branch', was appreciated and viewed as an improvement in democracy, and as an illustration of the principle of separation of powers and the system of checks and balances. Textual positivism and formalism came to be considered dangerous . . . The German Supreme Court now openly acknowledge their creative function and often make and change law overtly . . . German legal argumentation is heavily oriented on legal science [developed by academics] . . . One typical feature of the post-Stalinist Judiciary was its emphasis on the written law . . . in Western Europe extreme formalism and textualism is long gone. In the Western world after World War II, formalism was gradually overcome.
>
> (Kühn 2004: 535–540)

The legal professional elites cannot of course sustain that today's formalists caused the Second World War. Indeed, it has dawned on some observers, like Chesterton and Solzhenitsyn, that tyranny can come from any quarter.[5] But the Network Community's impatience with judicial restraint is no secret judging by the predominance of discourses discouraging it (Kühn 2004, 2011b; Cápeta 2005; for a nuanced analysis of formalism in CEE see Cserne 2015). Its entrepreneurs and missionaries tirelessly strive

[5] '[W]e have almost up to the last instant trusted the newspapers as organs of public opinion. Just recently some of us have seen (not slowly, but with a start) that they are obviously nothing of the kind. They are, by the nature of the case, the hobbies of a few rich men . . . The chieftain chosen to be the friend of the people becomes the enemy of the people; the newspaper started to tell the truth now exists to prevent the truth being told' (Chesterton 1908); And, in the words of Aleksandr Solzhenitsyn: 'Gradually it was disclosed to me that the line separating good and evil passes not through states, nor between classes, nor between political parties either – but right through all human hearts . . . And who is willing to destroy a piece of his own heart?' (Solzhenitsyn 1974: 615, 168).

to remould the thinking of non-activists. Their ideology has infiltrated everywhere in CEE. According to an officer of the Czech CC:

> [Networked-in judges such as those on the Court] have very much infected the legal order with ideas like 'the material concept of the rule of law', and 'you must not be formalist', and 'you must not be positivist'. [But] . . . every judge must be formalist and positivist, otherwise you are not a lawyer, you are a politician.
>
> (CC clerk and academician: Interviewee 50)

A potent way to propagate a hegemonic discourse like the living constitution is to let oracular bodies proselytize the new norms authoritatively and ubiquitously. Network entrepreneurs are hence keen to establish supranational fora such as the Consultative Council of European Judges, whose socialization nudges national jurists toward the Network consensus so that judges across jurisdictions 'can influence each other' (CoE Steering Committee member: Interviewee 3).[6]

As well as the comparison to judges in the Westminster system who have stuck to the 'old school' and accept as legitimate the jurisdictional bounds set by the acts or inaction of Parliament, it is also instructive to contrast the views of contemporary jurists in the more easterly CEE countries, which remain once removed from Western influence. They offer a glimpse of how judges classically thought:

> **Q:** Have the courts in Moldova ever ruled that the Executive has gone too far, that it has overstepped its boundaries? And have there been cases similar to the ones in Romania, where judges sued the Finance Ministry because they did not receive bonuses?
>
> **A:** No, there have not been such cases. . . . As long as I was a Constitutional Court judge [1995–98] nobody came with such cases. And the court does not have the power to file a petition itself. The Constitutional Court in Romania has at some point tried to create for itself the power to file a petition *ex officio*. No such attempts has happened here. From the beginning, they have been rejected even at the level of private discussions. If the Court did this, it would indeed be a tendency of assuming powers that would make it a super-power, a super-arbiter . . . this would be an attempt to situate itself above the other three powers [Executive, Legislative and ordinary Judiciary].
>
> (CC judge: Interviewee 29)

[6] This Network entrepreneur does not act in a vacuum. He belongs to a community of legal professionals who think along similar lines; he can therefore be assimilated to others like himself.

Formalist judges reject any idea that they have a prerogative to improvise new norms, especially those that would upset the norms of whole nations:

> In the USA, precedent is a source of law. Here [in CEE] precedent is not a source of law, and it would have no chance. Among experts in jurisprudence, voices can be heard arguing that [especially supranational] precedent can be recognized as a source of law, of national law; especially those who have a tendency to overestimate the role of the ECtHR, which is a total aberration, because a jurisdiction complementary and auxiliary [like the ECtHR's] is only that, and it cannot change the national jurisdiction.
>
> (CC judge: Interviewee 29)

The legal traditions of CEE do resist at the ground level the judicializing ethos of the Network Community. As noted above, the post-1989 constitutions exalted judicial power in order to set the stage for judicialization, but East European society enculturates people to defer to officialdom, and regards the exaltation of the Judiciary as alien (although this may be changing under the sway of the new magistrates' training academies, about which more below in Chapter 6). When Czech President Klaus defied the CC, a majority of judges rejected the Court's conclusion that the President, a dignitary of State, could be held in contempt:

> There was a controversy in the Czech Republic where the President refused to appoint a number of judges because they were too young. The case reached the Constitutional Court. The President refused to comply with the decision of the Court. There were different opinions on this point. Some said that the President cannot be executed to comply . . . they did not have the courage to take the decision to fine [the President's office for contempt for court] . . . They said, 'No, no, we think it is not possible.'
>
> (CC judge: Interviewee 34)

Transnational legal professional networks are discontent with the whole judicial culture of CEE, not just legal pedagogy. In the words of a law professor who has been involved in training judges in CEE:

> We are centuries away from judicial activism because judges [in CEE] are not even aware of their own power . . . EU law will change this because they will learn that they have to apply something other than the text of a written law. They have to apply case law and [learn] that the judges of the lowest court are entitled to communicate with a court as important as the ECJ, so the Minister or the legislature cannot do anything about it . . . no one can control whether they ask a question and whether they receive an answer . . . That would empower the judges, but we are still far from judicial activism as a *planned policy of the courts* . . . judges today are not aware that they do have this possibility.
>
> (Academician: Interviewee 49; emphasis added)

The same elites were disappointed that the Romanian Judiciary, when confronted with an outcry, backed down from the activism of restituting property on the basis of an abstract statement of principle in the Constitution. About the reluctance of most Romanian judges to proceed without a statute or an adequate, conducive body of case law, a networked-in local legal academician had this to say:

> Romanian judges did not act with sufficient alacrity to restitute property on the basis of the Constitution and of the ECHR, being frightened by the respect they had for parliamentary law, which provided that the abuses committed under Communism will be repaired through parliamentary law. They did not realize that, from a material standpoint, legality is no longer a unique and unifying principle, a principle that is abstract and undifferentiated, but that on the contrary as having certain specificities of a substantial nature, which evolve from one moment to another. Therefore, immediately after the 1991 Constitution entered into force, according to the principle of legality judges should have directly applied Constitutional provisions (Art. 21) and given course to constitutional provisions which gave priority to international law concerning human rights (Art. 20).
>
> (CC judge: Interviewee 38)[7]

And yet, amongst CEE elite jurists like those quoted herein who have exhorted younger judges to improvise, there is little heed to the problems of directly applying the general principles of law, which is a constitutional level of legal reasoning. Frank Emmert, a professor at Indiana University School of Law in the USA, who for almost a decade was deeply involved with courts and lawyers in CEE, witnessed the struggles of ordinary judges with lacunae in domestic law:

> The notion of general principles of law – of paramount importance in rapidly evolving systems such as European Union law, for example – is causing great difficulties for many jurists in transition countries. If they are not applied . . . this may well result in unjust rulings or even a complete denial of justice. However, if they are applied the outcome may not be much more satisfying . . . these general principles are inherently less clear and less accessible than statutory provisions, first and foremost because they are precisely

[7] Art. 20 of the 1991 Romanian Constitution stated '(1) Constitutional provisions concerning the citizens' rights and liberties shall be interpreted and enforced in conformity with the Universal Declaration of Human Rights, with the covenants and other treaties Romania is a party to; (2) Where any inconsistencies exist between the covenants and treaties on fundamental human rights Romania is a party to, and internal laws, the international regulations shall take precedence.'

> not written down in authoritatively legal instruments such as parliamentary legislation . . . Here may well lie another methodological problem, widely found among judges in the East and West: Using international law as inspiration for the resolution of cases for which national law does not provide clear-cut answers would obviously not require the direct applicability, let alone direct effect, of that international law. All it would require would be persuasive and consistent arguments by the national courts.
>
> (Emmert 2002: 406–407)

The 'general principles of law' are essentially contestable abstract inferences about which there would have been endless dispute but for the pre-existing elite Network consensus. The consensus is what provides the only solutions there are to the problems of applying the general principles of law. The main problem is that they lack any democratic sanction as a basis of law, and depend for their legitimacy on the quality of output.

Editing the constitution

Constitutions, including Bills of Rights, are legitimated by democratic consensus. That is why they must be ratified by a 'qualified' or super-majority. Judges who purport to find in silent or inexplicit constitutional texts novel rights that polarize the society whose consensus is supposed to undergird their legitimacy cannot be authentically reading it. Yet the Network's counter-consensus about the role of courts in democracy implies that the thinnest elite has jurisdiction to overwrite majoritarian-consensual texts or to read into them what they will, as a founder and ex-President of the Hungarian CC candidly admitted:

> [M]any European [Constitutional] courts may deliver an abstract interpretation of the constitution, that is, an advisory opinion, which is however binding. Although there is always a concrete – and mostly delicate – political issue in the background, the courts keep the opinion in abstract terms. It sounds as a law and has the force of a law. Such opinions usually *transgress the border between interpreting and writing the Constitution.*
>
> (Sólyom 2003; emphasis added)

The 'republican principle', as Madison (1787) called it, of majority rule requires that only legitimating super-majorities have any right to alter or add to a constitution's meaning; that no one else may add or subtract meanings that have not been ratified by an equally super majority. Constitutions contain provisions for their own amendment, and those never even mention judge-made law.

The editing and nullifying of constitutions by judges has reached a new level of overreach in the lively jurisprudence of courts now striking down even constitutional amendments for 'violating the spirit' of the Constitution. Carl Schmitt is the *locus classicus* invoked in justification, who posited a distinction between the constituent power and the amending power, arguing that the very basis of government, as democracy versus monarchy, may not be altered except by the constituent power (Roznai 2014). Be that as valid as it may, in theory, in practice Schmitt is wide open to abuse by judges disallowing constitutional amendments they do not prefer, especially those that disempower themselves.

The new paradox is that the CC on the basis of Schmitt has made itself more sovereign than anything but a constituent assembly – even more than a constitutional amendment the people still ratified by a majority but without an assembly, which it claims the right to strike down. A case of this rationale (if at a lower level of enactment) occurred in Romania in 2012. The newly elected Ponta Government moved to repeal powers ceded to the CC under a certain provision of the Constitution of 2003, that the CC shall 'carry out also other duties stipulated by the organic law of the Court', by implication however Parliament chooses to enact it (Art. 146 (l)). Romania's Court already controlled the 'Rules and Customs' (*Regulamente*) of Parliament, that is, parliamentary procedure in the abstract. By the early 2010s, Romanian politicians no longer kept themselves above a norm that the CC could be made omnipotent to the point of controlling the specific proceedings of Parliament in pursuance of its Customs. The minority Boc Government, unable to keep order within its own coalition, enacted into organic law a duty of the Court to do just that – control the Standing Orders (*'Hotărâri'*) of the Chamber of Deputies, the Senate, and the plenary (Act 177/2010) – that is, a marginal jurisdiction and the creature of statute.[8] The succeeding Ponta Government, fed up with the partisan, Boc-packed CC blocking even routine Standing Orders essential to governing, such as nominations of Chamber Presidents, etc., sought to emancipate itself by Executive Decree provisionally repealing the statute, subject to Parliamentary confirmation in accordance with Constitutional

[8] *Hotărâri* decisions are quotidian instances of *Regulamente*. In theory, they may be abused – for example, an Order by the Chamber of Deputies that the President shall be impeached by a three-fifths instead of the constitutional two-thirds majority. Presidents have the powers necessary to resist such an usurpation, however, without a Constitutional Court riding herd on both President and Parliament, with all the risks of abuse entailed by *that*.

provisions (Government of Romania 2012). The CC in Decision no. 727/9 July 2012 claimed, implausibly, that the very basis of the State was being altered, and held 'the legislative Act which excludes the Court's control of Standing Orders *affects constitutional values and principles*, and is unconstitutional. Definitive and compulsory' (Constitutional Court of Romania 2012; emphasis added). The cynicism of this decision signals that Judiciary empowerment is intended to be irrevocable. It defines the rule of law as co-extensive with the Court's self-empowerment, about which it may act as judge in its own cause; by design a double-bind without redress. It also puts paid to any idea that CCs are 'above politics' (for a similar interpretation see Selejan-Guţan 2016: Chapter 5, Section I.C. iii, para. 4).

Other avenues of self-defining jurisdiction rely on nothing but hegemonic discourses. Network entrepreneurs and judicial activists, whether in earnest or as part of shrewd public relations, commonly interpret challenges to their legitimacy as so many imputations of malice. By implication, judges have a legitimate right to make public policy without democratic input merely if they do not act out of malice:

> Is it right for a judicial decision to be taken on the basis of a vague principle in the constitution? Of course, and I am more than convinced about that even without entering into discussions about the theory of the Constitution. The Constitution is a directly applicable right and any judge has the right to use the Constitution, including a principle that has not been concretized through ordinary legislation. Does this give too much discretion to judges? No, it does not because there are few cases where the Constitution has a legal provision in it which is not contained in [parliamentary] law . . . We must not believe that all judges are evil and want to cause harm and are against legal order and of a low morality.
>
> (CC judge: Interviewee 29)

A near kin of this hegemonic discourse is the one that judges may not be disciplined (or even faulted) for their usurpations merely if they have committed none of the 'malfeasance and misbehaviour' (e.g. taking bribes, etc.) which were classic grounds for impeachment. But these were defined before judicial activism was known.

This is touted especially in connection with the supranational courts. The silence of the ECHR on many contemporary controversies is claimed by networked-in elite legal professionals to entitle them to 'find' in it those rights on which the Network have reached a consensus. Did the ECtHR go too far in the *Hirst* case on prisoners' voting rights? Did it stretch the Convention's meaning beyond what the UK government could have intended at ratification? Interviews of networked-in officials – for example, this senior civil servant and former Director of Political Affairs of the CoE's General Secretariat – evince this idealization, and expose a sometimes partial and confused grasp of the stakes:

> You cannot have democracy without human rights. And you cannot imagine human rights without democracy, the Chinese model. The interaction between democracy and human rights is extremely intertwined . . . and I cannot see how basic human rights can be protected in an autocratic system. That is the interpretation of the Court. Who shall define these rights? . . . The ECHR says nothing about voting rights . . . That is the interpretation of the Convention by the European Court of Human Rights, and this is done by the lawyers, by judges . . . it is important to have a body which has sufficient authority and which is able to interpret the provisions of a Convention or a Constitution. That is why also Constitutional Courts are very important.
>
> (CoE official: Interviewee 13)

When explicitly pressed, some of those who are networked-in do admit that the jurisdiction of courts ought in theory to be limited, such as this legal adviser to the Romanian government:

> On certain issues Parliament should have the last word, especially concerning the laws regarding budgetary cuts. The Constitutional Court . . . demand[ed] all kinds of documents regarding the economic situation of the country. I don't think it is the business of the Constitutional Court to establish whether the budget is well prepared or not given that . . . those laws were adopted by the Government . . . and that the Government risks its credibility. After it negotiates with the IMF, the World Bank, and the EU a reform package, it goes to Parliament, Parliament gives its vote of confidence to the Government . . . and then the Constitutional Court comes and says 'This is not good from a constitutional standpoint' . . . this is questionable . . . the Court meddles in an area which is not its business . . . in no country a Constitutional Court has the capacity to have a macro-economic vision, to know what the economic situation of a country is . . . in certain areas, the decisions of courts are questionable, because they decide on issues that are outside their competence. Plus, the Constitution does not give the Constitutional Court the power to verify the macro-economic situation of a country.
>
> (Senior Presidential adviser: Interviewee 32)

A minority element in the Network (possibly some of those with more administrative roles) have reservations about the over-empowerment of national Judiciaries, although this is unlikely to break out into open schism. One Venice Commission official in the Commission's Secretariat expressed concern for the enumeration of rights, lest it expands the jurisdiction of CCs to a fault:

> Constitution-makers are well advised to be very careful to which extent you put certain issues, especially social rights of a potential financial nature, into the Constitution. If you do it, then the consequence that there will be a constitutional judge using this is fairly logical . . . We [the Venice Commission] have always been quite sceptical about that.
>
> (Venice Commission official: Interviewee 8)

The Venice Commission's actual stance in concrete controversies tends to reflect the stance of the activists (especially academics) within the Network: to defend CCs' claims to power no matter, it would seem, how extreme, viz. the Hungarian Court's assertion of jurisdiction over the state budget against the Hungarian government's attempts to restore Parliament's independence. The academicians who wrote the Commission's Opinion in the Hungarian case conceded little to the sustainability of the public finances or to the macroeconomic consequences of judicial intervention nor even to Hungary's international commitments to the IMF (European Commission for Democracy through Law 2011a, 2011b).[9] These apparently typical representatives of the Network Community just presume the national welfare to be coterminous with judicial empowerment, the tacit corollary being an assumption of Judiciary omni-competence. In other words, there is no part of the constitution that the Network Community will not own.

In summary, the common agenda of judicial empowerment extends beyond enforcing consensus rights as understood when constitutions were ratified by qualified majority. The living constitution has empowered the self-empowered to empower themselves all the more, to the point that the legal professional networks and judicializing community can indulge themselves in reconstructing society without society's consent. It is a classic hegemonic discourse derivative of the Network consensus, the egocentrism of which shows every sign of being as unconscious as the

[9] The Venice Commission does not always speak with one voice, as the experts selected to write its opinions come from all over Europe, and transnational consensus on newer issues is still occasionally inchoative, but it should be noted that the personnel selection may none the less be inferred to reflect the Secretariat's agenda, both originating in the same transnational legal professional networks. Ideologically non-aligned jurists may not even try to enrol in the pool of experts the Venice Commission draws on. One UK scholar who has been amongst the most critical voices against judicialization, invited to attend a Commission workshop, found that his reasoning – that rights ought to be defined democratically – was not even understood, so alien was such a view to the legal professionals at the centre of the Network Community.

geocentrism of ancient astronomy. This discourse and its assumptions persist because they 'work' for the Network Community. Very many people, including politicians, think that judges are not merely ethically superior qua self-governing professionals but intellectually-morally superior in political settings as well. That it works is a social fact which in turn undergirds the assumption that it is justified. It is possible that the legal professional elites and their transnational and supranational Network 'constituents' do quite plausibly not even suspect that they have been re-creating the very thing they believe they are guarding against, an unchecked power prone to becoming tyrannical.[10] The contrast to ordinary folk, who are no less egocentric, is that the Network Community holds the 'high ground' by default in terms of both access to means of coercion and the appearance of superior morality; therefore, unlike ordinary folk, what they do has social repercussions like almost nothing else.

[10] Some might claim that certainly the CCs are consented-to, but tyrants are not, and that is the difference. 'Consent', however, is anything but that simple. The subjects of a tyrant consent to the tyranny by acquiescing in it, on the one hand; and on the other, the consent of the peoples and politicians of CEE to the transnational Template was manifestly not informed consent.

6

The Template

The transnational Network Community, encountering the events of 1989, proceeded to catalyse the progressive consolidation of its pre-existing, still inchoate consensus about governance of, by, and for the Judiciary into an institutional design Template that could be disseminated to the whole world. It has been propagated throughout CEE with virtually no resistance from the East European peoples who were suddenly liberated but unsure how to govern themselves. They are now pursuing, thanks to the Network and their extraordinary entrepreneurialism, none of their own pre-Communist traditions, but instead the Network's Template, all of the elements of which were chosen for their aptness to maximally empower the Judiciaries of CEE with the attributes of supremacy and autonomy. It may come as no surprise, then, if the seemingly eclectic provenance of its details is belied by the discovery that both its deep history and its overarching design bear the hallmarks of inspiration from twentieth-century American judicial practice. This Template is nowhere codified in a single document, however, and had to be reconstructed from the empirical evidence, hence the present chapter.

As demonstrated in the foregoing chapters, the transnational Template was not constructed in a vacuum. The paradigmatic assumptions which the Network Community 'shares' with the rest of society explain in part why *this* Template – why did the Network Community conceive it and to what end was it constructed? Many political actors in Eastern Europe and the EU have justified Judiciary revisions as necessary to build the state capacity of Eastern Enlargement member states to implement the *acquis* and the ECHR. But while this is true enough, the evidence argues that the Network Community has been aiming at broader goals. Having established that the 'final cause' of Judiciary revisions is the superintendence and reconstruction of democracy, the author proceeds now to unpack the Template to demonstrate how admirably it suits this end.

It can be fully fathomed only in the context of an even more ambitious transnational policy agenda, of which the Template is one 'instalment'.

Its diffusion to CEE may have been, developmentally, a pivotal event, yet proportionally it is a detail in the big picture of juridical dissemination which includes international law and human rights, unexceptionable compliance with supranational and international courts, turnkey constitutions in which separation of powers is always in the Judiciary's favour, transitional justice, and the transnationally mediated rule of law – all manifesting the Network Community's overarching judicialization of politics agenda (Meyer et al. 1997; Dezalay and Garth 2002, 2011; Law and Versteeg 2011). In fact, the Network Community's agenda may be more ambitious still, as witness its interventions in the design of institutions other than the Judiciary but equally fundamental to politics. The Venice Commission, for example, is advising countries on electoral laws, media regulation, and the powers of the elected branches (Sólyom 2003; Smilov 2012).

The Template is rooted in US practice (if not high theory), insofar as judicialization in the USA inspired the paradigm of Europe's Network Community.[1] A CC is not exactly the same thing as the US Supreme Court and a JC is not exactly the same thing as the inherent powers doctrine, but the historical influence is not disputed and the generic similarity unmistakable, and a noteworthy departure from the prior European doctrine and practice of the administration of justice in both the (English) common law and civil law tradition.

Apart from the Template's historical beginnings, however, its lack of rootedness in pre-war and post-Communist European national and popular debates, and its essentiality to the public policy agenda of a solidary elite, transpires in instances where it was observed that even the slightest deviation from it by national governments incensed the Network Community and was treated to zero tolerance. Even pre-Communist designs which did feature certain judicial review functions (but without *Marbury*-style supremacism) were put off limits. The details in Russia or Romania of the Template's set-up, over and above its sheer paradigmatic prerequisiteness, could have been taken from any one of many West European models. As a matter of fact, Russia was influenced by Germany, whilst Romania copied

[1] It might be said that US Judiciary practice is very different from European in featuring decentralized review. Although true, this does not detract from a finding of US influence on a higher level of abstraction. What has been identified is a more overarching influence which has been significantly transformed by the Europeans, who have creatively adapted the American instantiation of judicial supremacy and autonomy, and the consequent judicialization of politics.

Spain, but all were variations on an American *Gestalt*. It was imposed on CEE from the top down, not socially constructed from the bottom up in the context of a national consensus to imitate the West in these particulars. After 1989, the CC did not actually diffuse in a way properly called transnational, as it had been doing in Soviet times, when Western influence was haphazard, and crossed over directly from nation to nation. Once the Network began promoting it, the Template came more and more to be 'downloaded' from *supranational* institutions via elite local norm entrepreneurs who were already initiated into the Network Community and swayed by Strasbourg. The institutional support of the CoE invested these networked-in locals with an authority over ordinary politicians that they otherwise possibly could not have wielded.

This directly implicates the Template's legitimacy. Scharpf identified two orders of legitimacy: 'input', consisting of breadth of constituent participation in political decisions *versus* 'output', consisting of the objective public benefit of such decisions (Scharpf 1999). The Template conspicuously lacks input legitimacy (Bobek and Kosař 2014). Its output legitimacy, presumed in practice, is open to question on principle. As no East European people has ever had 'ownership' of the Template, none care if it is adulterated or abolished for institutions more recognizably, more traditionally 'theirs', (cf. Bugarič and Ginsburg 2016).

The Template has evolved beyond the CC, and beyond Western Europe. As an institutional design, the CC is 'old news'; less well known is that it has been supplemented by other, equally important and equally monopolistic institutions since 1989: the Judicial Council and the Magistrates' Training Academy. The two existed before 1989 in a few European countries, but were not formalized as pan-European norms of Judiciary design until afterwards. It is remarkable too how the Template has spread across the world. In the teeth of its legitimacy issues, the whole of Eastern Europe 'bought' it.[2] The globalization of the Network Community has positioned

[2] This finding suggests a new type of legitimacy complementary to Scharpf's two: 'reputational legitimacy' stemming from the sheer prestige of the author(s) of political decisions. In a kindred but distinct context, this echoes Walter Bagehot's 'dignified' *and* 'efficient' parts of the English constitution. The efficient part is the Prime Minster and House of Commons who take decisions, whilst the Monarchy is the dignified part, in whom alone most people in Bagehot's day invested any trust or respect (Bagehot [1867] 1963); a remarkable, earlier 'democratic deficit' that bears deeper investigation. Parliaments and other political actors who have lost or never had any reputational legitimacy may find both their input and output legitimacy challenged or subjected to exacting scrutiny. What is called 'representative democracy' nowadays

its entrepreneurs to put the Template on the political agenda of regions far beyond its origin. This surely explains in part why by 2009 over 60 per cent of the countries in the world had adopted some form of JC (Garoupa and Ginsburg 2009).

The political-historical origin of Constitutional Courts

The Constitutional Court originated in the early twentieth century, but gained momentum in Europe only after the Second World War. It was first introduced in Austria, then Germany, France and Italy, spreading to Spain and Portugal, and later throughout CEE, buoyed by a paradigm that, rightly or wrongly, taxed parliamentary democracy for the horrors of that war. It is rationalized as an essential check on 'untrammelled' democracy.

By 1911, the Supreme Courts of Norway and Greece were already imitating the US Supreme Court. Karin Bruzelius, former Justice of the Supreme Court of Norway, notes that in Norway 'courts were among the first in the world to practice judicial review (without any support in the constitution); starting as early as in the middle of the nineteenth century – inspired by the US Supreme Court' (Bruzelius 2014). It was likewise even in a country as marginal as Romania. The Romanian Constitution of 1866 had vested no powers of constitutional control in the Supreme Court; nevertheless, the Court struck down a parliamentary statute – also in 1911 (Parau 2013c). The judges were asserting no general constitutional jurisdiction as supposed by *Marbury*, merely disapplying inside their own courtroom an Act of Parliament they deemed unconstitutional. It was none

was by ancient Greek philosophy deemed 'oligarchy' (Aristotle, *Politics*) – and not without reason considering that the social class whence today's MPs, too, are drawn excludes 'the many' (especially the poor). Moreover, the quality of output of the most illustrious representative bodies is plainly uneven. To take one example, Parliament would not even consider the Reform Bill of 1832 until sentiment had boiled over and people were on the verge of revolt (Brock 1973). As the recent history of the royal family shows, reputational legitimacy lasts only so long as the spell is not broken. Ginsburg and others have noted how this has befallen the Judiciary as well (Garoupa and Ginsburg 2016); though this is undoubtedly true, one must not be distracted too much by reputational legitimacy (alone) as the reason for judicial power. The public have a self-interest in the benefit of a second (and with jury nullification, a third) opinion of their innocence, once the Legislative and Executive branches have joined in finding them guilty. Judicial power is functionally useful in itself, with or without policy-making power.

the less a radical departure from the civil law mould. Their audacity was the by-product of transnational networking, even that long ago: the plaintiff's attorney in the case, a Romanian graduate of the Law Faculty in Paris, had hired French jurisconsults, one of whom was Henri Berthélemy, an administrative law specialist and future Dean of the Law Faculty. His memorandum, disseminated via *Revista de Drept Public* ['Review of Public Law'], Romania's premier publication for academics and practitioners in the field, vindicated the Romanian Supreme Court (Conac 2000). Some legal analysts have opined that Berthélemy's reasoning 'manifestly echoed the arguments of Judge Marshall in *Marbury v. Madison* of 1803' (Conac 2000: 13).

Contemporary US jurists also noted the European trend. American scholars writing in the first decade of the 1900s noted that French elites, including lawyer-politicians, were advocating the American model of judicial review:

> it is argued that . . . the habits and the temperament of the French people are so different from those of the United States that the argument from American experience cannot be regarded as decisive. But there have always been able and distinguished advocates in France of the American doctrine and the number has steadily increased in recent years. In the national assembly which framed the present constitution [of 1875], Louis Blanc [Socialist politician and historian], speaking on the subject in the session of March 11, 1873, said, 'I say finally that in order to hold in check the despotism of a single assembly the better means would be that which would result from giving to the Judiciary the right to annul unconstitutional laws.' In the same assembly M. Naquet [left-wing politician and professor of chemistry] advocated the creation of a supreme court on the American model with similar powers in respect to unconstitutional legislation, and in 1894, while a member of parliament, he proposed an amendment to the constitution with this object in view. The question has in recent years provoked widespread discussion and the American doctrine has been defended by many jurists.
>
> (Garner 1915: 660, 661, 662)

Berthélemy was able to act with a free hand in Romania; in France, he would have been hemmed in by settled custom and a constitutional prohibition on judicial nullification of statutory law. Berthélemy's worldview and the Romanian Supreme Court's self-empowerment chimed with some of Romania's leading academic theorists, who were predisposed to accept judicial review and who seconded Berthélemy. They were known to have been following developments in the US (Conac 2000).

The year 1911 was one of serendipity.[3] The fact that the Supreme Courts of Norway, Greece, and Romania all converged as if by chance on the US lead brings up the question of transnational diffusion, either spontaneous or coordinated informally. It was evidently in play before Kelsen had begun to design his Court. Whether coordination or coincidence, it was a bellwether of the strength of American influence.

The original intent and its transmogrification

The CC's original main function was to nullify administrative even more than legislative acts. The risk was an Executive so empowered that it 'ran away with' the act of parliament in the midst of enforcing it (as by 'filling in the blanks' as suits its own institutional self-interests). Kelsen's motive was to defend the people from the Austrian administrative elite, who at the time were not accountable:

> The Austrian Constitution of 1920–30 provided for guarantees to assure the constitutionality not only of statutes but also of ordinances. The latter were general legal rules enacted by administrative organs and not by a parliament, that is by a legislative organ . . . the judicial review of ordinances is even more important than that of statutes, for the danger that administrative organs will exceed the limits of their power of creating general legal rules is much greater than the danger of an unconstitutional statute . . . the power of issuing these ordinances was of the greatest political importance. By a misuse of this power the administration could easily suppress the parliament and thus eliminate the democratic basis of the State.
>
> (Kelsen 1942: 183, 184, 188)

Kelsen intended to protect popular representation by controlling above all the *un*-democratic, potentially rogue element in the Austrian state, a legacy Imperial bureaucracy and, not coincidentally, a homologue of today's Judiciary – an autonomous, supremacist administrative apparatus that presumed to legislate from the bureau as from the bench (cf. Vinx 2007). The greater danger was the tyranny of an elite minority, not of the majority, which may be why he conceived his Court as a 'third chamber' of Parliament to vindicate its prerogatives with finality:

[3] 1911 was also the year in which the British House of Lords was disempowered to veto a bill of the Commons. Whether there is any causal connection between these seemingly disparate events, or not, is a question that merits further inquiry.

> The decision of the Constitutional Court by which a statute was annulled had the same character as a statute which abrogated another statute. It was a negative act of legislation. Since the Constitution conferred upon the Constitutional Court a legislative function, i.e. a function which, in principle, was reserved to Parliament, the Austrian Constitution of 1920 [drafted by himself], provided that the members of the Constitutional Court had to be elected by the Parliament and not like the other judges, to be appointed by the administration.
>
> (Kelsen 1942: 187)

The trauma of war, America's victory, and its occupation of Germany and role in rebuilding Europe impressed much more strongly on the minds of European elites the transatlantic influence. The kind of constitutional control introduced into Europe after the Second World War on the back of Kelsen's formal design was, however, less Kelsenian than supremacist – and moreover, a self-defining jurisdiction that races far ahead of the glacial expansion of common law writ in the English tradition through spill-over. This new, society-reconstructing kind of judicial review that is ambitious to affect what lies beyond the courtroom sprang up in the US only after the Civil War, based not on *Marbury* but on an exotic reading of the 14th Amendment to the US Constitution. The consequent body of jurisprudence overwrote the original intent of the 1787 Convention, substituting a purported power unilaterally to find the States of the Union and the people guilty of the Amendment without any specific prohibition having been enacted as per Section 5 of the Amendment itself. This self-empowering arrogation, a minority opinion hotly contested before the Civil War, was reinforced by Big Business pressure on the Federal Judiciary to shield it from popular local regulation, using the 14th to bypass Congressional or Presidential concurrence in condemning the offending States (Gillman 2002) (see *Lochner v. New York* 198 U.S. 45 [1905]). The dearth of popular alarm in the post-Civil War Reconstruction Era gradually inured all to a universal but misconceived acquiescence, and the Court's impunity emboldened it to assert supremacy over the rest of the Constitution, a stance which it consolidated in the twentieth century. The myth of *Marbury*, previously a historical footnote, was invented in retrospect as a pretext (Fallon 2003; Levinson 2003), which may explain why it did not enter without any specific prohibition into elite discourse generally before 1945, even though they had begun imitating American *practice* decades previously. In any event, European CCs would be progressively tweaked until they constituted a pervasive distortion of the US Supreme Court's role in the classical system of checks and balances.

CCs have expressly been made supreme over all other political actors in being given mastery over the master political document. Those with a legal professional majority, especially, are at least latently supremacist.[4] This supreme power is taken away from representative government and from the people who are represented, who would otherwise share in constitutional interpretation. This mighty shift is well on its way to becoming a globally accepted norm, a development which Eastern European elite jurists follow with interest:

> Most democracies are setting up Constitutional Courts. Recently [*ca.* 2010] . . . at the Royal Court of Justice in Britain . . . [there was] a debate regarding the establishing of a Constitutional Court so that ordinary judges no longer determine constitutional norms. The trend is very strong towards creating Constitutional Courts and supranational courts as well.
>
> (Senior Presidential adviser: Interviewee 32)

The supremacy of the Constitutional Court is proudly affirmed by CC judges, who in CEE are candid enough to concede (at least obliquely) that, logically, these courts suspend and effectively abolish popular sovereignty:

[4] The contention that the CC as it has evolved is not Judiciary but somehow still Legislative is highly vulnerable to refutation. The feature commonly cited in evidence is the appointment of its personnel by the political branches (Kelsen's original view). It is an unreliable differentiator from a comparative politics standpoint (the US Supreme Court is appointed by politicians, and is not the only polity where this is so). Kelsen betrays a commitment to the 'pure doctrine' of separation of powers (Vile 1998) and a want of appreciation of the Madisonian 'mixing' of the powers of the several branches. Other comparative considerations are also telling. The Constitutional *Court* is not called a 'court' for nothing; it follows judicial procedures to resolve cases between delimited adversarial parties, distinct from the open-ended, all-sided, patiently deliberative procedure of parliaments. The Network Community, too, has been quietly phasing out Kelsen's strict qualifications and phasing in almost a contrarian version of his prototype; nudging it toward judicial supremacy, for example, by excluding from CC membership anyone (e.g. elder statesmen) who is not also a legal professional. It is conceded that the elite academic jurists in CEE who had a decisive hand in drafting their respective organic laws of the CC stood it apart from the Judiciary power, as if to forestall a political contest over separation of powers. Then their discourses could tout the CC as an extraordinary power above all others, even (especially) when staffed exclusively by legal professionals. And this has been carried to the point where even legal professionals can find the contradictory claims puzzling: 'In some countries, the CC is a component part of the Judiciary power. In other countries, the CC is not part of the Judiciary branch, but something separate which has nothing do to with any power in the State. This is bizarre. If we admit that there are three powers in the State, then the CC belongs to which of them?' (ECtHR judge: Interviewee 23). The most that can be conceded to the *sui-generists* is that, insofar as legal professionals hold only a minority of seats, in the manner of the original French *Conseil d'État*, then arguably such a court or council should not count as judicial.

> **Q:** Is it true that the CC is inherently anti-democratic because it is an elite institution with monopoly over the meaning of the founding document of a polity, and that this is incompatible with popular sovereignty?
>
> **A:** The logical conclusion of such a thesis must be that the Constitutional Court should not exist.
>
> (CC judge: Interviewee 34)

A constitution with an instrumental separation of powers to the end of mutual checks and balances would entail the abolition of CCs, a truth that Kelsen himself admitted (Kelsen 1942). Even if one believed CCs should exist, this is the issue that must be faced. It will never go away so long as the democratic deficit can still be criticized. Of course CCs did not create the democratic deficit, but they contribute to devolving it, even when they sometimes uphold the 'popular' cause (as legal elites understand it).

Constitutional Courts in the East: from 'pre-history' to the contemporary scene

Before 1989 CC-like organs had been set up in Communist Yugoslavia and in the Soviet Union. Designed to avoid challenging Communist Party supremacy, a Constitutional Oversight Committee was championed by Gorbachev himself, a law school graduate who 'introduced not only perestroika but the beginning of a law-governed system' (Schwartz 2002: 113). The Gorbachev-led reformist faction and other 'educated elites' were in turn influenced by German constitutional scholarship and collaborated with their German peers to design it (Thorson 2012). That the selfsame Network that would promote judicial empowerment after Communism were already swaying Russia by the mid-1980s (Parau 2013a), and Yugoslavia as far back as the 1960s, is the simplest inference.

These early CCs behind the Iron Curtain were socializing legal professionals throughout the Soviet sphere into this particular institution long before Communism fell,[5] who then could act as a primer for the setting up of similar institutions in the former Yugoslav nations and Soviet Republics after the fall:

[5] This does not mean that the fall of Communism was planned by the Network Community, or by any other Western network; although it does hint that the Network foresaw its eventuality.

> Where did the idea of the CC come from in Moldova? It was an idea that was flying in the air in the entire world, in the whole of Europe. Even in the Soviet Union the Constitutional Committee was created in the 1980s, the first one, and each [Soviet] Republic designated to it one or two persons. From Moldova, the representative of the Soviet Republic of Moldova to the Constitutional Committee was Andrei Smochina, Professor at Universitatea Liberă Internaţională din Moldova [The Free International University of Moldova] and Chief of Department at the Institute for History, the State, and Law.
>
> (CC judge: Interviewee 29)

Ideas do not fly through the air unassisted; somebody or something makes them fly. In this case, German constitutionalists alongside domestic entrepreneurship were involved in originating the Oversight Committee. The contribution of Soviet Republics like Moldova in diffusing it kindled awareness of transnational precepts and what was in effect transnational constitutional practice. The Soviet Union was a federation of nations; what was learnt within its federal structures could trickle down to the independent states that succeeded the Republics. Today, only Turkmenistan of all the member states of the Commonwealth of Independent States (CIS), nominal successor of the Soviet Union, lacks a CC. It is a fixture of the CIS as well as the Eastern Enlargement – thus, right across the East as far as the eye can see; and now even in the whole of Europe, given its contemporaneous infiltration into the practices if not formalities of Western Judiciaries too. To take two examples, France's *Conseil constitutionnel* in the 1970s imposed constitutional review by fiat on a polity that expressly rejected such a practice when the Fifth Republic was founded (Stone Sweet 2000). And in the UK, the Supreme Court was set up to abolish the millennium-old sovereignty of the King in Parliament, by setting up a power independent of it, and contrary to the precepts and indeed the whole genius of Britain's customary constitution. The Network members have wasted no time in asserting the Court's supremacy jurisdiction, again by fiat, to subject parliamentary proceedings to their dispositive review, the Government obeying implicitly as if robotized (see also below in 'Conclusions').

The Network's key success – the 'Big Bang' that embodied their energy into material form – was the 1989 Revolution in CEE and its aftermath, when the formative influence of their norms on the constitution drafters tipped the balance of political forces decisively in favour of the Template, forged by and for the occasion. It was efficiently disseminated across CEE under transnational entrepreneurial influence, once they enlisted a critical contingent of local CEE initiates in the cause. After this momentous watershed, the *dénouement* has consisted largely of fine-tuning the details of the Template to maximally empower the Judiciary branch.

Immediately after 1989, the Network entrepreneurs did not enjoy the default support of more than a minority of local elites, usually only law school academics, who were amongst the first in CEE to be networked-in. Professor Herman Schwartz's classic on Eastern European CCs notes a pre-existing Western influence on Eastern academicians, many of whom had travelled and studied abroad during Communist times: Lech Garliki of Poland, László Sólyom and Gabor Halmai of Hungary, Evgeny Tanchev of Bulgaria, Petr Kresak of Slovakia, and Vojtek Cepl of the Czech Republic all studied in Germany, the United States, or Great Britain. They all played a major role in post-1989 developments, in some cases serving as CC judges, like Garliki, Sólyom, and Cepl (Schwartz 2000).

In the farther reaches of CEE, such as Romania, adoption of CCs was a process obliged to start from scratch by initiating into the *cultus* the academic experts to whom the task of drafting the first post-Communist constitutions was delegated, and who had been amongst the first to go West after 1989. There they met key norm entrepreneurs whose tutelage they were eager to accept: Antonio La Pergola, Italian CC judge, founder of the Venice Commission (also in 1989, not perhaps coincidentally) and its President until 2007; and Robert Badinter, President of the Constitutional Council in France and an enthusiastic member of the Venice Commission. That Commission was at this early date a CoE consultative body, though not yet incorporated into its formal structure.

The Romanian academicians, when they returned, distilled the West's advice in a document of twenty-six pages intended to 'serve as bibliographical material' to the (non-academic) others on the Drafting Committee (Iorgovan 1998: 112). The judicial governance paradigm of a still inchoate Template was deemed so authoritative that they devoted five pages of that report to it – even describing their personal voyage of discovery to the West. The pivotal precept laid down by La Pergola, according to the academician who chaired the Drafting Committee, was this:

> I don't believe that democracy in your country, which you are framing in the new Constitution, can be qualified as complete democracy unless you have a Constitutional Court . . . It is a symbol, is the key which opens the door to Europe's sympathy.
>
> (Iorgovan 1998: 112)

These academicians have cherished and nursed their transnational odyssey ever since, and the elite contacts made on the voyage, which initiated them into the Network Community:

> Romania's road towards the Council of Europe passed through the Constitutional Committee . . . The contacts that we established then, and without exaggeration the friendships which we established were of great help in the battle which we led at the time of convincing the Council of Europe that we are capable of adopting a democratic Constitution, and that Romania is heading towards a state with the rule of law . . . In Italy the discussions with Antonio La Pergola, on the 1st October 1990 remain the peak of our visit, being then that we established the fundamental strategic directions of the constitutional edifice in order to make it agreeable to the Council of Europe. Professor La Pergola, who had been the Justice Minister of Italy and the President of the Constitutional Court, was at that time the President of the Venice Commission . . . he remains the foreign personality who had the most important contribution . . . to the strengthening in Europe the prestige of the Romanian Constitutional Court later on.
>
> (Iorgovan 1998: 67)

These initiates became the Network's chief local entrepreneurial recruits. Back home they acted to download the first element of the Template into the 1991 Romanian Constitution. Here is one professor of constitutional law who advocated constitutional entrenchment of a CC. His testimony is crystal clear: he and his fellow academicians had a very different idea from the rest of the Constituent Assembly (even non-academic jurists):

> In our country, in the debates in the Constituent Assembly, it was hard to convince even the lawyers that we needed a distinct authority of this sort. They said, 'In 1923, the High Court of Cassation and Justice, which is similar to the Supreme Court today, was responsible for this [constitutional review], so let's go back to the way things used to be.' Then *we* [the networked-in academicians] explained that, in Western Europe, things were no longer the way they were in 1923. The present Constitutional Court was [thus] created.
>
> (Ion Muraru, Constitutional Court President, interviewed by Mungiu-Pipidi 1997: 78; emphasis added)

Step by step, CCs throughout CEE have taken where they were not given powers that set them up as influential yet unelected politicians. The Romanian CC had been given power *by statute* to review Parliament's internal proceedings. When a new government moved to repeal the statute, the Court found the repeal 'unconstitutional', effectively annihilating Parliament's independence and sovereignty. Several CEE CCs have moved to control the most essentially parliamentary prerogative of all, control of the budget, overwriting political discretion and fiscal prudence concerning funding the welfare state (Sajó 1996; Sadurski 2006). What the Network have succeeded in entrenching in CEE stands in thought-provoking contrast to Hans Kelsen's original vision.

Most CCs in CEE were vested with comprehensive constitutional-control jurisdiction *ab initio*. Romania and Poland were the holdouts, briefly retaining vestigial or legacy checks and balances external to the Judiciary qua Parliament's prerogative to reverse CC decisions by supermajority. This was abolished in both countries in 2003 and 1997, respectively, a move clearly in line with Network consensus, as witness the Venice Commission's approbation:

> It must be underlined that the possibility of Parliament to change, even with a qualified majority, a decision of the Constitutional Court, is an outlier in the field of comparative law and risks to tarnish the prestige of the Constitutional Court itself. Abolishing [that prerogative] . . . is therefore desirable.
>
> (Batliner et al. 2002: 4)[6]

In the case of Romania, the jurisdiction of the CC was concomitantly expanded beyond human rights to the policing of the other branches of government (Constitution of Romania, Art. 146e), a salient feature of the Template now, as observed by the Venice Commission itself: 'The Constitution will often confer to the constitutional court the power to deliver its opinion on issues concerning the separation of powers or the relationships between the organs of the State' (European Commission for Democracy through Law 1997: 30). By 1997, the trend had clearly become taken for granted in Europe as more usual than not. Contrast this with Romania's first post-Communist constitutions, and the emergent picture is one of creeping consolidation of CC power in accord with the Template: 'In 1991 nobody raised the issue of the Constitutional Court solving conflicts of a constitutional nature between public authorities. [By contrast], in 2003 no other possibility of arbitration was discussed' (CC judge: Interviewee 38).

[6] Art. 145.1 of the 2003 Romanian Constitution stated: 'In cases of unconstitutionality . . . the law or orders shall be returned [to Parliament] for reconsideration. If the law is passed again in the same formulation by a majority of at least two thirds of the members of each Chamber, the objection of unconstitutionality shall be removed, and promulgation thereof shall be binding.'

During all this time up till now, the mass of elected politicians has seemed almost hypnotically submissive to the hegemonic norms of the Network Community: ordinary MPs, especially those who are *not* lawyers, buy into the discourse even as it disempowers them. Commenting on Ponta's 2013 retreat from what seems a perfectly logical position, one non-lawyer MP lamented:

> This Executive Decree . . . represents a black spot on the government's activity. Why? It took away the power of the Constitutional Court to censure Parliament. The Court decided against it and now, a year later, we have to revisit and revise what we did wrong . . . I hope we will all learn . . . that there are limits to Parliament's legislative competence and that a State with the rule of law must be complied with obligatorily . . . .
>
> (Tinel 2013)

The impression of an elite transnational will to power is reinforced by the latest supranational trend: the exclusion of non-lawyers from the CC and judges' selection by an authority controlled only by legal professionals. It is on its way to becoming the norm for the Network Community, and implies the Community intends to make legal professionals the supreme actors in politics, if only in wielding an indefeasible veto. When in 2008 the General Secretariat of the CoE appointed, out of the legal professional networks, a transnational expert group to draft pan-European norms on Judiciary independence, the group recommended abolition of all elected-branch involvement in appointing CCs, by inserting a subtle but pivotal emendation to the original 1994 Recommendation on Judicial Independence, to extend its scope: 'This recommendation is applicable to all persons exercising judicial functions, including those dealing with constitutional matters' (Bureau of the European Committee on Legal Co-operation 2008: 7).[7]

The 2008 revision featured an additional and celebrated (within the Network) recommendation that CoE member states should set up an authority independent of the political branches – a 'High Council of the Judiciary' – to govern all or nearly all Judiciary affairs, including but not limited to CC appointments:

> Where, in this Recommendation, reference is made to an independent authority it is highly desirable, that it should be a single authority . . . The authority taking the decision on the selection and career of judges should be

[7] Incidentally, this inclusion entails a tacit acknowledgement by the Network Community that Constitutional Courts are Judiciary institutions after all.

> independent of the executive and legislative powers. With a view to guaranteeing its independence and its impartiality, the authority should have at least half its number made up of judges elected by their peers according to methods which guarantee their widest representation.
>
> (Bureau of the European Committee on Legal Co-operation 2008: 7)

The significance of this move did not escape the Ministries of Justice of certain member states, in particular Germany and Norway, who insisted on revisiting the 2008 version. *Even then*, the widening of scope to CCs was not retrenched; it was merely narrowed slightly to concede to member states the option of retaining their traditional arrangements in lieu of the Judiciary Council design. That was the version adopted by the member states in 2010:

> The Committee of Ministers, under the terms of Article 15.b of the Statute of the Council of Europe . . . *Wishing to learn from the diverse experiences in member states with regard to the organisation of judicial institutions* in accordance with the rule of law. *Having regard to the diversity of legal systems*, constitutional positions and approaches to the separation of powers . . . Noting that the constitutions or legal systems of some member states have established a council, to be referred to in this recommendation as a 'council for the Judiciary' . . . Recommends that governments of member states take measures to ensure that the provisions contained in the appendix to the present recommendation, which replaces the above-mentioned Recommendation Rec(94)12, are applied in their legislation, policies and practices and that judges are enabled to perform their functions in accordance with these provisions.
>
> (Council of Europe 2010a; emphasis added for irony's sake)

An 'independent authority' for judicial appointments that is independent of everyone but legal professionals and their peers will surely favour legal professionals for appointment. It follows that the aim was to exclude anyone else from appointment to CCs, and the Template must be understood as a revision of such Courts as exclusively legal professional organs.

This evolution has brought the CC 'half circle' to a position opposite Kelsen's original vision of a 'tie-breaking' institution wielded by the elected to solve intractable conflicts over constitutional meaning with the unelected. It now stands transmogrified into a vehicle for the self-empowering agenda of one class of the unelected. The Network Community's ambition as it has emerged from the evidence is one of an illimitable expansion of the power to settle all significant political conflicts yet, simultaneously, of its concentrated narrowing in the same few hands. It results from a process of elite self-empowerment indistinguishable in its practical consequences from the dominion over democracy by the unelected, which Hans Kelsen had tried to check by inventing the CC in the first place.

The drive for supremacy is augmented by a trend toward rendering the Judiciary autonomous through the CC-supplementary organs of the Template, which insulate it from the only effective mechanisms of democratic accountability. The 'new Template' is no kludge of sundries, but an elaboration of the common agenda that transformed CCs into engines of judicialization. All of the institutions fit together in a synergetic unity, and all are some of the best preconditions of the judicialization of politics.

Self-governance and self-perpetuation: the Judicial Council and the Magistrates' Training Academy

The Network Community has acted to radically revise the power relations of the Judiciary with democratically elected officials. In CEE, this has also been done through two other organs additional to the CC, which have become definitive aspects of the Template: firstly, the JC, a body ideally, per the Network, to be composed of 'magistrates' only (judges and prosecutors) with an open-ended mandate to govern judicial affairs from appointments to promotions to discipline autonomously, and secondly, an MTA to gatekeep the intake and shape the thinking of candidates for the magistracy.

The origins and diffusion of the Judicial Council

The raw material of the JC, like that of the CC, originated in the USA most probably. This would, if true, corroborate this monograph's conclusion that the trend toward judicial empowerment and judicialization of politics in Europe is one facet of American-driven globalization. At a minimum, the similarity of JC doctrine to institutions that have long existed in the USA is not lost on the Network entrepreneurs who worked on Judiciary revision in CEE:

> [We found that the judges in Eastern Europe are very different from what we were used to; they lack the 'inherent powers' of the US Judiciary.] The problem that we kept running into is that the courts are run by the Ministry of Justice, and this seems to paralyse them . . . [but] that has changed . . . they [have] adopted a new system . . . some of the US model for the administration

> of the courts, something called the Council of Judges [*sc*. JC] that operates like the Judicial Conference in the US.
>
> (ABA officer: Interviewee 31)[8]

Once the generic concept of inherent powers was absorbed from America, the European-style JC first evolved in and has come to be associated with France and, especially, Italy, which were the first nations to resonate to that influence – whether it was by serendipity or by political or cultural affinity or occupation in the Second World War or for some other reasons. From there it has been networked over into CEE with premeditation. Here is how an elite Croatian lawyer-politician learned of it:

> I became acquainted with the Italian model for the first time when we were discussing the setting up of the Judicial Council [*ca*. 1998], but this was not my idea. It was the opinion of the entire circle of people who were preparing the law, and participating in the passing of various laws . . . These were mostly professors from law schools, but also from political science. [The] politicians [who participated] were only those who at the same time also had a legal background.
>
> (Jurist and MP: Interviewee 47)

This evinces that the Template's Franco-Italianate origin is not merely the opinion of some authorities but not others. It is common knowledge in the Community's legal professional networks. When asked point-blank whether any of the institutions of the Template, especially the JC, which CoE norms have sought to promote, are modelled on Italy's or any particular country's, senior civil servants involved in policy making in Strasbourg emphatically deny it:

> **Q:** In CEE the template that has been adopted on the governance of the Judiciary seems to be modelled on the Italian system. Why is the CoE so open to the Italian rather than the Dutch or the Scandinavian model, especially given that many would say that the Italian model is not the best?
>
> **A:** Yes. In the discussions I was party to [in the CoE expert groups], nobody suggested that the system . . . proposed was modelled on the arrangements of any single country. It is clear that in many countries, some of the most important functions in relation to judicial careers were dealt with by Councils of the Judiciary and in terms of proofing these countries against the

[8] 'The Judicial Conference of the United States is the national policy-making body for the federal courts. The current name took effect when Congress enacted Section 331 of Title 28 of the United States Code. Before that, the body was known as the Conference of Senior Circuit Judges from its creation in 1922' (Administrative Office of the US Courts 2017).

> mischief that was perceived, that was a system that worked, because it put judicial appointments into the hands of other judges and out of the hands of government.
>
> (CoE Steering Committee member: Interviewee 3)

Career civil servants in the CoE General Secretariat are also keen to stress the non-specific, supranational origins of their norms on Judiciary power:

> **Q:** I have learnt that the French and the Italians have been particularly active in promoting their model of the Judiciary to CEE, compared to the British or the Dutch.
>
> **A:** I do not necessarily agree with that. I see very often the Germans being very, very active; we see the Americans, of course, and we use the expertise of all countries, and we . . . use more and more the expertise of the countries which have completed the transition or are in the process of transition . . . I don't think there is any policy to privilege one system over the other. In certain fields we have used more the Central European model of law, it is sometimes more the French and Italian system, but there is no central policy . . . we have forty-seven member states and use the expertise of the forty-seven member states.
>
> (CoE official: Interviewee 13)

Despite the disclaimers of these high officials, missionaries who were engaged in spreading the Template to CEE admit that what they are spreading does indeed derive from the Italian model:

> if we want to have a democracy in which people are equal in front of the law, the Italian system is the best, because . . . justice is justice for everyone, without any exception . . . if politicians commit crimes, there is no way to escape from prosecution . . . it is a very strong guarantee for equality in front of the law . . . if you look at the Italian system, I am convinced, from having compared our system with others, that with regard to independence [i.e., autonomy] the Italian model is the best you can find, and the demonstration is that the international sources regarding the independence of the Judiciary mention continuously the Italian model. It has been adopted by many opinions of the Consultative Council of European Judges for example, but also by the main recommendations of the CoE, because the Italian independence is a very, very good system.
>
> (Judge and EC adviser: Interviewee 40)

But the Franco-Italian model is itself a distillation of the main elements of latter-day American judicial practice. The doctrine of inherent powers is deeply entrenched in the structure of the American Constitution; and whilst Judicial supremacy over the political branches arose after the Civil

War in opposition to the Constitutional architecture, and had been advancing case by case for some time before the Second World War, it stands to reason that the connection between inherent powers and supremacy, though contingent, is none the less an established historical fact. It is also true that neither the French nor the Italians have ever actually instituted anything of the kind before a conquering American army had marched across their lands. Deliberate American agency may not have directly caused the European JC, but in the aftermath of the Second World War many Europeans did look to America as their saviour and a model to be imitated. By their own entrepreneurial agency, they took over much American doctrine and practice, but transformed it creatively and adapted it to their own circumstances.

French agency created Europe's first JC. French legal and political elites had been looking to America, using its example to buttress arguments for this or that institutional configuration according to the partisan make-up of the government *du jour* (Garner 1917). By the end of the First World War, French jurists were patently dissatisfied with their subordination compared to their American peers. This was remarked already in 1917 by James Wilford Garner, American professor of political science at the University of Pennsylvania and former editor-in-chief of the *American Journal of Criminal Law and Criminology*, who between 1907 and 1938 researched and wrote about French Judiciary governance. About his first-hand encounters with French jurists on his sojourns, he wrote that France's 'great jurists . . . strongly favoured' diminishing political involvement in judicial affairs, from recruitment to appointments to career promotion:

> In France as in most continental European countries, the Judiciary is not a constitutional creation. The organization of the courts, their jurisdiction, the mode of appointment and removal of the judges, their qualifications, and their tenure are all matters . . . regulated entirely by statute. The silence of the present constitution on this . . . is explained in part . . . by the view which still widely persists in France, that the Judiciary is merely a branch of the executive department. This . . . has called forth many expressions of regret from French writers . . . that the effect has been to degrade [the Judiciary] to the position of a *fonction* whereas it should be regarded as a *grande pouvoir* . . . and to diminish the great role which it should play in the life of the state. This dependence is one reason why, we are told, the French Judiciary has never asserted or exercised the right to declare unconstitutional acts of the legislature null and void . . . The influence exerted . . . especially by members of parliament in the appointment of judges has long been a subject of widespread complaint and protest. . . . [Even] W.V.J. Briand,

> minister of justice in 1912, declared that the judges had become the prey of politicians . . . and pleaded with his colleagues to renounce this 'dangerous confusion of powers' . . . each year, hundreds, almost thousands, of vacancies in the French magistracy must be filled annually by new appointments or transfers . . . In this way the independence of the Judiciary has been seriously impaired . . . All writers on the Judiciary without exception have inveighed against the evil of such a system . . . .
>
> (Garner 1917: 349, 350, 363, 364)

The end of the Second World War merely blazed a long-awaited opportunity for entrepreneurial French jurists to institutionalize their shared vision of judicial independence, if not full autonomy, entertained from decades before. They set up Europe's first JC in 1948 in hopes of fortifying their own Judiciary and insulating it from undue influence. It was a reaction against being 'dominated by the executive and the judicial hierarchy, that had been installed by the Consulate and Napoleon, redesigned by the Third Republic, and worsened by Vichy' (Bancaud 2006: 373; author's translation).

The *Conseil Superieur de la Magistrature* came to be imitated by Southern Europeans – Italy (1949), then Portugal (1974), then Spain (1978) – emerging from spates of undemocratic rule. At first it remained a minority concept, however, as many Central and West European countries declined to follow suit. Germany debated it in the 1950s, but its starkly decentralized federalism resisted adoption, and it hung onto its tradition whereby, for example, some *Länder* parliaments participate in deciding individual judicial careers (Guarnieri 2004).

The JC was introduced into Latin America under foreign, especially US, quite likely Network Community influence, if the network 'constituents' of judicialization and their legal professional collaborators in supranational organizations, like the World Bank, are reckoned in, during the democratizing decades of the 1980s and 1990s (Hammergren 2002).[9] After 1989, the JC was adopted across CEE, although the idea had already been becoming disseminated earlier through the IAJ:

> We [elite judges in the Czech Republic] started to collect information about this in the beginning of the 1980s. First we started with the International Association of Judges and with MEDEL – which is more or less the Social

[9] Dr Linn Hammergren herself is a long-term USAID and World Bank consultant under the aegis of the Law and Development programmes in democratizing countries (The Hague Institute for Innovation of Law 2018).

> Democratic Party and whose President was a representative of the revolution movement in 1968 in Germany – and they started to push this idea also through the Council of Europe.
>
> (High Court judge: Interviewee 59)

Network entrepreneurs were instrumental in disseminating it still further eastwards to the former Soviet Republics (and beyond). The power that the CoE and the EU, and the Network Community acting through them, have wielded over the Communist empire has been pivotal to this dissemination and subsequent consolidation, as witness the lack of a like sustained pressure, which has let several Latin American countries abolish their JCs (Neira Martinez 1996).

The JC, too, then, originated entirely outside CEE; it is an alien imposition on CEE's constitutional tradition. Jurists everywhere in CEE are aware of this: 'The Judicial Council is not a Romanian traditional institution . . . The question is, "Is it useful?" We were told that it is necessary so as to guarantee the independence of the Judiciary from the politic [*sic*]' (Jurist and career politician: Interviewee 17). 'The Judicial Council is something that nobody knows here [Croatia], even now when everybody is trying to introduce it' (Academician: Interviewee 54). And, 'there have been foreign experts advising policy makers in Moldova concerning the Judicial Council. I cannot say that we [Moldovan jurists] are the authors of these proposals' (SCt judge and JC official: Interviewee 21).

The growth of power of the Judicial Council and its consequences

JCs were at first poorly institutionalized (from the Network Community's standpoint), serving in the capacity of democratic fora for participation in judicial governance by parliaments and Justice Ministries, to which they were also answerable. Subsequent revisions have trended insistently away from these democratic beginnings toward the goal of judicial autonomy, precluding the rest of society from Judiciary governance. Intentionally or not (and the issue of intentionality is complex and multiform), the Network have objectively acted in a way that resembles the classic technique of bait and switch: selling the more attractive ware, then switching it for the less attractive after sale.

Parliaments were easily precluded, disempowered relative to Executives before the first post-Communist constitutions were ratified. The Executives, however, hung on to their prerogatives until the last minute before EU accession conditionality vaporized resistance. It was the latter that empowered the Network Community to disempower both elected branches relative to itself. For instance, the appointment of nominators of judges rested with the Croatian Parliament until 2010, when the Constitution was brought in line with the (actually 'extra-conditional') accession conditions imposed on EU candidate states – that is, a JC. In a straightforward instance of self-empowerment, elite Moldovan jurists, seconded by external pressures from the Network Community, succeeded in imposing Romanian-style autonomy, reducing to mere formality the role of Parliament and the Executive in appointing judges:

> The Parliament Act regarding the Status of Judges has been modified . . . so that everything that concerns the selection of candidates for the position of judge, their nomination, promotion, transfer . . . is all the prerogative of the Judicial Council. Since 2006, the Council decides . . . Once we decide on a candidate, if he is for a position at the Court of Appeal or lower, the proposal is made to the President of the Republic. If the candidate is for the position of Supreme Court judge the proposal is sent to Parliament. The decision of the Council is compulsory . . . The President can refuse [a candidate] but he has to argue and motivate his decision in writing. This is then sent to the Council which verifies to what extent the refusal of the President is founded, or if there are other reasons according to which he is right. The Council can propose the same candidate again . . . At this second proposal the President is obligated to appoint him. The same goes for Parliament and the Supreme Court judges . . . We were keen to borrow from the experience of Romania . . . All other things – whether you are promoted to an administrative post etc. – should be under the competence of the Council . . . Neither Mr [Nicolae] Timofti, former President of the Judicial Council [and President of Moldova since 2012], neither Mr [Mihai] Ghimpu [Speaker of Parliament, 2009–11, Acting President of Moldova, 2009–10, and leader of the Liberal Party], neither Mr Lupu who was Interim President would reject the Council-proposed candidate. They [all] said 'The Council decided, this is it' . . . Mr President Timofti used to be the President of the Judicial Council . . . *all of us* who know the system and care about it . . . know that that Presidential act is a formal act anyway, since the Judicial Council will get its way the second time. The same goes with Parliament.
>
> (SCt judge and JC official: Interviewee 21; emphasis added)

In CEE, the disempowerment of democracy did not stop with hollowing out its power to recruit judicial posts. All other competences over personnel, organization, etc., matters still determined democratically in the West, have been abolished or diminished to insignificance, or are in process of being so:

> **Q:** Does the Judicial Council decide the number of judges in a court? Or whether a court should be shut down?
>
> **A:** Yes. In Moldova the . . . original legal framework did not permit this. For example, as to judicial personnel touching clerks and assistants and consultants, these were all under the subordination of the Ministry of Justice . . . the new law stipulates that this will be transferred under the Council . . . Just now [2012] . . . we achieved much success . . . until now the law established clearly the number of judges and the number of judges for each court. The recent law stipulates that the Judicial Council has the right to establish the number of judges for each court, depending on the volume of work, and other necessities . . . The hands of the Council have been untied.
>
> (SCt judge and JC official: Interviewee 21)

At any point in time, a few countries in CEE may have gone farther than others in empowering their JCs, but design variation across the whole region is minimal. Revision may proceed at different rates, but the overall trajectory is uniform, and is pursued incrementally in premeditated stages, depending on how favourable national political circumstances are, or how feebly domestic veto players resist.[10] Even the Network's entrepreneurs admit there is a planned trajectory. In Moldova, where reform lagged behind until the EU intervened, the President of the JC observed:

> Today, *we* do not desire something maximal because we are aware that we will not be able to obtain it. We do have certain points of view, and some visions, which in time we will find space for . . . We could go further, but it is better to pursue a policy in small, but systematic and concrete steps.
>
> (SCt judge and JC official: Interviewee 21; emphasis added)

JCs in CEE are now the humming nodes of all judicial affairs. In one jurisdiction after another, they have been transformed from somnolent committees of part-time advisers to the Justice Minister (if that) to command-and-control centres with President, budget, and administrative apparatus, charged with essentially all judicial governance, from overseeing the MTAs to nominating new magistrates, to controlling career advancement, to disciplining misconduct. The last vestiges of transparency, even, were abolished in some countries by constitutionalizing a provision that

[10] Variation in the timing of Judiciary (re)design has misled external observers, some of whom perceive a variation of designs (Piana 2009), which might exist at the level of detail, instead of the uniformity of convergence that is clearly discerned in a macro-perspective.

JC decisions 'shall be taken by secret ballot . . . [which] shall be final and irrevocable' (Constitution of Romania, Arts. 133–135 and 133–137).[11]

Once etched in stone, JCs like other permanent bureaucracies proceed to aggrandize budgets and competences. The transition to bureaucracy has endowed JCs with greater reach inside the political system. The impression one gets when coming into contact with JC chieftains, even in CEE's most marginal countries, is of an ascendant power confident of its institutional prospects:

> We [Moldovans] have had a situation in which, until 2006, the Judicial Council was in majority made of judges, but they were not judges detached or with permanent activity in the Council. They would meet now and again, would come to a meeting when there was one scheduled . . . sometimes judges were not able to attend, and on many important questions the majority of the vote belonged to those who were not part of the judiciary corps . . . Under the current legislation, the Judicial Council is made of five judges with permanent activity out of twelve members . . . Many things have changed . . . Today we decided in the Council that we will summon an extraordinary meeting because we have to elect judges in two new colleges constituted within the Judicial Council.
>
> (SCt judge and JC official: Interviewee 21)

The Judiciary budget is the last remaining bastion of democracy that the Template's sway has not wholly transferred to the Council from the Ministry of Justice. At the time of going to press, democracy in CEE still retained partial or full competence over budget appropriations and how they are allocated amongst courts. The Network ambition is to see control transferred to its JC:

> **Q:** Why did Parliament decide to give the Judicial Council control over the Department of Judicial Administration, until then under the Ministry of Justice, and why did the President oppose it?
>
> **A:** Because the Judicial Council wants it. The Department puts together the budget of the judiciary. The Judicial Council has been successful at lobbying MPs to give it more autonomy. They argued that they were the best informed about what the judiciary needs in terms of finance . . . .
>
> (ABA officer: Interviewee 20)

What the judicializing community desires most is a general power to communicate directly to Parliament the budget they want – and ideally to dictate it: 'The administration of the [Romanian] Judiciary's budget is still

[11] Except for disciplinary decisions, which may be contested before the Supreme Court.

under the control of the Ministry of Justice . . . In future this competence should be transferred to a specialized department within the Judiciary' (Minister of Justice: Interviewee 52). Where no JC exists to be given budgetary control, the Network seek to transfer it to apex courts at least. Referring to the Czech CC, one of its former Deputy Chief Justices said:

> The Ministry of Justice controls the budget of courts . . . everything, everything in the budget is under the control of the Minister . . . This is not right. When the Court will create its budget, it will be . . . up to the [Court] President how to distribute it.
>
> (CC judge: Interviewee 34)

In this, the Template seeks to emulate the stature of the supranational courts, the ECJ especially. In the words of a MEDEL officer involved in Judiciary reforms in CEE:

> The autonomy of the Judiciary will make judges serious negotiators with the budgetary powers . . . in Luxembourg, the European Court of Justice is left to establish its own budget, and the Parliament will not touch a finger on it . . . They may even say 'Don't you need some more?'
>
> (MEDEL high official: Interviewee 2)

All of this has been 'downloaded' across the CEE region from the supranational level under the whip of EU accession conditionality (Magen and Morlino 2009; Piana 2009; Morlino and Sadurski 2010; Parau 2015b). But EU influence did not end with accession. Romania and Bulgaria were allowed to accede, as if provisionally, only on extra stipulations encompassing Judiciary revision, such as the make-up of the JC. These strictures have been transferred to accession candidates and aspirants like Moldova. Network entrepreneurs acting through the European Commission and the CoE on the basis of this after-conditionality have laboured tirelessly to fortify their peers:

> A new legislative package was adopted by Parliament in 2011 under the EU-negotiated Strategy for Judicial Reform. This included amendments to the Act on the Judicial Council. Before the amendment, the membership of the Judicial Council was made of five judges and four civil society members. Under the new Act, there are six judges and three civil society members, plus three members *ex officio*, viz. the [Executive] Minister of Justice, Supreme Court Chief Justice and General Prosecutor [both magistrates] . . . We think that due to our [legal professional] efforts . . . which led to the amendment of the law, the next Judicial Council . . . will be made of a majority of judges. There will be . . . one less professor and one more judge, so in total there will be a majority of judges . . . Before this change, only half were judges . . . one

> of them was the Supreme Court Chief Justice which here is elected by Parliament, and therefore we had a political element here.
>
> (SCt judge and JC official: Interviewee 21)

CoE experts advise countries without judge-dominated JCs to make them so:

> Cristi Danielet and Giacomo Oberto [of the CoE] who provided their expertise to us in the context of our recent constitutional revision have commented that it is not admissible for the Judicial Council to be made of less than half judges; we did what they recommended us.
>
> (MoJ civil servant: Interviewee 9)

The Network Community can be exacting; even the smallest detail is reserved from democratic discretion if it is politically significant. This membership purge follows the Network consensus, as evidenced by the position of the Venice Commission on this issue:

> **Q:** Is the Venice Commission sceptical of the Judicial Council given the negative experience with the Council in many CEE countries?
>
> **A:** That would be an overstatement . . . Our basic line on the composition of the Council has been that the substantial part or the majority of the Council should be composed of judges elected by their peers . . . while the other [transnational or supranational] texts now say, fairly uniformly, that it should be a majority.
>
> (Venice Commission official: Interviewee 8)

The JC paradigm admits a smattering of 'civil society'; however, these, too, are required by law or by convention to be jurists. For instance, parliamentary debates on the most recent Act on the JC in Romania focused on whether civil societals must belong to professional associations or not. That they must be jurists by training was taken for granted by the lawyer-politicians who alone bothered to engage with the details of design:

> The Bill provisions on civil society membership have triggered a lot of debates and discussions in the Standing Juridical Committee . . . The original text stated that any layman could be a member of the Judicial Council so long as he meets the eligibility criteria. The condition is indeed clear [since the revision]: he has to be a jurist.
>
> (Parlamentul României 2004b)

Appearances to the contrary notwithstanding, judicial autonomy was not rolled back in those CEE countries that recently saw controversial judicial reforms. The Hungarian JC's power was trimmed back only marginally, not even so far as to bring it in line with the German or Austrian model. In the words of one of the drafters of the 2011 Fundamental Law:

> [What we] created is a two-hat system. One is the Judicial Office which is running the management of the courts, and the other is the Curia, which is the Supreme Court. These are two different entities . . . What we did is a more pro-court system. We did not bring it back under the control of the administration, but created an independent body for managing the courts, a bit like the Prosecutor's Office, which is independent, and cannot accept any kind of orders . . . The government is only giving the money, but the management is . . . done by the government and the courts are doing the jurisdiction. The other is what we had [before the reform], the extreme, where everything was done . . . both the management of the courts and the jurisdiction of the courts [by a JC], which is not a good system . . . what we did was not bring it back under the government, which would be more in line with many European arrangements, but we created a third model . . . a midway rather than going back to the traditional European way . . . Germany, Austria . . . There is a Review Council also over the Judicial Office. This is a body elected by judges . . . Thus, there is a hierarchy in which you are proposing [for appointment] a higher judicial official . . . [whom] the courts have to approve.
>
> (Jurist and MEP: Interviewee 35)

Consolidation at the domestic level mirrors a prior consolidation at the supranational level of the CoE, where a pre-Enlargement trend was detected in the evolution of the Template qua CoE norms in the 1994 Recommendation on Judicial Independence. The trend culminated with the 2008 amendment of that Recommendation which, although scaled back in 2009 to allow leeway to carry on as before to those member states inured to their own Council-less systems, it yielded as a net result 'two steps forward, one step back' – a stronger political pressure (given the convention that member states conform to CoE norms) to consolidate the Template than exacted by the 1994 norms.

The fact remains that the problems never go away which JCs cause by dispensing from accountability and corporatizing that 'subtle corps of sappers and miners', hence the complaints about them are not going away either. In the CEE context, JCs have politicized the Judiciary by other means (than electoral politics) (Kühn 2011a).

The Network Community has responded to criticism by conceding the JC may be imperfect but only cosmetic adjustments to details of 'pluralism' are called for. Beyond twiddling, there is no sign that the Template is being rethought. According to the Venice Commission:

> we are aware that there is no ideal model, but that the essential is to adopt a system which combines in a harmonious way two imperatives – that of not succumbing to corporatism and that of not politicizing the institution . . . One can conceive of numerous modes of ensuring a satisfactory composition [of the JC] . . . [T]o avoid corporatism, it is not sufficient that the JC members elected by their equals are stars. Their presence must be counterbalanced by civil society (lawyers, law professors, legal advisers, university staff or scientists from any field) . . . In order to avoid politicization, political power must not be in control of nominations, careers, or discipline . . . politicization can be avoided if Parliament is charged only with confirming the election of magistrates.
> (Comisia Europeană de Democraţie prin Lege 2001: 2 *et passim*)

The Network exclusivity is such that 'pluralism' means a smattering of 'lay' professionals who happen not to be office-holding magistrates but are aligned with the Network consensus; and then it means as a placation, one or two Executive members *ex officio* (Comisia Europeană de Democraţie prin Lege 2001: 17). This inconveniences the legal professionals in no way, who under the Template retain a majority of votes no matter who else is appointed for decoration. Executives are easily, and frequently, outvoted by magistrates, as a matter of fact (General Prosecutor: Interviewee 55).

Even when civil societals are plain laity, this hardly opens JCs to external scrutiny and accountability. Who could such heavily outvoted persons influence? Maybe by 'blowing the whistle' out of doors – which always entails tremendous self-sacrifice to the whistleblower.

Evidence from the UK's Judicial Appointments Commission shows that laymen belong to the same broad white-collar elite class as experts, and invariably defer to them. Supposed to be conducive to a more open appointments process, the actual performance of lay members has disappointed many even in the legal profession. Their lack of qualifications (even though that is the very reason they were appointed) defeats any practical idea of challenging the experts, no matter how sorely needed. According to a member of one team of British researchers into this Commission:

> Most people can point to the fact that there's some lay involvement of the Judicial Appointments Commission. The Judicial Appointments Commission is a lay majority. But actually . . . the lay people are quite easily impressed by the judges, and understandably because they are very impressive, very bright. We haven't found any instance of a lay person standing up and saying, 'No, this appointment is one which shouldn't go through' . . . We've interviewed judges and lay people on these commissions and . . . one of them said something like, 'It's such an . . . honour to read the decisions and judgments of these people who are up for promotion to the Supreme Court.'

> And this person seemed so overwhelmed and impressed by the very sound intellect of these candidates. What one did wonder is to what extent they would be able to then argue with the Supreme Court President who sits on panel, the Deputy President who sits on the appointment panel and say, 'Actually, I disagree with your reading of these cases.' What do we mean by 'lay-ness' in this context? Are we actually talking about other very powerful, well, very prominent members of the elite? This idea that there's lay involvement is just another aspect of elite involvement, who have strongly aligned interests with judicial elites. I am very sceptical about the lay involvement in our appointment system.
>
> (Academician: Interviewee 56)

If failure of openness and accountability is routine in the UK, where the audacity to critique authority is entrenched, then a fortiori even less may be expected in CEE, where the social and political hierarchies are much steeper.

The consolidation of maximal judicial self-empowerment makes some local judges uneasy. Evidence in CEE comes from the 'old school', who are less networked-in and socialized into the consensus. Even amid spearheading Judiciary-empowering reforms in their own countries, a minority of these jurists remain sceptical:

> I don't know how correct [it] would be to remove Parliament's right to appoint at least some of the members of the Judicial Council . . . In the Scandinavian countries, the experience shows that there are designs that are quite different . . . and that the Ministry of Justice plays an important role.
>
> (SCt judge and JC official: Interviewee 21)

One also detects discomfort with JCs having a remit over and above protecting the independence of the Judiciary, such as promoting judicial self-interest, as if the JC were a powerful oligarch:

> The Romanian Constitution establishes clearly that 'The Judicial Council is the guarantor of the independence of the Judiciary.' . . . However, Art. 1 of the Bill [enacting this provision] states, 'The Judicial Council is the guarantor of the independence of the Judiciary, and the representative of the Judiciary power.' This is absolutely inadmissible . . . We cannot . . . attribute to the Council such a significant authority with such bewildering consequences . . . we [MPs] cannot allow such an unconstitutional absurdity.
>
> (Augustin Bolcas, lawyer and MP in Parlamentul României 2004a)

And, in fact, the JC has had perverse effects in CEE. Along with the rest of the Template, it has yielded a Judiciary insular and thus all the more corrupt, if not indeed incorrigible. Judges elect judges to a Council governing judges, a mode of self-perpetuating governance the actual net effect of which is to establish judicial self-government mainly qua immunity from democratic accountability.

Pierre Truche, a highly respected French jurist and former President of the French High Court of Cassation, when asked for advice in 2003 warned the Romanian government that maximizing empowerment of the JC would convert the Judiciary into 'a state within the state', and also an 'uncontrollable caste' (Minister of Justice: Interviewee 44; Truche 2009). Others have corroborated that this is actually what is happening (Bobek and Kosař 2014; Kosař 2016; Iancu 2017).

The present study has documented that such might actually be the intention – its very advocates describe the JC as a 'parliament of judges':

> **Q:** Critics say that the trend towards the institutional autonomy of the Judiciary is bad for democracy.
>
> **A:** If I dare ask you, what is bad in this?
>
> **Q:** In a democracy it is Parliament who should decide certain things with finality.
>
> **A:** But in what way does the Parliament of a country differ from our Parliament which is the Judicial Council, and which is elected by their professional peers?
>
> (CC judge: Interviewee 5)

And here is another lawyer-politician defending before the democratic Parliament the extreme version of autonomy, which he contributed to vesting in the Romanian JC:

> This Supreme Council of Magistrates is the Parliament of the Magistracy . . . The Romanian Parliament represents the Romanian people in relation to whomever. The Parliament of the Magistracy is the representative of the Magistracy. It is not a syndicate, it is a Parliament which debates important problems concerning justice in Romania.
>
> (Parlamentul României 2004a)

One can foresee the day when the Parliament of the Magistracy will be found entangled in a contest of power with the Parliament of all the people over fundamental public policy.

The Magistrates' Training Academy

Complementary to the JC is the MTA, which, too, has been inscribed in the transnational Template, and has spread throughout CEE, being entrenched in organic law. Originally modelled on France's *L'École nationale de la magistrature*, it was disseminated to CEE by a certain group of Network entrepreneurs: 'legal experts . . . who belong to a transfer network . . . [and] provide[d] not only a model . . . but also a link to an influential international network' (Piana 2007b). The 'transfer network' is the European Judicial Training Network, which has the moral and material support of the CoE and the European Commission (Institutul National al Magistraturii 2016). The Academy professes to solve problems besetting legal education in the region to render judges more professional, of better quality, with better skills and knowledge (Piana 2007b). Conspicuously overlooked is that such goals are better pursued by competitive decentralization of legal training in the manner of many if not all Western countries with a robust tradition of the rule of law.

The MTA not only standardizes legal education, it centralizes it in a single institution. Said the Director of one of the MTAs:

> The Judicial Academy in Croatia started in 2001 as a department in the Ministry of Justice. Since January 2010, it gained full independence as an entity of its own. The reason for creating it was to ensure that there is a centralized body which educates judges, prosecutors and that provides continuing training, clerks, and judicial trainees.
>
> (MTA official: Interviewee 45)

Centralization means no competition. Monopoly is the configuration most likely to transition from education to indoctrination. The parallel between (re-)education and Communism, which CEE was supposed to have left behind, is clear, yet the pattern is replicated. The door is opened to homogenizing the thinking of future magistrates to whichever ideology on the behaviour of new judges relative to the democracy is dominant. Transnational legal professional networks are not ideologically neutral just because they are not political parties. A common course of training can socially reproduce Network consensus in a way analogous in biology to ontogeny recapitulating phylogeny.[12] The legal professionals teaching at

[12] Embryos undergo a developmental process considered by some to mirror the development of the species; thus, for example, for a brief period, mammal embryos have structures resembling gills, supposed to mirror the evolution of air-breathing animals from fish. Indoctrination mirrors in miniature, if anything does, the process by which elite consensus may well have been achieved: negative and positive reinforcement of the trainee's personal views constitutes a bargaining process whereby the subject compromises himself in 'mere details' in exchange for admission into the club.

the Academy, if all or most are committed to activism (or formalism for that matter), risk narrowing young minds by the sheer omission of alternative ways of thinking and styles of judicial reasoning. This was one of the worries expressed by the Czech Supreme Court when an MTA was first proposed in 2001 (to be by default an organ of the Ministry of Justice, as the Czechs have no JC):

> The Supreme Court representatives objected to this concept by saying that it is harmful to monopolize education which . . . will . . . prevent judges from participating in educational events provided by other, including foreign institutions. The Ministry of Justice is not interested in training judges outside its own facilities, in topics not chosen by itself. This was demonstrated in a letter of autumn 2001, from the Deputy Minister to the American Bar Association's Central and East European Initiative, rejecting the participation of Czech judges in a seminar organized by the Institute.
> (Wagnerová 2003: 175)

As control by the Ministry of Justice, so control by the JC: neither monopolist will be 'interested in training judges outside its own facilities, in topics not chosen by itself'. The American Bar Association (and probably other 'foreign institutions') being part of the Network, the Czech Ministry *may* simply have misgiven their influence. Network-run MTAs might expose their trainees to more ABA seminars, but equally little diversity of ideas, if the same Network (which is, after all, transnational) determines to what level pupils will be trained, both at home and abroad. In either case, the existence of no other domestic training institutions is the root problem.

Legal professionals dislike indoctrination if under Executive aegis, but it becomes unproblematic in their own hands. Activism must be cultivated in case national parliaments default on EU law. According to one professor at the MTA in Zagreb:

> the EU dictates that you need judges who are more creative and are more capable of twisting the law, if you want [laughs] under the requirements of EU law, and conforming interpretation [to EU law] . . . judges are now starting to think about law . . . but they have not really been trained how to do [it] . . . What we need is for judges to realize . . . that they are doing a law-creating function . . . they are not [used to] looking at the law more broadly, and . . . they are hiding, in a way, behind the legislator. They actually are having a nice position, because it's easier for them to say, when something is not accepted by the public, 'This is not our fault. It is the legislature's fault because this is in the law. They have to change the law, not us.' So they are not taking on public responsibility for shaping the law in the end.
> (Academician: Interviewee 49)

Enough empirical evidence exists to let us infer that the MTA is indoctrinating the younger generation to think of their role in terms of activism and supremacy in the making of public policy. An academician in the Romanian MTA told the author that his courses centre on the jurisprudence of the supranational ECJ and the ECtHR, and train pupils to emulate their activist reasoning (*cf.* Piana 2007b). In fact, the Strategy of the Romanian MTA openly states that their purpose is to 'recruit and form' Romanian pupils as 'European magistrates' who are

> open to and integrated into the European juridical space as outlined in international documents, with all the consequences that this entails, the direct effect of EU law and of the jurisprudence of the ECJ and the ECtHR, so that judges and prosecutors are open to European and international law, and to human rights, as well as to cooperating with other European magistrates and courts.
> (Institutul National al Magistraturii 2016: 2; translated by the author)

That aim is vividly corroborated by a MEDEL officer:

> One needs to also indoctrinate them [the judges of post-Communist CEE] with the new values of the CoE and of the EU, otherwise it's just lost time . . . the young judges are not so highly skilled . . . judges as you would expect them to be, but nonetheless I think this is totally pardonable, this does not count. What counts is their courage.
> (MEDEL high official: Interviewee 2)

Indoctrination is by definition something that exceeds 'socialization' qua behaviour modification under probable yet haphazard peer pressure. 'Professional' training will hardly be questioned by trainees, especially in the hierarchical milieu of Eastern Europe. The new generation of judges may have institutional independence but not the independence of mind to 'draw the line' on EU law in the manner of the Germans' *Solange* doctrine.

The MTAs formalize the indoctrination begun under transnational elite influence directly after the fall of Communism. In some CEE countries, the methodology of judicial activism and the living constitution has been entrenched in domestic organic law. According to a top constitutional law professor in Romania who is a former CC judge, and president of an expert commission revising the Civil Code, 'A judge cannot refuse to adjudicate just because the law is silent, unclear or incomplete. See Art. 3 of the Civil Code and Art. 4 para 2 in Act 303/2004. In these situations *the judge acts as legislator*' (CC judge: Interviewee 38; emphasis added).[13]

[13] The doctrine that the judge must hear any complaint and improvise a remedy if the law gives none flies directly in the face of classical common law and plain common sense.

This is exactly how lawyers, trained after the fall of Communism, have been indoctrinated, as this Court of Appeal judge attests:

> A judge cannot refuse to hear a case on grounds of having no jurisdiction to grant relief. The 'denial of fair trial' legal provision stops a judge from refusing to solve a litigation on the basis that there is no law applicable to the case.
> (Appellate judge: Interviewee 57)

The MTAs in CEE now transmit a 'common' European juridical culture in the making of which they had no part, the history and origins of which are found in an elite Community beyond and prior to them. The MTAs operate to consolidate that culture by omitting to expose its roots to critiques that might prove subversive. An Italian judge and Network entrepreneur who has been involved in advising CEE countries on Judiciary reform noted concerning EU law that:

> there are clear rules which have . . . been accepted by all European countries, and that's surprising, because it means that we are very keen to accept the European system . . . This principle of the supremacy of the EU law was very difficult to be accepted [in the beginning] because of the traditional concept of the sovereignty of the state, but in the end . . . all the Constitutional Courts in the EU countries have accepted it. That means that the European project is very strong and . . . there is a European common culture. It is true that the common law system is very different from the civil law system, but in the end we have accepted the same principle . . . a very, very important incentive for all of us to know different systems and to interact with other judges in order to find a common culture . . . and it is not only my personal approach, because now we have many ways to exchange culture and experiences in Europe . . . so I do just what most Italian judges . . . from my generation are doing. It's just a normal approach; nothing extraordinary.
> (Judge and EC adviser: Interviewee 40)

Traditionally, defendants might 'demur' to answer complaints which failed to invoke a 'cognizable' cause of action, that is, a misdeed which the law (not the men who are judges) already recognizes as remediable. For example, in common law, children may not sue parents, or vice versa, for failure to fulfil a promise – for example, to buy a certain toy; not so much because trivial (cognizable causes can be more trivial) as because ancient precedent holds family ties to be more sacrosanct than mere contract. To train magistrates to let their idiosyncratic consciences be their guide is fraught with perilous unintended consequences. The author does not claim that the Network Community aims at such an outcome; rather, that it aims at Network consensus as a surrogate for idiosyncrasy, which may be even more perilous if it is true that odd, one-off miscarriages of justice tear the fabric of popular sovereignty less than systematic sapping and mining.

MTAs should also help reinforce the new insularity and self-perpetuation. According to a first-hand account of a lecturer at one of them:

> Judges do not like to be taught by anybody else but judges themselves . . . judges who act as trainers come in with suitcases of materials and these materials go to regional centres where they lecture and speak to other fellow colleagues, and although generally there is nothing wrong with that, this leads to the closing of judges in their own circle. They will not be subjected to any kind of outside view or criticism . . . There is no public accountability of the Judiciary or accountability to the elected branches, and this has been cemented through the [new] educational system . . . This leads to the formation of a closed circle of a privileged professional oligarchy that is accumulating both professional influence, and through that, political power.
>
> (Academician: Interviewee 54)

A parallel process of autonomizing the legal profession via education has been described in the West; in Canada, for instance:

> Accompanying the quantitative growth in law schools is a qualitative change in legal education: the displacement of the old vocational training approach by an emphasis on theoretical and constitutional issues. The social movements that were born in the 1960s were soon carried into the law school curriculum by the new cohort of young professors hired during the rapid post-war expansion. They introduced new courses that embraced a human rights curriculum . . . The new autonomy of the Canadian legal education coincided with the triumph of postmodernism among university based intellectuals.
>
> (Morton and Knopff 2000: 131)

Some evidence filters in from CEE that the MTAs' insularity may be alienating young trainees and stifling innovation, and may have been triggering a backlash:

> Young people who want to become judges are now opposed to the new Judicial Training Academy, because it makes access to the judicial profession very difficult, making the Judiciary even more professionalized and closed than it was . . . [Even] if you were an attorney with thirty years of experience in the courts, you still have to go through the Academy for another three years. This is making this group of lawyers pretty much untouchable. Some mobility within the legal profession would be useful because people who have been practicing law, such as attorneys or a public prosecutor, might perhaps have some fresh ideas which professional judges might not have.
>
> (Academician: Interviewee 51)

Whether or how much CEE judges actually exploit their MTA training on the bench is beyond the scope of this study. Judicialization in CEE may be most advanced in CCs, but this is an inference from available evidence to be treated as provisional because it is contingent on the dearth of empirical data about the ordinary courts. Even if the ordinary courts have been engaging less in public policy making, it is a state of affairs likely to be transitory. Generational changes in the mentality of judges under the influence of the Academies imply that ordinary courts will be making (further) inroads into democratic prerogatives.

A survey conducted by the author in Romania and Moldova in 2011 found that even then, even in the most marginal countries of Europe, the younger generation of judges now moving into the lower courts stood overwhelmingly against the German CC's nationalist position in *Solange*, but expressed very little nationalist sentiment of their own.[14] They would apply EU law even if it conflicts with the national constitutions (see Figures 6.1 and 6.2).

Likewise, very few thought that it would erode national sovereignty to regard the jurisprudence of the ECtHR as the supreme law. The Europeanizing commitment was so clear, a cynic might have quipped that judges in CEE are now wholly owned subsidiaries of the Network Community. The German CC's prestige could have shielded the MTAs had they wanted to teach that the national Constitution has ultimate priority; evidently, they have wanted to teach the opposite. It may be fairly inferred then that their training is heavily swayed by the transnational legal professional networks.[15] Whether for this or for other reasons, the drift of

[14] The survey was conducted with funding for 'The Europeanization of Legal Mentalities in Eastern Europe' by the British Academy Small Research Grants scheme. The project was held jointly by the author and Dr Manuel Guţan at Sibiu Law School, Romania.

[15] This would seem to contradict a prior claim made in 2010 of judges in CEE countries, who have been the most exposed to external influences, not least because of their geographic proximity to Western Europe (viz. the Czech Republic, Hungary, and Poland), that they 'have largely failed to respond to the incentives contained in the new constitutional frameworks. They continue to adopt the most-locally-applicable-rule approach and are reluctant to apply general principles of law or to rely on Dworkinian "policies" [as opposed to formalism] in deciding hard cases' (Matczak et al. 2010: 81). The survey, which I ran in Romania and Moldova, did indicate that this might be true, but the point made here is that the capacity for Dworkinian activism is already being nurtured through indoctrination within the monopolistic MTAs, yet there is still a time lag before this will manifest in concrete decisions, as determined by the career progression of the new generation of judges. The activism of lower court judges in CEE in resorting to the preliminary reference mechanism might be taken as additional evidence of this phenomenon; although, it is also possible that this is the by-product of a power struggle between apex and lower courts whereby the lower judges delight in circumventing the 'tyrants' at the top (Kornezov 2015). It is puzzling that MTAs

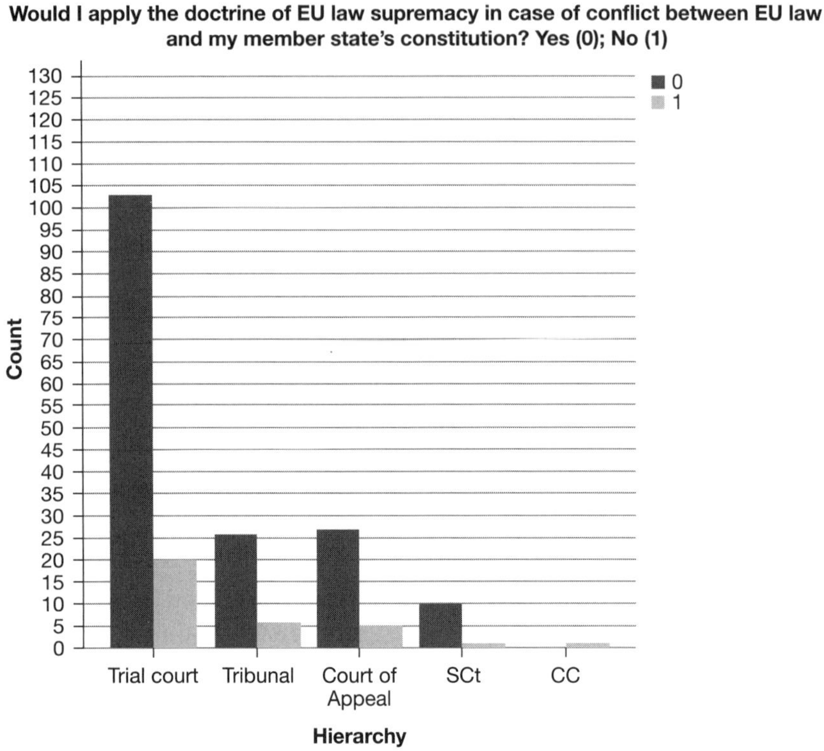

Figure 6.1 Orientation of Romanian judges respecting EU law in 2011, by hierarchical position

Note: Random sample size: 10 per cent of the population of judges in Romania, yielding a sample of 111 judges. The survey yielded no responses from the CC and very few from the SCt; therefore, no claims can be made about the attitudes of judges in these two courts. Although the attitudes of apex court judges matter supremely, as they have the last word, the scantiness of their response is irrelevant to the argument that the younger generation of judges currently staffing the lower courts, who over time will move up to staff the apex courts, nearly all have a mindset that is very favourable to EU law. The difference in response between the different levels of hierarchy are statistically significant at 95 per cent confidence levels.

do not feature in Kornezov's account. Perhaps their influence is invisible in the sense of not open to the public, escaping observation by others besides students and faculty (who might be vetted in advance). Kornezov's claim that Parliament itself stimulated the lower courts' partiality toward the ECJ by specially enacting the preliminary reference procedure into the Bulgarian Civil Code misses this author's finding that parliaments merely rubberstamp codes drafted by academicians networked into the Community (see Chapter 3).

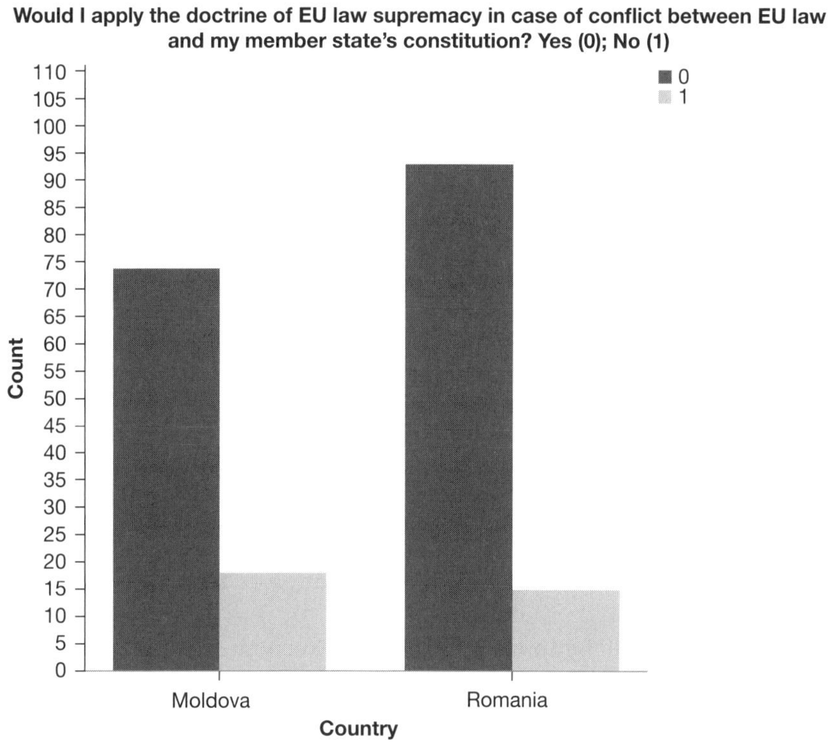

Figure 6.2 Orientation of Romanian and Moldovan judges respecting EU law in 2011

Note: Random sample size: 10 per cent of the population of both Romanian and of Moldovan judges, yielding a count of 111 and 93 judges, respectively. The independent variable 'Country' proved to be statistically insignificant at 95 per cent confidence intervals; that is, the probability of a 'Yes' response from a Moldovan judge is the same as that of a Romanian judge. This is contrary to the a priori expectation of the study that Moldovan judges would seek to imitate Russia/CIS more than the EU.

agent loyalty is happening even in West European states with strong traditions of parliamentary sovereignty (Stone Sweet 2000). In these far-flung developments, one fundamental fact remains: that the empowerment of judges sprang first from the self-empowerment of the transnational elites who conditioned their thinking – and the thinking of all other political actors as well.

A transnationally harmonizing Template

The Template's one-size-fits-all imperative razes the diversity of Judiciary designs in Europe in favour of standards set to harmonize them across the CoE member states in keeping with the Network Community's preferences. In the words of the CCEJ:

> There is *room for concern* that the *present diversity of approach* may tacitly facilitate the continuation of undue political influence over appointments. The CCEJ noted the view of the specialist, Mr [Giacomo] Oberto [judge, Turin Court of Appeal and Network entrepreneur], that informal appointment procedures and overtly political influence on judicial appointments in certain [CoE] States were not helpful models in other, newer democracies, where it was vital to secure judicial independence by the introduction of strictly non-political appointing bodies.
>
> (Consultative Council of European Judges 2001; emphasis added)

The inference must be that the Template is designed for the pan-European (and maybe too the worldwide) harmonization of judicial governance norms.

Moreover, one of the aims of the 2010 CoE Recommendation on Judicial Independence was to promote 'relations among judicial authorities and individual judges of different member states in order to foster the development of a common judicial culture' (Council of Europe 2010b). When queried about this 'common judicial culture', one of the legal professionals involved in drafting the Recommendation ventured a rationale that one ought perhaps to take *cum grano salis* as public relations packaging: it is 'a colourful point . . . included for emphasis . . . to give perspective, so that the Recommendation was not only about technical things, to give the text a bit more splendour' (CoE Steering Committee member: Interviewee 1). The effect of all of this is to make it easier for the apex of the Network to influence the thinking of apex judges across Europe.

Pan-European harmonization by transnational elite consenus is, for better and for worse, the new normal in solving problems of Judiciary governance as well as the content of justice in the nations of Europe. Note in the following excerpt that the interviewee, a Network entrepreneur in Strasbourg and high official of a Ministry of Justice in Western Europe, does not even try to refute the normative subtext of the author's query about uniformity (under elite supervision) as the Network Community's goal:

> **Q:** What drives the trend towards uniformization and standard setting? One can argue that we will end up with mediocre standards for everyone. Why is this desirable?
>
> **A:** This is all part of the continuing process of modernization . . . there are . . . areas where all member states can benefit from pooling expertise and best practice . . . What happened in CEPEJ [a legal professional network in Strasbourg] is a very good example of that, where information about [Judiciary] performance [is expressed] in sort of numerical terms. How many delays of justice are there? and how much does it cost? . . . what steps have been put in place in particular countries that have actually been shown to reduce delays, for example? [These measurements] throughout Europe have been analysed . . . and there are other things, too; there are new problems, new issues, IT, and the sharing of data. What issues does that give rise to privacy? and how should that work in the area of security, for example? where if you want to investigate crime and prevent terrorism you need police forces and other authorities to share information? How do these things chime together? New concepts in family law, for example – increasingly we are seeing registered partnerships rather than traditional marriages. What implications does that have for the way in which states work together? Does it have implications for what happens when people move to other countries? There are lots of issues out there. In the end, it comes to how much priority you want to give to things like that, and how much money do you want to spend on developing common European standards in these areas.
>
> (CoE Steering Committee member: Interviewee 3)

The CoE member states would have no reason to revisit the Template if it was only about innocuous things such as information technology or media relations, over which transfer of the power to make policy is less controversial because the issues are 'technical' (just as the technicalities of Single Market integration were less controversial than EU expansion into policy domains such as money and finance or extra-European immigration). But of course, this is not the whole story. The Template implicates a most fundamental transformation of power relations, as the Community itself admits in candid moments, as when the Bureau of the Steering Committee on European Legal Co-operation commented on the entrepreneurial revision of the 1994 CoE Recommendations on Judicial Independence:

> During its meeting on 7–9 April 2008, the Bureau examined the draft Recommendation and its draft Explanatory Memorandum [drafted by the Network entrepreneurs staffing CJ-S-JUST] . . . Some of the changes proposed . . . have constitutional importance for member states and would *entail changes to the very foundations of their legal structure.* The subjects dealt

> with . . . touch rule of law issues which lie at the core of the values of the Council of Europe.
>
> (Bureau of the European Committee on Legal Co-operation 2008: 2; emphasis added)

This is why the Template encounters the most resistance from robust Western democracies. A senior civil servant in Germany's Ministry of Justice noted, 'Not only Germany, Austria, but the Scandinavian countries too, and England, are completely against Judicial Councils. It is unacceptable' (CoE Steering Committee member: Interviewee 1). The author found the Template would have been imposed on these countries earlier, in more absolute form, but for the arousal of their veto players to resistance.

But the West has not remained immune. Network entrepreneurs acting on the domestic level have gradually been bringing their pressures to bear on Western states that had settled the rule of law and workaday decisional independence of the Judiciary centuries ago. And yet further scaled-back variants of the JC have been adopted in Norway and Britain lately, featuring less than autonomy and a modicum of democratic accountability compared to Southern Europe or CEE (where until lately virtually no resistance to the Template was observed). The Courts Administration in Norway and the relegation of the Lord Chancellor and creation of the Judicial Appointments Commission in the UK, in 2002 and 2006 respectively, are cases in point (Backer 2007; Gee et al. 2015). These developments go hand in hand with increased pressures and expectations that outliers such as the Scandinavian countries which are traditionally hostile to judicial supremacy should accede on demand to constitutional review of the kind exercised by the European and other supranational courts (Follesdal and Wind 2009; Wind 2010).

Other states are being made to feel the pressure. According to a Network entrepreneur:

> Austria and Germany are very important exceptions in Europe . . . there is a big debate in these countries, not only among judges but also among the academics, about the importance of judicial autonomy through Judicial Councils, and I don't exclude that in the future it's possible that a Judicial Council will be set up in Germany as well.
>
> (Judge and EC adviser: Interviewee 40)

Consolidated democracies where individual liberty is embedded in the political culture are thus being nudged to adopt a Template which ought to apply to democratizing regions at most, but is instead being applied across the EU and CoE member states. Why? The simplest explanation is the one that also explains the design features of the Template: it was designed and is being disseminated to empower the Judiciary for power's sake.

Eastern Enlargement justifies the impetus given these impositions on Western Europe, Network entrepreneurs claim, because the West needs to set an example. The relegation of the Lord Chancellor from Head of the Judiciary was reputedly a succumbing to Network pressure that Britain sets such an example:

> There were a number of issues [motivating the Constitutional Reform Act passed by the Blair Government in 2005] . . . how could I go off to places like Bulgaria or wherever, and say 'You should do this and this, you should have separation of powers, you politicians shouldn't have an influence on what the judges do', when you had the Lord Chancellor who had these three roles . . . it was one of the arguments.
>
> (High Court judge: Interviewee 42)

And, according to the Venice Commission:

> [There was] a general Council of Europe perception that . . . it was embarrassing with respect to new democracies, that on paper British solutions look quite bad . . . [although] I think they were working well in practice . . . but if you looked at them on paper and . . . compared that with what you would recommend to a country like Romania . . . it seems quite scandalous what is happening in Britain . . . it became a bit embarrassing for the British themselves.
>
> (Venice Commission official: Interviewee 8)

A similar argument was made by Carsten Smith, president of the expert group in Norway (the 'Courts Commission') who laboured to transfer competence over judicial governance away from the Ministry of Justice, and who is remembered for his enthusiam for the CoE and the idea that 'we had to be an example for Eastern Europe' (SCt judge and academician: Interviewee 46).

That a banal 'naming and shaming' tactic suffices for the demolition of venerable, effective, centuries-old institutions to 'set an example' for CEE is not the most convincing story. Everyone in Eastern Europe knows full well that the independence of the Judiciary is settled in the UK and other Western states. Dissemination of the Template is unnecessary for that purpose; therefore, it must serve some other purpose. The preponderance of the primary data weighs on the side of concluding that the purpose is transnational elite self-empowerment.

The Network Community has moved to ring-fence, after a manner, its maximal empowerment agenda by 'taking the offensive' – a proactive programme of expansion into realms where it is unneeded – in addition to vetoing deviations from and variations on it. This is achieved by disseminating it to the North and West of Europe. Network members insist that the Template addresses problems that Westerners experience as much as other Europeans:

> If you look at some of the member states who have been pretty much central to the Council of Europe, say France, Italy, and Spain . . . the UK and Ireland . . . there are issues around judicial independence that all have, for different reasons . . . pressure from the external media on judges to be talking more about their judgments . . . the pressure, as you have in the UK, around resourcing and partnership, arguments around efficiency, IT, and how far judges should be involved in court administration . . . .
>
> (MoJ official: Interviewee 28)

To proselytize via the Template implies marginalizing member states like the UK whose history proves judicial independence and the rule of law can be delivered without the Template; where before it existed, the Judiciary had decisional independence. The Constitutional Reform Act of 2005, widely interpreted as a step toward implementing some part of the Template, scrapped the tradition of a millennium to fix what was not broke, as a senior civil servant in the Department of Constitutional Affairs (now the Ministry of Justice) candidly admitted, who was an eyewitness to the change, and who has partaken in transnationally negotiating pan-European norms on Judiciary institutions in the CoE:

> **Q:** Why have these changes [Constitutional Reform Act] been made? Judges in Britain have had judicial independence for a long time.
>
> **A:** Judicial independence is enshrined in the constitutional format of the Constitutional Reform Act of 2005. The Act effectively put on the face of statute what has been regarded in Britain as a long-standing constitutional principle anyway . . . We have moved . . . in that direction [empowerment and autonomy] . . . but the sovereignty of Parliament is very strong here . . . The advantage that we have here is that judges are very clear, and ministers are very clear, *that there is a line which you do not cross*, and that line is particularly about judges' decisional independence in the case. Never go there . . . the fact that the principle [*sc.* constitutional convention] is so strong is a real help to making the system work.
>
> (MoJ official: Interviewee 28; emphasis added)

Alternatives are invariably presumed unsuitable. The Westminster model is eschewed even by entrepreneurs in the UK, who dismiss it as haphazard and as emerging 'for historical reasons'. The consensus is so tight that the

Network in Britain (a fortiori elsewhere) receive the opinion that the UK Judiciary model (if not some of its detailed workings) is off limits to export to the East, notwithstanding its illustrious success. In the words of a senior civil servant in the Ministry of Justice who has been closely involved in policy making in Strasbourg:

> **Q:** Why isn't Britain trying to export their model of the Judiciary institutional design to CEE? One of your colleagues in the CoE referred to the Italians and the French as being 'missionaries'. Why aren't the British missionaries?
>
> **A:** On this particular issue . . . our judges certainly . . . spend time talking with other jurisdictions but . . . we have the right model for us . . . we recognize . . . that the model we have has developed in the way our constitution has developed, in the way we [Britain] have our history of the Lord Chancellor who has three hats. We have a particular evolution . . . the Judiciary have . . . complete independence in how they organize themselves. So, given the degree of freedom that our judges have, exporting that as the model . . . I can think of lots of examples where it wouldn't work.
>
> (MoJ official: Interviewee 28)

In CEE, the Network Community does in fact face the daunting task of trying to transplant judicial independence and the rule of law in barren soil. It believes the Anglo-Saxon judicial independence cannot be exported because it could not survive a political culture where judges are intimidated. But the flip side of the problem is that if the political culture would defeat anything short of a Judiciary on steroids, then what would such a Judiciary do to democracy, the rule of law, the local quality of justice, and the ordinary people who seek to better themselves and their country? The danger is that the new seedling will grow up as polluted as the weeds it supplanted.

The great question now before the EU and CEE is 'What is the alternative, if any, to the Template?' Viable ones might include doing nothing but letting the locals work it out amongst themselves according to the principle of subsidiarity, which might entail a lengthy transitional membership status during which the institutional capacity to implement EU law would be empirically tested. One might also announce a project to think outside the box about good government under alien circumstances and inviting all interested parties to contribute, especially those who have lived through similar circumstances. This is how an EU and a CoE would proceed which concerned themselves not with their own empowerment, but with good government for its own sake – as both have sometimes done. And the Network Community, even if it can justify the Judiciary's operational autonomy because it is fighting real problems in a region with a hostile culture, can hardly justify its political (viz. policy-making) supremacy.

The Italian model too is not the great success it is touted to be. Those CoE member states which were first to implement the Template have been suffering problems with their Judiciaries for a long time. Legal professionals in CEE complain that they have been pushed to follow a model well known to produce a highly politicized Judiciary. The same outcome, only worse, may be expected in CEE given its political culture.

The Network Community knows the Template works poorly – the JC, especially, has a poor reputation in CEE as an 'uncontrollable caste' protecting its own rather than leading reform – but shows little interest in reforming it. The failure of the vaunted JC to deliver a better quality of justice on the ground even with maximal empowerment has made the Network more cautious lately; at least, the European Commission appears willing to learn a few lessons from the experience of new members like Romania and Slovakia, although it is unclear whether other models, and if any which, are being considered:

> With Montenegro they, the European Commission, have been discussing the Judicial Council . . . The Commission doesn't like what it sees, but doesn't quite know what [else] to propose . . . so there is now a dialogue on what . . . model to propose to the Montenegrins . . . the proposed solution or model of giving the majority to judges elected by their peers is the usual advice . . . [but] we are a bit worried that it may lead to the appointment of the cousins and nephews of the sitting judges . . . the politicians are concerned . . . it was very clear that they . . . were adamant not to give too much power to the judges for reasons of corruption and excessive self-rule.
>
> (Venice Commission official: Interviewee 8)

It seems to have dawned on some elements of the Network Community that self-empowerment and judicialization will fail if the institutional undergirding is unsustainable. It risks awakening dormant politicians who can reverse outright everything the Network have laboured to achieve to let egregious deficiencies persist. And yet generally, they have become stricter in disallowing deviations from the Template. The underlying consensus, in the making in the West well before the collapse of Communism, already precludes the Westminster and US models. This preclusion was cinched at a critical conjuncture in CEE: the very earliest stages in the drafting of its first democratic constitutions after Communism.

Alternatives were not only debated in Romania; they were preferred – at first. At least one – to vest the power of constitutional review in Parliament

– differed profoundly from the Network paradigm (CC judge: Interviewee 38). Strikingly original alternatives existed before the Template in other CEE countries. In Moldova, judges used to be elected by the people, which ensured a degree of democratic accountability, and in the Eastern context might have been more effective in reforming the Judiciary than the Template. The election of judges was abolished only a year before Moldova's JC was set up; it did not conform to the Network's peculiar conception of the separation of powers:

> I was a judge elected by the people . . . in a district in Transnistria . . . in 1987. This method of election would not be a problem. We have many problems with colleague judges and I ask them, 'If you were to stand for elections, with this behaviour, do you think you would stand any chances of being re-elected to this post?' . . . [But] if we are to rely on those principles that we learnt in school, in the Law Faculty, [then] separation means [absolute] separation . . . this procedure [was] eliminated . . . in 25 February 1995 . . . The Judicial Council was created in 1996.
>
> (SCt judge and JC official: Interviewee 21)

Other institutional designs for delivering justice are not even oppositional to the Template, only tangential, but are squelched anyway. This suggests at the outside that the networked-in elites aim at concentrating judicial power in their own hands; at a minimum, it catches the Template precluding (where it does not prohibit) alternatives that might deliver justice with popular input as well or better than autonomy without it:

> Until 25 February 1995, there also existed lay judges [in Moldova] – two assistants to the judge, lay people of different professions with no legal background, but with some life experience, who knew certain realities of their social environment. Their role was sort of intuitive. This was not a bad arrangement. The society's perception was that 'the people judge' because two of the judges were not dependent on the Judiciary system . . . [A] young man was suspected of manslaughter, an intentional act: he killed his stepfather, and it was due to those two lay judges, who were in some ways more attentive and more careful . . . to the defendant . . . the file was very complicated, but they took things very positively in the sense that they wanted to establish the truth, not to protect the young defendant. He was acquitted, but I have to say that in 1989 acquitting somebody of a crime was a big thing. Acquittal in a case of manslaughter was a delicate thing then [under Communism] . . . the Supreme Court affirmed the acquittal. This was my only dossier that ended up before the Supreme Court of the Soviet Union, and they affirmed the decision. There were many cases of this kind.
>
> (SCt judge and JC official: Interviewee 21)

Another illustration is the abolition in 2003, under Network pressure, of *recurs in anulare*, a traditional Romanian check and balance on the ordinary Judiciary. Since then, those internal to the Judiciary – appeal to the national apex courts and the ECtHR – are the only 'checks and balances' on judicial errors and abuses left standing. If an apex court decision is itself unjust, no mechanism at the disposal of the democracy can now correct it. Even local Network entrepreneurs who were once at the forefront of Judiciary empowerment in Romania lament its passing:

> **Q:** Was *recurs in anulare* a check and balance on the Judiciary?
>
> **A:** They hurried to take it out. There are many judicial errors which cannot be repaired any longer. The mechanism of 'recourse in the interest of the law' (*recurs in interesul legii*) is aimed at unifying judicial practice but it cannot be exercised in individual cases. For example, right now you have a former magistrate suing the Procuratorate for some rights. The court decides and then in appeal a new pleading is introduced, and the court that judges the appeal decides differently. Nobody can correct a case like this . . . Yes, *recurs in anulare* could have been used to attack [*sc.* check and balance] a decision of the Supreme Court. No such mechanisms exist at present.
>
> (JC high official: Interviewee 41)

The Chief Procurator may be a very remote popular representative, but the abolition of his power epitomizes the drive for that autonomy and supremacy which the Template demands. This is corroborated by the act of the European Commission 'vetoing' an alternate version of *recurs in anulare*, that shortened the time limit on its exercise so as to reduce legal uncertainty, and to satisfy the objections of the ECtHR (CC judge: Interviewee 58).

Beyond a reasonable doubt, the Network Community has purposely rejected alternative designs which afforded fewer opportunities for judicial self-empowerment than the Template. It follows that the motive behind it is not judicial independence but something over and above that. The legal professionals label that over-and-above 'judicial independence' too, as if every aspect and detail of self-empowerment were essential to the basic functioning of a Judiciary. Such an expansive (and uncritical) definition of independence has the effect, whether intended or not, of casting the democracy that revolts against judicialization in the role of the aggressor, whilst the Judiciary is typecast as the innocent, aggrieved victim of its Defence of Human Rights. It is never explained why the self-determination of peoples is not a cardinal one of those rights, and maybe the most important.

To conclude, the three-pronged transnational Template transfers public policy-making power to the Judiciary by minimizing, where it cannot altogether eliminate interference by all other political actors in interpreting the constitution and governing the Judiciary. It seems the main prize is to eliminate anything more than ceremonial, or very marginal involvement by the people and their elected representatives in public policy making, or at a minimum to vest the Judiciary with an absolute veto over them. This conclusion is less speculative than it may appear to some. Judges are currently being empowered by being made: (1) supreme over elected representatives, wielding the last word over all legal and constitutional meanings, which democracy is precluded to contest; and (2) autonomous to the popular will as expressed through the political branches, their accountability to democracy for their internal governance and their public policy making having been abolished. Conformity with the judicial activist paradigm that the Template enables is inculcated in the younger generations of judges by training in the jurisprudential paramountcy of supranational courts. (Whether this centralizing, nation-shrinking tendency is perceived by local judges as a constraint on their own power, or as a price well worth paying to empower the whole Network Community, or as something else, is a question worth inquiring into.)

Given such a *dénouement* to our age of judicialization and the empowerment of non-elected bodies at the expense of elected ones, it is a singular paradox that 'accountability' should have become the ubiquitous mantra, whilst older, more effectual concepts such as checks and balances, now affected to be obsolete but which spoke directly to power relations between branches of government, are superseded in favour of . . . wind.

Conclusions

The Judiciary revisions that have taken place in CEE since 1989 and lately in Western Europe, exhibit an unmistakable common pattern: to transfer political power away from majoritarian and over to non-majoritarian institutions, from elected officials to judges, excluding popular sovereignty from the make-up of Judiciary organs, and insulating judges from accountability and democratically determined boundaries. Contrary to transnational media narratives, even episodes of 'rebellion', such as the recent constitutional adjustments in Romania and Hungary, never even purported to deconstruct the Network Community's Template but merely tinkered with it at the margins. Its consolidation at the domestic level is in lock-step to its prior consolidation at the supranational level in the Council of Europe. A similar trend was observed in the evolution of norms on Judiciary governance, which have also been 'tightened up' by Network Community members at the apex of the Network's fora like the General Secretariat of the CoE, the CCEJ, and the Venice Commission.

The transnational Template is a more radical development than merely setting pan-European but ultimately non-binding norms out of the CoE. Once entrenched in domestic constitutions, the Template is not only legally binding but also politically difficult to repeal or even modify insofar as amending constitutions requires a supermajority, and also requires domestic elites to attain self-transcendence from their own transnational socialization. After having been invented by legal professional networks to achieve European integration to prevent another World War, the CoE and the EU have latterly become a goad to whip the 'backward' countries of Europe into line with what the Network Community has unilaterally defined as universal values. This strategy has demonstrably slipped reasonable bounds; the whip is used for good but also evil, exposing Northern and Western Europeans to seemingly irresistible pressure to sacrifice their most sacred, indeed robust traditions.

The Europeanization of American-style judicial politicking is most puzzling. The Network Community in Europe imitated the US transmogrification of its own governing principles that features the overriding supremacy of judicial output, and adapted it to the European context by super-adding the autonomy of judicial input. When exemption from input accountability is combined with output supremacy, autonomy becomes indistinguishable from autocracy. The Judiciary becomes a state within the state, the illimitable arbiter of all other political actors.

The causal nexus discovered to explain this puzzle – why this Template and its unfathomable widespread distribution? – reflects the dual, mutually reinforcing nature of causation which in social science is encountered at the intersection of agency and structure, and of the material and the mental social constructs. One and the same cluster of determinants was found to explain, in fact, the whole phenomenon of Judiciary empowerment in CEE and, potentially, farther afield – a causal nexus involving agency, structure, and omission of agency. The causal processes were top-down and elite-driven, and cut across all the nations of Europe, even 'blowing back' to their origin in the West.

Agency is multi-level and collective, and supported by the networking of elite national and supranational actors, non-State as well as State. The elites in question were encountered in their 'native [transnational] habitat' (as revealed by empirical research), having overleapt the confines of the nation-state long ago (as inferred from secondary research). Intriguingly, although it is judges who become empowered, the agents who bring this about, especially those who may be considered the grand strategists, are by no means all judges. Neither are they elected politicians, certainly not the mass of elected representatives in parliaments, despite parliaments having entrenched Judicial empowerment in constitutions and organic legislation. It is this puzzling omission of agency or, if you like, this 'dormancy' of the national polity's main veto players which has enabled the Network Community to advance and consolidate its power, especially since 1989.

The transnational elite is a class of people who share a collective identity and a sense of solidarity – paradigmatic assumptions that originate in network consensus, like their revision of the separation of powers and assumption of the Judiciary's moral superiority – and who disseminate hegemonic discourses that (effectively) coerce the general public. Bringing to the fore the existence of such an elite is itself a contribution that brings fresh perspective to a 'law and politics' literature which rarely ventures outside the confines of the nation-state (via the law of nations tradition) or the agency of elected politicians (via the rational choice paradigm).

Had the Network Community's assumptions and discourses been different, no Template would have been constructed, or a very different one. Paradigmatic thinking and discourse is revealed to go a long way toward a sufficient explanation of the judicialization of politics in Europe, and elsewhere, and the continuance of the American original despite marked popular disaffection. The story of Judiciary empowerment in Europe is a textbook example of how the normative is causative, as the constructivists imply (cf. Berger and Luckmann 1984).[1] But it also goes a long way toward sufficiently explaining what (or who) causes the normative.

Discovering the usual material causes, whilst normatively critiquing the normative as also a cause (but not just a cause), does not merely add to our theoretical understanding of the phenomenon, it also elevates the reader above the hegemonic influence of the very discourses under study, to which academic researchers are all too susceptible. Exposing the Network Community's normative paradigm can potentially put future social inquiry on a sounder footing, so that instead of falling into step with the elites we are studying, we can construct a vantage point from which to see reality anew. This does not mean an a priori commitment to some other ideology, however, which would merely substitute one prison for another. Such a commitment was the downfall of the Critical Theory movement, whose potential to enlighten by clarifying the pervasive influence of normative assumptions, was shackled by its Marxist, anti-European adhesion.

The original aim of this research project was to explain the Template, but it was discovered in the field that a causal nexus is unable to be thus limited. Mounting, undeniable evidence does compel the conclusion that the Template was not constructed for a 'middling' strategic goal like building the capacity to enforce the EU *acquis* upon accession only. It is the agenda of a grand strategy. The paradigmatic assumptions coded in Network Community discourses, and the Template's (or certain elements') blowback to member states like the UK whose capacity to implement the *acquis* is beyond cavil, evince that this exceptional degree and kind of empowerment is purposed to subserve the judicialization of politics for its own sake. Judges are catapulted into a position of superintendence of government and society though a capital cornerstone of the Network

[1] That the normative is causative and the causative normative is the core Constructivist insight. See in the EU context, for example, Diez (2013), Manners (2002), Nicolaidis and Howse (2002).

agenda. The Template's remote origin, its lack of rootedness in national and civil societal debates (transpired in so many instances of intolerance of the slightest deviation from it), likewise intimates that it is the non- (even the anti-)majoritarian fulcrum of the judicialization agenda: elite superintendence, or universal veto at a minimum, over popular self-government itself.

Counterfactual reasoning suggests it would have been simpler and less costly for our elites to have let the national Judiciaries be, and to decline becoming involved in matters as politically thorny and institutionally path-dependent as Judiciary revision. Even the masses of ordinary judges revealed signs of not wishing to be boosted in the way elite networks deem desirable. In CEE, this would have meant treating the debility of the Judiciary as a national problem and letting the newly elected parliaments in the region figure out how best to reform it; or letting the peoples of those countries pressure their domestic governments for adequate justice in the courts of law. Or the Network Community could have decided that this was not a problem for it to solve, just as it decided to do little to reform post-Communist parliaments. Or, the Network Community could have encouraged creation of an East European League to enable those countries to work in concert with each other. Such a League could have merged with the EU at a later date, when problems like the functioning of the Judiciary had been resolved. These are the kinds of alternatives that an actor not interested in self-empowerment would prefer. All this and the high transaction costs of nudging domestic Judiciaries away from their traditional moorings, not only in CEE but right across Europe, implies a pay-off to those bearing the costs, such that these institutions are not alone in being empowered.

The agency in question must be at its irreducible level individual: the Network entrepreneurs who spearhead it and the missionaries who propagate it may feel empowered when their policy ideas succeed. They are drawing none the less on the social capital of many. Bonded by collective identity (*esprit de corps*), they resemble d'Artagnan and the musketeers raising their cry, '*Un pour tous, tous pour un*'. Empowerment is of more than individual judges, or a few norm entrepreneurs. It is not the individual empowerment of a Napoleon, but collective empowerment (Bourdieu 1987). The Network Community is empowering itself; it is the one choosing judicialization as means to its own ends. Networked elite self-empowerment is the keystone of the arch of causes explaining the phenomenon and more parsimonious than the same design plan was arrived at spontaneously, independently in each of so many European states. It required a collective decision imposed from the top down.

The construction of a concrete institution like the Template is more than an outcome to be explained; it is in fact a cause in itself. It works in tandem with the propagation of its ideational paradigm and ruling discourse justifying to itself and all interested parties the Network Community's entrepreneurship. These are in fact the causes of something else, that is, the revisions of CEE constitutions and their legal, political, and social consequences. The Network Community did not construct them for their own sake. In Aristotelian terms, the Template is a Formal Cause; the Final Cause is the Network Community's self-empowerment conceived as a sovereign remedy for society's injustices.

Inferences about the Template can be generalized to the whole of the Network's agenda, the most celebrated component of which is human rights. Though beyond the scope of this study, it is worthwhile to observe for future research's sake that judicial activism, both national and supranational, exhibits certain puzzling features, including in the field of human rights, which seem inexplicable except on the premise of the consensus-driven networking of transnational elites. How should mere judges show such boldness in flouting public opinion? Why do they conform so exactly to each other over the content of the 'new rights'? Why do so many non-judicial elites leap to their defence, whilst nobody defends the majority's right to play by the rules of self-government? Inferences from the Judiciary design Template can be generalized to explain the transnational human rights agenda; it is more than just plausible that the same transnational, elite, collective agency is causing the sameness of output in both domains. All apex judges are networked-in nowadays and are enacting the common agenda *tout court*. If so many judges with so much discretion were acting *sua sponte* instead of from the Network identity and consensus that discourses constructed for them, they should be expected to rule in idiosyncratic ways when extrapolating the living constitution and extemporizing rights, given the degree of impunity from democratic discipline available for them to exploit, And would activists be reflexively supported by a larger Network Community of policy 'constituents', if they were acting *sua sponte*? As the American lawyer Schwartz candidly admits (see Chapter 2), judges deploy legalistic discourses as *ex post* rationales for getting what Ego wants, and *individual* egos want different things. The expected outcome of the living constitution meme stands in marked contrast to Original Intent, which would be expected to crystallize a more uniform interpretation. The international human rights agenda too seems a Network consensus phenomenon, not a spontaneous convergence on The Truth by the individual agency of egos independent of the influence of interested parties at all levels of governance. The (rebuttable) inferential presumption must be that the causal nexus found in this study – that is, a solidary Network Community plying its common agenda – applies to every agendum, not the Template alone. Regardless of whether courts are empowered by the Template or by designs derived from the same paradigm, the judicial Ego who is empowered is not individual but collective.

The Template reflects the Network's ambition to rule through the Judiciary, not only in Europe, but globally, as the evidence herein suggests, corroborated by other sources (Dezalay and Garth 2002, 2012). As so much of the Network consists of governmental actors who with the legal professional networks converge on revisiting the power relations in and between nation-states, it is not amiss to describe the Network Community as an informal State amid the formal, territorial ones. Its global reach and ambition suggests it is conceived or conceives itself as an incipient global government, or 'new world order' (Slaughter 2004; see also Helfer and Slaughter 1997), or 'cosmopolitan governance' (Held 1995). At a minimum, the Network Community, perhaps in tandem with others of its kind, may be deemed a 'new Great Power' in international affairs and ought to be theorized as such.

European integration stands revealed as a process at least partly dependent upon the Network Community, whose power is ever more consolidated with the 'ever closer' interdependence and policy coordination between the CoE and the EU (cf. Coman 2016; Dallara and Piana 2016). It cannot be stressed too often that the stability of this arrangement depends on a pre-existing meeting of the minds: the EU's dependence is tacitly contingent on 'good behaviour' in furnishing the EU the expertise it believes and the kind of advice it wants to hear. The glue is the pre-secured but informal Network consensus that pre-dates both formal institutions. This arrangement notably precludes democratic choice except if the people just so happen to agree with the elite networks. The old Soviet joke mocked that in America you are free to denounce President Reagan, and in the Soviet Union you are also free to denounce President Reagan. Asymmetrical inter-organizational dependency brings up the issue of dependency on solidary expertise generally. If society believes it cannot forgo the expertise, it is a lucky opportunity structure and a power resource for the corps of experts, if they are well enough organized to exploit it. But it is a 'fraught' political relation that enables the networked-in to overreach. The Network Community could have prevailed in any conflict-that-never-was over judicial empowerment because CEE believed that it needed its expertise. The conflict runs on underground none the less and may erupt unpredictably, from the revolt against activism in the USA to the (largely) counterfactual case if the EU faced CoE advice it disliked.

It is clear, if only from the latest developments in European and American politics, that the Template is one of many instances where the Network Community and its entrepreneurs pursue a judicializing governance agenda incompatible with democracy. Backbenchers and the people they represent often have quite different ideas about minority rights, the death penalty, or the regulation of political parties. Some indeed have argued that there is more wisdom in the multitude (Aristotle, *Politics*, Book III; Waldron 1995), particularly if elites are going to sacrifice significant portions of their independence of mind (in effect, compromising their otherwise superior enlightenment) for the sake of availing themselves of policy-making power through Network solidarity and consensus. The whitest of 'white hats' are not driven solely by the aspiration to solve the problems of humankind, but also by the all-too-human will to power, as Nietzsche called it. The Siren of self-empowerment by networking to unanimity convinces the networkers that they are doing nothing so crass as empowering Ego, but rather that Community into which they have been accepted, who is on the side of the angels. But the evolution of self-empowering legal professional networks feeds back to a correlative hollowing-out of national democratic institutions. The changes wrought by the Template are potent enough to contribute to the stillbirth of genuine democracy in the East and the deepening of the democratic deficit in the West.

The Template is an exemplary case of elite networking to sway democracy toward revising its governing institutions away from democracy to elitism. It is a window onto the farther-reaching processes of transnational self-empowerment by consensus and coordination, which can gain the Judiciary but also the whole of society (yet through the Judiciary). Parallel developments are the civil service reforms that worried Eastern Enlargement throughout the 1990s and early 2000s, also driven by Western agencies and transnational networks which might well be joined up with our Network Community, or the independent central bank craze which is now normalized across Europe, not just in the East. International development, too, appears to show a very similar pattern (Jackson 2005). These interventions, too, appear prima facie to exhibit the same patterns of elite self-empowerment as this study found, which future research ought to examine on the conjecture that both are instances of a much wider pattern (see e.g. Kauppi and Madsen 2013). Do the policy decisions these actors take at different times and places show any convergence hinting at transnational Network consensus? Is the collective identity or Network consensus or common agenda (if any) amongst senior civil servants, or bankers, the same as that of the legal professionals found in this study? That is, are national civil servants and central bankers members of the same Network Community, or a separate one of their own? On a more general level, why does the magic word 'professional' have so much power over the minds of men when the monopoly of experts shuts out competition, rendering justice, reverting to judicial affairs, too expensive for the average person? The one constant in all of the non-majoritarian reform programmes which the author observed in CEE is the 'independence' agenda. Does it entail ensconcing bankers and bureaucrats beyond accountability to elected representatives, as Judiciary revisions are doing? If so, why is it being done? Why have these models been recommended by international and supranational organizations such as the OECD in preference to all others? Could it be that the Network Community is motivated to want to make public policy through politically insulated institutions?

All of these institutional templates are best understood as manifestations of a power contest at the material and ideational level between pre-existing national and rising transnational elites. Recasting the analysis from the power-neutral terms that merely receive the discourses of one party to the contest, to terms that feature precisely all of the parties' power relations with each other, opens the door to a holistic perspective on the causal processes in play. Our Template, too, redistributes power from new member states to the EU, but also from majoritarian to non-majoritarian institutions.

The (re-)distribution and consolidation of powers by way of judicialization is one issue given short shrift in the European integration literature, though academics and commentators across the Atlantic confronted it long ago. 'When, in the name of a "right," a court strikes down the desire of the majority expressed through laws, freedom is transferred from a larger to a smaller group, from a majority to a minority' – to the *elite* minority confabulating the rights, above all (Waldron 1998; Bork 2003).

The Network's internal power resources of agency and expertise – from collective identity and solidarity to hegemonic discourses – all are necessary but none would suffice to empower the Network Community unless the public and their representatives accepted it. The Template has triumphed in part because the Network Community's paradigm had bewitched politicians and constituents alike, before it was ventured, to the point that veto players could omit to veto their own disempowerment. The assumption of intellectual-moral superiority is pivotal to get the public to practically presume politicians are the Class Enemy. The meek acquiescence of ordinary politicians whose misdemeanours are all too publicly known, and whose credibility with the public might therefore crater if not for their submission to a (self-appointed) 'higher control', is clearly part of the causal nexus of why the Network agenda and its embodiments are tolerated on the ground. A complete exploration and explanation of this fork of causation, however, must await future research which may draw on more constructivist approaches that seek to understand how norms come to be socially constructed through the agency of network multitudes and not always the genius of a few great men.

Except for the unicorn of zero veto, the causal picture is complete to the best of the author's knowledge; though questions remain about the nature of some of the causes in play, and still puzzling aspects of their interrelationships. One of the most difficult is the variable degree of deliberation wherewith large numbers of individuals pursue self-empowerment, who amongst themselves share much but far from all. Have all (or any) Network Community members been plotting to empower themselves over all other political actors? Are all (or any) aware that autocracy not democracy will result from how they think and act? Self-empowerment may be furthered unconsciously, just as the assumption of intellectual-moral superiority may be partly unwitting. Given that intentionality of large numbers is variable, definitive answers lie outside the scope of this inquiry. The most that can be said here is that the intentionality of Network agents may be expected to span the gamut from conscious to unconscious, and the relevant political actors may be more or less aware of the disempowerment of democracy. It is *not* disputed that European elites desire peace as sincerely as do ordinary Europeans, and that their primary motive is to secure peace amongst the nations of Europe (themselves in fact). On the other hand, insofar as certain entrepreneurs and other interested parties within the Network exploit their leverage to advance an agenda whose ambit surpasses what is really necessary for peace, they may be suspected to harbour motives that are all too human.

The theme of (self-)empowerment, which implicitly preconditions utility-maximization, is certainly familiar in the Rational Choice tradition.

The Network Community certainly does pursue its self-empowerment strategically to some extent, just as the rationalist logic would predict: networking, collective identity, and consensus to forestall internal disharmony; interdependency, coordination, and personnel is policy to efficiently implement the common agenda; favourable structural conditions to exploit, such as the trauma of Communism, and the yearning to integrate with the West; paradigmatic discourses to induce the public to take for granted – all these have a strategic dimension to them (although causally, some of these processes originate in less intangible forms of social construction).

The strategic dimension of self-empowerment of the whole Network Community clearly does not aim at a material coercion (whether or not it factors into the motives of this or that actor) which would achieve the social justice of the Marxists (Hirschl 2004). It is rather the intellectual-moral authority to arbitrate between all other political actors which the Network desire. A question for future research is, What all then explains the drive for *collective* self-empowerment? Anything is possible, from an inner circle of masterminds to the universal ego-centrism, however unconscious, of human nature, all interacting with the consciousness of one's intellectual therefore moral superiority in relation to other (but in reality no more flawed) human beings. Unconscious ego-centrism manifests as the drive to self-empowerment resting on the assumption that self-empowerment will actually achieve the betterment of humanity. Every human ego (who thinks about such things at all) is tempted to believe that if only Ego ruled, the world would be well in order.

Might such a complex explain certain other intangible features of the Network Community? Some quite well-informed academics baulk at the very concept of a Network consensus, for instance, owing to the lack of an obvious motive-force driving and holding it together. But it was seen how collective identity filters out 'undesirables' – unsuitable paradigms, agendas, and templates, as well as members – from the Network's undertakings, almost as if excluding them from private property.

If the same ego-centrism were acknowledged as operative in the disciplines of social science, not just political affairs or ancient astronomy, it could profoundly transform our endeavours both substantively and methodologically. Academic studies of transnational elites often verge on idealizing and crediting them with championing all good things, from the rule of law to human and minority rights, and they are esteemed for not resorting to violent, obvious coercion (Checkel 2012). In reality, as this study also documents, transnational elites dispose of many means of non-violent coercion: they are networked-in with media, political, and commercial elites at multiple levels of governance and need not use naked force to prevail.

The foregoing highlights the need for further inquiry into both the causal role of the spectrum of intentionality, from unconscious to conscious, in social phenomena, and the methodology of collecting data on it; drawing on (social) psychology insights from the psychic economy of pleasure and pain, to the social construction of Ego out of the reinforcement of others. Media are irresistible arbiters of public reputation, thus behavioural reinforcement, in contemporary politics. Social media have profoundly altered but not abolished (if anything, have amplified) the power of the media to reinforce political behaviour. These issues were necessarily left outside the scope of this study, but the author's informal observations along the way of her field work has been that the discourses of elite media invariably cast courts and judges, especially those at the apex, in a positive light compared to politicians, whose generally negative portrayal is a stratagem most readers find persuasive, as demonstrated by political psychology (Arceneaux 2012). Research into such phenomena needs to be supported if we would understand more fully why the success of judicial empowerment and the judicialization of politics has been so facile.

If the competences of apex courts, and if the Network Community's common agenda went no further than enforcing individual rights as understood when ratified by supermajority, with no agenda to engineer a 'better society' with or without the same consent, then judicialization (if that is what it would still be) might be bearable. As this study has documented, the ambition of the Network Community is further overreaching than that. It is, in fact, as limitless as the jurisdiction to which they have already laid claim. All-too-human ego seeks security in self-empowerment,[2] yet the only certainty is that absolute power corrupts absolutely. The transnational legal professional elite, and their non-jurist 'constituents', are, unbeknownst to themselves, recreating the very beast they were hoping to guard against: an unchecked power prone to tyranny. In the process, they are surely planting the seeds of their undoing.

[2] A homologous precept is found, for example, in the Realist school of international relations, one of whose basic premises is that nations seek security in self-empowerment (Morgenthau 1948; Waltz, 1959).

Of all of the political actors who have disrupted 'normal' politics in recent years, from Fidesz and Ponta to Brexit and Donald Trump, none have made a dent in the ongoing judicialization of politics. Only Fidesz managed to carry their agenda, and only in part. Ponta was forced to back down, and both Prime Minister May and President Trump have yielded to the overreaching of judges without giving any thought to the legitimacy of their jurisdiction. Neither the Declaration of Independence embedding the American Republic in the law of nations, nor the Constitution which did not contradict it, nor US statutory law gives to federal judges any jurisdiction to overrule presidents on matters of national security and entry by foreigners, yet judges ten out of thirteen of whom were appointed by partisan opponents exhibiting the 'violence of faction' awarded themselves jurisdiction no court had ever claimed in the history of the Republic, and purported to nullify a presidential act in international affairs on the subjective, personalistic grounds that it was not 'really' about security, but 'drips with religious intolerance, animus, and discrimination' (*International Refugee Assistance Program et al. v Trump* [2017]: 12).

Less dripping with animus but even more amazing was the UK Supreme Court's '*Marbury* Moment' in *R(Miller) v Secretary of State for Exiting the EU* [2017]. The English courts had never before claimed jurisdiction of foreign relations, but now assumed it on the grounds that use of the Queen's prerogative power to execute Article 50 of the Treaty of Lisbon affected the rights of British subjects (under the EU Treaties, not in the common law of England). The Court ruled that it may not be executed except by an enabling Act of Parliament, even though Parliament by the European Communities Act 1972 had already done just that: enabled the prerogative to be used to execute not only Article 50, but any article of any EU treaty.[3]

[3] The judicial precedent that only an Act of Parliament may defeat 'rights' (except if it is the 1972 Act, it would seem) conflates plaintiffs demanding treaty entitlements with defendants whom Crown prosecutors have put in jeopardy. The rights of British subjects under the EU Treaties are not common law rights where the jurisdiction of the law courts is settled, but 'rights' in the more technical sense of creatures of foreign powers which stand or fall with their acts of State. The Lisbon treaty is one such act, authorizing any member state to exit unilaterally through Article 50 (and per the European Communities Act). Courts exempt defendants from loss of prior liberties unless Parliament sanctions it. At no time did the Government take away rights of English citizens under the laws of England. Hardly less incredible than the UK Supreme Court's assuming the powers of a constitutional court was how the twisting of an ancient rule meant to protect English citizens from the royal prerogative is countenanced to mean courts now control Government execution of treaties, even to

With no case to answer, the Government should have responded to neither complaint nor summons, yet the PM and Parliament both sheepishly submitted to the outlandish assertion of judicial supremacy. So was the elites' discourse that the Court intervened to vindicate Parliament. A private citizen complained, not Parliament, which needs no judicial affirmation of its powers; it holds them in contempt of courts. What courts can make, courts can break. At a stroke, the Court overrode both Government and Parliament, in effect nullifying Parliament's delegation of the prerogative power by its 1972 Act. The hue and cry about parliamentary sovereignty has positioned the legal professional elite to assume a jurisdiction, the ulterior end of which is to put paid to Parliament's sovereignty. And the public, triggered by the word 'rights', seem incapable of defending its sovereignty by reflecting on the insecurity of founding its rights on transnational councils beyond veto or vote. Achieving discursive hegemony to such a breathtaking pitch is surely the Network Community's greatest victory.

nullifying a statutory exercise of the prerogative to exit a compromise of national sovereignty just because it was swapped for 'rights' in the tribunals of foreign powers. Now there will be no end to courts' finding rights in treaties as pretexts to nullify foreign policy that a judge (or a plaintiff) disprefers.

Annexe: Interviewees

Interviewee	*Position at the time of the interview*	*Organization*	*Transcript availability*
Interviewee 1: CoE Steering Committee member	Senior civil servant	CoE Steering Committee on Legal Co-operation	Yes
Interviewee 2: MEDEL high official	Career civil servant	MEDEL	Yes
Interviewee 3: CoE Steering Committee member	Jurist and senior civil servant	CoE Steering Committee on Legal Co-operation	Yes
Interviewee 4: Academician and political adviser	Jurist, academic, and political adviser	Law Professor, Lóránd Eötvös University, Hungary	No
Interviewee 5: CC judge	Judge and MP	CC, Romania	Yes
Interviewee 6: SCt judge	Judge and academic	SCt, Czech Republic	Yes
Interviewee 7: OSCE officer	Jurist	OSCE, Moldova	
Interviewee 8: Venice Commission official	Senior civil servant	Venice Commission, Strasbourg	Yes
Interviewee 9: MoJ civil servant	Senior civil servant	MoJ, Moldova	Yes
Interviewee 10: Jurist and MP	Jurist and career politician	Political adviser, Office of the Presidency, Romania	Yes
Interviewee 11: EJA officer and CoE adviser	Judge	EJA and CoE	Yes
Interviewee 12: CoE civil servant	Career civil servant	General Secretariat, CoE	Yes
Interviewee 13: CoE official	Senior civil servant	Director, General Secretariat, CoE	Yes
Interviewee 14: EC official	Jurist and senior civil servant	DG Enlargement, EC	Yes
Interviewee 15: EC official	Jurist and Head of Unit	DG Enlargement, EC	Yes

Interviewee	*Position at the time of the interview*	*Organization*	*Transcript availability*
Interviewee 16: EC official	Jurist and Head of Unit	DG Enlargement, EC	Yes
Interviewee 17: Jurist and career politician	Jurist, private lawyer, and career politician	Parliament, Romania	Yes
Interviewee 18: ECJ clerk	Jurist and clerk	ECJ	Yes
Interviewee 19: JC official	Judge	JC senior official and SCt judge, Croatia	Yes
Interviewee 20: ABA officer	Jurist	ABA-CEELI, Moldova	Yes
Interviewee 21: SCt judge and JC official	Judge	SCt judge and JC senior official, Moldova	Yes
Interviewee 22: OSCE officer	Jurist	OSCE, Moldova	Yes
Interviewee 23: ECtHR judge	Judge	ECtHR	Yes
Interviewee 24: ABA officer	Jurist	ABA-CEELI, Romania	Yes
Interviewee 25: Lawyers for Human Rights officer	Jurist and human rights activist	Lawyers for Human Rights and Soros Foundation, Moldova	Yes
Interviewee 26: EC official	Jurist	DG Justice, EC	Yes
Interviewee 27: MoJ senior official	Jurist and career civil servant	MoJ, Norway	Yes
Interviewee 28: MoJ official	Career civil servant	Constitution and Judiciary Division, MoJ, UK	Yes
Interviewee 29: CC judge	Judge and academic	CC, Moldova	Yes
Interviewee 30: Trial Court judge	Judge	Judge, Municipal Criminal Court, Croatia	Yes
Interviewee 31: ABA officer	Jurist	ABA, International Judicial Academy, and the National Centre for State Courts	Yes
Interviewee 32: Senior Presidential adviser	Jurist, academic, and political adviser	Adviser on Constitutional Law, Office of the Presidency, Romania	Yes

Interviewee	*Position at the time of the interview*	*Organization*	*Transcript availability*
Interviewee 33: Jurist and academician	Jurist and academic	Lecturer, Department of International and European Law, Moldova State University, Chişinău	Yes
Interviewee 34: CC judge	Judge	CC, Czech Republic	Yes
Interviewee 35: Jurist and MEP	Jurist and career politician	Fidesz MEP, European People's Party	Yes
Interviewee 36: EC career civil servant	Civil servant	DG Enlargement, EC	Yes
Interviewee 37: EC career civil servant	Civil servant	EC Delegation, Moldova	Yes
Interviewee 38: CC judge	Judge and academic	CC, Romania	Yes
Interviewee 39: EC official	Jurist and career civil servant	DG Justice, EC	Yes
Interviewee 40: Judge and EC adviser	Judge and EC expert on judicial reform	Court of Appeal, Italy	Yes
Interviewee 41: JC high official	Judge	JC and Court of Appeal, Romania	Yes
Interviewee 42: High Court judge	Judge and academic	Royal Courts of Justice, UK	Yes
Interviewee 43: CoE Steering Committee member	Jurist, academic, and CoE civil servant	CoE Steering Committee on Legal Co-operation	Yes
Interviewee 44: Minister of Justice	Jurist	MoJ, Romania	Yes
Interviewee 45: MTA official	Jurist	MTA, Croatia	Yes
Interviewee 46: SCt judge and academician	Judge and academic	SCt, Norway	Yes
Interviewee 47: Jurist and MP	Jurist and career politician	Parliament of Croatia	Yes
Interviewee 48: Academician	Jurist	Law Faculty, Sibiu, Romania	Yes
Interviewee 49: Academician	Jurist and academic	Law Faculty, Zagreb, Croatia	Yes
Interviewee 50: CC clerk and academician	Clerk and academic	CC, Czech Republic	Yes
Interviewee 51: Academician	Jurist and academic	Law Faculty, Zagreb, Croatia	Yes

Interviewee	*Position at the time of the interview*	*Organization*	*Transcript availability*
Interviewee 52: Minister of Justice	Jurist	MoJ, Romania	Yes
Interviewee 53: ECJ judge and academician	Judge and academic	ECJ, Luxembourg	Yes
Interviewee 54: Academician	Jurist	Law Faculty, Zagreb, Croatia	Yes
Interviewee 55: General Prosecutor	Jurist	MoJ, Romania	Yes
Interviewee 56: Academician	Jurist	University College London, UK	Yes
Interviewee 57: Appellate judge	Judge	Court of Appeal, Romania	Yes
Interviewee 58: CC judge	Judge	CC, Romania	Yes
Interviewee 59: High Court judge	Judge	High Court and the Union of Judges, Czech Republic	Yes

Bibliography

Abrams, I. (1957). 'The emergence of the International Law Societies.' *The Review of Politics* 19(3): 361–380.

Administrative Office of the US Courts. (2017). 'Governance & the judicial conference.' Retrieved 23 March 2017, from www.uscourts.gov/about-federal-courts/governance-judicial-conference

Adunarea Constituantă. (1991). 'Dezbateri parlamentare. Sedinta din ziua de 13 February 1999. Stenograma.' *Monitorul Official* II(1).

Alexander, L. and F. Schauer (1997). 'On extrajudicial constitutional interpretation.' *Harvard Law Review* 110(7): 1359–1387.

Allen, V. L. and J. M. Levine (1969). 'Consensus and conformity.' *Journal of Experimental Social Psychology* 5(4): 389–399.

Alter, K. J. (2001). *Establishing the Supremacy of European Law: The making of an international rule of law in Europe.* Oxford, Oxford University Press.

Alter, K. J. (2007). 'Jurist social movements in Europe: The role of Euro-law associations in European integration (1953–1975).' *EUSA Review* 20(4): 6–12.

Alter, K. J. (2008). 'Jurist advocacy movements in Europe and the Andes: How lawyers help promote international legal integration.' Retrieved 5 July 2011, from http://ssrn.com/abstract=1270075

Alter, K. J. and L. R. Helfer (2010). 'Nature or nurture? Judicial lawmaking in the European Court of Justice and the Andean Tribunal of Justice.' *International Organization* 64(4): 563–592.

Alter, K. J. and L. R. Helfer (2017). *Transplanting International Courts: The law and politics of the Andean Tribunal of Justice.* Oxford, Oxford University Press.

American Bar Association. (2002). 'Judicial reform index for Romania.' Retrieved 10 January 2008, from http://unpan1.un.org/intradoc/groups/public/documents/UNTC/UNPAN017567.pdf

Anderson, T. and W. Twining (1991). *Analysis of Evidence: How to do things with facts.* London, Weidenfeld and Nicolson.

Antonić, S. (2008). 'New purge of judges?' Retrieved 4 November 2012, from www.sudije.rs/en/actuals/news-articles/new-purge-of-judges

Arceneaux, K. (2012). 'Cognitive biases and the strength of political arguments.' *American Journal of Political Science* 56(2): 271–285.

Aristotle (1885). *Politics*, translated by Benjamin Jowett as *The Politics of Aristotle*. Oxford, Clarendon Press. Retrieved 20 January 2018, from https://archive.org/details/politicsaristot05arisgoog

Atran, S. and J. Henrich (2010). 'The evolution of religion: How cognitive by-products, adaptive learning heuristics, ritual displays, and group competition generate deep commitments to prosocial religions.' *Biological Theory* 5(1): 18–30.

Backer, I. L. (2007). 'The Norwegian reform of civil procedure.' *Scandinavian Studies in Law* 51: 41–75.

Bagdikian, B. H. (1983). *The Media Monopoly*. Boston, MA, Beacon Press.

Bagdikian, B. H. (2004). *The New Media Monopoly*. Boston, MA, Beacon Press.

Bagehot, W. ([1867] 1963). *The English Constitution*. Oxford, Oxford University Press.

Bains, J. W. (2011). 'Ground due process and the unconstitutionality of the Fourteenth Amendment jurisprudence.' Unpublished manuscript.

Baird, V. A. and A. Gangl (2006). 'Shattering the myth of legality: The impact of the media's framing of Supreme Court procedures on perceptions of fairness.' *Political Psychology* 27(4): 597–614.

Ball, M. M. (1959). *NATO and the European Union Movement*. London, Stevens.

Bancaud, A. (2006). 'Normalisation d'une innovation: le Conseil supérieur de la magistrature sous la IVe Republique.' *Droit et Société* 63–64: 371–391.

Bánkuti, M., G. Halmai and K. L. Scheppele (2012). 'Hungary's illiberal turn: Disabling the constitution.' *Journal of Democracy* 23(3): 138–146.

Bánkuti, M., T. Dombos, Z. Fleck, G. Halmai, K. Rozgonyi, B. Majtényi, L. Majtényi, E. Polgári, K. L. Scheppele, B. Somody and R. Uitz (2012). 'Opinion on Hungary's new constitutional order: Amicus brief for the Venice Commission on the transitional provisions of the fundamental law and the key cardinal laws.' Retrieved 2 February 2018, from http://lapa.princeton.edu/hosteddocs/hungary/Amicus_Cardinal_Laws_final.pdf

Batliner, G., J. Robert and J.-P. Massias (2002). *Proiect de Aviz Complementar Asupra Revizuirii Constitutiei României CDL (2002)138*. Bucharest, Parlamentul României.

Bellamy, R. (2007). *Political Constitutionalism: A Republican defence of the constitutionality of democracy*. Cambridge, Cambridge University Press.

Berger, P. and T. Luckmann (1984). *The Social Construction of Reality: A treatise in the sociology of knowledge*. London, Penguin.

Berggren, N. and N. Karlson (2003). 'Constitutionalism, division of power and transaction costs.' *Public Choice* 117(1/2): 99–124.

Blackmore, P. and C. B. Kandiko (2011). 'Motivation in academic life: A prestige economy.' *Research in Post-Compulsory Education* 16(4): 399–411.

Blacksell, M. and K. M. Born (2002). 'Private property restitution: The geographical consequences of official government policies in Central and Eastern Europe.' *The Geographical Journal* 168(2): 178–190.

Blackstone, W. ([1765] 1809). *Commentaries on The Laws of England (15th edition)*. London, A. Strahan.

Blaustein, A. P. and A. H. Field (1958). '"Overruling" opinions in the Supreme Court.' *Michigan Law Review* 57(2): 151–194.
Bobek, M. and D. Kosař (2014). 'Global solutions, local damages: A critical study in judicial councils in Central and Eastern Europe.' *German Law Journal* 15: 1251–1292.
Boffey, D. (2017). 'European commission criticises Romania over prisoner pardon plan.' *Guardian*, 27 January.
Bork, R. H. (2003). *Coercing Virtue. The worldwide rule of judges*. Washington, DC, AEI Press.
Boulanger, C. (2006). 'Europeanization through judicial activism? The Hungarian Constitutional Court's legitimacy and the "return to Europe".' In W. Sadurski, A. Czarnota and M. Krygier (eds). *Spreading Democracy and the Rule of Law*. Dordrecht, Springer: 263–280.
Bourdieu, P. (1987). 'The force of law: Toward a sociology of the juridical field.' *Hastings Law Journal* 38(July): 805–853.
Bourdieu, P. (1996). *The State Nobility. Elite schools in the field of power*. Stanford, CA, University of Stanford Press.
Brady, H. E. and D. Collier (eds) (2004). *Rethinking Social Inquiry*. New York, Oxford, Rowman & Littlefield Publishers, Inc.
Brock, M. G. (1973). *The Great Reform Act*. London, Hutchinson.
Bruzelius, K. (2014). 'The Nordic constitutions and judicial review.' Retrieved 15 September 2015, from www.constcourt.md/public/files/file/conferinta_20ani/programul_conferintei/Karin_Bruzelius_2.pdf
Bugarič, B. and T. Ginsburg (2016). 'The assault on postcommunist courts.' *Journal of Democracy* 27(3): 69–82.
Bureau of the European Committee on Legal Co-operation. (2008). 'View of the Bureau of the CDCJ on the follow-up to be given to the initial revision of Recommendation n° R (94) 12 on the independence, efficiency and role of judges and its Draft Explanatory Memorandum, CDCJ-BU (2008)7.' Strasbourg, Bureau of the European Committee on Legal Co-operation.
Burley, A.-M. and W. Mattli (1993). 'Europe before the court: A political theory of legal integration.' *International Organization* 47(1): 41–76.
Caldeira, G. A. (1987). 'Public opinion and the U.S. Supreme Court: FDR's court-packing plan.' *American Political Science Review* 81(4): 1139–1153.
Cápeta, T. (2005). 'Courts, legal culture and the enlargement of the EU.' *Croatian Yearbook of European Law & Policy* 1: 23–55.
Centre Virtuel de la Connaissance sur l'Europe. (2018). 'The Congress of Europe in The Hague (7–10 May 1948).' Retrieved 1 March 2018, from https://www.cvce.eu/en/
Checkel, J. T. (1999). 'Norms, institutions and national identity in contemporary Europe.' *International Studies Quarterly* 43(1): 83–114.
Checkel, J. T. (2001). 'Why comply? Social learning and European identity change.' *International Organization* 55(3): 553–588.

Checkel, J. T. (2003). '"Going native" in Europe? Theorizing social interaction in European institutions.' *Comparative Political Studies* 36(1–2): 209–231.

Checkel, J. T. (2012). 'Norm entrepreneurship: Theoretical and methodological challenges.' Paper presented at Wolfson College, University of Oxford, January 2012.

Chesterton, G. K. (1908). 'Orthodoxy.' Retrieved 5 May 2015, from www.gutenberg.org/files/16769/16769-h/16769-h.htm

Chrisafis, A. (2011). 'Sarkozy under pressure as French judges take to the streets.' *Guardian*, 10 February. Retrieved 15 May 2013, from www.theguardian.com/world/2011/feb/10/sarkozy-french-judges-protest

Coase, R. H. (1988). *The Firm, the Market, and the Law*. Chicago, IL, University of Chicago Press.

Cohen, A. (2007). 'Constitutionalism without constitution: Transnational elites between political mobilization and legal expertise in the making of a constitution for Europe (1940s–1960s).' *Law & Social Inquiry* 32(1): 109–135.

Cohen, A. and A. Vauchez (2007). 'Law, lawyers, and transnational politics in the production of Europe.' *Law & Social Inquiry* 32(1): 75–199.

Coke, E. (1628). 'Petition of Right.' Retrieved 23 March 2017, from www.constitution.org/eng/petright.htm

Collier, D. (2008). 'Introduction to symposium: Case selection, case studies, and causal inference.' *Qualitative and Multi-method Research* 6(2): 2–4.

Collier, D. (2011). 'Understanding process tracing.' *PS: Political Science and Politics* 44(4): 823–830.

Coman, R. (2014a). 'Quo vadis judicial reforms? The quest for judicial independence in Central and Eastern Europe.' *Europe-Asia Studies* 66(6): 892–924.

Coman, R. (2014b). 'The normative power of the EU and contentious Europeanization: The case of judicial politics.' *Journal of European Integration* 36(6). DOI: 10.1080/07036337.2014.894036.

Coman, R. (2016). 'Strengthening the rule of law at the supranational level: The rise and consolidation of a European Network.' *Journal of Contemporary European Studies* 24(1): 171–188.

Coman, R. and C. Dallara (2009). 'Judicial independence in Romania.' In A. Seibert-Fohr (ed.). *Judicial Independence in Transition*. Heidelberg, Springer: 835–885.

Coman, R. and J.-M. De Waele (2007). *Judicial Reforms in Central and Eastern European Countries*. Bruges, Vanden Broele.

Comfort, K. J. (2003). *Power, Politics and the Ego*. Cohoes, NY, The Public Administration Institute of New York State, Inc.

Comisia Europeană de Democraţie prin Lege. (2001). *Anteproiect de aviz consolidat asupra proiectului de revizuire a Constitutiei României, CDL (2002)96*. Bucharest, Parlametul României.

Comisia Prezidenţiala de Analiză a Regimului Politic şi Constituţional din România. (2009). *Raport al Comisiei Prezidenţiale de Analiză a Regimului Politic şi Constituţional din România – Pentru consolidarea statului de drept*. Bucharest, Preşedinţia României.

Committee of Ministers of the Council of Europe. (1999). '22nd conference of European Ministers of Justice Chisinau (17–18 June 1999).' Retrieved 23 June 2011, from https://wcd.coe.int/ViewDoc.jsp?id=417393&Site=CM

Committee of Ministers of the Council of Europe. (2010). 'Resolution CM/Res(2010)26 on the establishment of an advisory panel of experts on candidates for election as judge to the European Court of Human Rights.' Retrieved 5 February 2015, from https://wcd.coe.int/ViewDoc.jsp?id=1704555&Site=CM&BackColorInternet=C3C3C3&BackColorIntranet=EDB021&BackColorLogged=F5D383#P36_2535

Conac, G. (2000). 'O anterioritate română: controlul constituţionalităţii legilor în românia de la începutul secolului XX până în 1938.' Retrieved 19 March 2012, from https://www.ccr.ro/ccrold/events/2000/ro/Conac.pdf

Connolly, W. (1983). *The Terms of Political Discourse*. Oxford, Martin Robinson.

Constitutional Court of Austria. (2015). 'History of the Constitutional Court.' Retrieved 6 August 2014, from https://www.vfgh.gv.at/cms/vfgh-site/english/history.html

Constitutional Court of Romania. (2012). 'Press release (03.07.2012).' Retrieved 13 July 2012, from www.ccr.ro/comunicate/COMUNICAT-DE-PRES-27

Consultative Council of European Judges. (2001). 'Opinion N° 1 (2001) of the Consultative Council of European Judges (CCJE) for the attention of the Committee of Ministers of the Council of Europe on standards concerning the independence of the judiciary and the irremovability of judges.' Retrieved 14 April 2012, from www.coe.int/t/dghl/cooperation/ccje/textes/Avis_en.asp

Consultative Council of European Judges. (2014a). 'Chair of the CCJE from January 2004 to December 2005: Alain Lacabarats.' Retrieved 5 December 2014, from www.coe.int/t/dghl/cooperation/ccje/presentation/Bio-Lacabarats_en.asp

Consultative Council of European Judges. (2014b). 'Chair of the CCJE in 2012 and 2013: Gerhard Reissner.' Retrieved 5 December 2014, from www.coe.int/t/dghl/cooperation/ccje/presentation/Bio-Reissner_en.asp

Consultative Council of European Judges. (2014c). 'Member states.' Retrieved 5 December 2014, from www.coe.int/t/dghl/cooperation/ccje/presentation/MembresCCJE.asp

Costa, J.-P. (2012). 'Jean-Paul COSTA, President of the European Court of Human Rights, C.V.' Retrieved 22 May 2015, from www.echr.coe.int/Documents/CV_Costa_ENG.pdf

Council of Europe. (1949). 'Statute of the Council of Europe.' Retrieved 6 March 2015, from www.coe.int/en/web/conventions/full-list/-/conventions/rms/0900001680306052

Council of Europe. (2010a). 'Recommendation CM/Rec(2010)12 of the Committee of Ministers to member states on judges: independence, efficiency and responsibilities.' Retrieved 2 March 2013, from https://wcd.coe.int/ViewDoc.jsp?id=1707137

Council of Europe. (2010b). 'Recommendation of the Committee of Ministers to member states on judges: independence, efficiency and responsibilities, CM/Rec(2010)12.' Retrieved 12 January 2013, from https://wcd.coe.int/wcd/ViewDoc.jsp?id=1707137&Site=CM

Council of Europe. (2010c). 'Reform of European Court of Human Rights: Protocol No.14 enters into force. Press release – 437(2010).' Retrieved 16 April 2013, from https://wcd.coe.int/ViewDoc.jsp?id=1628875&Site=DC&BackColorInternet=F5CA75&BackColorIntranet=F5CA75&BackColorLogged=A9BACE

Council of Europe. (2012). 'Prisoner human rights breaches puts Romania prisons in spotlight.' Retrieved 11 March 2016, from www.humanrightseurope.org/2012/06/prisoner-human-rights-breaches-puts-romania-prisons-in-spotlight/

Croxton, D. (2013). *Westphalia: The last Christian peace*. New York, Palgrave Macmillan.

Cserne, P. (2015). 'Formalism in judicial reasoning: Is Central and Eastern Europe a special case?' In M. Bobek (ed.). *Central European Judges Under the European Influence: The transformative power of the EU revisited*. Oxford, Hart Publishing: 23–43.

Curtea Constitutionala a României. (2012). 'Comunicat de presa [Press release].' Retrieved 12 January 2014, from https://www.ccr.ro/comunicate/COMUNICAT-DE-PRES-27

Dahl, R. A. (1971). *Polyarchy: Participation and opposition*. New Haven, CT and London, Yale University Press.

Dallara, C. (2012). 'The definition of "best judicial practices" by judicial and legal expert networks and commissions.' In A. Vauchez (ed.). *The Fabric of International Jurisprudence. An interdisciplinary encounter*. Florence, European University Institute: 21–31.

Dallara, C. and D. Piana (2016). *Networking the Rule of Law: How change agents reshape judicial governance in the EU*. London, Routledge.

Davies, C. (2017). 'Polish MPs pass judicial bills amid accusations of threat to democracy.' *Guardian*. Retrieved 10 January 2018, from https://www.theguardian.com/world/2017/dec/08/polish-mps-pass-supreme-court-bill-criticised-as-grave-threat

Davis, R. (2011). *Justices and Journalists: The U.S. Supreme Court and the media*. Cambridge, Cambridge University Press.

Davis, T. (2010). 'The Council of Europe – the best kept secret in Europe.' Retrieved 20 March 2012, from www.dmu.ac.uk/news_events/news/archive/100107_Terry_Davis_DLS.jsp

Dawidson, K. E. K. (2004). 'Conflicts of interest in the restitution and privatisation of housing since the fall of socialism: The case of Central Timisoara City: A problem of democracy?' *Europe-Asia Studies* 56(1): 119–141.

de Visser, M. and M. Claes (2013). 'Courts united? On European judicial networks.' In A. Vauchez and B. de Witte (eds). *Lawyering Europe: European law as a transnational social field*. Oxford, Hart Publishing: 75–101.
Dezalay, Y. and B. G. Garth (2002). *Global Prescriptions: The production, exportation, and importation of a new legal orthodoxy*. Ann Arbor, University of Michigan Press.
Dezalay, Y. and B. G. Garth (eds) (2011). *Lawyers and the Construction of Transnational Justice*. Abingdon, Routledge.
Dezalay, Y. and B. G. Garth (2012). *Lawyers and the Rule of Law in an Era of Globalization*. Abingdon and New York, Routledge.
Diamond, L., J. J. Linz and S. M. Lipset (eds) (1995). *Politics in Developing Countries: Comparing experiences with democracy*. Boulder, CO and London, Lynne Rienner.
Diez, T. (2013). 'Normative power as hegemony.' *Cooperation and Conflict* 48(2): 194–210.
Dimitrova, A. L. (ed.) (2004). *Driven to Change: The European Union's enlargement viewed from the East*. Manchester, Manchester University Press.
Directorate General of Human Rights and Legal Affairs. (2009). 'Group of Specialists on the Judiciary (CJ-S-JUST) Composition.' Strasbourg, Council of Europe.
Directorate of Legal Advice and Public International Law. (2015). 'Role of the Advisory Panel.' Retrieved 2 September 2015, from www.coe.int/en/web/dlapil/advisory-panel
Dowding, K. (1995). 'Model or metaphor? A critical review of the policy network approach.' *Political Studies* 43(1): 136–158.
Dwyer, D. (2009). 'Looking for a bailout? Just call your Congressman.' Retrieved 3 January 2015, from http://abcnews.go.com/Politics/congress-private-laws-bailout-americans-special-cases/story?id=8995047
Dye, T. R. (2008). *Understanding Public Policy*. Upper Saddle River, NJ, Pearson Prentice Hall.
Easterbook, F. H. (1989). 'Presidential review.' *Case Western Reserve Law Review* 40: 905–929.
Eckhardt, C. C. (1937) *The Papacy and World Affairs as Reflected in the Secularization of Politics*. Chicago, IL, University of Chicago Press.
Ellicott, S. (2011). 'British newspaper representations of the judiciary in connection with coverage of the Human Rights Act 1998 and the European Convention on Human Rights.' London, The UCL Constitution Unit.
Elster, J. (1995). 'Forces and mechanisms in the constitution-making process.' *Duke Law Review* 45: 364–396.
Emmert, F. (2002). 'The independence of judges – a concept often misunderstood in Central and Eastern Europe.' *European Journal of Law Reform* 3(4): 405–409.
Engdahl, D. E. (1992). 'John Marshall's "Jeffersonian" concept of judicial review.' *Duke Law Journal* 42(2): 279–339.
Epstein, L., A. D. Martin, K. M. Quinn and J. A. Segal (2007). 'Ideological drift among Supreme Court Justices: Who, when, and how important.' *Northwestern University Law Review* 101(4): 1483–1542.

Erdos, D. (2010). *Delegating Rights Protection – The Rise of Bills of Rights in the Westminster World*. Oxford, Oxford University Press.
Etzioni-Halevy, E. (1993). *The Elite Connection: Problems and potential in Western democracy*. Boston, MA, Basil Blackwell.
European Commission. (2013). 'Recommendation for a Council Recommendation on Hungary's 2013 national reform programme and delivering a Council opinion on Hungary's convergence programme for 2012–2016 /COM/2013/0367 final.' Retrieved 11 May 2016, from http://eur-lex.europa.eu/legal-content/EN/TXT/?uri=CELEX:52013DC0367
European Commission. (2015). 'European neighbourhood and enlargement negotiations. TAIEX.' Retrieved 15 June 2016, from http://ec.europa.eu/enlargement/tenders/taiex/index_en.htm
European Commission for Democracy through Law. (1997). *The Composition of Constitutional Courts*. Strasbourg, Council of Europe.
European Commission for Democracy through Law. (2011a). 'Opinion on three legal questions arising in the process of drafting the new Constitution of Hungary.' Adopted by the Venice Commission at its 86th Plenary Session (Venice, 25–26 March 2011). Retrieved 5 October 2014, from http://tasz.hu/files/tasz/imce/2011/opinion_on_hungarian_constitutional_questions_enhu.pdf
European Commission for Democracy through Law. (2011b). 'Opinion on the new constitution of Hungary.' Adopted by the Venice Commission at its 87th Plenary Session (Venice, 17–18 June 2011). Retrieved 4 January 2018, from www.venice.coe.int/webforms/documents/default.aspx?pdffile=CDL-AD(2011)016-e
European Commission for the Efficiency of Justice. (2013). 'Abridged report of the 21st plenary meeting (20–21 June 2013).' Retrieved 24 May 2013, from https://wcd.coe.int/ViewDoc.jsp?id=2081651&Site=
European Committee on Legal Co-operation. (2014). 'At a glance.' Retrieved 5 March 2014, from www.coe.int/t/DGHL/STANDARDSETTING/CDcj/default_en.asp
European Communities Act 1972 c. 68, 2(2). Retrieved 15 March 2017, from www.legislation.gov.uk/ukpga/1972/68/contents
European Council. (1993). 'Presidency conclusions. Copenhagen European Council – 21–22 June 1993.' Retrieved 13 May 2003, from www.europarl.europa.eu/enlargement/ec/pdf/cop_en.pdf
European Council. (1995). 'Madrid European Council 15 and 16 December 1995. Presidency conclusions.' Retrieved 10 May 2008, from www.europarl.europa.eu/summits/mad1_en.htm
European Council of the European Union. (2015). 'Judges appointed to the Court of Justice and the General Court.' Retrieved 2 October 2015, from www.consilium.europa.eu/en/press/press-releases/2015/09/16-judges-appointed-to-ecj-and-general-court/
European Court of Human Rights (Fourth Section). (2005). 'Case of *Hirst v. The United Kingdom* (No. 2) (Application no. 74025/01).' Retrieved 20 January 2018, from http://hudoc.echr.coe.int/eng?i=001-61680

European Court of Human Rights (Second Section). (2009). 'Case of *Lautsi v. Italy* (Application no. 30814/06).' Retrieved 13 June 2014, from http://hudoc.echr.coe.int/eng?i=001-95589

European Court of Justice. (1998). 'Press release no 57/98, 17 September 1998. Two new judges appointed to the court of first instance of the EC.' Retrieved 21 June 2015, from http://curia.europa.eu/en/actu/communiques/cp98/cp9857en.htm

European Court of Justice. (2014). 'Opinion 2/13 of the Court (Full Court) (18 December 2014).' Retrieved 13 March 2017, from http://curia.europa.eu/juris/liste.jsf?num=C-2/13

European Movement International. (2015). 'Who we are. History.' Retrieved 3 June 2015, from http://europeanmovement.eu/who-we-are/history/

Fairbrass, J. and A. Jordan (2001). 'Protecting biodiversity in the European Union: National barriers and European opportunities?' *Journal of European Public Policy* 8(4): 499–518.

Fallon, R. H. J. (2003). 'Marbury and the constitutional mind: A bicentennial essay on the wages of doctrinal tension.' *California Law Review* 91(1): 1–57.

Follesdal, A. and M. Wind (2009). 'Introduction – Nordic reluctance towards judicial review under siege.' *Nordic Journal of Human Rights* 27(2): 131–141.

Foucault, M. (2000). *Power*. London, Allen Lane.

Franklin, B. ([1868] 1996). *The Autobiography of Benjamin Franklin*. Mineola, NY, Dover Publications.

Gant, S. E. (1997). 'Judicial supremacy and nonjudicial interpretation of the Constitution.' *Hastings Constitutional Law Quarterly* 24: 359–440.

Garner, J. W. (1915). 'Judicial control of administrative and legislative acts in France.' *American Political Science Review* 9(4): 637–665.

Garner, J. W. (1917). 'The French Judiciary.' *Yale Law Journal* 26(5): 349–387.

Garoupa, N. and T. Ginsburg (2009). 'Guarding the guardians: Judicial councils and judicial independence.' *American Journal of Comparative Law* 57: 103–134.

Garoupa, N. and T. Ginsburg (2011). 'The comparative law and economics of judicial councils.' *Berkeley Journal of International Law* 27(1): 52–82.

Garoupa, N. and T. Ginsburg (2016). *Judicial Reputation: A comparative theory*. Chicago, IL, University of Chicago Press.

Gaventa, J. (1980). *Power and Powerlessness: Quiescence and rebellion in an Appalachian valley*. Oxford, Clarendon Press.

Gearty, C. (2013). *Liberty and Security*. Cambridge, Polity.

Gee, G., R. Hazell, K. Malleson and P. O'Brien (2015). *The Politics of Judicial Independence in the UK's Changing Constitution*. Cambridge, Cambridge University Press.

Georgakakis, D. (2012). *Le champ de l'Eurocratie. Une sociologie politique du personnel de l'U.E.* Paris, Economica.

Gerring, J. (2004). 'What is a case study and what is it good for?' *American Political Science Review* 98(2): 341–354.

Gillman, H. (2002). 'How political parties use the courts to advance their agendas: Federal courts in the United States, 1875–1891.' *American Political Science Review* 96(3): 511–524.

Ginsburg, T. (2003). *Judicial Review in New Democracies*. Cambridge, Cambridge University Press.

Glaser, B. G. (2013) 'Introduction: Free style memoing.' *Grounded Theory Review* DOI: http://groundedtheoryreview.com/

Glaser, B. G. and A. L. Strauss (1967). *The Discovery of Grounded Theory: Strategies for qualitative research*. New Brunswick, NJ and London, Aldine Transaction.

Glendon, M. A. (1993). *Rights Talk: The impoverishment of political discourse*. New York, The Free Press.

Glendon, M. A. (1996). *A Nation Under Lawyers*. Cambridge, MA, Harvard University Press.

Glickstein, J. (2013). 'After midnight: The circuit judges and the repeal of the Judiciary Act of 1801.' *Yale Journal of Law and the Humanities* 24(2): 543–577.

Goetz, K. H. (2005). 'The new member states and the EU: The challenge of adapting to Europe.' In S. Bulmer and C. Lequesne (eds). *Member States and the European Union*. Oxford, Oxford University Press: 254–285.

Goldstone, L. (2008). *The Activist. John Marshall,* Marbury v. Madison, *and the Myth of Judicial Review.* New York, Walker & Company.

Government of Romania. (2012). 'Emergency Ordinance amending Law 47/1992 concerning the organisation and functioning of the Constitutional Court [OUG 38/2012 pentru modificarea Legii nr. 47/1992 privind organizarea si functionarea Curtii Constitutionale].' Retrieved 4 April 2018, from www.dreptonline.ro/legislatie/oug_38_2012_modificarea_legii_47_1992_organizarea_functionarea_curtii_constitutionale.php.

Grabbe, H. (2006). *The EU's Transformative Power: Europeanization through conditionality in Central and Eastern Europe*. Basingstoke, Palgrave Macmillan.

Grabenwarter, C. (no date). 'Christoph Grabenwarter, Constitutional Judge.' Retrieved 8 February 2018, from https://www.vfgh.gv.at/cms/vfgh-kongress/downloads/en/CV_Grabenwarter.pdf

Group of Specialists on the Judiciary (CJ-S-JUD). (2009). 'First meeting, Strasbourg, 26–27 March 2009, Meeting Report (CJ-S-JUD(2009) 9).' Retrieved 4 March 2010, from www.coe.int/t/dghl/standardsetting/cdcj/CJSJUD/CJ-S-JUD%20_2009_%209%20E%20-%20report%20of%201st%20meeting.pdf

Guarnieri, C. (2004). 'Appointment and career of judges in Continental Europe: The rise of judicial self-government.' *Legal Studies* 24(1–2): 169–187.

Guarnieri, C. and P. Pederzoli (2002). *The Power of Judges*. Oxford, Oxford University Press.

Gulyás, G. (no date). 'Dr. Gulyás Gergely.' Retrieved 3 June 2014, from www.parlament.hu/kepv/eletrajz/hu/g053.pdf

Gurin, P., A. H. Miller and G. Gurin (1980). 'Stratum identification and consciousness.' *Social Psychology Quarterly* 43(1): 30–47.

Haas, E. B. (1958). *The Uniting of Europe: Political, social and economic forces (1950–1957)*. London, Stevens & Sons Limited.
Haas, E. B. (1961). 'International integration. The European and the universal process.' *International Organization* 15(3): 366–392.
Haas, P. M. (1992). 'Introduction: Epistemic communities and international policy coordination.' *International Organization* 46(1): 1–35.
Habermas, J. (2012). *The Crisis of the European Union: A response*. Cambridge, Polity.
Hague Institute for Innovation of Law. (2018). 'Dr Linn Hammergren.' The Hague, The Hague Humanity Club. Retrieved 1 February 2018, from http://www.hiil.org/index.php?pageID=200
Hailsham of St Marylebone, Quintin Hogg, Baron (1990). *A Sparrow's Flight: The memoirs of Lord Hailsham of St Marylebone*. London, Collins.
Halmai, G. (2017). 'The early retirement age of the Hungarian judges.' In F. Nicola and B. Davies (eds). *EU Law Stories: Contextual and critical histories of European jurisprudence*. Cambridge, Cambridge University Press: 471–488.
Hamilton, A. (1788a). 'The Federalist Papers No. 76: The appointing power of the executive.' Retrieved 5 May 2014, from http://avalon.law.yale.edu/18th_century/fed76.asp
Hamilton, A. (1788b). 'The Federalist No. 78. The Judiciary department.' Retrieved 20 February 2018, from http://avalon.law.yale.edu/18th_century/fed78.asp
Hammergren, L. (2002). 'Do judicial councils further judicial reform? Lessons from Latin America.' Retrieved 2 March 2010, from https://media.law.wisc.edu/s/c_8/zfmfw/lhdjc.pdf
Hancké, B. (2009). *Intelligent Research Design. A guide for beginning researchers in the social sciences*. Oxford, Oxford University Press.
Harlow, H. F. (1958). *The Nature of Love*. Retrieved 29 August 2015, from http://psychclassics.yorku.ca/Harlow/love.htm
Hay, C. (2002). *Political Analysis: A critical introduction*. Basingstoke, Palgrave Macmillan.
Hazlitt, H. ([1946] 1979). *Economics in One Lesson*. New York, Crown Trade Paperbacks.
Held, D. (1995). *Democracy and the Global Order: From the modern state to cosmopolitan governance*. Cambridge, Polity.
Helfer, L. R. and Slaughter, A.-M. (1997). 'Toward a theory of effective supranational adjudication.' *Yale Law Journal* 107(2): 273–391.
Hirschl, R. (2004). *Towards Juristocracy: The origins and consequences of the new constitutionalism*. Cambridge, MA and London, Harvard University Press.
Hirschl, R. (2008). 'The judicialization of politics.' In K. E. Whittington, R. D. Kelemen and G. A. Caldeira (eds). *The Oxford Handbook of Law and Politics*. Oxford, Oxford University Press: 119–142.
Hirschl, R. (2013). 'Epilogue: Courts and democracy between ideals and realities.' *Representation – The Journal of Representative Democracy* 49(3): 361–373.

Holzner, B. and J. H. Marx (1979). *Knowledge Application: The knowledge system in society*. Boston, MA and London, Allyn and Bacon.
Hood, C. (1983). *The Tools of Government*. London, Macmillan.
House of Commons. (2005). 'Constitutional Reform Bill [Lords] (17 January 2005). Hansard Debate.' Retrieved 3 December 2013, from www.publications.parliament.uk/pa/cm200405/cmhansrd/vo050117/debtext/50117-07.htm
Iancu, B. (2017). 'Perils of sloganised constitutional concepts notably that of "judicial independence" – [Review of] David Kosař, *Perils of Judicial Self-Government in Transitional Societies* (Cambridge University Press 2016) 470pp.' *European Constitutional Law Review* 13(3): 582–599.
Ingram, M. (2016). *Crafting Courts in New Democracies: The politics of subnational judicial reform in Brazil and Mexico*. New York, Cambridge University Press.
Institute for European and International Law. (2015a). 'Christoph Grabenwarter.' Retrieved 4 May 2015, from www.wu.ac.at/eir/mitarbeiter/teamgrab/grabenwarter/en/
Institute for European and International Law. (2015b). 'Matti Pellonpää.' Retrieved 4 May 2015, from www.wu.ac.at/eir/mitarbeiter/ehemalige-mitarbeiter/matti-pellonpaeae/en/
Institutul National al Magistraturii. (2016). 'Strategia Institutului National al Magistraturii pentru perioada 2013–2016.' Retrieved 2 August 2016, from www.inm-lex.ro/fisiere/d_286/Strategia%20INM_2013_2016.pdf
International Association for Court Administration. (2014). 'Maja Tratnik. Advisory Council – Slovenia.' Retrieved 5 October 2014, from www.iaca.ws/maja-tratnik.html
International Association of Judges. (2014). 'History.' Retrieved 2 January 2015, from https://www.iaj-uim.org/
International Refugee Assistance Program et al. v. Trump, United States Court of Appeals for the Fourth Circuit, Appeal No. 17-1351 [2017].
Iorgovan, A. (1998). *Odiseea elaborării Constituţiei*. Târgu Mureş, Vatra Românească.
Ip, E. (2010). 'The Supreme People's Court and the transformation of judicial politics in contemporary China.' Master's thesis, Studies in Legal Research, Centre for Socio-Legal Studies, University of Oxford.
Jackson, A. (1832). 'President Jackson's veto message regarding the Bank of the United States, July 10, 1832.' Retrieved 10 October 2009, from http://avalon.law.yale.edu/19th_century/ajveto01.asp
Jackson, T. J. (2005). *The Globalizers. Development workers in action*. Baltimore, MD, Johns Hopkins University Press.
Jefferson, T. (1784). 'Notes on the State of Virginia. Query XIII: Constitution.' Retrieved 1 March 2018, from https://constitution.hillsdale.edu/document.doc?id=235
Jefferson, T. (1804). 'Letter from Thomas Jefferson to Abigail Adams, Monticello, 1 September 1804.' Retrieved 20 February 2018, from https://founders.archives.gov/documents/Jefferson/99-01-02-0348

Johnston, A. I. (2001). 'Treating international institutions as social environments.' *International Studies Quarterly* 45(4): 487–515.

Joint Liberal/SDP Alliance Commission on Constitutional Reform. (1983). 'Towards a new constitutional settlement: Second report of the Joint Liberal/SDP Alliance Commission on Constitutional Reform.' London, Poland Street Publications.

Jupille, J., J. A. Caporaso and J. T. Checkel (2003). 'Integrating institutions: Rationalism, constructivism, and the study of the European Union.' *Comparative Political Studies* 36(1–2): 7–40.

Kang, Y. H. R., F. H. Petzschner, D. M. Wolpert and M. N. Shadlen (2017). 'Piercing of consciousness as a threshold-crossing operation.' *Current Biology*. Retrieved 29 July 2017, from http://dx.doi.org/10.1016/j.cub.2017.06.047

Kant, I. (1795). 'Perpetual peace: A philosophical sketch.' Retrieved 10 February 2013, from https://www.mtholyoke.edu/acad/intrel/kant/kant1.htm

Kauppi, N. and R. M. Madsen (eds). (2013). *Transnational Power Elites. The new professionals of governance, law and security*. London, Routledge.

Keck, M. E. and K. Sikkink (1998). *Activists Beyond Borders: Advocacy networks in international politics*. Ithaca, NY, Cornell University Press.

Kelemen, D. R. (2013). 'Judicialisation, democracy and European integration.' *Representation – Journal of Representative Democracy* 49(3): 295–308 (Special Issue on Courts and Representative Democracy).

Kelsen, H. (1942). 'Judicial review of legislation: A comparative study of the Austrian and American Constitution.' *Journal of Politics* 4(2): 183–200.

King, A. (1981). 'The rise of the career politician in Britain – and its consequences.' *British Journal of Political Science* 11(3): 249–285.

King, G., R. O. Keohane and S. Verba (1994). *Designing Social Inquiry: Scientific inference in qualitative research*. Princeton, NJ, Princeton University Press.

King's College London. (2015). 'Supporting the House of Commons Political and Constitutional Reform Committee inquiry into whether or not to pursue a codified or written constitution for the UK, through a literature review and future project planning.' Retrieved 13 March 2016, from https://kclpure.kcl.ac.uk/portal/en/projects/supporting-the-house-of-commons-political-and-constitutional-reform-committee-inquiry-into-whether-or-not-to-pursue-a-codified-or-written-constitution-for-the-uk-through-a-literature-review-and-future-project-planning(9d4243ac-450f-4c9a-b264-d3b741ae8272).html

Kingsbury, B. (1999). 'The proliferation of international tribunals: Piecing together the puzzle.' *New York University Journal of International Law and Politics* 31(4): 679–991.

Kornezov, A. (2015). 'When David teaches EU law to Goliath: A generational upheaval in the making.' In M. Bobek (ed.). *Central European Judges under the European Influence: The transformative power of the EU revisited*. Oxford, Hart Publishing: 242–265.

Kosař, D. (2016). *Perils of Judicial Self-Government in Transitional Societies: Holding the least accountable branch to account*. Cambridge, Cambridge University Press.

Kosař D. (2017) 'Politics of judicial independence and judicial accountability in Czechia: Bargaining in the shadow of the law between Court Presidents and the Ministry of Justice.' *European Constitutional Law Review* 13(1): 96–123.

Kosař, D. (2018). 'The Strasbourg Court and domestic judicial politics: Disciplining judges and beyond.' In M. Wind (ed.). *International Courts and Domestic Politics.* Cambridge, Cambridge University Press.

Koskenniemi, M. (2001). *The Gentle Civilizer of Nations: The rise and fall of international law.* Cambridge, Cambridge University Press.

Kramer, L. (2004). *The People Themselves: Popular constitutionalism and judicial review.* New York, Oxford University Press.

Kühn, Z. (2004). 'Worlds apart. Western and Central European judicial culture at the onset of the European Enlargement.' *American Journal of Comparative Law* 52: 531–567.

Kühn, Z. (2011a). 'Judicial independence in Central and Eastern Europe: The experience of 1990s and 2000s.' *The Lawyer Quarterly* 1(1): 31–42.

Kühn, Z. (2011b). *The Judiciary in Central and Eastern Europe: Mechanical jurisprudence in transformation?* Leiden and Boston, MA, Martinus Nijhoff Publishers.

La Pergola, A. (1993). 'Italy and European integration: A lawyer's perspective.' *Indiana International & Comparative Law Review* 4: 259.

La Pergola, A. (1997). 'Introductory statement on the constitutional heritage of Europe.' *The Constitutional Heritage of Europe, Montpellier (France) 23–24 November 1996. Proceedings.* Strasbourg, Council of Europe.

Lafave, W. R. (1970). 'The prosecutor's discretion in the United States.' *The American Journal of International Law* 18(3): 532–548.

Lahusen, C. (2008). *Law and Lawyers in Brussels' World of Commercial Consultants.* Florence, European University Institute.

Landes, W. and R. Posner (1975). 'The independent judiciary in an interest-group perspective.' *Journal of Law and Economics* 18(3): 875–901.

LaRowe, N. (2010). 'On and off the Supreme Court beat: A content analysis of newspaper coverage of the Supreme Court from 1997–2004.' Retrieved 1 March 2012, from http://ssrn.com/abstract=1642697

Lasch, C. (1978). *The Culture of Narcissism: American life in an age of diminishing expectations.* New York, W. W. Norton.

Lasch, C. (1995). *The Revolt of the Elites and the Betrayal of Democracy.* New York and London, W. W. Norton.

Lash, K. T. and A. Harrison (2007). 'Minority report: John Marshall and the defense of the Alien and Sedition Acts.' *Ohio State Law Journal* 68(2): 436–516.

Law, D. S. and M. Versteeg (2011). 'The evolution and ideology of global constitutionalism.' *California Law Review* 99(5): 1163–1257.

Lemmens, K. (2015). '(S)electing judges for Strasbourg. A (dis)appointing process?' In M. Bobek (ed.). *Selecting Europe's Judges: A critical review of the appointment procedures to the European Courts.* Oxford, Oxford University Press: 95–119.

Lester, A. (1984). 'Fundamental rights: The United Kingdom isolated?' *Commonwealth Law Bulletin* 10(2): 955–971.

Leucht, B. (2010). 'Expertise and the creation of a constitutional order for Core Europe: Transatlantic policy networks in the Schuman Plan negotiations.' In W. Kaiser, B. Leucht and M. Gehler (eds). *Transnational Networks in Regional Integration. Governing Europe 1945–1983*. Basingstoke, Palgrave Macmillan: 18–37.

Levinson, S. (2003). 'Why I do not teach *Marbury* (except to Eastern Europeans) and why you shouldn't either.' *Wake Forest Law Review* 38: 553–578.

Levinson, S. (2006). 'Identifying "independence".' *Boston University Law Review* 86: 1297–1308.

Levitsky, J. E. (1994). 'The Europeanization of the British legal style.' *American Journal of Comparative Law* 42(2): 347–380.

Lieberson, S. (1991). 'Small N's and big conclusions: An examination of the reasoning in comparative studies based on a small number of cases.' *Social Forces* 70(2): 307–320.

Lippmann, W. (1922). *Public Opinion*. New York, Allen & Unwin.

Ludlow, N. P. (2010) 'Governing Europe: Charting the development of a supranational political system.' In W. Kaiser and A. Varsori (eds). *European Union History: Themes and debates*. Basingstoke, Palgrave Macmillan: 109–127.

Lukes, S. (1974). *Power: A radical view*. London, Macmillan.

Lukes, S. (ed.) (1986). *Power*. New York, New York University Press.

MacMullen, A. (1997). 'European Commissioners 1952–1995: National routes to a European elite.' In N. Nugent (ed.). *At the Heart of the Union. Studies of the European Commission*. London, Macmillan: 27–48.

MacMullen, A. (2004). 'Intergovernmental functionalism? The Council of Europe in European integration.' *Journal of European Integration* 26(4): 405–429.

Madison, J. (1787). 'The Federalist No. 10. The same subject continued: The Union as a safeguard against domestic faction and insurrection.' Retrieved 23 May 2014, from http://thomas.loc.gov/home/histdox/fed_10.html

Madison, J. (1788a). 'The Federalist No. 47. The particular structure of the new government and the distribution of power among its different parts.' Retrieved 1 January 2018, from http://avalon.law.yale.edu/18th_century/fed47.asp

Madison, J. (1788b). 'The Federalist No. 48. These departments should not be so far separated as to have no constitutional control over each other.' Retrieved 12 January 2018, from http://avalon.law.yale.edu/18th_century/fed48.asp

Madison, J. (1788c). 'The Federalist No. 49. Method of guarding against the encroachments of any one department of government by appealing to the people through a convention.' Retrieved 1 October 2008, from http://avalon.law.yale.edu/18th_century/fed49.asp

Madison, J. (1788d). 'The Federalist No. 51. The structure of the government must furnish the proper checks and balances between the different departments.'

Retrieved 23 February 2018, from http://avalon.law.yale.edu/18th_century/fed51.asp

Madsen, M. R. and A. Vauchez (2005). 'European constitutionalism at the cradle: Law and lawyers in the construction of a European political order (1920–1960).' In H. Schepel and A. Jettinghoff (eds). *In Lawyers' Circles. Lawyers and European legal integration*. The Hague, Elsevier Reed: 15–36.

Magalhães, P. C. (1999). 'The politics of judicial reform in Eastern Europe.' *Comparative Politics* 32(1): 43–62.

Magalhães, P. C., C. Guarnieri and Y. Kaminis (2006). 'Democratic consolidation, judicial reform, and the judicialization of politics in Southern Europe.' In R. Gunther, P. N. Diamandouros and D. A. Sotiropoulos (eds). *Democracy and the State in the New Southern Europe*. Oxford, Oxford University Press: 138–197.

Magen, A. and L. Morlino (eds) (2009). *International Actors, Democratization and the Rule of Law: Anchoring democracy?* Abingdon, Routledge.

Mahieux, E. (2014). 'European economic governance and its contestation: Conflict in the European Semester from 2011 to 2013.' MPhil thesis, European Politics and Society, Department of Politics and International Relations, University of Oxford.

Maitland, F. W. and F. Pollock (1899). *The History of English Law Before the Time of Edward I*. Cambridge, Cambridge University Press.

Manners, J. I. (2002). 'Normative power Europe: A contradiction in terms?' *Journal of Common Market Studies* 49(2): 235–258.

Manning, J. F. (2011). 'Separation of powers as ordinary interpretation.' *Harvard Law Review* 124(8): 1941–2040.

Marquand, D. (1979). *Parliament for Europe*. London, Jonathan Cape.

Matczak, M., M. Bencze and Z. Kühn (2010). 'Constitutions, EU law and judicial strategies in the Czech Republic, Hungary and Poland.' *Journal of Public Policy* 30(1): 81–99.

McNamara, K. R. (2003). 'Rational fictions: Central Bank independence and the social logic of delegation.' In M. Thatcher and A. Stone Sweet (eds). *The Politics of Delegation*. Portland, OR and London, Frank Cass: 47–77.

MEDEL. (2012). 'Declaration of Medel on the re-appointment procedure of judges and prosecutors in Serbia.' Retrieved 5 June 2013, from www.medelnet.eu/index.php?option=com_content&view=article&id=135:declaration-of-medel-on-the-re-appointment-procedure-of-judges-and-prosecutors-in-serbia&catid=57:europe&Itemid=179&lang=en

Mény, Y. (2003). 'De la démocratie en Europe: Old concepts and new challenges.' *Journal of Common Market Studies* 41(1): 1–13.

Merryman, J. H. and R. Perez-Perdomo (2007). *The Civil Law Tradition. An introduction to the legal systems of Europe and Latin America*. Stanford, CA, Stanford University Press.

Meyer, J. W., J. Boli, G. M. Thomas and F. O. Ramirez (1997). 'World society and the nation-state.' *American Journal of Sociology* 103(1): 144–181.

Meyer-Sahling, J.-H. (2009). 'Transnational communication in the European public sphere. The summit of The Hague 1969.' In W. Kaiser, B. Leucht and R. Morten (eds). *The History of the European Union: Origins of a trans- and supranational polity 1950–72*. New York, Routledge: 110–128.
Moravcsik, A. (1995). 'Explaining international human rights regimes.' *European Journal of International Relations* 1(2): 157–189.
Moravcsik, A. (2000). 'The origins of human rights regimes: Democratic delegation in postwar Europe.' *International Organization* 54(2): 217–252.
Moravcsik, A. (2014). 'Transparency in qualitative research.' *PS: Political Science & Politics* 47(1): 48–53.
Morgenthau, H. J. (1948). *Politics Among Nations: The struggle for power and peace*. New York, Knopf.
Morlino, L. and W. Sadurski (2010). *Democratization and the European Union. Comparing Central and Eastern European post-Communist countries*. London and New York, Routledge.
Morris, W. N. and R. S. Miller (1975). 'The effects of consensus-breaking and consensus preempting partners on reduction of conformity.' *Journal of Experimental Social Psychology* 11(3): 215–223.
Morton, F. L. and R. Knopff (2000). *The Charter Revolution & the Court Party*. Peterborough, Ontario, Broadview Press.
Mosca, G. (1939). *The Ruling Class*. New York and London, McGraw-Hill.
Moustafa, T. (2007). *The Struggle for Constitutional Power: Law, politics, and economic development in Egypt*. New York, Cambridge University Press.
Munck, G. L. (2004). 'Tools for qualitative research.' In H. E. Brady and D. Collier (eds). *Rethinking Social Inquiry*. London, Rowman and Littlefield: 105–121.
Mungiu-Pipidi, A. (1997). 'Interview with President of the Romanian Constitutional Court, Ion Muraru.' *East European Constitutional Review* 6(1): 78–83.
Murray, D. (2017). *The Strange Death of Europe: Immigration, identity, Islam*. London, Bloomsbury Publishing.
Nagel, R. F. (1993). 'Disagreement and interpretation.' *Law and Contemporary Problems* 56(4): 11–33.
Neira Martinez, N.-H. (ed.) (1996). *Judicial Councils in Latin America. Lessons learned. Proceedings of the Second Judicial Reform Roundtable*. Williamsburg, Virginia, 19–22 May 1996, National Centre for State Courts, US Agency for International Development, Inter-American Development Bank.
Nicolaidis, K. and R. Howse (2002). '"This is my EUtopia": Narrative as power.' *Journal of Common Market Studies* 40(4): 767–792.
Open Society Foundations. (2017). 'Staff.' Retrieved 20 May 2017, from https://www.opensocietyfoundations.org/people/heather-grabbe
Open Society Institute. (2001). 'Monitoring the EU accession process: Judicial independence.' Retrieved 12 March 2008, from https://www.opensocietyfoundations.org/sites/default/files/judicialind_20011010.pdf

OSCE. (2016). 'Human rights.' Retrieved 13 February 2016, from www.osce.org/what/human-rights

Parau, C. E. (2009). 'Impaling Dracula: How EU accession empowered civil society in Romania.' *West European Politics* 32(1): 119–141.

Parau, C. E. (2010). 'East side story: How transnational networks contested EU accession conditionality.' *Europe-Asia Studies* 62(9): 1527–1554.

Parau, C. E. (2012). 'The drive for judicial supremacy in Central and Eastern Europe.' In A. Seibert-Fohr (ed.). *Judicial Independence in Transition*. Heidelberg, Springer: 619–667.

Parau, C. E. (2013a). 'Book review: Thorson, Carla (2012) *Politics, Judicial Review, and the Russian Constitutional Court*, Palgrave Macmillan.' *Law and Politics Book Review* 23(6): 268–271.

Parau, C. E. (2013b). 'The dormancy of parliaments: The invisible cause of judiciary empowerment in Central and Eastern Europe.' *Representation – The Journal of Representative Democracy* 49(3): 267–280 (Special Issue on Courts and Representative Democracy).

Parau, C. E. (2013c). 'Romania's transnational constitution: A tradition of elite learning and self-empowerment.' In D. Galligan and M. Versteeg (eds). *The Social and Political Foundations of Constitutions*. Cambridge, Cambridge University Press: 497–532.

Parau, C. E. (2015a). 'Environmental network governance in Romania.' In L. Stan and D. Vancea (eds). *Post-Communist Romania at Twenty-five*. Lanham, MD and Boulder, CO, Lexington Books: 241–259.

Parau, C. E. (2015b). 'Explaining judiciary governance in Central and Eastern Europe: External incentives, transnational elites and parliament inaction.' *Europe-Asia Studies* 67(3): 409–442.

Parau, C. E. (2015c). 'The Politics of a Written Constitution for Britain.' Retrieved 20 February 2015, from http://politicsinspires.org/politics-written-constitution-britain/

Parau, C. E. (2015d). 'Constitutional ferment in Britain. Towards a republican constitution?' Unpublished manuscript.

Parau, C. E. and J. W. Bains (2012). 'Constitutional designs: Lessons we can learn from the early American Republic.' *Romanian Journal of Comparative Law* 3(2): 348–382.

Parau, C. E. and R. Bellamy (2013). 'Introduction: Democracy, courts and the dilemmas of representation.' *Representation – The Journal of Representative Democracy* 49(3): 255–266 (Special Issue on Courts and Representative Democracy).

Pareto, V. (1916). *Trattato di sociologia generale*. Florence, G. Barbèra.

Pareto, V. ([1901] 1991). *The Rise and Fall of Elites: An application of theoretical sociology*. New Brunswick, NJ and London, Transaction Publishers.

Parlamento Italiano. (no date). 'Governo De Mita (13.04.1988–22.07.1989).' Retrieved 4 April 2018, from http://storia.camera.it/governi/i-governo-de-mita

Parlamentul României. (2003). *Stenograma lucrărilor şedinţei Comisiei pentru elaborarea propunerii legislative privind revizuirea Constituţiei din 7.02. 2003*. Bucharest, Parlamentul României.

Parlamentul României. (2004a). 'Dezbateri Parlamentare. Şedinţa Camerei Deputaţilor din 25 mai 2004. Dezbateri asupra Proiectului de Lege privind Consiliul Superior al Magistraturii.' Retrieved 3 June 2011, from www.cdep.ro/pls/steno/steno2015.stenograma?ids=5681&idm=2&idl=1

Parlamentul României. (2004b). 'Şedinţa Camerei Deputaţilor din 25 mai 2004. Dezbateri asupra Proiectului de Lege privind Consiliul Superior al Magistraturii.' Retrieved 3 June 2011, from www.cdep.ro/pls/proiecte/upl_pck.proiect?idp=5547&cam=2

Parliamentary Assembly of the Council of Europe. (2014). 'Election of judges. How are judges of the European Court of Human Rights elected?' Retrieved 5 April 2015, from http://website-pace.net/en GB/web/as-jur/echr-judges-election

Paulsen, M. S. (1993). 'The Merryman Power and the dilemma of autonomous executive branch interpretation.' *Cardozo Law Review* 15: 81–111.

Paulsen, M. S. (1994). 'The most dangerous branch: Executive power to say what the law is.' *Geo L. J.* 83: 217–345.

Peirce, C. S. (1902). 'Application for support for his logic Memoir 19, Draft E: "On Arguments".' Retrieved 10 May 2015, from www.iupui.edu/~arisbe/menu/library/bycsp/L75/ver1/l75v1-06.htm

Phillip, A. and S. Larimer (2015). '"He has guts": David Bunning, the same-sex marriage decision's unlikely enforcer.' Retrieved 1 October 2015, from https://www.washingtonpost.com/news/post-nation/wp/2015/09/04/he-has-guts-judge-david-bunning-the-same-sex-marriage-decisions-unlikely-enforcer/

Piana, D. (2007a). 'Judges and legal experts in the European policy of rule of law promotion.' In R. Coman and J.-M. de Waele (eds). *Judicial Reforms in Central and Eastern European Countries*. Bruges, Vanden Broele: 23–73.

Piana, D. (2007b). 'Unpacking policy transfer, discovering actors: The French model of judicial education between enlargement and judicial cooperation in the EU.' *French Politics* 5: 33–65.

Piana, D. (2009). 'The power knocks at the court's back door: Two waves of postcommunist judicial reform.' *Comparative Political Studies* 42(6): 816–840.

Piana, D. (2010). *Judicial Accountabilities in New Europe*. Farnham, Ashgate.

Pinker, S. (2002). *The Blank Slate: The modern denial of human nature*. London, Allen Lane.

Pinker, S. (2015). 'Professor Steven Pinker in conversation with Wolfson graduate students.' Retrieved 13 December 2015, from https://www.wolfson.ox.ac.uk/news/pinker-conversation-students

Pinto-Duschinsky, M. (2011). 'Bringing human rights back.' Retrieved 13 March 2012, from https://policyexchange.org.uk/publication/bringing-rights-back-home-making-human-rights-compatible-with-parliamentary-democracy-in-the-uk/

Political and Constitutional Reform Committee. (2014). 'Political and constitutional reform – Second Report. A New Magna Carta?' Retrieved 14 December 2014, from www.publications.parliament.uk/pa/cm201415/cmselect/cmpolcon/463/46302.htm

Posner, R. A. (1993). 'What do judges and justices maximize? (The same thing everybody else does).' *Supreme Court Economic Review* 3: 1–41.

R(Miller) v. Secretary of State for Exiting the EU [2017] UKSC 5. Retrieved 10 May 2017, from https://www.supremecourt.uk/cases/docs/uksc-2016-0196-judgment.pdf

Ramseyer, M. J. (1994). 'The puzzling (in)dependence of courts: A comparative approach.' *Journal of Legal Studies* 23(2): 721–747.

Reichertz, J. (2007). 'Abduction: The logic of discovery of grounded theory.' In A. Bryant and K. Charmaz (eds). *The SAGE Handbook of Grounded Theory*. London, SAGE Publications.

Reinke, G. (2010). 'The European Information Society: Governance and the decision-making process for ICT policy and standards.' Doctoral thesis, Department of Politics and International Relations, Royal Holloway College, University of London.

Reinke, G. (2012). *Industry Governance and Regulatory Compliance: A theoretical and practical guide to European ICT policy*. London, Gold Rush Publishing.

Rekosh, E. (2002). *Emerging Lessons from Reform Efforts in Eastern Europe*. Washington, DC, Office for Democracy and Governance. US Agency for International Development.

Rhodes, R. A. W. (1996). 'The new governance: Governing without government.' *Political Studies* 4(4): 652–668.

Rich, A. (2004). *Think Tanks, Public Policy, and the Politics of Expertise*. Cambridge and New York, Cambridge University Press.

Rios-Figueroa, J. and J. K. Staton (2009). 'Unpacking the rule of law: A review of judicial independence measures.' *Law School Symposium, The Rule of Law*. Retrieved 10 March 2008, from http://ssrn.com/abstract=1434234

Risse, T. and K. Sikkink (1999). 'The socialization of international human rights norms into domestic practices: Introduction.' In T. Risse, S. C. Ropp and S. Kathryn (eds). *The Power of Human Rights: International norms and domestic change*. Cambridge, Cambridge University Press: 1–38.

Roper, S. D. (2002). 'The impact of Moldovan parliamentary committees.' In D. M. Olson and W. E. Crowther (eds). *Committees in Post-Communist Democratic Parliaments: Comparative institutionalization*. Columbus, OH, Ohio State University Press: 154–171.

Rosenn, K. S. (1987). 'The protection of judicial independence in Latin America.' *University of Miami Inter-American Law Review* 19(1): 1–35.

Rothkopf, D. J. (2008). *Superclass: The global power elite and the world they are making*. London, Little, Brown.

Rozenberg, J. (2014). 'Codification conundrum.' *Law Society Gazette*. Retrieved 12 December 2014, from www.lawgazette.co.uk/21-july-2014/92.issue?cmd=ChangeSortOrder&val=4

Roznai, Y. (2014). 'Unconstitutional constitutional amendments: A study of the nature and limits of constitutional amendment powers.' PhD thesis, Department of Law, The London School of Economics and Political Science. Retrieved 13 June 2015, from http://etheses.lse.ac.uk/915/

Russell, P. H. (1983). 'The political purposes of the Canadian Charter.' *Canadian Bar Review* 61: 30–54.

Russell, P. H. (2001). 'Towards a general theory of judicial independence.' In P. H. Russell and D. M. O'Brien (eds). *Judicial Independence in the Age of Democracy: Critical perspectives from around the world*. Charlottesville, VA and London, University Press of Virginia Press: 1–25.

Sacriste, G. and A. Vauchez (2007). 'The force of international law: Lawyers' diplomacy on the international scene in the 1920s.' *Law & Social Inquiry* 32(1): 83–107.

Sadurski, W. (2006). 'Solange, chapter 3: Constitutional courts in Central Europe – Democracy – European Union.' *European University Institute Series/Report no. EUI LAW; 2006/40*. Retrieved 12 June 2013, from http://hdl.handle.net/1814/6420

Sadurski, W. (2008). *Rights Before Courts. A study of constitutional courts of post-Communist states of Central and Eastern Europe*. Dordrecht, Springer.

Sadurski, W. (2012). *Constitutionalism and the Enlargement of Europe*. Oxford, Oxford University Press.

Sajó, A. (1996). 'How the rule of law killed Hungarian welfare reform.' *East European Constitutional Review* 5(Winter): 31–41.

Sajó, A. (2012). 'Courts as representatives.' Lecture. Retrieved 20 May 2013, from www.fljs.org/content/are-courts-representatives-0

Salamon, L. (2015a). 'Dr. László Salamon (1947).' Retrieved 12 February 2015, from www.alkotmanybirosag.hu/members/dr-laszlo-salamon-1947

Salamon, L. (2015b). 'Dr. László Salamon. Parliamentary profile.' Retrieved 27 August 2014, from www.parlament.hu/internet/plsql/ogy_kpv.kepv_adat?p_azon=s201&p_ckl=39

Salsich, P. W., E. O. Switzer, S. Schmitz and J. Munich (1980). *The Revolving Door: Ethics in government service*. St Louis, MO, St Louis University School of Law.

Scharpf, F. W. (1997). *Games Real Actors Play. Actor-centered institutionalism in policy research*. Boulder, CO, Westview Press.

Scharpf, F. W. (1999). *Governing in Europe: Effective and democratic?* Oxford, Oxford University Press.

Schepel, H. (2007). 'The European brotherhood of lawyers: The reinvention of legal science in the making of European private law.' *Law and Social Inquiry – Journal of the American Bar Foundation* 32(1): 183–199.

Scheppele, K. L. (2011). 'Hungary's constitutional revolution.' *New York Times*, 19 December. Retrieved 20 February 2018, from https://krugman.blogs.nytimes.com/2011/12/19/hungarys-constitutional-revolution/

Scheppele, K. L. (2013). 'Beware of Hungarians bearing gifts.' Retrieved 3 March 2018, from https://krugman.blogs.nytimes.com/2013/06/09/beware-of-hungarians-bearing-gifts/

Scheppele, K. L. and V. Perju (2012). 'Guest post: Separating law and politics in Romania.' Retrieved 12 June 2014, from http://krugman.blogs.nytimes.com/2012/07/12/guest-post-separating-law-and-politics-in-romania/

Schimmelfennig, F. and U. Sedelmeier (eds) (2005). *The Europeanization of Central and Eastern Europe*. Ithaca, NY and London, Cornell University Press.

Schwartz, H. (2000). *The Struggle for Constitutional Justice in Post-Communist Europe*. Chicago, IL, University of Chicago Press.

Scruton, R. (2010). 'Viktor Orbán's triumph.' Retrieved 3 May 2014, from https://www.opendemocracy.net/democracy-newright/article_381.jsp

Scruton, R. (2011). 'The rebirth of nations.' Retrieved 2 October 2014, from http://spectator.org/37503_rebirth-nations/

Seibert-Fohr, A. (ed.) (2012). *Judicial Independence in Transition*. Heidelberg, Springer.

Selejan-Guţan, B. (2012). 'The illusion of the Romanian Constitution?' Retrieved 3 July 2014, from www.iconnectblog.com/2012/12/the-illusion-of-the-romanian-constitution/

Selejan-Guţan, B. (2016). *The Constitution of Romania: A contextual analysis*. Oxford, Hart Publishing. Retrieved 12 December 2017, from https://bodleian.ldls.org.uk/accessnow/start.html

Shapiro, I. (2005). *The Flight from Reality in the Human Sciences*. Princeton, NJ, Princeton University Press.

Shepsle, K. A. and M. S. Bonchek (1997). *Analyzing Politics. Rationality, behaviour, and institutions*. New York and London, W. W. Norton.

Simpson, B. (2004). *Human Rights and the End of Empire: Britain and the genesis of the European Convention*. Oxford, Oxford University Press.

Skinner, B. F. (1971). *Beyond Freedom & Dignity*. Indianapolis, IN and Cambridge, Hackett Publishing Company.

Slaughter, A.-M. (1994). 'A typology of transjudicial communities.' *University of Richmond Law Review* 29: 99–134.

Slaughter, A.-M. (2004). *A New World Order*. Princeton, NJ and Oxford, Princeton University Press.

Slotnik, E. E. and J. A. Segal (1998). *Television News and the Supreme Court: All the news that's fit to air?* Cambridge, Cambridge University Press.

Smilov, D. (2012). 'Hard law, soft law and the politics of standards: Regulating political parties in Europe.' Paper given at the conference 'The evolution of international norms and norm entrepreneurship: The Council of Europe in comparative perspective', Wolfson College, University of Oxford, 11 January.

Smith, T. (2008). 'The first decade of Charter 88: Fruitful interaction with the Joseph Rowntree Reform Trust.' In P. Facey, B. Rigby and A. Runswick (eds). *Unlocking Democracy: 20 years of Charter 88*. London, Politico's Publishers.

Sólyom, L. (2003). 'Constitutional justice – some comparative remarks (CDL-JU (2003) 30).' Retrieved 24 June 2014, from www.venice.coe.int/webforms/documents/?pdf=CDL-JU(2003)030-e

Solzhenitsyn, A. (1974). *The Gulag Archipelago*. London, Collins/Harvill Press.

Sowell, T. (2010). *Intellectuals and Society*. New York, Basic Books.

Stein, E. (1981). 'Lawyers, judges and the making of a transnational constitution.' *American Journal of International Law* 75(3): 1–28.

Stone Sweet, A. (1992). *The Birth of Judicial Politics in France*. Oxford, Oxford University Press.

Stone Sweet, A. (1994). 'Judging socialist reform: The politics of coordinate construction in France and Germany.' *Comparative Political Studies* 26(4): 443–469.

Stone Sweet, A. (2000). *Governing with Judges*. Oxford, Oxford University Press.

Stone Sweet, A. (2002). 'Constitutional courts and parliamentary democracy.' *West European Politics* 25(1): 77–100.

Stone Sweet, A. (2004). *The Judicial Construction of Europe*. Oxford, Oxford University Press.

Stone Sweet, A. (2010). 'The European Court of Justice and the judicialization of EU governance.' *Living Reviews in European Governance* 5(2). Retrieved 4 April 2018, from https://ssrn.com/abstract=1583345 or http://dx.doi.org/10.2139/ssrn.1583345

Tansey, O. (2007). 'Process Tracing and elite interviewing: A case for non-probability sampling.' *PS: Political Science and Politics* 40(4): 765–772.

Tate, N. and T. R. Vallinder (eds) (1995). *The Global Expansion of Judicial Power*. New York, New York University Press.

Telegraph, The. (2014). 'Coalition rules out giving prisoners the vote.' Retrieved 4 January 2015, from www.telegraph.co.uk/news/uknews/crime/11306002/Coalition-rules-out-giving-prisoners-the-vote.html

Teles, S. M. (2009). *The Rise of the Conservative Legal Movement: The battle for control of the law*. Princeton, NJ, Princeton University Press.

Thatcher, M. and A. Stone Sweet (eds) (2003). *The Politics of Delegation*. London and Portland, OR, Frank Cass.

Thorson, C. L. (2012). *Politics, Judicial Review and the Russian Constitutional Court*. Basingstoke, Palgrave Macmillan, in association with St Antony's College, Oxford.

Tinel, G. (2013). 'Parliamentary debates. Sittings of the Chamber of Deputies of May 8, 2013 [Reexaminarea Legii privind aprobarea Ordonanţei de urgenţă a Guvernului nr.38/2012 pentru modificarea Legii nr.47/1992 privind organizarea şi funcţionarea Curţii Constituţionale, ca urmare a Deciziei Curţii Constituţionale nr.738/19.09.2012 (PL-x 283/2012/9.10.2012)].' Retrieved 12 May 2014, from www.cdep.ro/pls/steno/steno.stenograma?ids=7262&idm=6&idl=2

Tomiuc, E. (2012). 'Romania's top court says government threatening rule of law.' Retrieved 3 December 2014, from www.rferl.org/content/romania-ponta-basescu-court-rule-of-law/24634313.html

Toulmin, S. E. (1958). *The Uses of Argument*. Cambridge, Cambridge University Press.

Truche, P. (2009). President of the French Court of Cassation (1996–1999); Honorary President of the Court of Cassation (since 1999). Written correspondence with the author.

Turner, K. (1961). 'The midnight judges.' *University of Pennsylvania Law Review* 109(4): 494–523.

Tushnet, M. (1999). *Taking the Constitution Away From Courts*. Princeton, NJ, Princeton University Press.

Unlock Democracy. (2013). 'The original Charter 88.' Retrieved 5 June 2013, from http://unlockdemocracy.org.uk/pages/the-original-charter-88

Vauchez, A. (2008). 'The force of a weak field: Law and lawyers in the government of the European Union (for a renewed research agenda).' *International Political Sociology* 2(2): 128–144.

Vauchez, A. (2015). *Brokering Europe: Euro-lawyers and the making of a transnational polity*. Cambridge, Cambridge University Press.

Veblen, T. ([1899] 1934). *The Theory of the Leisure Class: An economic study of institutions*. New York, The Modern Library.

Venice Commission. (2014). 'Members of the Venice Commission.' Retrieved 7 June 2015, from www.venice.coe.int/WebForms/members/default.aspx

Vibert, F. (2007). *The Rise of the Unelected. Democracy and the new separation of powers*. Cambridge, Cambridge University Press.

Vile, M. J. C. (1998). *Constitutionalism and Separation of Powers*. Indianapolis, IN, Liberty Fund.

Vinx, L. (2007). *Hans Kelsen's Pure Theory of Law: Legality and legitimacy*. Oxford, Oxford University Press.

Voeten, E. (2007). 'The politics of international judicial appointments: evidence from the European Court of Human Rights.' *International Organization* 61(4): 669–701.

Voeten, E. (2013). 'Public opinion and the legitimacy of international courts.' *Theoretical Inquiries in Law* 14(2): 411–436.

Vromen, A. (2010). 'Debating methods: Rediscovering qualitative approaches.' In D. Marsh and G. Stoker (eds). *Theory and Methods in Political Science*. Basingstoke and New York, Palgrave Macmillan: 249–266.

Wagnerová, E. (2003). 'Position of judges in the Czech Republic.' In J. Přibaň, P. Roberts and J. Young (eds). *Systems of Justice in Transition*. Aldershot, Ashgate: 163–180.

Waldron, J. (1993). 'A right-based critique of constitutional rights.' *Oxford Journal of Legal Studies* 13(1): 18–51.

Waldron, J. (1995). 'The wisdom of the multitude: Some reflections on Book 3, Chapter 11 of Aristotle's *Politics*.' *Political Theory* 23(4): 563–584.

Waldron, J. (1998). 'Judicial review and the conditions of democracy.' *Journal of Political Philosophy* 6(4): 335–355.
Waldron, J. (2012). 'Separation of powers or division of power?' *NYU School of Law, Public Law Research Paper No. 12-20*. Retrieved 22 May 2014, from http://ssrn.com/abstract=2045638 or http://dx.doi.org/10.2139/ssrn.2045638
Waltz, K. N. (1959). *Man, the State, and War: A theoretical analysis*. New York, Columbia University Press.
Ward, K. (2006). 'Legislative primacy: A neglected alternative to judicial supremacy.' Retrieved 15 December 2017, from https://ssrn.com/abstract=899607 or http://dx.doi.org/10.2139/ssrn.899607
Weiler, J. (1991). 'The transformation of Europe.' *Yale Law Journal* 100(8): 2403–2483.
Weiler, J. (1994). 'A quiet revolution: The European Court of Justice and its interlocutors.' *Comparative Political Studies* 26(4): 510–534.
Weir, S. (2008). 'Tilting at windmills. The first years of Charter 88.' In P. Facey, B. Rigby and A. Runswick (eds). *Unlocking Democracy. Twenty years of Charter 88*. London, Politico's Publishing.
Wessels, W. (1997). 'An ever closer fusion: A dynamic macro-political view of integration process.' *Journal of Common Market Studies* 35(2): 267–299.
Wessels, W. (1998). 'Comitology: Fusion in action. Politico-administrative trends in the EU system.' *Journal of European Public Policy* 5(2): 209–234.
White, S. D. (1979). *Sir Edward Coke and 'the Grievances of the Commonwealth', 1621–1628*. Chapel Hill, NC, University of North Carolina Press.
Whittington, K. E. (2000). 'Herbert Wechsler's complaint and the revival of grand constitutional theory.' *University of Richmond Law Review* 34: 509–538.
Whittington, K. E. (2002). 'Extrajudicial constitutional interpretation: Three objections and responses.' *North Carolina Law Review* 80: 773–852.
Whittington, K. E. (2007). *Political Foundations of Judicial Supremacy. The Presidency, the Supreme Court, and constitutional leadership in U.S. history*. Princeton, NJ and London, Princeton University Press.
Wind, M. (2010). 'The Nordics, the EU and the reluctance towards supranational judicial review.' *Journal of Common Market Studies* 48(4): 1039–1063.
Woods, P. J. and L. Hilbink (2009). 'Comparative sources of judicial empowerment: Ideas and interests.' *Political Research Quarterly* 62(4): 745–752.
Wright Mills, C. (1956). *The Power Elite*. New York, Oxford University Press.
Yanow, D. (2009). 'What's political about political ethonography? Abducting our way toward reason and meaning.' *Qualitative and Multi-method Research* 7(2): 33–37.

Index